KANONIKA
9

THE SYNOD OF DIAMPER REVISITED

KANONIKA

All correspondence concerning manuscripts should be addressed to the Editor; all other correspondence to the Managing Editor.

KANONIKA
9

THE SYNOD OF DIAMPER REVISITED

Edited by
George Nedungatt, S.J.

PONTIFICIO ISTITUTO ORIENTALE
PIAZZA S. MARIA MAGGIORE, 7
00185 ROME, ITALY
2001

ISBN 88-7210-331-2

Finito di stampare nel mese di febbraio 2001
dalla Tipolitografia 2000 sas di De Magistris R. & C.
Via Trento, 46 - 00046 Grottaferrata (Roma) - Tel. e Fax: 06.941.04.73
E.mail: rdemagistris@pelagus.it

Contents

Preface

When the Academic Council of the Pontifical Oriental Institute, Rome, deliberated about organizing a symposium on the Synod of Diamper on the occasion of its fourth centenary (1599-1999), it was aware of the fact that the topic was a controversial one. While this synod is highly praised by some as a great achievement of the Portuguese Padroado and a positive contribution to the Church in India, it is roundly condemned by some others as the organized latinization of an Oriental Church by a colonial power destroying its true identity. The Pontifical Oriental Institute did not want to take sides in this controversy or even appear to do so but conduct a seminar on the purely academic level. This neutral stance was expressed in the following manner in the convocation notice.

> In the history of the Church of the Thomas Christians of Kerala, the Synod of Diamper (20-26 June 1599) is a necessary point of reference. It deserves to be remembered, if not celebrated. After four centuries, its consequences are still with us, for better or for worse. A symposium on the Synod of Diamper will be held at the Pontifical Oriental Institute, Rome, on 18 November 1999.

The above distinction between *remembering* and *celebrating* was implicit in the topic chosen for the symposium: "The Synod of Diamper 400 Years After: Lessons of History."

Kanonika keeps to the same neutral stance in publishing the present volume containing the papers of that symposium and entitled *The Synod of Diamper Revisited*. Revisiting an ancient monument or place of historical interest is a different experience from the first visit. If the first impressions were global and sensational, on a later visit we are more likely to get a better idea of the setting, proportion, and details and be in a position to make a more objective evaluation. The original sense of discovery, awe and wonder, or the opposite feeling of apathy or revulsion, has given way to a more seasoned perception and we are prepared for a more balanced critical appraisal. The present volume presupposes that the readers are not newcomers to the Synod of Diamper but are already familiar with its history: the volume is in the nature of a guided tour on a second visit.

Besides the papers presented at the 1999 symposium by Benedict Vadakkekara, Vincenzo Poggi, Jacob Kollaparambil, Jacob Vellian, and Paul Pallath there are four other studies in the present volume. The first is an introductory, hermeneutical essay, "Interpreting Diamper and the Lessons of History" by the organizer of the symposium and editor of the papers. The second study entitled "Menezes on the Road to Diamper," is by Dr. K. J. John (Ochanthuruth), lecturer of Archeology and Ancient History in the Postgraduate Department of History, Calicut University, and member of Kerala Latin Catholic History Association. This study first appeared in his recent book *The Road to Diamper: An Exhaustive Study of the Synod of Diamper and the Origins of Roman Catholics in Kerala* (Cochin, Kerala Latin Catholic History Association: House of Providence), 1999, pp. 115-148. It presents Menezes as the hero of Diamper, whereas in some other studies his image may be less rosy. The editor's wish, as said above, is to present a volume that is *supra partes*. Of the two other studies by the editor included in this volume the first was written as a communication to the seminar and bears the title "The Union of Brest and the Synod of Diamper: A Comparison;" and the second is the conclusive study entitled "Return to Pre-Diamper Traditions."

The volume contains also five related documents as appendices. Appendix I is the Pontifical Bull of Pope Julius III on the reception of John Simon Sulaqa into the Catholic communion and appointing him Patriarch of the Chaldean Church (20 February 1553). The text is taken from Samuel Giamil, *Genuinae Relationes inter Sedem Apostolicam et Assyrorum Orientalium seu Chaldaeorum Ecclesiam*, Roma, Loescher, 1902, pp. 15-23, with some slight editing. In Appendix II we present an English translation of a document written less than five years before the Synod of Diamper and containing Francis Ros's denunciation of Mar Abraham as an incorrigible Nestorian prelate, who should be deposed by the pope. Appendix III is an enthusiastic report in Latin on the Synod of Diamper written soon after in November 1599 by Giovanni Campori, a young Jesuit missionary. In Appendix IV we publish for the first time the full text of a Portuguese manuscript (British Library, formerly British Museum, MS. Add. 9853, ff 86-99[v]), by Francis Ros, setting the Synod of Diamper in its historical context. We publish the Portuguese original accompanied by an English translation. Appendix V is the Common Declaration of Pope John Paul II and Patriarch Dinkha IV of the Assyrian Church of the East on 11 November 1994, which recognizes that historical Nestorianism and Roman Catholicism have always professed and do profess the same christological faith, a declaration that resets the theological parameters of past appraisals of orthodoxy and Nestorian heresy.

After the symposium of 18 November 1999 the speakers met in a follow-up session for sharing, for fraternal correction and for mutual help. This enabled them to avoid unnecessary repetitions as far as possible. On the question of orthography of proper names it was noted that different writers use different forms. Thus we find in the sources and in the literature, for example, Ros, Roz, and Rox; so also Menezes, Menezez, Menezis, Meneses, Menesis, etc. After a short discussion it was agreed to use the original form, except in textual citations where a different form occurs. Hence, in this volume we use Ros, since Francis Ros was a Catalan whose name was Francisco Ros (not Roz, as is found generally in Portuguese documents and writers); similarly, Menezes (not Menezez, etc.), whose Portuguese name is Alejio de Menezes.

Another point that came up for discussion was the lack of a critical edition of the authentic text of the decrees of the Synod of Diamper. The text that was read out to the participants and was signed by them at the end was the Malayalam text, and so it is the *authentic* text of the decrees of the Synod. Though the Portuguese text was, from the literary point of view, the *original* text (of which the Malayalam text was a translation), it does not represent the text approved by the synod, even apart from the problem created by later additions made by Menezes to the synodal decrees. Such additions may be Menezian, but was not synodal. Although it was the Portuguese version that gained currency in the West through the Portuguese propaganda, and asserted itself juridically in a Latin translation, from a historical standpoint the synodal decrees are to be sought in the Malayalam version. All the speakers agreed, therefore, that the lack of a critical edition of the Malayalam version making use of *all* the available manuscripts, was a real lacuna, although we already have two editions made on the basis of a *few* manuscripts. Hence the decision was taken to explore the possibilities of such a critical edition. This project is now already under way. Copies have been acquired of 3 MSS of the Vatican Library, 2 MSS of the library of Dharmaram College, Bangalore, 1 MS each of the CMI monasteries of Mannanam and Ambazhakad, Kerala. It is needless to underscore the fact that the studies contained in the present volume still bear the marks of the lack of such a critical edition of the decrees of the Synod of Diamper.

The editor wishes to thank all the learned contributors to the present volume. Grateful acknowledgement is hereby made of permission to publish Additional MSS 9853 ff 86-99 of the British Library. Thanks are also due in particular to Dr. K. J. John for permission to include his study of Dom Alexis Menezes as well as a picture of the same archbishop (Archbishop's Palace, Braga), published in his recent book *The Road to Diamper*. Finally, a word of thanks is due to Sunny Kokkavavalayil, S.J., for his patient work in preparing the Index.

Rome,
21 December 2000

George Nedungatt, S.J.
Editor

George Nedungatt, S.J.

Interpreting the Synod of Diamper and the Lessons of History

The Synod of Diamper has been hailed as a great achievement on the one hand, and on the other condemned or lamented as a great tragedy. At a midway between these two extreme standpoints is probably the sober truth that it was a watershed in the chequered history of the Thomaschristian Church, but not an unmixed blessing or unmitigated evil. The Synod of Diamper marks the beginning of the Latin period (third period) in the periodization of the Thomaschristian church history with reference to the hierarchy; it ends the Chaldean period (second period) that had followed the first period called the Indian period comprising the first four or five centuries. The Synod of Diamper gave impetus and hierarchical sanction to a process of change in the lifestyle of Eastern Christianity in India, a process that had begun already with the arrival of the European missionaries at the beginning of the sixteenth century. The gale-waves released by the Synod gradually lulled in the course of centuries, but the ripples have not ceased to ebb and flow.

Diamper consolidated and introduced many changes in the life and mores of the Thomaschristian community, changes that were charged with a latent explosive potential destined to detonate after half a century around the Coonan Cross of Mattancherry, leaving behind cataclysmal ecclesial debris. The Thomaschristian community had been a single Church for sixteen centuries, in spite of Northist-Southist ethnic rivalries, at times even reaching bloody paroxysm, and the caste-like separation of local communities congregating in separate churches for worship and the inflexible social interdict of intermarriage. Today, that Church is divided into seven or eight Churches or ecclesial communities. Though the Synod of Diamper was intended by its organizers as a union synod, unity proved to be its gravest casualty in the end. What is more, it continues to be seen and evaluated differently, the judgements varying from the most positive on the extreme right to the most negative on the extreme left. Is Diamper condemned to be a dialogue between the deaf in historical hermeneutics? The fourth centenary of this historical event bids us to look for the basic principles in interpreting it and the lessons to be learnt from it.

The present introductory study is conceived as an experiment in hermeneutics, a signpost to revisit Diamper at the threshold of the third millennium. After taking stock of the divergent interpretations of the Synod of Diamper in the first section, we shall in the next section raise the question of its identity: was it a Thomaschristian *yogam* or a diocesan synod on the Latin model? In the third section then we shall discuss a basic problem regarding its authentic acts. Fourthly, we shall consider the role of Nestorianism in the unfolding of the drama of Diamper and stress the need to cast off outdated parameters of evaluating Nestorianism from an ecumenical perspective. Related to this is the question dealt with in the fifth section if the Church of the Thomaschristians was already in the Catholic communion at the time of the synod. A distinction between latinization and catholicization is necessary for a correct appraisal of the achievement of the Synod of Diamper (sixth section). In the seventh and last section we shall draw attention to the novelty of revisiting the Synod of Diamper.

1. Historical Hermeneutics

The Synod of Diamper belongs to the history of Christianity in India as a whole. The dramatis personae were foreign missionaries and native Christians, Portuguese colonisers and Indian kinglets, “Latins” and “Syrians,” clergy, religious and laity. The history of this dramatic event has been told again and again in various versions. History is not a mere narration of facts, which is chronicles. Even chronicles are seldom a simple record of facts and often bear the imprints of the narrator handpicking the facts. The historian not only narrates but interprets. At the end of the Fourth Gospel we read that, if all that Jesus ever did and said were to be chronicled, the written volumes might well fill the whole world — a rhetorical hype to make the writer's point. He chose to write history, that is, history with an interpretation — indeed, a highly theological interpretation. Historical interpretation is the burden of most of the studies included in the present volume.

To look at an event after four centuries is to see it through the telescope of the intervening space-time. Thus, for example, since the Catholic Church officially changed its traditional stand on historical

Nestorianism in 1994, this christological doctrine and its upholders are seen today (at least by those who are theologically and ecumenically alert) in a different light than was the case at the time of Diamper. This new perspective, or the lack of it, will condition and differentiate one's appraisal of the Synod of Diamper today. It would indeed be intriguing to ask how Menezes, who took to the road to Diamper like a hero to kill the dragon of Nestorianism, would react if, like the legendary Maveli, he were to return to Diamper after four centuries. The present volume entitled *The Synod of Diamper Revisited* might well be a souvenir of that visit.

Conflicting historical appraisals are not uncommon. If Alexander's invasion of India in the fourth century B.C. was acclaimed by Greek historians as a victory of the great conqueror, his mysterious retreat was hailed as the triumph of the formidable phalanx of Indian elephants by the Indian chronicler. *Quidquid recipitur ad modum recipientis recipitur*, the Scholastic philosophers used to say. The subtle role of the subject in perception has been well expressed by Albert Einstein in his reply to felicitations on his discovery of the theory of relativity: If my theory is proved false (which can well happen if it is found not applicable in a single instance), the Germans will say, "Einstein is a Jew!" and the French will say "Einstein is a German!" But if it is verified, the Germans will say "Einstein is a German" and the French will say "Einstein is a citizen of the world."

In the traditional Protestant view, the Thomaschristians were as good as anonymous Protestants who detested the pope till the Synod of Diamper, but their Nestorianism was only a veneer.[1] According to most Portuguese and Spanish authors,[2] and like-minded Indian writers, the Synod of Diamper rescued the Thomaschristians from their allegiance to the Patriarch of Babylon and the perfidy of Nestorianism, thus putting them on the way of salvation in the bosom of the Catholic Church. On the other hand most Thomaschristian writers hold that their ancestors had always professed the true faith, although their liturgical books contained Nestorian names and formu-

[1] Thus (Anglican) Michael Geddes, *The History of the Church of Malabar*, London, 1694; Maturin Veyessière de la Croze, *Histoire du christiansme des Indes*, Den Hague, 1724; James Hough, *History of Christianity in India,* vol. 1, London, 1839.

[2] António de Gouvea, *Jornada do Arcebispo de Goa Dom Frey Aleixo de Menezes…*, Coimbra, 1606; António da Silva Rego, *Documentaçao para a Historia das Missoês do Padroado Portugues de Oriente-India,* 12 vols., Lisbon, 1947-1958; Idem, *Portuguese Colonization in the Sixteenth Century*, Johannesburg, 1959; Carlos Alonoso O.S.A, *Alejo de Meneses O.S.A. Arzobspo de Goa (1595-1612): Estudio biográfico*, Valladolid, 1992.

lae, and that they had always been in communion with Mārpāpa, the pope of Rome, through or in spite of the Patriarch of Babylon, to whom they were subject hierachically; and that they were victimised by the Portuguese through forced Romanization (latinization, westernization). A middle critical position eschews such blanket generalisations and recognizes the lights and shades, points out the variations and exceptions. But this midway critical position is not a meridian that passes necessarily between India and Portugal.[3] Nor are the various interpretations to be differentiated rite-wise.[4]

Quidquid percipitur ad modum percipientis percipitur is a variation of the Scholastic dictum cited earlier. Perception is conditioned by the perceiver. Historical interpretation differs not only because of the nearness or distance of the perceiver in time and space but also inevitable precomprehensions, dogmatic or philosophical presuppositions, subtle or gross emotional involvement that detracts from scientific detachment, unconscious conditioning by dominant or complex ideologies. It will be for the reader to judge whether and how far such factors condition the divergent interpretations of the Synod of Diamper. Though law is dispassionate ("reason without passion") according to Aristotle, the *jurisprudentes* (the "knowers" or interpreters of law) can be impassioned. So we shall not be surprised that there is no uniform answer to the juridical question about the canonical validity of the Synod of Diamper, as may be seen in the final study by Paul Pallath. At any rate, seeing the enormous impact this synod has had on the Thomaschristian Church, for better or worse, this question about validity might seem otiose to the general reader — like the discussion of the validity of a marriage when the baby born of it has already become a full-grown man and is presiding over the destiny of a nation.

---

[3] A refreshingly critical view of the Portuguese policy, dissociating from the traditional Portuguese laudatory standpoint, may be found in João Paolo Oliveira e Costa, "Os portugueses e a cristandade siro-malabar (1498-1530)," *Studia* [Lisboa, Centro de estudios históricos ultramarinos] 52 (1994) 121-178.

[4] For an overview of the writers on the Synod of Diamper across the centuries see Josef Wicki, "Die Synode von Diamper in Malabar (1959) und ihre Beurteilung (1600-1975)," *Annuarium Historiae Conciliorum* 9 (1977) 190-205. The writers examined are Antonio Gouvea, Jean Baptiste de Glen, Michael Geddes, Eugene Renaudot, Maturin Veyssière de la Croze, Joseph S. Assemani, J. F. Raulin, W. Germann, Samuel Giamil, Giusppe Beltrami, L. W. Brown, Gregorio Magno Antão, Jonas Thaliath, and Joseph Kuzhinjalil.

The present volume has not set itself the impossible task of quarantining the Synod of Diamper into a historical "epoche" and appraising it "in vacuo." No one can be impersonally "objective," free of all precomprehension, but all will do well without bias and bigotry. The ghost perceptions of Ros and Menezes need no more beguile us as we appraise their achievement at Diamper from a fresh perspective, different from theirs and from that of Gouvea, the admiring biographer and the adoring painter of the icon of Menezes the Great.

With the claim of having rescued the Thomaschristians from the Nestorian heresy and brought them under obedience of the pope in the Catholic Church the Synod of Diamper was touted all over Europe as a union council.[5] Whether it was really a union council is examined in a separate study in this volume, comparing the Synod of Diamper and the Union of Brest. Just as "non-theological factors" were behind most Church divisions and they still continue to block Church union, there are non theological factors that lie behind the dynamics of the Synod of Diamper. This forms part of the problem of its hermeneutics, rendered more complex by the fact that we need to look at it through the bifocal lens of history. Here we cannot linger long over the diverse interpretations and divergent appraisals of the Synod of Diamper[6] but may draw attention to works that qualify as scientifically detached exposition of this epoch-making event.[7]

---

[5] "Diamperitana Synodus in Malabaria, qua Christiani S. Thomae, vulgo dicti, fidem catholicam amplexi sunt et disciplina in tota Malabaria instituta." Such is the extended title of the Synod of Diamper in Mansi, *Sacrorum conciliorum...*, (op. cit. n. 14), col. 1161-1162.

[6] Gregorio Magno de Antão, *De Synodi Diamperitanae natura atque decretis*, Goa, Typ. Rangel-Bastora, 1952; Jonas Thaliath, *The Synod of Diamper* (Orientalia Christiana Analecta, 152), Rome, Pontifical Oriental Institute, 1958 (reprint: Bangalore, Dharmaram Publications, 1999). Two other more recent authors are: Scaria Zacharia, *Udayampērūr Sūnahadōsinte Kānōnakal*, (Malalayam), Edamattam, Indian Institute of Christian Studies, 1994; Idem, *The Acts and Decrees of the Synod of Diamper, 1599*, Edamattam, Indian Institute of Christian Studies, 1994; K. J. John, *The Road to Diamper: An Exhaustive Study of the Synod of Diamper and the Origins of Roman Catholics in Kerala* (Cochin, Kerala Latin Catholic History Association: House of Providence), 1999.

[7] For a detached exposition and critical appraisal of the Synod of Diamper by a Swiss Jesuit historian, see Joseph Wicki, "Die Synoden der Thomaschristen (auch Syromalabaren genannt) (1583-1603)," *Annuarium Historiae Conciliorum* 18 (1986) 333-447, on the Synod of Diamper see pp. 343-440. The *Documenta Indica* bears witness to the admirable scholarship of Joseph Wicki, who completed the last volume XVIII (1595-1597), (= Monumenta Historica Societatis Iesu, 133), in 1988 before his death in 1993. He died before publishing the documents regarding the Synod of Diamper.

2. The Synod of Diamper a *Yogam* or Synod?

The Synod of Diamper was conducted from 20 June to 25 June 1599[8] by Alexis Menezes, O.S.A., the young (forty-year old), dynamic and daring Latin Archbishop of Goa, who was both a Portuguese patriot and dedicated pastor of the Roman Catholic Church.[9] He had it convoked through the reluctant Archdeacon George of the Thomaschristians as a Thomaschristian *yógam*[10] but it was conducted as a *diocesan synod* of the Latin Church, following the *Rites of Councils* by Cardinal Charles Borromeo. Was it then a synod or a *yogam*?

Overtly, the Synod of Diamper was a pastoral attempt to promulgate and apply the decrees of the Council of Trent, as had already been done in the provincial councils of Goa, and to clear the Christianity of the Serra (Malabar) of Nestorian heresy and other evils. But these religious motives were not the only ones that moved Menezes. Understandably so in pre-modern times when Church and society, religion and politics, bishops and dukes were inseparable. Not the least of Menezes' motives in conducting a synod during the vacancy of the See of Angamaly (thus making hay while the sun shines), was to take over the Thomaschristian Church and integrate it into the Padroado regime. For this he pursued an astute policy of diplomacy (as some see it) or duplicity (as others perceive it).[11] For example, Menezes acted as if the See of Angamaly were already suffragan to Goa, although it would be made a suffragan see only six months after the Synod on 20 December 1599 by Pope Clement VIII (1592-1605), which his successor Paul V (1605-1621) would regret and annul in response to the complaints of the Thomaschristians. Menezes acted as if the Thomaschristians were already under the Padroado, al-

---

[8] J. Thaliath, *The Synod of Diamper,* op. cit., n. 6, p. 31, n. 90; Andrews Thazhath, *The Juridical Sources of the Syro-Malabar Church*, (OIRSI, 106), Kottayam, Paurastya Vidyapitham, 1987, p. 136, n. 119.

[9] In 1558 Goa had been elevated as the primatial see of All East for the Latins, a qualification that was also a restriction. But this restriction did not count in practice at that time in India as the Portuguese Padroado advanced its claim to the rights of conquest (see note 12 below).

[10] On the Thomaschristian *yōgam,* which was an ancient institution of clergy-laity cooperation in Church government, see George Nedungatt, *Laity and Church Temporalities: Appraisal of a Tradition*, Dharmaram Canonical Studies, 1), Bangalore, Dharmaram Publications, 2000, pp. 127-157.

[11] Cf. Joseph Thekkedath, *History of Christianity in India*, vol. 2, (CHAI History of Christianity in India, vol. 2), Bangalore, Theological Publications, 1982, "The Synod of Diamper....". pp. 64-75, at p. 75.

though the Padroado jurisdiction would be extended over Angamaly by the pope only on 4 August 1600, more than one year after the Synod of Diamper. It is, therefore, difficult to avoid the suspicion that the Synod was covertly a dramatic ploy to execute the plot of Portuguese political hegemony over Malabar, nursing the hope of enlisting an additional army of 30,000 Thomaschristian soldiers and ensuring the monopoly of trade and commerce with the Serra.[12] To overcome the resistance of the archdeacon and forestall any native interference by the protective secular arm, Menezes pulled up his sleeves and showed the Portuguese military muscle.

> Menezes went to the King of Cochin, spoke very harshly to him, without giving any opportunity for reply, insulted his gods and threatened him with hell. The king swallowed the Archbishop's insults along with his own rage, and did what Menezes required of him. The archdeacon now learned that any further resistance by him might end up with his elimination from the scene. He, therefore, decided to surrender to the Archbishop.[13]

Clearly, Archbishop Menezes was relying on the military might of the Portuguese colonial power. Before that power the king of Cochin, currently the petty protector of the Christians, who were living scattered in seventeen tiny principalities, could only cow down and do obeisance, whatever be the insult to his person and the dent to his sovereignty. This dramatic episode in the palace of the King of Cochin is emblematic of the Portuguese conquest of the Serra, striking terror into the native kinglets with superior cannon power. The lesson was not lost on the archdeacon. He saw that his choice now lay between two alternatives: "elimination from the scene" or "surrender to the Archbishop." Not being made of the stuff of martyrs, he chose the latter alternative. With that the Thomaschristian Church was also virtually surrendered to Menezes and to the Portuguese forces for a surgical operation to save her from the mortal malignity of Nestorianism as some see it, for an ecclesial rape as others see it. Where is the truth?

---

[12] Already in 1499 King Manuel I (reigned 1495 to 1521) had made the tall claim that he was the "Lord of the Conquest, Navigation and Commerce of Ethiopia, Arabia, Persia, and of India." The Portuguese regarded it their divine mission to conquer the lands of pagans and of heretics for Christ and for the Roman Catholic Church by planting the cross behind the sword and thus reaping a harvest of souls. See C. R. Boxer, *The Portuguese Sea-Borne Empire, 1415-1825*, London, 1969.

[13] K. J. John, *The Road to Diamper,* op. cit. (note 6), pp. 140-141.

Menezes knew that without the cooperation of the archdeacon a general assembly of the Thomaschristians, called traditionally *Mahāyogam,* could not be convoked and that his cooperation could not be secured except under duress. But then, according to the law about force and fear, the convocation of the *Mahāyogam* itself would be invalid, casting doubt about the validity of the "yogam/synod" itself. We do not, however, wish to enter here into the question of validity, which is dealt with elsewhere in this volume by Paul Pallath.

The assembly at Diamper had all the semblance of a *Maháyógam* (the precursor of the present Major Archiepiscopal Assembly), except the substance, in that it lacked any deliberative voice. It is significant that it is not called *yógam,* in spite of the protocol, but "synod" — in a diocesan synod the only legislator, by law, being the diocesan bishop. But Menezes was not the diocesan bishop, nor was he an apostolic administrator, *sede vacante.* That again raises the question of the validity of the synod, which, however, need not detain us.

The Synod of Diamper was assembled at a strategic place, Udayamperur (or Diamper, which is the westernised form of this village in today's central Kerala), a stronghold of the Southists, not too far from Cochin and Cranganor (Kodungallur). It was a massive assembly of over 800 participants, of whom 153 were clerics and 660 laymen, mostly delegates, swelled by the local population and the Portuguese Captain and entourage. We do not know the exact number of the participants since admission was not restricted to the delegates: four lay delegates (*notabili,* in the terminology of Francis Ros, that is "prominences") elected by the *Palliyógam* from each parish and all the priests who were summoned to attend under pain of excommunication, though not all of them actually came. Of the 153 clerics more than 100 were the newly ordained priests who owed allegiance to Menezes and supported him promptly in the Synod, thus stifling any incipient opposition.

What has come to be known as the Synod of Diamper saw through an ample agenda to promulgate and apply the norms and reforms of the Council of Trent.[14] If some changes were of the nature of catholi-

---

[14] "The Synod of Diamper was a concerted effort by the Portuguese to westernize the Eastern Christians of Kerala," so writes Scaria Zacharia, *Ranṭu prācīna gadyakrtikal,* Changanacherry, 1976, pp. XVIII, LXXXIII. This is a reductive view that does not do justice to the overriding religious factor, though it is true that the Portuguese did westernize, as did the other colonial powers with their sense of the superiority of the western culture and civilization.

cization, most were latinization, especially in the matter of liturgy and the sacraments. The Synod also corrected several abuses and made good many lacunae, though some decrees prohibited morally neutral customs and mores that were factors of social and cultural integration.

3. The Authentic Decreess of the Synod

There is some confusion regarding the authentic decrees of the Synod of Diamper. The decrees were first formulated in Portuguese by Dom Menezes, for some of which he surely had at hand a dossier prepared by Francis Ros. Menezes had them then translated into Malayalam. It was this Malayalam text that was read out in the synod to the participants and signed by them at the end of the sessions. However, the Malayalam version of the decrees is significantly different from the Portuguese version, which is larger in contents chiefly because it contains thirty-five canons lacking in the Malayalam text. The Portuguese version was published by Antonio Gouvea and was translated into Latin by John F. Raulin, and this Latin text was reproduced in Mansi.[15] It is this Latin version that has been cited in the official Church documents including the *Code of Canons of the Eastern Churches*.

A preliminary methodological task is to ascertain the authentic text of the decrees of the Synod of Diamper: is it the Malayalam text or the Portuguese text? According to some authors it was the Portuguese text that was read out in the Synod. But this hypothesis is preposterous. Menezes was zealous but not crazy. He himself had drafted the Portuguese text for the most part but then had it translated into Malayalam *before* the Synod sat, a move which hardly makes sense if what was to be read out to the participants was the Portuguese text. Moreover, Portuguese would not have been understood by the participants except for a few, most of whom had been taught in the Vaipicotta seminary of the Jesuits. And to keep such an assembly from becoming unruly for a week Menezes would have needed police force, turning the synod into a self-defeating farce. Finally, it was at the end of the Malayalam text that the participants

[15] J. D. Mansi (et alii), *Sacrorum conciliorum nova et amplissima collectio* ..., 53 vols., Florence, etc., 1759-1927; for the Synod of Diamper see vol. 35, Paris, Welter, 1902, cols. 1161-1368.

put their signatures.[16] And so it clearly represents the *synodal* acts and the *authentic text* of the decrees of the Synod of Diamper, while the Portuguese text with an extra thirty-five canons represents the *Menezian* acts.

The Malayalam text was made out in two scripts then in use, Malayalam and Karsuni (that is, Malayalam written with Syriac characters). The signatures were appended to both, of the priests probably to the latter, and of the laity to the former. The sheets with the signatures were later detached and sent to Rome, but the Malayalam and the Karsuni texts were not transmitted. These mostly got lost after the Synod of Diamper, which was not generally received by the Thomaschristians and was in part, though minimally, overruled by the 1603 Diocesan Synod and the 1606 Statutes of Ros.

How are we to explain the presence in the Portuguese text of these canons that are lacking in the Malayalam text? According to Francis Ros, who wrote later about the Synod to the Jesuit General in Rome, Menezes added some canons to the synodal decrees after the Synod was over. There is no good reason to discount this testimony, but Ros does not indicate or identify the additions. The thesis or rather hypothesis ("it is possible") of a recent writer instead is as follows. These are not post-synodal additions to the Portuguese text. The Malayalam translation is only a "cursory translation" with some portions "deleted" and some other portions only "summarised," chiefly because the sixteenth century Malayalam was still "in its infancy" without "sufficient vocabulary."[17] This explanation might well hold good in a few instances but not in all. A textual comparison does not confirm this benevolent hypothesis, which seems to labour under the preoccupation to exonerate Menezes of all possible blame of interpolation. But such a preoccupation is misplaced. Being the only lawful legislator of the synod, Menezes was fully free to determine the text he wanted to promulgate without the fear of the charge of falsification or interpolation. The textual difference between the Malayalam text and the Portuguese text is, therefore, no reason either to dress up Menezes as a villain or to look for far-fetched hypotheses to shield him from all blame. From the canonical point of view, however, it is the Malayalam text that counts for the acts of the Synod of Diamper.

---

[16] For the Malayalam text of these Statutes with an introduction, see Scaria Zacharia, *Ranṭu prācīna gadyakrtikal*, Changanacherry, 1976, pp. 111-177.

[17] See K. J. John, *The Road to Diamper*, op. cit. (n. 6), p. 179.

One serious difficulty, however, remains. We are far from having established the Malayalam text that was read out in the Synod of Diamper. The earliest MS now available is a copy made more than 150 years after the synod. We cannot be sure of being able to reconstruct the original even with the help of the other known MSS. For in 1603 Bishop Francis Ros conducted a diocesan Synod, in which he weeded out those provisions of the Synod of Diamper that had most grieved the Thomaschristians. After this event only archivists would have kept the original Diamper text, while the copies that circulated among the parish priests would be the "expurgated" version. It is quite possible that the few Malayalam MMS that have been identified so far are all of this kind. The archivist's version, if it is still extant, may well be in Vattezhuth or Karson, which can make the work of less equipped researcher's harder. In any case, in the present state of our knowledge, it is hazardous to speak of thirty-five "additional decrees" in the Portuguese text of the Synod of Diamper that are lacking in the Malayalam text. All this bids us to be cautious in identifying the authentic *synodal* acts simply with the latter as well.

As long as there is the shadow of a question mark on the authenticity of the synodal text the interpretation of the Synod of Diamper itself must bear the marks of that shadow.

4. Diamper and Nestorianism

One of the overt aims of Menezes in conducting the Synod of Diamper was to purge the Thomaschristian Church of Nestorianism. Before focusing on this question we have to be clear in our own minds about Nestorianism, since its Catholic understanding today has changed profoundly from that of the sixteenth century. As a result of serious and dispassionate research studies, conducted chiefly in the postconciliar ecumenical climate, it has been recognized in non-official as well as official ecumenical statements by Catholics as well as Orthodox that both historical Monophysitism and historical Nestorianism have professed the same true *faith* as contained in the christological dogmas defined by the ecumenical councils of Ephesus and Chalcedon, in spite of differences in terminology and *theological expressions* which caused misunderstandings and did give rise to mutual anathemas.

a) *Common Papal-Patriarchal Declatation (1994)*

An official common declaration was signed on 11 November 1994 by Pope John Paul II, representing the Catholic Church, and by Patriarch Dinkha IV as the spokesman of the Assyrian Church of the East, traditionally called the Nestorian Church. This Common Declaration recognizes the orthodoxy of the faith of both of these Churches, though expressed in different theologies. See the full text in Appendix V. Here are the key sentences of this Common Declaration.

> Our Lord Jesus Christ is true God and true man, perfect in his divinity and perfect in his humanity, consubstantial with the Father and consubstantial with us in all things but sin. His divinity and his humanity are united in one person, without confusion or change, without division or separation. In him has been preserved the difference of the natures of divinity and humanity, with all their properties, faculties and operations. But far from constituting "one and another," the divinity and humanity are united in the person of the same and unique Son of God and Lord Jesus Christ, who is the object of a single adoration.
>
> .... The humanity to which the Blessed Virgin Mary gave birth always was that of the Son of God himself. That is the reason why the Assyrian Church of the East is praying the Virgin Mary as 'the Mother of Christ our God and Saviour.' In the light of this same faith the Catholic tradition addresses the Virgin Mary as 'the Mother of God' and also as 'the Mother of Christ.' We both recognize the legitimacy and richness of these expressions of the same faith and we both respect the preference of each Church in her liturgical life and piety.
>
> This is the unique faith we profess in the mystery of Christ. The controversies of the past led to anathemas, bearing on persons and on formulas. The Lord's Spirit permits us to understand better today that the divisions brought about in this way were due in large part to misunderstandings.
>
> Whatever our christological divergences have been, we experience ourselves united today in the confession of the same faith in the Son of God....[18]

With this declaration the Catholic Church has officially recognized that the true faith in Christ was preserved in historical Nestorianism all through the past centuries. By "historical Nestorianism" is meant Nestorianism as professed and explained by its own adherents and theologians and synods. For the most part it does not coincide

---

[18] *L'Osservatore Romano*, 12 November 1994, p. 5; *Acta Apostolicæ Sedis* 87 (1995), July, pp. 685-687; *Christian Orient* 16 (1995) March, pp. 38-41; *Enchiridion Oecumenicum*, vol 3, Bologna, Edizioni Dehoniane, 1995, pp. 345-348; *Enchiridion Vaticanum*, vol 14, Bologna, Edizioni Dehoniane, 1997, pp. 1014-1016 (NN. 1823-1825). For the full text of this Common Declaration see Appendix V.

with "theological Nestorianism" sketched in polemical manuals of theology and church history of outsiders, or even in conciliar anathemas. These conciliar anathemas, geared to theological Nestorianism, are not necessarily an obstacle to the reunion of the Churches.[19] This is one of the more significant fruits of ecumenical dialogues and studies undertaken above all in the decades following the Second Vatican Council. These dialogues and studies of the christology of the divided Churches cross-fertilized each other and produced astounding, not to say 'revolutionary,' results. Both historical Monophysitism and historical Nestorianism (Dyophysitism) have therefore been reconsidered and redefined more objectively.[20] One thinks of the monumental work of Aloys Grillemeir, who wrote in 1985: "One is delighted to have established that despite all the differences, conditioned as they are culturally and intellectually, the great regions of the *orbis christologicus*, whether Eastern or Western, are one in their faith in Christ."[21] As regards Nestorius in particular,

> Recent scholarship questions whether Nestorius was himself a 'Nestorian', and maintains that his position was orthodox and that his differences with his great rival Cyril of Alexandria, are to be explained more by the confusion of terminology from which both suffered, particularly the failure to distinguish clearly between 'person' and 'nature,' rather than from any departure from the Church's faith on Nestorius's part.[22]

Nestorius was in fact more sinned against than sinned. He declared that his own position was well expressed by Pope Leo the Great, and "he quite often affirmed even that Christ is 'in two natures,' or 'a sole *prosōphon* in two natures.'"[23] It has even been said that Nestorius was not a Nestorian! In order to affirm that Jesus Christ is truly and fully God and truly and fully man, against the Arians and the Apollinarians misleading his flock in Constantinople, Nestorius, Patriarch of Constantinople, speaks of the *prosōpon* of God

---

[19] John H. Erickson, "Anathema: An Obstacle to Reunion?" *St. Nersess Theological Review* 3 (1998) Nos. 1-2, pp. 67-75.

[20] For a lucid and synthetic overview, Sebastian Brock, "The Importance of the Syriac Traditions in Ecumenical Dialogue and Christology," *Christian Orient* 20/4 (1999) 189-197.

[21] Aloys Grillemeier, *Christ in Christian Tradition*, second revised ed., 2 vols., London & Oxford, Mowbray, 1975/1985, at vol. 2, part one, Preface, p. v.

[22] *The New Dictionary of Theology*, ed. Joseph A. Komonchak, Mary Collins, Dermot A. Lane, Wilmington, Glazier, 1987/1989, p. 715.

[23] Luigi I Scipioni, *Nestorio e il concilio di Efeso: Storia, dogma, critica*, Milano, Università Cattolica del Sacro Cuore, 1974, pp. 431-432.

and the *prosōpon* of man but in the sense of complete divine and human natures, which are manifested only through a *prosōpon*. His objection to the Marian epithet *Theotokos* (literally, "God-bearer," Mother of God) was not dogmatic but pastoral, not to seem to sanction its Apollinarian abuse. Unfortunately, he could not anticipate the post-Chalcedonian precision in the use of the three key terms *physis*, *hypostasis*, and *prosōpon*, and he lost his case at the Council of Ephesus owing more to the wily ecclesiastical politics of Cyril of Alexandria than to any deviation from orthodoxy.[24]

According to the latest competent critical comment to date, it is in fact difficult to find Nestorians who have really upheld what their adversaries have attributed to them as their doctrine, namely that there are not only two natures in Christ but two persons, one divine (Logos) and the other human, united in a sort of moral union.[25] Seemingly more for political than dogmatic reasons, the East Syrian Church embraced Nestorianism since 486, but as expounded by its patronymic teacher Theodore of Mopsuestia († 428), *the* Exegete, who was condemned posthumously at the Second Council of Constantinople (553) on the basis of interpolated texts, a victim of imperial politics. The christology of Babai the Great (ca 551 – ca 628), the premier theologian of the East Syrian Church, comparable in this regard to Thomas Aquinas of the Latin Church, professed and defended the same true faith in Christ as the Catholic Church, albeit using different terminology.[26] Barhebraeus declared in the thirteenth century, that after much study and experience of christological dialogue he was convinced that the three traditional church divisions around christology (Chalcedon, Monophysite, and Dyophysite/Diphysite) preserved and expressed the same true faith in Christ, true

---

[24] Ibid., pp. 409, 417, 420.

[25] Edward G. Farrugia, "Nestorianesimo" in Idem, ed., *Dizionario enciclopedico dell'Oriente cristiano*, Roma, Pontificio Isituto Orientale, 2000, p. 522.

[26] Geevarghese Chediath, *The Christology of Mar Babai the Great*, Roma 1982. "For the Persians Babai's christology was the christology of their Church." (p. 193). "He avoids Nestorianism (teaching of two sons, one natural and adoptive son joined together only externally and morally. ... Babai's christology expresses the very same truth as the Cyrillian christology, although the same words meant different things to different people" (p. 195). Indeed, "The history of theology and the church history of the "Nestorian Church" have to be rewritten" (p. 196).

God and true man, right through their polemics.[27] The divided Churches needed seven more centuries to come to the same realisation and, alas, are as yet unable to make a common declaration in an ecumenical council, exorcising the ghosts of perception of the past.

In short, the christological faith professed by the East Syrian Church (alias Chaldean Church, Persian Church, Assyrian Church of the East) was misunderstood in the past and was condemned unfairly as heresy, although it coincided essentially with the Ephesian orthodoxy of the universal Church. The mutual anathemas of the past are as a rule ecumenically regretted today as unfortunate.

b) *Nestorianism in Malabar*

In Kerala, where historical Nestorianism undoubtedly had and still has its habitat, the above mentioned epoch-making Common Declaration of John Paul II and Patriarch Mar Dinkha IV (1994) is still not generally known. This is sad. To refer to it is often like breaking fresh news! Not surprisingly certain Catholic writers still carry on dutifully beating the carcass of Nestorianism![28] Some others see Nestorianism in the current text of the Syro-Malabar Qurbana and express their "Catholic" shudder! By contrast, as a follow-up of the 1994 Common Declaration, efforts are afoot chiefly in Iraq and in the United States of America for the reunion of the Assyrian and Chaldean Patriarchal Churches. According to a communiqué released after a joint session held on 13-14 August 1997 in Chicago, the concrete measures decided upon include preparation of a common catechism and common liturgical books, as well as the foundation of a common institute in Chicago for the formation of priests and deacons.

The current understanding of Nestorianism came four centuries too late for the Synod of Diamper and especially for its prime mover, Archbishop Menezes and his aide Francisco Ros. No one can of course be blamed for not being ahead of his or her times. However, Menezes practically ignored the fact that the Church of the Tho-

---

27 For the text of Barhebraeus see Sebastian Brock, "The Importance of the Syriac Traditions in Ecumenical Dialogue and Christology," *Christian Orient* 20/4 (1999) 189-197, at p. 197.

28 K. J. John, *The Road to Diamper* (op. cit, n. 6) is a recent example. This author does not mention the 1553 East Syrian Church union with the Catholic Church (see Appendix I) nor does he show awareness of the 1994 Common Declaration of Pope John Paul II and Patriarch Dinkha IV (see Appendix V).

maschristians was already in the Catholic communion (see below). Surely, he had seen papal documents to this effect in the files of the Archbishop of Goa, which showed the papal respect for the Babylonian Patriarch's jurisdiction in Malabar. The Jesuits in Malabar would have rather worked with and through Mar Abraham (who had landed in Malabar as a Nestorian bishop in 1556 but later became a Catholic making the profession of faith in Rome) as long as he was pliant and executed the decrees of the Third Council of Goa. But when he demurred or resisted the correction of Nestorian "errors" (and now we know he was not wrong, rather had a right and duty to ecclesial resistance!), they turned against him and denounced him wanting to engineer his ouster. Menezes, strong with the persuasion that he had the ear of the pope, acted as one better informed than the pope and the papal curia, "duped" by the "sly" heretic! And he brusquely brushed aside the Jesuits who had been active in Malabar for a quarter of a century and advised caution, temporising and moderation. Father Francisco Dionysio, for example, who came to India in 1563 and was Rector of the Jesuit residence in Cochin (1576-1578), had written the following in his "Information on the Christianity of St. Thomas" on 4 January 1578:

> In general these Christians believe in all the articles of the Nicean Creed and the equality of the divine persons, and the two natures of Christ in one person. And so do also the Archbishop and the Archdeacon. The pope they regard as the Vicar of Christ our Redeemer on earth, and their patriarch as subject to the pope, from whom he has received his powers.[29]

Another Jesuit Antonio Montserrate saw the continued dependence of Malabar on the Patriarch as an open possibility for the evangelization of India.[30] But Francis Ros, S.J., well versed in Syriac and professor of that language in the Jesuit seminary of Vaipicotta, detected errors in the Syriac books that were found in the Serra. He wrote a treatise about the "errors of the Nestorians in Malabar" and sent it to Rome in 1586-1587.[31] He stated his thesis at the outset: "The

---

[29] Ioseph Wicki, *Documenta Indica*, XI (1577-1580), (= Monumenta Historica Societatis Iesu, 103), Rome, 1970; Doc. 10, "Relatio P. Francisci Dionysii S. I. de Christianis S. Thomae," pp. 131-143, at p. 139.

[30] St. Augustine's *compelle entrare* principle was adopted by the Portuguese for the evangelization of Goa. Reconciling heretics was after all only a step away in the same direction.

[31] Irénée Hausherr, ed., "De erroribus Nestorianorum qui in hac India orientali versantur," *Orientalia Christiana*, vol. XI/1 (1928), N° 40, Rome, Pontifical Oriental Institute, pp. 15-36.

Nestorians who are the inhabitants of Eastern India have professed the Catholic faith, but their books are awash with the teachings of Nestorius, Diodore of Tarse and Theodore of Mopsuestia."[32] As proof of this thesis he collected a number of texts and translated them from Syriac into Latin. This proof-text method, till recently much used in biblical theology as well as dogmatic theology has been found wanting.[33] Ros quaintly qualified the Thomaschristians as "Nestorians" who "profess the Catholic faith."[34] His real purpose in writing the above treatise was probably to have Mar Abraham deposed by the pope: this is betrayed by his tone and final statement.[35] Ros wrote still another more detailed and harsher denunciation of Mar Abraham in 1594 (see Appendix II). Menezes chose to follow Ros's judgement regarding Nestorianism in Malabar rather than that of his confreres. He determined that the time had come to draw the curtain on the Nestorian drama in Malabar. He peremptorily demanded the Thomaschristians to abjure their "Nestorian" faith and their "Nestorian" Patriarch of Babylon. He silenced the remonstrance of those Jesuits whose temporising policy would have delayed a Portuguese prelate enter the scene and occupy the see of Angamaly, which had to be part of Padroado territory. His was the Hidalgo's service to the Portuguese imperial-ecclesiastical design, "to win lands and people for the Roman Catholic Church and the King of Portugal."[36] The Synod of Diamper was that service.

---

[32] "Nestoriani, qui Orientalem Indiam degunt, quamvis Romanam fidem catholicam fuerint professi, ipsorum tamen libri, Nestorii, Diodori Tarsensis et Theodori Mopsuestheni, dogmatibus scatent" (p. 15).

[33] "Evidently, the real and full doctrine of an author or of a period regarding the mystery of Christ is not to be determined on the basis of terms and formulas only." — P. Galtier, *De incarnatione ac redemptione*, Paris, Beauchesne, 1926, p. 80; cited by Hausherr in the original Latin, op. cit., p. 13.

[34] "It is regrettable that the Synod relied too much on the knowledge of Father Ros without any protest from those who took part in it; he should have been more careful in denouncing heresy in as much as he lacked the necessary scientific background." So writes Joseph Wicki, "Die Synode der Thomaschristen," (art. cit. n. 7), p. 375.

[35] "quamobrem, re ad Summum Pontificem delata, optimum plane esset ab ecclesiastico gradu archiepiscopatusque sede illum deturbare" ("De erroribus..." , op. cit. (note 31), p. 35).

[36] "To win lands and people for Roman Catholic Church and the King of Portugal was the ideal that motivated his Indian mission." So is the frank and clear statement of K. J. John, op. cit., (n. 6), p. 116.

5. Ecclesial *Koinonia*

Long before the Synod of Diamper sat, the East Syrian Patriarch John Sulaqa had made the profession of the Catholic faith before Pope Julius III on 20 February 1553 and renounced Nestorianism[37] at a time when the Council of Trent was still in session. This profession of the Roman Catholic faith was not probably motivated purely for reasons of faith. In any case on his return from Rome Sulaqa died a martyr of union at the hands of the "traditionalists," who in their turn would, however, enter into union with Rome in the next century. Two Jesuit theologians, Laynez and Salmeron, were active during the Council of Trent as papal theologians. Consequently their confrères in Malabar could have also more easily known that the Thomaschristians under the Catholic Patriarch of Babylon were in communion with the See of Rome, just like themselves. The Jesuit missionaries starting with St Francis Xavier, who had worked for and among the Thomaschristians, were conscious of belonging to the same Catholic fold as the Thomaschristians. It is enough to think of the Jubilee indulgence of the Holy Year 1575 which the Jesuits arranged to be sent to Mar Abraham and his Church with a Roman rescript dated 28 October 1579. It is unlikely that the Jesuits would have presented Nestorians to the pope for indulgences, and even more unlikely that the pope would have granted them to Nestorians!

There is further documentation about the Roman view of the orthodoxy of the Chaldean patriarchs, of Mar Abraham, and of the Thomaschristians. After receiving Mar Abraham's profession faith, Pope Pius IV had written to Sulaqa's successor Patriarch Abdisho on 23 February 1565 *suggesting* the division of the Church of the Thomaschristians into two circumscriptions and entrusting them to Mar Abraham and Mar Joseph. And on 28 February 1565 Pope Pius IV wrote also to the Archbishop of Goa asking him to respect the jurisdiction of the Chaldean Patriarch in Malabar. Later Pope Gregory XIII wrote to Mar Abraham on 29 November 1578 asking him to attend the provincial synod of Goa seeing that he himself had no suffragan bishops to hold a provincial synod. The Third Provincial Council of Goa (1585), in which Mar Abraham also took part, decreed in its third session that any future bishop of the Thomaschristians

[37] See Samuel Giamil, *Genuinae relationes inter Sedem Apostolicam et Assyriorum orientalium seu Chaldæorum Ecclesiam*, Rome, 1902, pp. 23-27; Giuseppe Beltrami, *La Chiesa caldea nel secolo dell'unione*, (Orientalia Christiana, 29, n. 83), Rome, 1933. The date of the profession of faith is wrongly given here as 15 February (p. 5).

appointed by the pope, *or by the East Syrian patriarch,* should first present his letters of appointment to the Archbishop of Goa, the Primate of India.[38] Finally, less than five years before the Synod of Diamper, the Jesuits held their fourth Provincial Congregation at Goa (22-29 October 1594), which requested the Father General to propose to the pope the appointment of Archdeacon George as the future successor of Mar Abraham (*Documenta Indica,* XI, pp. 650-652). Thus, from the mid-sixteenth century there was not only hierarchical communion between the See of Rome and the East Syrian patriarchate, from which the Thomaschristians used to receive their bishops, but also papal documents recognizing this patriarchal jurisdiction in Malabar and requiring its respect by Goa and the Portuguese missionaries, among whom at least the Jesuits wanted the episcopal succession to pass finally to the Thomaschristians with the papal appointment of a native priest.[39] Undoubtedly, we can conclude that the Latin missionaries were aware of the fact that the Thomaschristians belonged to the same Catholic Church as governed by the pope as the supreme common pastor and that the Patriarch of Babylon was long since in the Catholic communion and had pontifically approved jurisdiction in Malabar.

As early as 1525, as Benedict Vadakkekara points out, candidates for priesthood were recruited from among the Thomaschristians. After ordination they used to exercise the sacred ministry along with the Padroado clergy. Menezes himself ordained, contrary to law and without pastoral need, about a hundred young Thomaschristians as priests, making them abjure "Nestorianism" and making them "Catholics," who would considerably increase the number of his supporters at the Synod of Diamper. "He gave the sacrament of Confirmation to the greater part of this Christianity," as Bishop Ros wrote.[40]

Did Menezes really believe that the Thomaschritians were indeed Nestorian heretics? Or was there some make-believe in his dire stand on Nestorianism at the Council of Diamper and after? The "Decree

[38] Paiva Manso, *Bullarium Patronatus Portugalliae Regum,* Lisbon, 1872, Appendix I, pp. 73-76.

[39] For these and other documents see Giamil, *Genuinae Relationes*, op. cit., documents V-XXVI, pp. 15-100; Giuseppe Beltrami, *La chiesa caldea* (op. cit.), 141-272. For a summary of these and other documents (papal, patriarchal, and synodal including the Provincial Synods of Goa of 1575 and 1585 as well as the First Synod of Angamaly of 1583) see Andrews Thazhath, *The Juridical Sources of the Syro-Malabar Church,* (OIRSI, 106), Kottayam, Paurastya Vidyapitham, 1987, pp. 121-133.

[40] See Appendix IV, 25.

for the Armenians" issued by the Council of Florence (1438-1452) had already been received by the First Synod of Angamaly (1583).[41] Since then there were several papal bulls and communications to the Archbishop of Goa respecting and instilling respect for the jurisdiction of the Chaldean Patriarch. Besides there was the on-the-spot counsel of the Jesuits who knew the people, their language, their faith, their bishops and their relations with the Patriarch of Babylon. Against their counsel Menezes demanded of the Thomaschristians to abjure their Patriarch. It was an age that burnt heretics as an act of homage to God. Then it was enough to cry heresy to make martyrs of Hus and Savanarola at the pyre. The Thomaschristian Archdeacon George of the Cross did not have the blood of martyrs in his veins. Menezes had his way to daunt, to subjugate and appropriate under the veneer of liberation from heresy. Notwithstanding all the Catholic *koinonia*, the emissaries of the Patriarch of Babylon had to be ousted and prevented from coming to Malabar in the future if the Portuguese imperial-ecclesiastical agenda had to be put through. Whatever their profession of faith before the pope and his curia, on the evidence of their books as read by Ros — neither Menezes or any other foreign missionary knew Syriac well —, they were "heretics" and "thieves" who had sneaked into the sheepfold of Christ.[42] The Inquisition of Goa, zealous with the *Zeitgeist* of heresy-hunting, had hounded the patriarchal emissary Mar Joseph out. And it harassed Mar Abraham, who had to use all his Chaldean wiles to evade time and again the Portuguese tentacles and reach or return to his episcopal see in Malabar.

Celebrated as a "union synod," the Synod of Diamper singularly advanced the Portuguese imperial-ecclesiastical design. Lisbon and Rome were apparently pleased with the achievement of Menezes.[43] Neither reproached Menezes for acting *ultra vires* in conducting the Synod. As some see it, this argument from silence in Rome and Lis-

[41] See DzSch 1300, introductory note.

[42] The title "Universal Pastor" translated the Greek "Ecumenical Patriarch," (*patriárchēs oikonomikós*), and indicated suprametropolitan powers, and was applicable to all patriarchs, whether of Constantinople or of Rome or Seleucia-Ctesiphon ("Babylon" in the Acts of Diamper) without any claim to universal jurisdiction, as would instead be claimed by the Pope of Rome. Ignorance of this fact vitiated Menezes' judgement about the Patriarch of Babylon and it continues to vitiate the judgement of authors in our own times (See K. J. John, *The Road to Diamper*, op. cit. (n. 6), pp. 130, 131).

[43] So Gregorio M. Antão, *De Synodi Diamperitanae natura atque decretis*, op. cit. (n. 5), pp. 42-57.

bon would leave the validity of the Synod of Diamper still an open question.[44] This is hardly convincing since there were reasons for silence both in Lisbon and in Rome other than tacit recognition of validity. In Lisbon, the Apostolic Nuncio Fabius probably opted for silence if only not to pour water on the ardour of the *conquista* celebrations. And in Rome, for Cardinal Santorio to raise the objection of invalidity would have been to unleash a *casus belli* with the formidable Potuguese crown. The fact that Menezes' right hand collaborator at Diamper, Francis Ros, S.J., stood for the invalidity of the Synod after he became the first Latin Bishop of Angamaly, is not a negligible argument. So, too, in the light of the theology of reception, the fact that the Synod was not received generally by the Church of the Thomaschristians is of no little weight. But there is also the subsequent multicentennial custom of applying most of the provisions of the Synod of Diamper, which is not without canonical significance. Some would even add that this synod has now been equivalently approved by Pope John Paul II by promulgating CCEO, which cites the Synod of Diamper fifty-three times, which could be regarded as an equivalent *sanatio in radice*. However, it should be noted that the papal approval of the canons of CCEO in 1990 does not extend to the *fontes* subsequently added in 1995 by the Council for the Interpretation of Legislative Texts. But this is to digress.

It is hazardous to venture to peep into people's conscience, especially when motives are mixed. Menezes was both a religious leader and a politician who was energized by what served *Ad Majorem Dei et Portugalliae Gloriam*. As the Portuguese historian João Paolo Oliveira e Costa observes, "the behaviour of the dignitaries of the Kingdom and of many members of the clergy deluded the Indians... as the Portuguese acted with authoritarianism even contrary to the dispositions of the King."[45] Does that hat fit Menezes? If, like the ardent Saul of Tarsus, Menezes, too, erred, did he err "in ignorance" and good faith like Saul?

To dress up Menezes as a villain, as some Thomaschristian writers do, however, would be to do him an injustice. He personally led an evangelically poor life and was charitable to the poor (though some would question the real motive behind his largesse in Malabar). Not

---

[44] So Joseph Wicki: "Die Synode der Thomaschristen," op. cit. (n. 7), p. 438.

[45] João Paolo Oliveira e Costa, "Os portugueses e a cristandade siro-malabar (1498-1530)," *Studia* [Lisboa, Centro de estudios históricos ultramarinos] 52 (1994) 121-178, at pp. 168-169.

many would see him adorned with the halo of a saint, as he is painted by his devotees. He walked a middle ground. He was the hero of Diamper, an able leader, a thundering orator, a persuasive diplomat, a courageous prelate, a sly politician, a shrewd schemer, zealous *pro Ecclesia et Rege*. The contradictions in his personality are sunk in the "conquest-for-Christ" ideology. And the ambiguities of his policy are blurred behind the equivocation between "Catholic" and "Roman Catholic,"[46] so that certain Portuguese writers can speak of the "reduction" of the Thomaschristians to the Catholic fold. This has worked so well that even certain Thomaschristian writers are blinkered into believing that the Synod of Diamper was a union synod in which their ancestors really abjured the Nestorian Patriarch of Babylon and quit the Nestorian faith to become members of the Catholic Church.

6. Catholicization and Latinization

While the Synod of Diamper has been credited for having catholicized the Thomaschristians on the one hand, it has been condemned for having them break with their Eastern tradition on the other hand. How is one revisiting Diamper to find one's way here?

The Eastern Christian communities entering into union with the Holy Apostolic See of Rome were required not only to accept the dogmas and decrees of the ancient ecumenical councils but also the teachings and decrees of the Council of Florence and the Council of Trent. This has indeed involved some *latinization* of the Eastern Catholic Churches. But not all conformity to Florence and Trent was plain and simple latinization, especially where these councils drew on the earlier ecumenical councils. In this latter case we have to speak of *catholicization*. There is thus an important distinction between latinization and catholicization (see the last essay in this vol-

[46] Synod of Diamper, Session III, decree 19, is a good example of this confusion. "Catholic Church at Rome/of Rome" or "Roman Catholic Church" meant at first the local Church of Rome that was "catholic," meaning "true to the faith of the Council of Nicea I" and as such was "universal." The later identification of the "Roman Catholic Church" with the "Catholic Church" was due both to the Western exclusion of "the heretical East" from the Church and to the papal claim of universal jurisdiction. So Yves Congar speaks of "l'espèce de absorption de 'catholique' par l'Église de Rome en raison de pape." See his "Romanité et catholicité" *Revue des sciences philosophiques et théologiques* 71 (1987) 161-190: reprint in Idem, *Église et Papauté*, Paris, Cerf, 1994, 31-64, at p. 61.

ume). The ideology and policy of latinization has lost whatever official or non-official commendation it had prior to the Second Vatican Council, for which all rites are to be fostered equally. Thus the Synod of Diamper has been overtaken and dated by the Second Vatican Council. However, to condemn the Synod of Diamper for its many latinizations without distinguishing what is catholicization is shortsighted. And a study of the Synod of Diamper from the perspective of latinization and isolating it from the wider Catholic framework is to be regarded as inadequate and even misleading.

In spite of much undeniable, unwarranted and deleterious latinization, especially in liturgy and discipline as dealt with in other studies in this volume, attention may be drawn to one ultimately positive contribution of the Synod of Diamper, for which the "Syrians" should be grateful to the "Latins." The Synod of Diamper marks the beginning of the liberation of the Thomaschristian Church from its Dark Ages which had lasted over a millennium, during which the remissive East Syrian bishops had functioned mostly as cultic figureheads but not as pastors, keeping the Church perpetually retarded through nongovernance.[47] If it were not for the Latin intervention, those Dark Ages of the Thomaschristian Church might well have lasted into our own days. Latinization was the prize the Thomaschristians had to pay in the logic of things, though not in the logic of law. The alternative to latinization would probably have been the same splintering trauma as plagued the breakaway group, which finally turned to the Antiochene patriarchate to ensure valid episcopal succession. Eventually this group split up again on the question of autonomy under the thunderbolt of patriarchal excommunication, and finally formed the Malankara Orthodox/Malankara Syrian Church. Instead, the Syro-Malabar Church has reached its hierarchical autonomy, albeit through a long zigzag Latin route, but all in one piece, under the aegis of the Petrine ministry of the Holy See of Rome.

With the Second Vatican Council *delatinization* has become a conciliar imperative. First of all latinization needs to be understood for what it is and not mistaken for catholicization, and vice versa. Delatinization is not as simple a matter as the term might suggest. These problems need to be handled if revisiting the Synod of Diamper is to be different from a mere tourist trip and be productive of solid and beneficial results.

---

[47] George Nedungatt, *Laity and Church Temporalities,* op. cit. n. 10, pp. 122-123.

7. Revisiting Diamper Today

To revisit Diamper today one has first of all to come alive to the truth about historical Nestorianism as different from the Nestorianism of the Catholic theological treatises Menezes had studied at Coimbra. Surely, he could not reasonably be expected to have had Pope John Paul II's positive appraisal of historical Nestorianism, anticipating four centuries . Today, in the event of union between the Assyrian or East Syrian Church and the Catholic Church, Patriarch Dinkha IV would not be required to correct the liturgical books of "Nestorian errors" any more than the pope would be asked to do likewise, reciprocally. We may fancy Menezes revisiting Kerala, like the legendary King Maveli, for the fourth centenary of the Synod of Diamper. We can see him reel to hear of the 1994 papal-patriarchal declaration revising the traditional condemnation of Nestorianism. After that shock he would surely not ask Mar Aprem, Metropolitan of Trichur, or any other member of the Assyrian Church of the East, to abjure his/her "Nestorian" Patriarch Dinkha IV. Nor would Menezes set up a committee to "correct" their liturgical books — much less organize an auto-da-fé to burn them! Today Catholic canon law excludes any abjuration of any Eastern patriarch as a heretic in the event of reception into full Catholic communion of Eastern Christian faithful.[48] But Menezes lived and died four centuries too early, for no fault of his. It was his Catholic zeal that set him on a crusade for the destruction of heretical books, as was prescribed by the canon law of the times. So he held auto-da-fés of "Nestorian" books everywhere in Malabar with the help of two Jesuit correctors, Ros and Campori. Love's labour lost! And what a loss for the Thomaschristian Church, though not perhaps for Europe's libraries! We need these distinctions to move beyond uncritical adulation and sheer vituperation.

The 1994 papal-patriarchal Common Declaration has of course no retroactive effect nor does it annul the mutual anathemas of the past, much less erase them from human memory. But it provides us with a valuable theological key for the interpretation of Nestorianism and its history without judging past events in the light of present day standards or criteria. Thus, for example, the fact that in his last years Mar

---

[48] "The Christian faithful of an Eastern non-Catholic Church is to be received into the Catholic Church with only the profession of the Catholic faith, after a doctrinal and spiritual preparation suitable to each one's condition" (CCEO c. 897). The phrase "with only the profession of the Catholic faith" excludes in particular abjuration of hierarchs and 'heresyarchs,' formerly in vogue.

Abraham refused to cooperate with the Jesuit "correctors" of his Nestorian "errors" does not mean, as the Jesuits interpreted it then, and some writers uncritically repeat it today, relapse into Nestorian heresy. As Mar Abraham saw it, there was simply no heresy and no errors to correct! He possessed and professed the same faith as did the Jesuits. The difference was only verbal. What was really in question was the more or less apt theological expression, not faith. In condemning the faith of the "Nestorians of Malabar" expressed in their liturgical and other books as tarnished by "errors" it was Ros and Menezes who were in error!

Avowedly, this might sound shocking. It is hindsight buttressed by the 1994 papal-patriarchal declaration, which is in its turn the fruit of the post-conciliar progress of ecumenical dialogue. It enables us to see things differently today, though it does not authorise us to make judgements on Ros and Menezes from a moral point of view. That does not mean, however, that their understanding of and approach to the "Christianity of the Serra" was simply all right. Today's revised view of Nestorianism was not theirs, sure enough. But it was already the view of those whom they condemned as Nestorians! True, the view of Ros and Menezes carried the victory at Diamper. But it was not simply the victory of truth but of power.

If an analogy is needed here we can say: surely, Vasco da Gama cannot be blamed for having spent several months of sea voyage to reach India. Nor can he be credited anachronistically with having reached India in a steamer in less than two weeks or in a jet plane in six hours. Likewise writers who continue to qualify simply as Nestorian heretics Mar Abraham and his Thomaschristians and to claim for the Synod of Diamper the merit of having "reduced" the Nestorian heretics of the Serra to the Catholic Church, may be innocently sailing the Indian ocean in the galley of Vasco da Gama. They have not looked up to the sky and seen the jumbo jets rise aloft and roar by. They have not been awake to the progress of ecumenical theology and are blessedly ignorant of the 1994 common declaration of Pope John II and Patriarch Dinkha IV. They are stuck with Pope Julius III.

"Return to Pre-Diamper Traditions" is on the ecclesial agenda of the Thomaschristians of the Syro-Malabar Church. For those who revisit the Synod of Diamper this return constitutes an indirect judgement of this epoch-making event. As will be seen in the last study, this return to "ancestral traditions" following the directive of the Second Vatican Council is a very complex and delicate agenda, and has been confused from the start by the fact that the conciliar directive is often misread in the English speaking world and is misapplied. The return to ancestral traditions is, however, no regression like setting the clock back but organic progress in a "double fidelity" — in the words of Pope John Paul II — "to God and to man." That is to pursue a fidelity passing by the Synod of Diamper.

Pontifical Oriental Institute
Piazza S. Maria Maggiore, 7
Roma

George Nedungatt, S.J.

Benedict Vadakkekara, O.F.M. Cap.

THE SYNOD OF DIAMPER IN HISTORICAL PERSPECTIVE

The occurrence of the Synod of Diamper (20-26 June 1599) in the history of the Community of India's St Thomas Christians is all of a piece with the Church's bimillenary story line. It was in the normal course of things that the path of these Indian Christians should one day cross those of their brethren in other lands. Right from its inception the Community of Jesus' disciples has had the consciousness that it is duty-bound on the one hand to carry through the Lord's commission to make disciples from all nations and on the other to remain united in fellowship. But as the communities that had mushroomed the length and breadth of Asia, Africa and Europe through the instrumentality of the apostles and their disciples were finding themselves face to face with one another, the end-point of being in communion began proving to be an uphill task. There were instances of local Churches being bulldozed into conforming to proffered patterns, having to sacrifice some of their cultural patrimonies in the process. The ill-starred stories of the Gallican and Celtic rites exemplify the dark side of inter-ecclesial encounters in Europe in the first millennium of Church's history. In the second millennium the contacts between Christian peoples took place on a far wider range as there was an upward climb in regular intercourse between Rome and the outer world towards the East. At the close of the fifteenth century the seaway from Europe to India circumventing the Cape of Good Hope was discovered. Thanks to this maritime feat of the Portuguese, it was now the turn of India's St Thomas Christians to respond to the frontal and direct advances being made by the Church of the Latin tradition represented by the personnel of the Portuguese Padroado.

I. INDIA'S ST THOMAS CHRISTIANS AT THE DAWN OF XVI CENTURY

Though today the St Thomas Christian Community of India finds itself evolved into various distinct ecclesial formations due to diverse historical circumstances, till past the middle of the seventeenth century it had remained one and united. These divisions notwithstanding, they all have certain common constants running through them, which give them a shared social identity. When the Portuguese encountered them in the sixteenth century these elements, which are briefly outlined hereunder, were much more pronounced.

1. *Sharers of a Communal Memory*: The conviction that the Apostle St Thomas in person gave origin to the Community of the St Thomas Christians of India has been so profoundly embedded in the participated memory of its members that it has kept all along conditioning their relationship with their compatriots as well as with their fellow-Christians from other lands. This communal consciousness was something more than an idea that they shared in common; for the Community it was an experiential partaking of one and the same patrimony, and as far as the individuals were concerned, it was a concrete reality of everyday significance. In one voice the members jointly eulogise certain definite locations and particular families as having been especially privileged by their Apostle. That they had no ancient written documents in confirmation of this communal consciousness of theirs did not in any way unsettle them while proudly upholding their Community's origin. Therefore, when they declare as is their wont that it is their communal *tradition* that the Apostle Thomas is the founder of their Church, they have in mind a reality that differs substantially from what the same term *tradition* would signify, say, for a European.

The unanimity in assigning the pride of place to specific locations and families on the sole belief that the same had been in direct contact with St Thomas, vested this tradition of theirs with precision and concreteness. The name of a locality like Nilakkel, even centuries after it had become inaccessible, has retained its exact identity in their traditional accounts, and the far-off Mylapore has always been venerated as the burial spot of their Apostle. It was a definite family, precisely because of its acknowledged link with the Apostle Thomas, that had been providing the Community with leadership in the person of the *Jathikukarthavyan*. The rock-steady sureness of theirs about their origin not only rendered them secure in their remote existence away from the other centres of Christendom but also made them resilient to every form of pressure and allurement, as the later events like the unfolding of the Synod of Diamper would confirm.[1]

[1] *The Acts and Decrees of the Synod of Diamper. 1599*, ed. Scaria Zacharia, Edamattam 1994, 93, Session 3, Decree 7: "Condemns the error, that St Thomas and St Peter published two different laws; and maintains that there is but one law for the Universal Church of Christ." The decree speaks about the "one only universal pastor, to

Hence it was the unanimously participated consciousness of the members about their common origin, regardless of how undocumented it might have been, that has served the Community of the St Thomas Christians as the underpinning while it has withstood all the vicissitudes of history and maintained its identity through its multi-centennial existence.

2. *One and Undivided*: The fact that internally there are no divisions in this five-million and odd strong Community betraying caste vestiges, is an added corroboration that its nucleus is so ancient in origin as to antedate the rigidification of casteism in Kerala. Irrespective of the financial strength of the families the members address one another in the familial style, employing terms like brother, sister, uncle and aunt. Before casteism got consolidated and the pecking order was determined, the Community of the St Thomas Christians had already taken shape in Kerala. This aspect stands out in contrast with the members of the Moslem, Latin Christian and Sikh religions in India, who still have the caste label sticking to sections of them precisely because their respective religious formations had come into being after they had been stereotyped into tight systems of caste. Despite the centuries that have elapsed since their progenitors embraced these acknowledgedly egalitarian religions, the members' caste background has refused to scale off, while the St Thomas Christians remain internally indistinctive on the basis of caste. Unlike Kerala's ancient Jewish community that suffers an internal segregation into "White Jews" and "Black Jews," the St Thomas Christians present themselves as a native-born social entity of coequality.[2] Sure enough consequent upon the outgrowth and the consolidation of casteism, the St Thomas Christians too found themselves walled in, with the result that their societal mobility, together with that of their

---

whom all other prelates owe obedience, the Pope and Bishop of Rome, successor in the chair of St Peter, the prince of the Apostles; to whom our Lord Jesus Christ bequeathed that supreme authority, and by him to his successors...." Thus it was only after expressly recognising the apostolic origin of the Community of the St Thomas Christians that the promoters of the Synod were able to make the St Thomas Christians understand the logic of obeying "the only universal pastor" of the Church.

[2] A numerically inferior and exclusive grouping within the same Community, consistently identify themselves as those who had gone all the way from the Middle East (Babylon or Persia according to some versions) to India to tide the Church of the Apostle Thomas over some contretemps. The persistence of this minor aggregation within the wholeness of the Community instead of debilitating the explanation of the original St Thomas Christians regarding their origin, is actually a vigorous restatement of their case.

compatriots, too came to be defined along the lines of caste. And willingly succumbing to the dynamics of caste, ever since they too have stubbornly resisted the entry of fellow-believers of other castes into their midst. Before the wall of their opposition the personnel of the Latin and the Anglican Churches had no other go than opt for a half-way house. Their Christian faith failed to melt down their caste prejudice.

Before the caste system got unyieldingly strait-jacketed in Kerala the St Thomas Christians had secured for themselves a high perch in the societal hierarchy and which they jealously safeguarded against all intrusions. While scrupulously insulating themselves against all ritually impure touches, they cultivated fraternal intercourse especially with the militarised caste of Nairs, even though en bloc they attributed a Brahmanic origin to themselves. Visitors from Europe have reported not only instances of Brahmins joining the St Thomas Christians but also of some of them being promoted to priesthood. While subsisting as a solitary clan far-off from all other Christian strongholds, they were all too conscious of their Christian identity and doggedly clung to their Community's traditions and practices, which they described as the *Law* or *Path of Thomas*, because, to their collective mind, these had attached to them the sanction of their Apostle.

3. *Physically Circumscribed*: The physical whereabouts is a potent factor that also helped determine the course of the history of the St Thomas Christians. The enormous distance that separated their homeland on the south-west stretch of India from the Christian nerve-centres condemned them to a state of practical seclusion and at the same time shielded them from being torn apart by sectism. The physical isolation goes to explain the vagueness and the imprecision that characterise the allusions to the Indian Christians in the sources at the disposal of the other Churches. Contrastively, the volumes of extant epistolary and reportorial material originating in India through the instrumentality of European visitors from the sixteenth century onwards, mirror distinctly the essentials of the shared memory that the St Thomas Christians had been for centuries nurturing. Their latter-day relationship with other Churches, instead of thinning out their communal conviction and persuasion, has in fact turned out to be a whetstone for clear-cutting their ecclesial individuality. The particular terrain of Kerala too exerted its influence on the evolution of their mind-set. This homeland of theirs, coated with the luxuriance

of the monsoon forest, is nestled in between the Arabian Sea and the Western Ghats. The land is interspersed with rivers that can swell to great levels in the rainy season and spill over undeterred into the bordering areas. Roads, bridges and wheeled transport are only recent innovations. Thus the surroundings did have a crippling effect on the physical mobility of the local populace.

4. *Relatively Closed*: In contradistinction to most of the ancient Christian Communities, the St Thomas Christians lost in the course of time their zeal for proselytising, as they entertained the belief that everyone had his or her own way of salvation; this view of theirs was spotted by the Padroado missionaries and was expressly condemned at the Synod of Diamper:

> That everyone may be saved in his own law; all which are good, and lead men to heaven. Now this is a manifest heresy; there being no other law upon earth in which salvation is to be found, besides that of Our Saviour Jesus Christ, for that he only teacheth the truth; so that all that live in any other sect, are out of a state of salvation, and shall be condemned to hell; there being no other name given to men, by which we can be saved, but only the name of Our Lord Jesus Christ the Son of God, who was crucified for us....[3]

The minority group (the *Southists*) within the Syro-Malabar Church, which was constituted into the Diocese of Kottayam in 1911, to date maintains rigidly this social exclusivity. When someone from the *Southist* group marries a member of another diocese of even the Syro-Malabar Church, he or she is regarded as having become alien to the Diocese of Kottayam. This vestigial practice is emblematic of the way in which communal exclusivism came to be formerly practised and perpetuated by the entire St Thomas Christian Community.

5. *Related with East Syriac Church*: The spatial separateness of the St Thomas Christians from Christian centres in other lands was not in every way absolute, as at an early stage of their history they found themselves in rapport with the East Syriac Church. Neither their traditions nor their posterior documents exhibit any sign of constraint or bad blood occasioned by such a relationship. On the other hand everything goes to show that it was a happy working arrangement. Their being in dire straits early on in their history and the arrival on the scene of the progenitors of the present-day "*Southists*" as benefactors, appears to coincide with the Community's acceptance of fellowship with the East Syriac Church. The St Thomas Christians

[3] *The Acts and Decrees of the Synod of Diamper*, 90: Session 3, Decree 4.

undoubtedly took pride in worshipping after the manner of these allies of theirs and held in highest regard East Syriac as being the language of Jesus. They used to send for an East Syriac Metropolitan as and when their cultic exigencies demanded and in return various largesses of provision and rich emoluments used to be regularly forwarded to the Patriarch. The ministering Metropolitan used to be welcomed and accommodated as their most honoured guest.

6. *Ecclesially Distinct*: A close reading of this give-and-take arrangement between the St Thomas Christians and the East Syriac Church that prevailed till the close of the sixteenth century, that is till the Synod of Diamper, is quite illuminating.

Firstly, the Apostle Thomas is known in the entire East Syriac tradition as Judas Thomas and never simply as Thomas, while such a double name is totally unheard of among the St Thomas Christians in India. They always preferred to refer to him in the sacred language Syriac as Mar Thoma and introduced themselves as Mar Thoma Christians. They described their way of life as the *Thoma Margam* or *Way/Law of Thomas*. Unquestionably the total extraneousness of the double name "Judas Thomas" to the St Thomas Christians postulates that they have an origin that is independent of and anterior to their entry into fellowship with the East Syriac Church.

Secondly, the common architectural style of the churches of the St Thomas Christians with the Hindu temples and the conspicuous absence of the bema in their churches, signify that the East Syriac cult came actually to be celebrated in a pre-existing locale of worship. Otherwise it does not make sense why the texts alone were faithfully transferred to India, while the liturgical settings prescribed for the enacting of the same texts were left aside. Thus it was not a case of cultic transplantation into a liturgical vacuum when the East Syriac liturgy came to be introduced into the Church of the St Thomas Christians.

Thirdly, one cannot but note the incongruity of the prelate's official designation of "Metropolitan of All-India" in reference to the real radius of his jurisdiction. The East Syriac Church's prolific missions had given rise to a network of Metropolises across the length and breadth of Asia and the title Metropolis of India, though very much an overblown title for a relatively small community confined to a nook of the Subcontinent, was to make it distinguishable from the others. The task entrusted to the 4 East Syriac bishops who reached India had been "to go to the countries of India and the islands of the sea, that are between Dabag (Java) and Sin (China) and Masin (Maha China or Great China)."[4]

Fourthly, it was the *Jathikukarthavyan* of the St Thomas Christians who held the reins of his Community's governance. For his faithful, his office had an aureole attached to it precisely because of the Apostle Thomas' special preference for his family. His leadership, unanimously acknowledged as the *Jathikukarthavyan* or "Head of the Community," by far antedated the entry of the East Church into Malabar. Christening his office as "Archdeacon of All-India" by the East Syriac Church did not for all practical purposes add anything to it. That it was not merely a part of the apparatus of the Metropolis, may be seen from the fact that there used to be only one Archdeacon for the whole Community even when more than one Metropolitan were active in Kerala. In his letter of 16 September 1577 to his General Fr Alexandro Valignano recommends that Archdeacon George of Christ be nominated auxiliary to Mar Abraham, because he was more powerful than the Archbishop and that it was he who was actually maintaining the Archbishop.[5]

Fifthly, despite the centuries of cordial fellowship between the East Syriac Church and the Church of the St Thomas Christians, the former's acclaimed monastic tradition and enterprising evangelisation thrust, did not find their way to Kerala. The St Thomas Christians had their own forms of asceticism, rules of ablution and purification, and rites of initiation.

Sixthly, the doctrinal options of the East Syriac Church and its official disposition to the Bishop of Rome did not have any reverberation in the collective mind of the St Thomas Christians. In Malabar there were contemporaneously in circulation formulas typical of the Catholic faith[6] as well as those of the creed of the Church of the East.

---

[4] Mathias A. Mundadan, *History of Christianity in India*, I: *From the beginning up to the middle of the sixteenth century*, Bangalore 1984, 89.

[5] *Documenta Indica*, X: *(1575-1577)* (Monumenta Historica Societatis Iesu, 98), ed J. Wicki, Romae 1968, 884-885: "La otra cosa que se á de hazer que mucho puede ayudar al caso, es que Su Sanctidad haga Obispo y coadjutor suffragáneo del dicho Arcebispo al arcediano de Angamale, porque, allende de ser él persona más poderosa en aquella tyerra que el mismo Arçobispo, es persona muy prudente y entre ellos religiosa y enfín es él que manda, govierna y sustenta el mismo Arçobispo."

[6] G. C. Alapatt, *La devozione alla Madonna nella Chiesa siro-malabarese*, Trichur 1950, 7. This booklet lists the many ways and forms in which the Syro-Malabar Church has been manifesting its devotion to the Blessed Virgin. One of such is the fact of the dedication of the ancient church of Kuravilangad to the Blessed Mary Mother of God, as may be gathered from the Syriac inscription on the bell cast in

And ecclesiastics from Rome used to find a warm welcome in Malabar even in that dim and distant past.

And seventhly, the relational bond between India's St Thomas Christians and the East Syriac Church instead of eclipsing the Indian Christians' communal consciousness of their Church's apostolic origin, in fact only cemented it. The East Syriac Church not only wholly subscribed to their tradition, but also joined them in holding ceremoniously the memory of the Apostle. It also looked to the tomb of Mylapore as the Apostle's original tomb and venerated the dust from there as relic. As distinct from the Syriac Church which celebrated liturgically the memory of St Thomas with a mere feast, the St Thomas Christians embellished the Solemnity, the *Dukhrana,* with an octave. For the Indian Christians, the customary pilgrimage to the mountaintop of Malayattur and to Mylapore on the Easter Octave continues to be a popular way of honouring their Apostle who had acknowledged the Risen Lord as "My Lord and my God" (Jn 20,28). At the same time the Syriac language, the Syriac Liturgy and the physical presence of a Syriac prelate in their midst, had gone far towards confirming them in their conviction that they were in direct contact with the primordial source of faith which they had received from the Apostle Thomas.

This is a profile of the Church of the St Thomas Christians at the start of the sixteenth century when the Portuguese Padroado personnel encountered it. But for the lone figure of the Metropolitan from the East Syriac Church, there were no other institutional representatives of the East Syriac Church stably in residence in India. And it was the Head of the Community (*Jathikukarthavyan*), a linear descendant of the family held to have been especially privileged by the Apostle Thomas, who led the Community; the East Syriac Church too recognised his leadership role by bestowing on him the title of Archdeacon. The St Thomas Christians who had remained one and united under their *Jathikukarthavyan* right from their inception, would continue this unity even after their ecclesial linkage with the East Syriac Church would formally be dissolved once and for all at the close of the sixteenth century. And as the bishops of the Padroado jurisdiction would effectively assume their centric position in the life of the

---

1584, and which the author renders into Italian as: "Venne fusa questa campana — per la chiesa di S. Maria Madre di Dio — nel villaggio benedetto di Kuravilangad — la fonte di ogni mio soccorso amen — nell'anno 1584 della nascita di N.S.G.C. — in giugno."

Community, the *Jathikukarthavyan* would find himself displaced. While the Community would continue worshipping in the language of Jesus, its cultic patrimony would be notably enriched by elements of the Latin Church. And during the whole while the deep-seated awareness of being a Fellowship called into being by the Apostle Thomas, served as the rallying point for the whole Community and it would be the same communal consciousness that would enable it to weather all the storms on its way and make it emerge as a reinvigorated ecclesial body in the bosom of the Universal Church.

II. Eastbound Christians from Europe

The landing of the Portuguese at Kappad in the neighbourhood of Calicut on 20 May 1498 represents the acme of success of the various endeavours of the peoples of Europe to voyage to India. The navigational success of the Portuguese would have an enduring bearing on the relationship between the Christians of Europe and their counterparts in India. While this success story of Portugal began in 1415 with the conquest of the City of Ceuta in Morocco, the Portuguese had the tried and tested experiences of many a sailor and trader to fall back on.[7] In 1488 the Portuguese were already able to have the waterway till the Cape of Good Hope delineated. In the last analysis, it was on the heels of these expeditions that the Christians in the West came to have precise information about their brethren-in-faith in India and later to establish ecclesial communion with them.

Thanks to these overseas newcomers, their permanence in India occasioned the production of a considerable quantity of archival material on the St Thomas Christians. Hence the historiographic importance of the landing of the Europeans in India cannot be overestimated, though the reading of the events and the reporting on them were from the angle of the visitors. Even the few correspondential items forwarded to Europe in the name of the local Christians too were materially shaped by their newly-found allies from the West. A perusal of the volumes of the reports of the Europeans brings out the stark fact that from the part of the St Thomas Christians there had been no historical compilations that would help dispel the mists of

[7] M. N. Pearson *Os portugueses na Índia* (Colecção de Cabo a Cabo), Lisboa 1987, 24, mentions particularly the accounts of the voyages of Marco Polo and John Mandeville.

time with regard to their early history.[8] They have kept no track of a pastoral visit by Bishop David (250-300), or a Bishop John the Persian (who was deputed by the Council of Nicea to promulgate its decrees in Greater India), or of a Cosmas Indicopleustes who visited them.[9]

A quick survey of the accounts of the presence of traders and visitors from abroad at the locations in India associated with the Apostle Thomas and his disciples there, casts light on the frame of mind of the Portuguese when they launched out into the East in search of India. These reports also reflect the complex nature of inter-ecclesial contact between the St Christians in India and their co-religionists from Europe, and which would be the forerunner of the lasting and direct relationship that would be effectuated through the instrumentality of the Portuguese at the Synod of Diamper.

1. *Visitors and pilgrims*: Even though anciently Europe did not have detailed information on India, it was generally held there that the Apostle Thomas had preached in India and that he had suffered martyrdom at the hands of the Indians. In the same vein the various accounts of the arrival of visitors and pilgrims from Europe at the tomb of St Thomas in Mylapore, represent the then contemporary belief in the Christendom about the existence in India of the first tomb of the Apostle.[10]

---

[8] In all the versions of their communal tradition the person of the Apostle Thomas preponderate, leaving little room for the memory of other personages of their Community or of those churchmen from other lands who had arrived in their midst. While they have not preserved for the posterity a list of their great leaders, some of their priests, side-stepping all such names, are wont to identify themselves according to the serial number they represent in the generations of priests that have followed from the time of the Apostle Thomas.

[9] Most books of history on Christianity in India discuss the various contacts that have taken place between the Christians in India and their counterparts elsewhere. Eg, Mundadan, *History of Christianity in India*, 67-108, 116-144; Stephen Neill, *A history of Christianity in India. The beginnings to AD 1707*, London – New York – New Rochelle etc. 1984, 68-86. Cosmas spoke of communities of faithful along the Indian coastline and on the islands of Socotra and Sri Lanka (Taprobana), ministered to by the Persian clergy.

[10] Gregory of Tours in his *Gloria martyrum* (ca 590), writes of Monk Theodore's visit to the tomb of the Apostle Thomas in India. Egeria's diary had been very much in circulation in the West. The *Anglo-Saxon Chronicle* (ca 892) and the *De gestis regum anglorum* (ca 1143), Book V, refer to the embassy sent to India by King Alfred of England with offerings to the Apostle Thomas in India and its having returned home with precious stones and odoriferous essences.

2. *Fortune-seekers and Glob-trotters*: Besides these predominately religious grounds, there were others that served as the mainspring for the undertaking of hazardous voyages to India. From the days of the ancient Greeks India was fabled for its mysteries and oddities. The land's fame for spices, perfumes and silks too was proverbial, thus making it a dream destination for voyagers and other adventurists. The St Thomas Christians and the tomb of the Apostle at Mylapore too were among the attractions in India.[11]

3. *Emissaries and Evangelisers*: The sweeping success of the Mongolian military campaigns westwards urged the Christian leadership in Europe to try to block these marauders from venturing further towards them. As the geopolitical initiatives of the papal authority showed results, the idea of building up an alliance with the Christians in the eastern parts began gaining ground. The legends surrounding the Priest-King John in the East too raised hopes in the West of creating such a coalescence.[12] There was wide consensus in the Christian West that liquidating the threats poised by the growing Islamic power was indeed a matter of great urgency. The Minorite and the Dominican friars had already got a foothold in the Middle East, and their respective *Societas peregrinantium* were regarded as handy instruments for translating the new project into a reality.[13] One of the papal letters that Jordanus of Severac had been entrusted with was addressed to the leader of the "Nascarini (Nazarani) Christians and his Community." The pope wanted all the Christians to come together "in oneness of orthodox faith, under one shepherd, and in the solid and untainted union of one flock, the one, holy, catholic and universal

---

[11] Marco Polo seems to have made two visits to India (1288 and 1298).

[12] António da Silva Rego, *História das missões do Padroado português do Oriente Índia*, I: *(1500-1541)*, Lisboa 1949, 379. The Dominican friar Philip (ca 1237) spoke of the many letters that had reached him from a prelate whose territorial jurisdiction "extends over greater India and the kingdom of Presbyter John."

[13] In 1289 Pope Nicholas IV made John of Montecorvino his legate to Kublai Khan; John together with Nicholas of Pistoia was in India between 1292-3 en route for China. He carried with him 26 papal missives, including the ones addressed to the Persian king Argun, Qubilai Khan and Patriarch Jaballaha III of the East Syriac Church. He spent 13 months in India, visited the church of St Thomas and baptised about 100 persons. The Dominican friar John Catalani of Severac and 4 Franciscan friars arrived in Thana in 1321 but he alone proceeded to Quilon (the Frairs Minor were martyred in Thana). In his *Mirabilia descripta*, he says that he had won over to the Catholic faith about 10,000 persons in India. To get more collaborators he returned to Europe. He reached Avignon and was received by the pope. On 9 August 1329 the diocese of Quilon was created and Jordan was made its bishop.

Roman Church." In 1338 as a diplomatic reciprocity Pope Benedict XII deputed the Minorite John of Marignolli to accompany the emissaries of the Great Khan back to Khanbaliq. The papal delegation reached its destination in 1342 and after 3 years the legate embarked for Quilon where he landed on 23 March 1346 to be accorded a stirring welcome. The St Thomas Christians presented him "as a perquisite of his office as Pope's delegate, every month a hundred gold *fanams*" and a thousand when he left. Indeed John of Marignolli was fully conscious of being a papal legate and of his right to receive obeisance from the Indian Christians.

4. *Merchants, Warriors and Missionaries*: The arrival of Vasco da Gama in Calicut was to ring up the curtain on a new era in the history of Asia in general and the Christians in particular. "We are looking for Christians and spices" was the reply that one of Gama's crews gave, when queried about the purpose of their expedition.[14] They had been so conditioned by the preoccupation of meeting Christians that they mistakenly took the Hindu temples and images for Christian churches and statues.[15] However, their search for spices brought them to head-on collision with the Islamic traders from the Middle East, who then held a monopoly over trade. The age-old rivalry and animosity between Christians and Moslems in the West suddenly found itself transported into the distant eastern emporium of Calicut.[16] The local chieftain, the Zamorin, trying not to dish his long-standing clients, the Moslems, and not to disillusion the European newcomers, found himself treading a tightrope. The eagerness to outwit the other and to control the market of spices fanned the flames of reciprocal aversion between the Portuguese and the Moslems. Thus outbreaks of horrid violence and massacre were to accompany the carving out of the Portuguese colonial enclaves in India. The course of events had taken an irretrievable turn and the Portuguese had already this blood-stained reputation when they encoun-

[14] M. N. Pearson, *Os portugueses na Índia*, 22. Besides, it was then a commonplace to say: "servir a Deus e obter lucros para nós." Silva Rego, *História das missões*, 38: "Al diabro que te doo! Quem te traxo acá? — Vimos buscar cristãos e especiaria."

[15] Silva Rego, *História das missões*, 379: "Como se sabe, os portugueses de Vasco da Gama tomaram os pagodes por igrejas e a imagem da deusa Bhavagti pela de Nossa Senhora, ajoelhando-se reverentes perante a mesma, julgando ouvir a palavra 'Maria' nas orações dos seus devotos."

[16] Silva Rego, *História das missões*, 45: refers to the Portuguese attitude to Moslems: "... os eternos inimigos dos Portugueses: os Mouros."

tered the St Thomas Christians and later embarked on their evangelisation activities.

III. Padroado and India's St Thomas Christians

The fact that in the history of the St Thomas Christians the Synod of Diamper triumphantly dominates the end-point of the sixteenth century has created the general impression that the century-long presence of the Portuguese in India is very much all of a piece with the Synod itself. It is thus from the angle of the Synod that the policies and the strategies of the Portuguese often come to be viewed and assessed. Neill's study is emblematic of this slant: "The attempts of the Portuguese to bring the Thomas Christians into conformity with every detail of Roman doctrine and practice seem to have begun with Fr Álvaro Penteado, a priest who came to India in 1510 or 1511...." He speaks about Fr Vicente de Lagos who reached India in 1538: "Vincent, as convinced as any of his contemporaries that the Thomas Christians must be brought into complete conformity with Rome at every point, had seen that the only way in which this could be brought about was the replacement of the old race of *cattanārs* (priests) ... by a new race of young priests...."[17] Despite this all too explicit deduction, the fact of the matter is that in the documents neither Penteado nor Lagos appears as representing their contemporaries nor championing the idea of bringing the St Thomas Christians "into complete conformity with Rome at every point." Neill seems to discover a thread linking Penteado and Lagos with the Synod of Diamper, during the course of which Menezes' behaviour is marked with ruthlessness and he is faulted for "the rigidity with which he excluded everything that did not exactly conform to Roman usage."[18]

When seen against the backdrop of the widespread historiographic position as exemplified in Neill,[19] the recent study by Oliveira

---

[17] Neill, *A History of Christianity in India*, 196-197.

[18] Neill, *A History of Christianity in India*, 215.

[19] Neill, *A History of Christianity in India*, 200, seems to take a mellow attitude when it comes to evaluating the overall behaviour of the Portuguese towards the St Thomas Christians: "The first half century of relations between the Portuguese and the Thomas Christians were, in spite of misunderstandings, on the whole marked by cordiality and good will. Mar Jacob had maintained good relations with the Westerners throughout the long period of his episcopate...."

e Costa[20] appears to be a new and refreshing evaluation of the events of the first decades of the sixteenth century in the history of India's St Thomas Christians. Oliveira e Costa judiciously comments, "this exaggerated uniformization of the attitude of the Portuguese disfigures the historical truth and ignores as much the sixteenth century European culture as the complexity of the Portuguese ultramarine policies." The abundance of documents of the second half of the sixteenth century that "clearly show the intolerance of the great part of the Latin hierarchy towards the Syro-Malabar clergy" has also its part to play in the creation of this overly one-sided view.[21] Since the sources for the first five decades are relatively not so forthcoming, there has been the tendency to read these few-and-far-between ones in the light of the plentiful testimonies of the latter half of the century. Thus a study of the historical background of the Synod of Diamper calls for the clarification whether or not there was an overall strategy from the start to place the St Thomas Christians under the Padroado yoke, and what all factors ultimately entered into Archbishop Menezes' stage-managing of the Synod of Diamper.

A. *Earlier Decades of Sixteenth Century*

The reciprocal delight that resulted at the encounter between India's St Thomas Christians and their Portuguese brothers-in-faith was in the course of time to give way to diverse sentiments, making it resemble a love-hate relationship. Even those who tend to inculpate the Portuguese of harbouring right from the very beginning ulterior motives behind their smooth exterior, agree that initially the relationship between the St Thomas Christians and the Padroado personnel was on the whole neighbourly and collaborative.[22] With the exception of the few and intermittent encounters, no formal meeting took place

---

[20] João Paulo Oliveira e Costa, *Os portugueses e a cristandade siro-malabar (1498-1530)*, in *Studia* 52 (1994) 121-178. "Sumário das cartas que vieram da Índia no ano de 1525 e respostas d'el-rei a elas," which is the text of the ten inedited papers that Prof. Oliveira e Costa gives as appendix to this study (p.170-178), is indeed illuminative. These papers cast new light on the Portuguese history in India in the first part of the sixteenth century.

[21] Oliveira e Costa, *Os portugueses e a cristandade siro-malabar*, 123: "Esta limitação facilitou a conclusão de que logo os primeiros homens desembarcados na Índia consideraram a cristandade local herética e passaram a desenvolver uma acção concertada que teria tido o seu desenlace natural na intervenção de D. Alexio de Meneses, em 1599."

[22] Mundadan, *History of Christianity in India*, 287-347.

between the two till November 1502. By then the Portuguese had already successfully challenged the commercial dominance of the Moslems and had got established in Cannanore and Cochin. It was thus after the scales had tipped in favour of the Portuguese that a delegation of the St Thomas Christians from Cranganore, a territory belonging to the Zamorin of Calicut, in the name of 30,000 of its brethren, presented itself before Gama on 19 November 1502, and handing over to him "the rod of justice which they possessed" requested to be taken under the Portuguese king's aegis. Gama acceded to the request, promising the delegation Portuguese protection. The minutiae apart, one cannot ignore the all too visible political import of this gesture, even though both Gama and his Indian friends recognised themselves as Christians. What was to follow in the space of the following three decades was in fact an exercise in sizing up reciprocally, each party with an eye to accruing benefits. At this stage the comportment of the Portuguese does not betray anything to indicate that they intended to be the harbingers of the Synod of Diamper.

Oliveira e Costa makes out a strong case when he says that in the first half of the sixteenth century the prevailing cultural atmosphere in Europe was principally humanistic and that there was a concomitant critical posture towards the Church. But in the second half of the century the wind of Counter-Reformation whisked away the ideological reservations towards the institutionalised Church and ushered in a spirit of submission and reverence to churchmen especially in the regions like the Iberian peninsula. The emphasis now was on religious and social conformism, and everything that was diverse doctrinally and liturgically was suspected. While uniformity in religious observances became normative, a certain intolerance towards differing traditions crept in. This perspectival evolution in Europe also reverberated in the unfolding of the events in Portuguese India. Actually in the early part of the sixteenth century there were instances of the actualisation of this Renaissance humanism even towards the Hindus.[23] On the one hand they showered lavish praise on the St

[23] Oliveira e Costa, *Os portugueses e a cristandade siro-malabar*, 138-140. In 1510 the Portuguese captain of Cannanore gifted two "fardos" of sugar to the local Hindu chieftains on the occasion of their "Páscoa," and in 1514 in Calicut the captain gave 25 fardos of rice to different people in connection with their feast. See also *Documentaçao para a História da missões do Padroado Português do Oriente*, I, 98; 208-209. At the same the Portuguese clergymen in India were the butt of the criticism of the humanists. It was the pre-Reformation era.

Thomas Christians for their zeal in religious observances and on the other criticised the clergy and bishop for charging heavy fees for the administration of baptism and the other sacraments. Here they were right in levelling these criticisms and were not indulging in mud-slinging in order to prepare the way for a Synod of Diamper. At this stage no accusation of heresy is put forward against the St Thomas Christians.

1. "Christians and Spices": Mar Jacob and the Portuguese

The second Portuguese expedition to India commanded by Pedro Alvarez Cabral that reached Calicut on 30 August 1500 showed more promise than the first one. But when the Portuguese discovered that the Muslims had outmanoeuvred them, they avenged themselves on the Moslems. Much blood was shed on both sides. The vindictive cannonade of a village by the Portuguese for the Zamorin's neutrality created many victims. But in Cochin Cabral received a warm welcome, and there began a long drawn-out hostility between the Portuguese patronised by the king of Cochin and the Moslem traders seconded by the Zamorin of Calicut. And on occasions the St Thomas Christians too would find themselves caught up in the blood-letting exchanges between the two sides.

To their great satisfaction, the Portuguese found that early on their relationship with the St Thomas Christians was paying rich dividends. In 1502 itself a certain Mathias of Kayamkulam took the lead in procuring them quality pepper. The first consignment took place in January 1503 when two of Gama's ships were sent to Quilon to take delivery of the merchandise.[24] There was even an epistolary exchange between this Mathias and the Portuguese king. Mathias was positively impressed by the Portuguese clergy and thought that their ministration would be advantageous to his community.[25] In 1503 when the Portuguese returned to Quilon to found the trading station, they were enthusiastically welcomed by the St Thomas Christians, who invited them to hold a solemn High Mass in their church. And in the following year it was the turn of the four East Syriac prel-

---

[24] *Documentaçao para a História da missões do Padroado Português do Oriente*, I, 25. The letter dated 18 December 1504, begins as: Senhor Mathias christão, modador em Quaequolam [Kayamkulam]."

[25] *Documentaçao para a História da missões do Padroado Português do Oriente*, I, 27.

ates Mar Thomas, Mar Jabballaha, Mar Denha and Mar Jacob to be entertained by the Portuguese in Cannanore for nearly three months. The St Thomas Christians used to receive the Portuguese priests into their churches and take part in the ceremonies officiated by them. In 1510 the Portuguese governor Alfonso de Albuquerque had 1000 *fanams* given to the *Abunas* of Cranganore.[26] There was no talk of a religious domination on the part of the Portuguese. The honeymooning between the Portuguese and the St Thomas Christians was seasoned with pepper and religious fellow-feeling, to the benefit of both the parties.[27]

But in the course of time a certain delusion crept in, as the Portuguese and the St Thomas Christians reassessed their respective positions in terms of benefits in kind. Vasco da Gama's promise of royal patronage to the delegates of the St Thomas Christians had failed to come up with the goods. The common courtesy exchanges between Mar Jacob and the Portuguese like providing hospitality too was leading nowhere. Though the trade between the Portuguese and the St Thomas Christians had acquired a regular pattern, the latter felt that earlier they had been receiving a better deal when selling their products to the Moslems. To the St Thomas Christians, the leading planters and suppliers of pepper, the Portuguese did not seem to have the credentials for being their dependable trading partners. They remonstrated against the underpricing of their goods and the double-dealing of their new patrons from Europe, and openly showed their preference for transacting with their customary clients, the Moslems.[28] In 1523-1524 the forces of Zamorin attacked Cranganore and destroyed the houses of some of the Christians and some of the churches as a retaliation for their dealing with the Portuguese. This is a clear example to show how they were pressurised into keeping away from the Portuguese. It helps one understand the resistance on their part to enter into commercial transactions with the Portuguese, especially if it meant it would be less lucrative than with the Mos-

---

[26] *Documentaçao para a História da missões do Padroado Português do Oriente*, I, 106 in October 1510 to the "abunas cristâos" in Cranganore.

[27] Oliveira e Costa, *Os portugueses e a cristandade siro-malabar*, 137: "Tal como se nota para os anos anteriores, os Portugueses viam-se não como disciplinadores de comunidades heréticas, mas acima de tudo come resgatadores de cristandades perdidas."

[28] *Documentaçao para a História da missões do Padroado Português do Oriente*, II, 356: "Quanto a esmolla, Deus te de ho pagamento della e eu ho pagarei com orações e melhorando estes serviços que tenho dito."

lems.[29] The Portuguese had miserably failed to rise up to the occasion and respond to the violence inflicted by the Moslems on their brothers-in-faith in India.[30]

It did not take the Portuguese many summers to realise that they could not have access into the inner circles of the Community of the St Thomas Christians. The breakthrough in this stalemate came when Mar Jacob began accepting royal emolument, as offered by King John III. Thus Mar Jacob was on the payroll of the Portuguese king and, in this capacity, he went about urging the St Thomas Christians to sell their products to the Portuguese. In this way the Portuguese got their money's-worth, and Mar Jacob even volunteered to take along with him Portuguese clergymen during his pastoral-commercial journeys. According to Mar Jacob, after such a personal introduction from his part, the St Thomas Christians would no longer have any reservation towards the Portuguese priests and they would feel welcome to function among them. But there was already a group within the Community that took objection to these new policies of Mar Jacob.[31] At this stage while there was a certain openness on the part of the St Thomas Christians towards members of the Portuguese and their way of worshipping, there was no concerted move yet for making them conform to the ways of the Portuguese.

Mar Jacob's succumbing to the pecuniary enticements of the Portuguese represents a turning point in the history of the St Thomas Christians. Till then it had been the St Thomas Christians themselves who had been taking the initiative to approach the Patriarch for the

---

[29] From their part the Moslems avenged themselves for this breach of trust by burning down the St Thomas church at Cranganore. Georg Schuhammer, *Three letters of Mar Jacob. Bishop of Malabar. 1503-1550*, in *Gregorianum* 14 (1933) 74-75. Mar Jacob writes to the Portuguese king: "And now it is necessary more than ever, for, because I served thee as I have said, the *Moors* have robbed and killed me many people and also burnt our houses and churches, by which we are much distressed and disgraced."

[30] Silva Rego, *História da Missões*, 388-389: "Rafael Catanho, vindo da China, tentou ainda convencer D. Luís a auxiliar os cristãos de S. Tomé, mas nada conseguiu."

[31] Georg Schurhammer, *Three letters of Mar Jacob*, 78-86, gives the Portuguese original and the English translation of the third letter of Mar Jacob. It is addressed to King John III of Portugal and is dated 16 December 1530. Regarding the difficulties he faces in moving around among his faithful for promoting Christian faith and the cause of the Portuguese king, he says: "And this journey to that place is very arduous, for we go through enemies' land, in whose power & land they dwell, & they [the enemies] favour some, who are hard of heart, & others, that have good will to go over to the usage of the Church of Rome, but have not the courage to do it for fear of them...."

service of a Metropolitan. It was considered as an honour for them to accompany their new Metropolitan to Kerala and then to generously maintain him. One of the duties of the *Jathikukarthavyan* was to regularly collect the money from the whole Community for this purpose as well as to forward an honorarium to the Patriarch. But with Mar Jacob the situation changed. Mar Jacob remained a faithful recipient of Portuguese gratuity and used to report to the Portuguese governor in Cochin. He had as his advisers the Franciscan Observant friars there. On account of this compromising attitude of Mar Jacob, it appears that his faithful's affection for him too waned.

In contrast, an identical overture to a younger colleague of Mar Jacob then present in Kerala had an altogether different effect. He turned down the royal subsidy but enjoyed highest regard in the eyes of the St Thomas Christians. The Portuguese decided to get rid of this recalcitrant bishop and got him aboard a ship in order to deport him. On learning of their designs, he openly said that he too would become a salaried man of the Portuguese monarch and that like his senior, he too would be accommodating to the Portuguese clergy. These were only empty promises and as soon as the opportunity provided itself, he gave his captors the slip and found again the warmth of the hospitality of the St Thomas Christians. Later he was again apprehended and was shifted to Goa and kept in confinement for a year and finally deported to Ormuz. From here too he escaped and got back to Kerala. In 1536 he made his confession to Father Guardian of the St Anthony's Friary in Cochin and received Communion and accepted to be on the payroll of the Portuguese. Thus if Mar Jacob's pliancy and pragmatic approach had rendered him a persona grata to his new benefactors, it was his colleague's refusal to be a stooge that made him stand out like a sore thumb to the Portuguese.

Once Mar Jacob's collaboration was assured, the political bigwigs in Lisbon looked for ways of making hay while the sun was shining. The importance that Mar Jacob newly acquired in the Portuguese politics in India is reflected in the archival sources also. While the documents for the period before 1522 make only four references to him, those for the subsequent years have Mar Jacob occupy a more central place. In his letter of 1524 to the Portuguese sovereign Mar Jacob is seen assuming the role of a patriot of the Portuguese kingdom and goes as far as to promise the king "twenty-five thousand men of war." Thus finally after two decades a new situation now presented itself to the Portuguese king: his officials were now able to negotiate directly with the local Christians and their bishop was offering him 25,000 soldiers.[32] Meanwhile alarming reports of Moslem attacks on the Portuguese bases along the Malabar Coast were reaching Lisbon. The king's letters of 1526, to the Governor of India and to his three confidants in India, Fr João Caro, Mar Jacob and Fr Álvaro Penteado, show unmistakably that the monarch was seeing in the Christians of St Thomas a precious help for the solution of his problems. His plan was to prevent the Moslems from having access to the trade in spices, and to extend unconditional support to Mar Jacob as head of the St Thomas Christians. He asked Fr Penteado to help Mar Jacob, and to get the bishop's support in carrying through this project, without however giving scandal. The king renewed his trust in Penteado in his capacity as his personal representative to the St Thomas Christians. There was no doubt that the king was already regarding the Indian Christians as his allies, as those who had to be helped on the religious plane, but whose hierarchy had to be respected. He underscored this point in his letter to Mar Jacob.[33]

The Portuguese leadership never fully lost sight of the chief objectives of their expedition to India, including the one of mobilising a Christian force that could neutralise the threats from the Moslem world. Thinking that Vasco da Gama had already met "the Indian Christian king" in the person of the Zamorin of Calicut, the Portuguese king had written to the Zamorin proposing to him the idea of creating a new alliance between the Indian and Western Christianities in order to effectively contain the expansionism of Islam.[34] There are occasional reports of the Portuguese that explicitly make reference to the strength of the Community of the St Thomas Christians and to the number of its battleworthy men. But there does not seem to have been any serious attempt to bring together the soldiery of the

---

[32] Oliveira e Costa, *Os portugueses e a cristandade siro-malabar*, 162, expresses "many doubts regarding the sincerity of the offer of Mar Jacob in 1524": the St Thomas Christians were dispersed in various chiefdoms and it would not have been easy to mobilise an army of such a size; in order to translate such a project into reality Mar Jacob had to count upon the communal leadership. As a matter of fact in the years that followed Mar Jacob would get sidelined in the Community.

[33] See "Sumário das cartas que vieram da Índia no ano de 1525 e respostas d'el-rei a elas," in Oliveira e Costa, *Os portugueses e a cristandade siro-malabar*, 170-178.

[34] *Documentaçao para a História da missões do Padroado Português do Oriente — India*, I, ed. António da Silva Rego, Lisboa 1947, 15-21: letter of King Manuel to "El-Rey de Calecut," dated 1 March 1500.

St Thomas Christians in defence of the Portuguese interests.[35] In 1525 "the war of Calicut" had taken priority over all the other needs of the Portuguese *Estado da Índia* and the king despatched a number of letters to India to prepare the ground for a punitive expedition against the Zamorin. It was expected that Mar Jacob's promised army of 25,000 men would turn the scales in favour of the Portuguese. While in Portugal the details were being meticulously worked out the situation in India was getting out of control. Complying with the order that had been issued through Vasco da Gama in 1524, Governor Henrique de Menezes abandoned the Fort of Calicut towards the end of 1525. And soon after, that is in February 1526 the Governor died suddenly, and there began a long struggle for succession, which came to an end only with the arrival of Nuno da Cunha in 1529. This crisis also affected adversely the relationship between the Portuguese and the Christians of St Thomas, preventing, among other things, the reconstruction of the St Thomas church of Cranganore.[36]

Meanwhile Goa was fast developing in such a way as to eclipse Cochin in strategic importance for the Portuguese. Their territory centred around Goa actually consisted of five islands (*Ilhas*) which formed the midpoint of the south-west coast of India. The Portuguese had definitively captured the area way back in 1510 after spilling much blood. Following the successful implementation of a policy of encouraging the Portuguese to take wife locally, there was already a sizeable community of Christians of Indo-Portuguese origin. The capital Goa could be defended with relative ease. And so it was in the scheme of things that the Portuguese base in India be shifted to Goa from Cochin. This took place in 1530 and three years later, that is, in 1533 Goa was created a diocese. Its range of jurisdiction extended all the way from Cape of Good Hope in South Africa to China. In the emerging network of the Portuguese colonies, Goa acquired such a pivotal position that in 1557 it was made an archdiocese, with Cochin and Malacca as its suffragans. Thus as Goa gained in importance for

---

[35] Oliveira e Costa, *Os portugueses e a cristandade siro-malabar*, 162-163: "Com efeito, os cristãos de São Tomé nunca participaram nas guerras travadas pelo Estado da Índia, embora as dezenas de milhares de guerreiros que podiam mobilizar tenham sido consideradas por alguns estrategas portugueses." In Cochin when the Portuguese capitulated on 8 January 1663 to the Dutch, the St Thomas Christians did not in the least bother to take sides. They remained dispassionate spectators to the event.

[36] *Documentaçao para a História da missões do Padroado Português do Oriente*, II, 176-177: the letter of João Carcere to the Portuguese king, with the dateline "Cochim, 2 de Janeiro de 1529."

the Portuguese colonies in Asia, Cochin's political and economic significance declined. Consequently from the middle of the first half of the sixteenth century the Portuguese are not seen going out of the way in cultivating a political and economic relationship with the St Thomas Christians.[37] On the other hand their preoccupation was more with digging themselves in and fortifying the City of Goa in every way. It was again in Goa that the Inquisition or the Tribunal of the Holy Office for the whole of East was established in 1560, as a bulwark of the Portuguese colonial power.[38]

As long as the Metropolitan of the St Thomas Christians was ready to be a dependant of the Portuguese Crown, it appears that the Portuguese were prepared to respect him as the authoritative spokesman of the Community. "This attitude may be seen, to our understanding, as a structural behaviour of the Portuguese Crown, which runs from the beginning of the century till at least its integration into the patrimony of Philip II of Spain in 1580. Dom Manuel I effectively established an institutional relation with Mar Jacob."[39] Mar Jacob's relatively long episcopate among the St Thomas Christians (1503-1552), was a period in which the Portuguese authorities felt reassured that they had achieved their objective of finding "Christians and spices." The Portuguese regarded Mar Jacob as a loyal subject and dealt with him directly and there was no move to replace him or to circumvent his authority. On the other hand they were grateful to him and wanted him to continue his services.[40] At the same time neither the Portuguese Bishop of Goa nor the ecclesiastical authorities are seen playing any part in the affairs of the St Thomas Christians or those of

[37] Oliveira e Costa, *Os portugueses e a cristandade siro-malabar*, 149, footnote 90: "Empenhado numa estrategia que abarcava todo o Oceano, Albuquerque não via grande utilidade na cristandade siro-malabar, dispersa pelo interior dos reinos hindus e sem armadas de guerra nem frotas mercantis."

[38] Ana Cannas da Cunha, *A Inguisição no Estado da Índia. Origens (1539-1560)* (Estudos & Documentos, 1), Lisboa 1995, analyses the countless discussions that preceded the setting up of the Inquisition in Goa. The selection of the headquarters too was significant.

[39] Oliveira e Costa, *Os portugueses e a cristandade siro-malabar*, 160.

[40] King João's letter sent through the fleet of 1526 testifies to the profuseness of his thanks to "Abuna Yacob" for his services in getting the St Thomas Christians sell their pepper to the Portuguese. The king wants Mar Jacob to continue this service of his: "... que lhe encomendo muyto que continuy de nisto me serujr e o trazer a todo boom fim porque nam me podia com nenhua cousa mais obrigar pera folgar de lhe fazer merce de que com esta." See Oliveira e Costa, *Os portugueses e a cristandade siro-malabar*, Documentary Appendix, 174-175.

Mar Jacob. It was generally with the consent and approval of Mar Jacob that the Portuguese clergymen moved around among the St Thomas Christians.

2. "Approximation to the Portuguese": Penteado and Lagos

Even though Mar Jacob was conducting himself in a manner becoming a faithful subject of the Portuguese king, the charge of Nestorianism brought up against the St Thomas Christians and the activities of the two Portuguese clerics Penteado and Lagos in Kerala call for an explanation. The first Portuguese who appears to cast doubt on the Catholic faith of the St Thomas Christians is none other than Vasco da Gama himself. As a matter of fact on landing at Calicut, he and his fellow-voyagers were cocksure that they had set foot in a Christian land. After all they had come in search of Christians. And so they did not have to think twice about paying obeisance to a multi-limbed statue with protruding teeth, believing that it was a saint of some Christian heretics.[41] The correspondence material of 1499 and 1500 shows that the Portuguese had absolutely no doubts about India being a Christian land. And that is the reason why King Manuel I gave voice to the conviction of his voyagers in his letter to the Cardinal Protector, that the people of India were heretical Christians.

> The earliest reference to errors and imperfections among the Indian Christians seems to be that of King Manuel in his letters to the sovereigns of Castile, to the Cardinal protector, in the instructions he gave to Cabral before the latter's voyage to India, and in his letter to the Samorim of Calicut. Probably the king had no intention of imputing schism or heresy to them but was more prone to consider their imperfections more as the result of isolation than of separation.[42]

---

[41] Pearson, *Os portugueses na Índia*, 129: "Os primeiros anos são especialmente interessantes, pois foram dominados por um desejo muito humano e compreensível de encontrar coisas conhecidas na Ásia. Isso explica a tão falada incapacidade de Gama, durante três meses, no Malabar, de compreender que o Hinduísmo era diferente do Cristianismo."

[42] Mundadan, *History of Christianity in India*, 505. But Oliveira e Costa, *Os portugueses e a cristandade siro-malabar*, 127, criticises this interpretation of Mundadan: "Para Mundadan esta atitude de *Venturoso* è a chave que explica todo o comportamento futuro dos Portugueses para com os cristãos de São Tomé, pois estes foram considerados desde logo como 'imperfeitos'. Esta teoria parece-nos, contudo, insustentável, pois a relação com a cristandade siro-malabar não assentou neste equívoco, come veemos da seguida." On the other hand, Oliveira e Costa says that "... it appears to us that to regard a Hindu temple as a temple of the Christians, although heretics,

Inasmuch as the king's view was based on a mistaken identity, he cannot be cited as a proof that from the beginning onwards the Portuguese considered the faith of the St Thomas Christians as deficient. Since the persons whom Gama had met in Kerala on his first expedition were not Christians, his comments or those of others based on this wrong impression of his, cannot be applied to the St Thomas Christians. It was again this misapprehension that made the king address the Zamorin of Calicut as his brother-in-faith. He, therefore, wanted the "Indian brothers" to return to orthodoxy.[43]

It would be only in January 1501 during the course of the expedition led by Pedro Álvares Cabral that the Portuguese would realise that the natives of India were predominantly non-Christians. On his home voyage Cabral would have the fortune to take aboard with him the two Indian priests, Joseph and Mathias of Cranganore. It is actually at this point that the relationship between the two Christian traditions begins and hereafter the considerations that would be made by Manuel I on the St Thomas Christians differ substantially from what he had expressed on Gama's return from his maiden voyage to India. Soon the king would speak commendably of the Church founded by the Apostle Thomas in the Kingdom of Cochin.[44] In the first decades of the sixteenth century the Portuguese are not seen assuming the role of converters of heretics; on the other hand they present themselves as benefactors of a community that was at a low ebb.

Actually it was around this period that one sees another attempt to label the St Thomas as Nestorians. This time it was not a question of mistaken identity. The doctrinal charge appears in a letter written in Lisbon in 1515 by a certain Valentin to a merchant of Nuremberg. Speaking of the lands already reached by the Portuguese, Valentin speaks of Quilon where "there is a great number of Nestorian Christians." As no such allegation is seen in any of the then contemporary sources arising in India, Valentin must have had some other foun-

---

does not signify intolerance, but rather a relatively open spirit." See also *Documentaçao para a História da missões do Padroado Português do Oriente*, I, 11.

[43] *Documentaçao para a História da missões do Padroado Português do Oriente*, I, 11.

[44] Mundadan, *History of Christianity in India*, 505, adds: "His [King Manuel's] attitude towards the Christians of St Thomas, when he actually came to know of them through Cabral and the two Indian Christians whom Cabral brought to Portugal, was rather one of respect and esteem for them."

tainheads to go by. As a matter of fact Odorico of Pordenone (c. 1330) and a century later Nicholas of Conti (c. 1440) had affirmed that Indian Christianity was Nestorian.[45] Valentin must have certainly had access to Conti's work because it had been published in 1502 precisely from Lisbon along with the work of Marco Polo.[46] At any rate Valentin's remains an individual and hackneyed consideration which could not at all have been based on any epistolary sources originating in India.

Now Fr Álvaro Penteado's mission among the St Thomas Christians too needs a comment. It was in 1516 that he received the posting to Cochin, after serving in Madagascar and Goa. On his visit to Cranganore he was well received by the St Thomas Christians there. He moved around the Christian pockets in the neighbourhood of Cranganore. Penteado does not make any adverse remark on the St Thomas Christians or on their faith or on their praxis of it. But he pointed the finger straight at their clergy for leaving so many of the children and even adults unbaptised. His virulent attack is understandable, granted the absolute importance attached to the reception of the sacrament of baptism. "Although Penteado suggests that the King should take under his charge the governance of that Christianity, for the purpose of making it more approximate to the Portuguese, we think that there do not exist elements that point to a manifest will of subordinating authoritatively the Christians of St Thomas."[47] It was more the desire to rush to the aid of a Church in need, which had remained cut off and abandoned, and in which baptism was not readily available to the faithful. It would not be fair to read into Penteado's letters any intention to set in motion a programme of latinization. That he had an insight into the intricacy of the issue may be gauged from his own words: "... because we are among them like the English and the Germans among us."[48]

---

[45] Mundadan, *History of Christianity in India*, 143: "One common attribute assigned to them by the foreign visitors is 'Nestorian'."

[46] Oliveira e Costa, *Os portugueses e a cristandade siro-malabar*, 141-142: holds that though from 1502 this work had been in circulation in Lisbon, it was the only source that referred to the St Thomas Christians as being tainted with Nestorianism. See also *Cart escrita da Lisboa (1515) pelo alemão Valentim* [Fernandes] *da Morávia a um mercador de Nuremberga*, in *Deambulations of the Rhinoceros (Ganda) of Muzafar, King of Cambaia, from 1514 to 1516*, ed. A. Fontoura da Costa, Lisboa 1937, 33-40.

[47] Oliveira e Costa, *Os portugueses e a cristandade siro-malabar*, 147.

[48] This incident has been diversely interpreted. Oliveira e Costa, *Os portugueses e a cristandade siro-malabar*, 148, holds that some scholars have not been fair to Pen-

With great facility Penteado was able to move around the Christian communities in and around Cranganore. Seeing that the priest in charge at Cranganore, Fr Joseph, had been away on pilgrimage to Mylapore, he took the occasion to administer sacraments to the faithful. But as soon as Fr Joseph was back, Penteado bowed to the wishes of the local authority.[49] At this stage Penteado, however, is not the central figure; in fact the real protagonists of the project for bringing the Portuguese and the St Thomas Christians closer were Mar Jacob and Fr João Caro.[50] In the same way Oliveira e Costa sees the initiative of Lopo Soares de Albergaria in 1517-1518 for promoting "institutional approximation" between the Portuguese and the St Thomas Christians, as a way of bypassing the intermediary Moslems and thus guaranteeing themselves the direct access to the producers of the spices, namely the St Thomas Christians.[51] This was intended to be more a commercial strategy than an ecclesiastical measure. The fact that the Castilian Dominican friar João Caro was able to strike a close friendship with Mar Abraham won the approval of the Portuguese king.[52] One cannot blink the fact that neither the ecclesiasticl leadership back in Portugal nor their representatives in India had any

---

teado: "Notamos, assim, um cuidado em respeitar a hierarquia local que não condiz com a imagem assaz intolerante que autores come Schurhammer e Mundadan nos dão deste clérigo… Parece-nos, contudo, que dum ponto de vista estritamente cristão nunca è um abuso administrar os scramentos a uma comunidade que está sem sacerdote durante meses, e mesmo tendo em atenção os interesses político-comerciais dos Portugueses na zona, não notamos nenhum abuso, pois Penteado subordinou-se à vontade do padre local, assim que este regressou." He further makes the observation in the footnote No 86: "Estranhamente Schurhammer dá uma versão diferente desta passagem…." For the original text see, *Documentaçao para a História da missões do Padroado Português do Oriente*, I, 546.

[49] *Documentaçao para a História da missões do Padroado Português do Oriente*, I, 546.

[50] Schurhammer, *Three letters of Mar Jacob*, 72: In his letter (ca. 1523) to King John III of Portugal, Mar Jacob says about Fr Caro: "It may be 4 years since a Father Master *Joam Caro* came to this country. From him I received many instructions for my salvation and that of this my people and also about the things of thy service. One of the things of thy service, which he taught me, was, that the Christians I am ruling, got all the pepper from the hands of the farmers who collect it and that they dared not bring it to thy factory for fear, which the Moors instilled into them telling them falsehoods and deceit …."

[51] Oliveira e Costa, *Os portugueses e a cristandade siro-malabar*, 148-149.

[52] *Documentaçao para a História da missões do Padroado Português do Oriente*, II, 352: Mar Jacob says that the service of Fr Caro has been greatly beneficial to him and to his flock. See also Schurhammer, *Three letters of Mar Jacob*, 72.

role to play in the evolution of this relationship between Mar Abraham and Fr Caro.

While Mar Jacob forcibly defended the correctness of his way of administering baptism, a manner that had found favour in Fr Caro's eyes, he warned the Portuguese king that should the king order him to allow Fr Penteado to baptise, there would be the risk that the Portuguese would lose the friendship of the St Thomas Christians. The mind of Mar Jacob was to begin a progressive approximation of his faithful to the mores of the Portuguese and to their clergy.

> We observe, in this way, that the prelate did not admit that they were questioning his competence, but he was accepting the royal orders, although he sought to influence them... . Then it was the Chaldean bishop himself who was offering in a medium term the integration of his Church into the bosom of the Portuguese one.[53]

Oliveira e Costa sees the altercation between Mar Denha and Fr Penteado regarding the administration of baptism very much in the same way. Penteado's words "more damaging than Nestor" and "the Nestorian baptism" used in reference to Mar Denha are to be seen in the context of the embittered relationship between the two individuals. What is curious is that this accusation appears to be a cry in the wilderness and it does not find echo in any of Penteado's contemporaries either in India or in Portugal. This signifies that these Indian Christians were still being complimentarily regarded as the faithful disciples of the Apostle St Thomas. Thus Penteado's indictment at this stage appears more as the outburst of one individual's fury and frustration over the stubborn refusal of the St Thomas Christians to follow his lead than the common opinion of the Portuguese concerning the doctrinal tenets of these Indian Christians.[54]

Chronologically it is here that the establishment of the St James Seminary (College) in Cranganore (*Colegio do Apostolo Samt'Iaguo*) by Friar Vicente de Lagos can be situated. During the third decade of the sixteenth century a certain polarisation had already taken place within the Community of the St Thomas Christians. On the one hand there was the group that remained faithful to Mar Jacob and his adviser Fr Penteado and on the other there was the younger bishop Mar Denha (*O bispo moço*) who had the backing of another group that did not approve of Mar Jacob's innovations. Mar Jacob's accept-

---

[53] Oliveira e Costa, *Os portugueses e a cristandade siro-malabar*, 156-157.

[54] Oliveira e Costa, *Os portugueses e a cristandade siro-malabar*, 165-166.

ing of salary from the Portuguese king could have been seen as a sell-out. Sometime early in 1530 Penteado, realising that he had become all too unpopular in India and that his life itself was in danger, called it quits and returned to Portugal. And it was now the turn of the Franciscan Observant friars in Cochin to advise Mar Jacob. He was now directly answerable to the Portuguese governor. Fr Mundadan describes the political constraints on Mar Jacob as:

> We have already seen that King John III by granting to Mar Jacob a state subsidy had tried to bring him and his Christians under his direct jurisdiction. In this second letter he appears to take that subjection for granted and officially gives the charge of the St Thomas Christians to the East-Syrian bishop as if they were his subjects in some way or other. Further, he orders the bishop to give an account of his ministry to his representative.[55]

And faithfully Mar Jacob reported to the Portuguese Governor in Cochin, "on whose advice he had brought to Cochin seven boys who read well and had made a good beginning and had great desires"

At long last the Portuguese authorities decided to oblige Mar Jacob and his faithful by constructing a fortress in Cranganore. While such a structure would enable the Portuguese to keep an eye on the flow of pepper, it was seen by the St Thomas Christians as a reassuring presence. They were being haunted by the fear of the vindictive measures of the Moslems for their having diverted the sale of pepper to the Portuguese. In December 1536 the fortress was already under construction. The fortress' proximity was one of the reasons why Friar Vicente de Lagos, a Franciscan Recollect friar, preferred Cranganore for the erection of the seminary (college). As a matter of fact he had been sent to Cochin to found a seminary by his confrere, Juan de Albuquerque, the first bishop of Goa.[56]

---

[55] Mundadan, *History of Christianity in India*, 311.

[56] The two of them had together reached India in 1538 and belonged to the newly constituted Custody of Piedade, a jurisdiction of the Recollect Branch sprung up within the Franciscan Observant Movement. This Branch goes back to Peter of Villacreces, who withdrew to a desert cave, thereby initiating a reform movement in Spain at the very close of the fourteenth century. This movement officially referred to as *Recollectio Villacresciana*, came to be known popularly in Portugal as *Capuchos*; here they were constituted into the *Custodie da Piedade* in 1505 and into a Province in 1517. This explains both why Fr Vicente is also alluded to as being of the *Capuchos* as well as to the fact he did not wish to start the seminary in Cochin, where the Observant friars already had a house.

The choice of the institution's heavenly patron too was significant. The Apostle James, the patron saint of the Iberian peninsula, would be on a par with the Apostle Thomas, whom the St Thomas Christians cherished as their progenitor, and to whose sanction they appealed whenever it came to making any change in their religious and social mores. The St James Seminary was to offer to a select group of young men of the St Thomas Christian Community a thorough schooling in the traditions of the Latin Church. The horarium was patterned on the strict conventual life that the Franciscan Recollect friars were wont to live. The Portuguese clergy and officials were all in admiration for the way the Seminary functioned. "Friar Vicente's enthusiasm in conducting the seminary impressed Mar Jacob, who encouraged the Thomas Christians to entrust their children to Friar Vicente."[57] The St James Seminary opened in 1540/1 and it enjoyed the backing of those St Thomas Christians who approved the policies of Mar Jacob. The seminary had a good start.[58]

Qualifying St James Seminary of Cranganore as "the first seminary which was founded in India, this honour going entirely to Fr Vicente de Lagos," António da Silva Rego states, "We only say in conclusion that it was Fr Vicente de Lagos who gave the start to the real evangelisation of the Christians of St Thomas."[59] But judging from the results, one should add that this brainchild of Fr Vicente was not of any significance for the St Thomas Christians, even though it contributed to the birth and growth of the Latin Church in Kerala and beyond.[60] "In the 50 years since priests were being trained there, we read that many had been ordained, but none of them worked among the Thomas Christians. If the candidates were to

---

[57] Gervasis J. Mulakara, *History of the Diocese of Cochin*, I: *European Missionaries in Cochin (1292-1558)*, Rome 1986, 61.

[58] Georg Schurhammer, *Francis Xavier. His Life, His Times*, II: *India (1541-1545)*, Rome 1977, 485, speaks of the appreciation that St Francis Xavier had for the nascent institution and says that the seminary "had quickly flourished as a promising nursery of future missionaries for the whole of Malabar."

[59] Silva Rego, *História da Missões*, 398-399. Though the author promised "to refer to this institution in the following volume," the project has not made any headway.

[60] Josef Wicki, *Der einheimische Klerus in Indien (16. Jahrhundert)*, in *Der einheimische Klerus in Geschichte und Gegenwart. Festschrift P. Dr. Laurenz Kilger OSB zum 60. Geburtstag dargeboten von Freunden und Schülern*, hrg. von Johannes Beckmann (Neue Zeitschrift für Missionswissenschaft. Supplementa, 2), Schöneck-Beckenried 1950, 43: "Dieses Verbleiben im Verband der lateinischen Kirche ist denn auch der Hauptgrund, weswegen wir dieses Kolleg den andern gleichstellen und es nicht zum syro-malabarischen Ritus zählen."

know Latin, they would be taken by the Bishop of Cochin and ordained, and they gladly stayed with him because with the Portuguese they would have better food and other things."[61] What is known for certain is that from the first half of the sixteenth century onwards there have been young men of the Community of the St Thomas Christians who entered the ranks of the Padroado missionaries[62] and toiled away in the establishment of the various Latin dioceses in Kerala and beyond.

But for the active involvement of Mar Jacob the St James Seminary would not have got materialised. It was Mar Jacob who had been visiting the strongholds of the St Thomas Christians in order to recruit the suitable candidates for the seminary. Thus this seminary cannot be seen merely as a Trojan horse created by the Portuguese in order to Latinize the St Thomas Christians, inasmuch as right from the start it had the blessing of Mar Jacob. While it was the Bishop of Goa who had deputed Fr Vicente to undertake the project of the seminary, the Metropolitan of the St Thomas Christians was actively involved in finding out candidates for the seminary. Hence Fr Vicente was not the only villain of the piece.

---

[61] Wicki, *Der einheimische Klerus in Indien*, 43; Mundadan, *History of Christianity in India*, 341: "To conclude: the college was a success in the sense that it produced many well-trained and good Latin priests from the community of St Thomas Christians. But it failed miserably in its ultimate purpose, namely, of influencing the community of St Thomas Christians through these Latinized priests and of 'converting' them to the acceptance of Latin customs, jurisdiction and Rite."

[62] Stephen Neill, *A History of Christianity in India*, 199, speaks of the St James College got up by the Franciscan Friars (*Capuchos*) at Cranganore, where in 1548 there was "a flock of seventy pupils, many of them from the best families among the Thomas Christians." Since these and others were not welcome in the churches of the St Thomas Christians for officiating at the liturgy because of their inexperience in the Syriac form of worship, they were posted among the Latin communities. Neill comments: "Many of the Indian priests mentioned in the records of the next forty years of the mission seem to have been waifs and orphans of this type; they remain shadowy and inconsiderable figures." As early as 1525 there were instances of recruiting candidates for priesthood from the Community of the St Thomas Christians by the Padroado clergy. In his letter of January 1525 Fr Penteado requested the Portuguese king to sponsor the "dez ou xij filhos," whom the St Thomas Christians were ready to make available for being trained to receive priestly ordination. Since the rich families would not send him their children for this purpose, Penteado was forced to take recourse to the poor families. See Penteado's letter of January 1525 to the Portuguese king, in the Documentary Appendix, Oliveira e Costa, *Os portugueses e a cristandade siro-malabar*, 171.

B. *Later Decades of Sixteenth Century*

Subsequent to his becoming a stipendiary of the Portuguese king, Mar Jacob's sphere of activities gravitated more towards Cochin. By 1542 he, already a greybeard, moved house to Cochin, to the St Anthony's Friary, where he breathed his last in 1552. His death was seen by the Franciscan Observant friars as the cue for bringing to completion their new scheme for fully bringing the St Thomas Christians under the Portuguese umbrella both politically and ecclesiastically. They not only tried to coerce the St Thomas Christians into further falling in line with the Latin ecclesial traditions but also determined to pre-empt the arrival of another East Syriac bishop in India. But as was their wont, the St Thomas Christians appealed to the Patriarch of the East Syriac Church for a bishop. Since in the meantime there had taken place a vertical split in the hierarchical set-up of the East Syriac Church, both the factions responded positively to the petition from India. It was Mar Abraham from the hierarchical line of leadership, in union with the See of Rome since 1553, who first reached Malabar. He reached his destination in 1556. But by this time, contextually many things had changed; the then prevailing circumstances were quite different from those of the early decades of the century.[63]

If previously the main worry of the Portuguese had been to dodge the Moslem middlemen from having direct access to the source of the spices and to form an alliance with the St Thomas Christians, in the second half of the sixteenth century they felt a compulsion to make the St Thomas Christians conform to their own way of Church-life. Hence, as far as the sixteenth-century history of the St Thomas Christians of India is concerned, it is very much in place to draw a line of demarcation across it, making the early decades distinct from the rest. However thin the line may be, it neatly evidences aspects that make the one stand apart from the other. In sum, one may say that it is the emergence of two new realities in the second phase that distinguishes it from the first. The two events are the coming of the members of the Society of Jesus on the scene and the celebration of the Council of Trent.

---

[63] Oliveira e Costa, *Os portugueses e a cristandade siro-malabar*, 169.

1. Arrival of Jesuits on the Scene (1542)

By the time Francis Xavier and his two companions reached India in 1542 the Minorite and Dominican friars were already in service there as missionaries, vicars, apostolic commissaries and bishops. While the Minorites had established themselves in Goa (1518) and Cochin (1521), it was only in Goa (1548) that the Dominicans had their house. Sequel to the entry of the Jesuits into the picture the ecclesiastical landscape of Kerala underwent profound changes. "The militant character and the dynamism of the Society, as well as its rapid expansion in the *Estado da Índia*"[64] enabled the Jesuits to make their presence felt in India. In 1584 there were 349 Jesuits in the Indian Province.[65] Though they were late-comers on the scene, on account of their methodological preparedness and numerical superiority, for various decades they were able to occupy the centre-stage in the history of the St Thomas Christians. "During Mar Abraham's second stay in India [1568-1597] the Jesuits were able to commence their activities among the Thomas Christians and supersede the Franciscans."[66]

Though the Jesuits had opened a base in Cochin way back in 1548, it was only in 1576 that they began operating among the St Thomas Christians. Their earlier contacts were individual missions and did not form part of a strategy. The ingress of the Jesuits into the sphere of the communal life and thinking of the St Thomas Christians took place in a fortuitous manner. In his capacity as visitor to the East, Fr Alessandro Valignano toured the various mission stations of the Society in South India. The impenetrable wall of casteism in vogue in India struck him as one of the obstacles to evangelisation. To his mind, the Community of the St Thomas Christians would provide the right personnel for taking the Gospel to the upper castes. And he was looking out for the auspicious moment for enabling his Fathers to function among the St Thomas Christians. By a happy coincidence, Mar Abraham too was then contemplating the idea of approaching the Jesuits for help. He was badly in need of outside help in order to

---

64 Cunha, *A Inquisição no Estado da Índia*, 121.

65 *Documenta Indica*, XIII: *(1583-1585)* (Monumenta Historica Societatis Iesu, 113), ed. J. Wicki, Romae 1975, 599-658, is the catalogue of the members of the Province of India.

66 Joseph Thekkedath, *History of Christianity in India*, II: *From the middle of the sixteenth century to the end of the seventeenth century*, Bangalore 1982, 36.

neutralise the efforts of Mar Simon, his rival, to get himself accepted as bishop by the St Thomas Christians.

Thus when Fr Dionysius, the Rector of the Jesuit College of "Madre de Dios" in Cochin called on Mar Abraham, the latter saw it as a godsend occasion. The visit paved the way for the creation of a close rapport between the two. On his part the Archbishop reciprocated the visit on 18 April 1577, the feast of Corpus Christi. He was favourably impressed by his hosts and became well-disposed towards them. Consequently he allowed the Jesuits to minister to his faithful. And without further ado Fr Valignano set about finding out an ideal location for their centre. Vaipincotta appeared well suited for their activities. And in the same year two Jesuits, one of them a Keralite Brahmin, took up their residence there. And using Vaipincotta as their base they were able to move around undeterred among the surrounding pockets of the St Thomas Christians. In general they were warmly welcomed everywhere especially because of their reputation as priests who administer baptism and other sacraments without charging fees. They used to move from one community to another, celebrating the Eucharist, blessing marriages, instructing children etc., all after the manner of the Latin ecclesiastical tradition. Great emphasis would be placed on making the faithful aware of the need to be in fellowship with Rome both in faith and in the form of worship.

In 1578 in Vaipincotta they constructed a church and alongside it also a house to serve as a seminary. The seminary was meant exclusively for the children of the St Thomas Christian Community.[67] With the aid of the Viceroy in Goa, in 1587 the construction of a more spacious seminary was begun. Besides the theological subjects the clerics were taught Latin, Syriac and Portuguese. However the entire system of formation was based on the Latin ecclesial tradition, including the Tridentine accentuations. Thanks to the generous collaboration of Mar Abraham there was no dearth of candidates for joining the seminary.

The Jesuits knew exactly what had to be done, because they had clearly done their homework, as the dissertation of Fr Ros,[68] who was

---

[67] J. Wicki, *Der einheimische Klerus in Indien*, 33.

[68] Thekkedath, *History of Christianity in India*, 54: "On the other hand, the Jesuits began to suspect more and more that Mar Abraham was at heart a Nestorian, seeing that he was so slow in getting the liturgical books corrected and in introducing the changes which he had promised at the Council of Goa. This suspicion is clearly ex-

then teaching Syriac at the seminary of Vaipincotta, would go to show. Fr Thekkedath accurately sums up the prevailing mind of the Jesuits in India as regards the future of the St Thomas Christians:

> The Jesuits were convinced that the hierarchical and liturgical dependence of the St Thomas Christians on the Chaldean Church was the source of most of the errors found among them. Hence many accepted the opinion of the predecessors and contemporaries that it was necessary to prevent the Chaldean bishops from going to Kerala and also to bring the Malabar Church under the Portuguese *Padroado*. To many of these missionaries, anything that did not accord with the usages of the Roman (Latin) Church was corruption and abuse and heresy. Hence they sought to get such things changed. Some of the Jesuits wanted to change things immediately, others wanted to do it gradually. This trend culminated in the Synod of Diamper, where under the pressure of contemporary thought and the demands of the Council of Trent, almost complete Latinization of the Church of the St Thomas Christians was effected.[69]

Even though there was no formal rupture between Mar Abraham and the Jesuits, the initial level of cordiality and friendship just could not be sustained for long. Notwithstanding the fact they had no incontrovertible grounds for calling into question Mar Abraham's Catholic faith and his allegiance to the Pope, he was just tolerated as an unavoidable obstruction. How genuinely some of the Jesuits longed for the day when they would be free of that headstrong Chaldean! And they were not to wait long, for Mar Abraham died in January 1597.

2. Council of Trent (1545-1563)

The Council of Trent, which had as its objectives the refutation of the errors of the Protestant Reformation, the clarification of the doctrinal tenets, and the promoting of genuine reform of the whole Church, impacted the entire Catholic Church profoundly. Of the twenty-five sessions of the Council seventeen were concerned specifically with doctrine and reform. The invigorating of the Counter-Reformation, the Roman Catechism (1566) and the reformed Missal (1570) too were the fruits of this reform. The broad movement of reform (1500-1648) and especially the Catholic Church's response to the Protestant Reformation is generally known as the Catholic Ref-

---

pressed by Ros in the opening sentences of the little treatise entitled *De erroribus Nestorianorum qui in hac India Orientali versantur*, which he wrote in 1586 or 1587."

[69] Thekkedath, *History of Christianity in India*, 59.

ormation or the Counter-Reformation. The constitution and the rapid diffusion and development of the Society of Jesus served the Holy See as an effective vehicle for the launching of this Catholic Reformation the world over.

Practically every aspect of Church-life was covered by the Council of Trent, leaving little space for divergence in believing and worshipping. In the same way everyone in a position of ecclesiastical authority was in conscience bound to contribute to the translation of the Conciliar mind into actuality. The following citation from the Bull of Approval of the Conciliar Canons and Decrees goes to corroborate this:

> Moreover, in virtue of holy obedience and under the penalties prescribed by the holy canons, and others more severe, even of deprivation, to be imposed at our discretion, we command each and all of our venerable brethren, patriarchs, archbishops, bishops, and all other prelates of churches, whatever may be their state, rank, order and dignity, even though distinguished with the honour of the cardinalate, to observe diligently the said decrees and ordinances in their churches, cities and dioceses both in and out of the court of justice, and to cause them to be observed inviolably, each by his own subjects whom it may in any way concern; restraining all opponents and obstinate persons by means of judicial sentences, censures and ecclesiastical penalties contained in those decrees, every appeal being set aside, calling in also, if need be, the aid of the secular arm.[70]

This spirit of the Counter-Reformation too had a determining effect on the missionaries the whole world over. And individuals and groups who had pledged themselves to be committed spokespersons of the Church naturally felt impelled to be vigilant in implementing the Church's policies across the globe. The Synod of Diamper with its excesses in the details too had as its mainspring the Tridentine and the Counter-Reformation mind-set.

The Synod of Diamper is unequivocal in declaring its ultimate purpose, namely, to make the Church of the St Thomas Christians fully conform to the pattern of ecclesial life approved and promulgated by the Council of Trent. According to the promoters of the Portuguese Counter-Reformation, the observances of the St Thomas Christians on the whole were clearly adulterated with Hindu and

[70] From the "Bull of our Most Holy Lord, Pius IV, by the Providence of God, Pope, concerning the confirmation of the Ecumenical and General Council of Trent," in *The Canons and Decrees of the Council of Trent*, translated and introduced by H. J. Schroeder, Rockford 1978, 270.

Nestorian influences, in other words, they were tainted or quasi heretical.[71] The faculty to preach exercised by the priests of the St Thomas Christians was en bloc withdrawn with the synodal Decree entitled "None are to preach to the people without licence from the bishop or the rector of Vaipicotta, and without having subscribed to the doctrines of Trent."[72] Another Decree of the Synod carries the caption: "Resolves to be governed in all things by the last Council of Trent" and it reads:

> Furthermore, this present Synod, with all the priests and the faithful people of this diocese, doth embrace the last holy and sacred council of Trent, and does not only believe and confess all that was determined and approved of therein, and reject and anathematize all that council rejected and condemned; but doth moreover receive and embrace the said council as to all matters therein determined, relating to the reformation of the church, and all Christian people, promising and swearing to govern itself according to the rules thereof, and to observe the same forms that are observed in the catholic church, and as are observed in this province of the Indies, and in all the other provinces and suffragans to the metropolis of Goa; in order to the removing of all abuses and customs that are contrary to the decrees of the said council of Trent; by which only it is resolved to govern itself as to all matters relating to the government of the church, and the reformation of the manners of this faithful and catholic people, any customs, though immemorial, in this bishopric, to the contrary notwithstanding.[73]

Some of the doctrinal elaborations contained in the Syriac books in the possession of the St Thomas Christians did not fully square with the teachings of the Catholic Church. Fr Francis Ros's compilation of *De erroribus nestorianorum qui in hac India Orientali versantur* and the Synod of Diamper's order to purge the liturgical texts of such anomalies and the burning of other heretical books are evidences that elements of *"Nestorianism"* were in fact present at least on the academic level, even though the St Thomas Christians were not aware of any theological option they or their forefathers had ever made against the Catholic creed.[74] What they were cocksure about

---

[71] Pearson, *Os portugueses na Índia*,132.

[72] *The Acts and Decrees of the Synod of Diamper*, 105: Session 3, Decree 17.

[73] *The Acts and Decrees of the Synod of Diamper*, 108: Session 3, Decree 21.

[74] Jesuit Provincial Francisco Cabral's letter of 20 November 1595 to the Jesuit General speaks about the doctrinal errors and the corrections already introduced into the books in use: "... o arcediago tinha entregues os livros ao Padre Ros per os emmendarem des erros que tinhão": *Documenta Indica*, XVII: *(1595-1597)* (Monumenta Historica Societatis Iesu, 132), ed. J. Wicki, Romae 1988, 230.

was that their primogenitors had received the Christian faith from the Apostle Thomas and had, despite everything, preserved ever since that faith. According to them their association with the East Syriac Church only corroborated them in their faith as this ecclesial fellowship had enabled them to worship in Jesus' own language. The fact remains that the East Syriac Church with its cultic modalities, dogmatic tenets and theological literature, reflecting the Nestorian line of thinking, was very much present among them. Hence it did not require much time and effort for those trained in the scholastic categories and doctrinal subtleties of the Latin Church to smell out those divergencies in circulation in this ancient Church in India.

While the missionaries remained one-idea'd to stamp out "*Nestorianism*" from the Community of the St Thomas Christians, as the epistolary and reportorial sources originating from the missionaries evidence, instances are aplenty to show that they were deliberately ignoring the incontrovertible proofs that the bishops of the St Thomas Christians were not Nestorians at least from the middle of the sixteenth century onwards. In 1555 when Mar Joseph, escorted by Metropolitan Elias, Mgr Ambrose Buttigeg and Antoninus Zahara, both Maltese Dominicans, landed in Goa en route for Kerala to take possession of his See, the whole group was forcibly detained. Mar Joseph was deported to the Portuguese colony of Mozambique and then taken back to Salesette in India. The others were kept under vigilance in Goa. On his second arrival Mar Abraham did not fare any better. In order to avoid every equivocation and to make himself doubly sure of the rightness of his status, on special authorisation from Pope Pius V, he had got himself re-ordained by the Patriarch of Venice. Fortified with letters from the Pope, his Patriarch, the General Superiors of the Franciscans, Dominicans and the Jesuits to their respective representatives in India, he disembarked in Goa. He too was apprehended but he was smart enough to make good his escape. And thereafter he took good care to steer clear of the Portuguese.

Both the Synod of Angamali (1583) and the Third Provincial Council of Goa (1585) did not effectively make the St Thomas Christians conform fully to the Latin Church-life, as the champions of the Counter-Reformation would have wished. The conclusion was therefore drawn that such a goal would be attained only if the St Thomas Christians, after their Chaldean links had been severed, were to be placed under the jurisdiction of a bishop of the Latin Church. Fr Ros's list of the Nestorian errors of the St Thomas Christians had already been compiled in 1586/7. And it meant that the ecclesiastical tacticians in Goa and Vaipincotta needed merely to bide their time. With the death of the elderly Mar Abraham in the beginning of January 1599, the stage was set for the Archbishop of Goa to descend into Kerala and deal the mortal blow to the spectre of *Nestorianism* there. And it was killing two birds with one stone because in the wake of the Synod of Diamper Archbishop Alexis de Menezes was able to get the Church of the St Thomas Christians placed directly under the jurisdictional power of his Archdiocese of Goa.[75]

RETROSPECT

What originally appeared to be a bipartite contest was in fact a polygonal trial of strength. Firstly, there were the St Thomas Christians who remained headstrong never to leave the beaten track that they tenaciously believed had been traced by the Apostle Thomas. At the same time they unabashedly fought for their caste privileges and vigorously resisted the entry of others from the bottom rungs of the social ladder into their privileged club. Their caste consciousness blinded them from recognising the evangelisation initiatives of the missionaries and from accepting the newly converted as brothers in faith.

Secondly, there were the Portuguese personnel who reached India, armed "with the sword and the cross" in their capacity as traders and missionaries. When they did not scruple to have recourse to violence and bloodshed in order to displace the Moslem traders and to spread the colonial tentacles, they were depriving Christianity of the Gospel flavour. Indian Christianity still labours under this hangover. In their overenthusiasm to get the St Thomas Christians under the Padroado umbrella the Portuguese trampled underfoot legitimate ecclesiastical traditions, disgraced authorities, and perpetrated violence and injustice on individuals and groups.

Thirdly, there were the Chaldean high-ups, who would keep on trying as late as the second decade of the twentieth century to bring back the St Thomas Christians under their hegemony. They were

[75] Thekkedath, *History of Christianity in India*, 75: "In this way, the synod of Diamper achieved one of the aims of Portuguese policy in Kerala, viz., to separate the Syrian Christians of Malabar from the Chaldean patriarch and to extend the influence of his Catholic Majesty over those parts. Soon the king of Portugal would have the right of nomination to the see of Malabar."

more keen to preserve their jurisdiction in India and to have the economic advantages accruing to them than about the welfare and growth of the St Thomas Christians. The vertical split in the leadership of the East Syriac Church in 1552 only aggravated the situation.

Fourthly, the role of the twenty princes and chieftains of Kerala in whose domains lived the St Thomas Christians, cannot be undervalued in the unfolding of the story of these Christians. The Christian strongholds were mainly in the kingdoms of Cochin, Kaduthuruty (Vadakkumkur) and Kottayam (Thekkumkur). Some of these princes were only too eager to fish in troubled waters, readily changing patronage depending on the size of the bribes proffered or on the prestige of the interlocutor.

Fifthly, there were the authorities in distant Rome and Lisbon, the Franciscan Observant and Recollect friars, the Dominicans and the Jesuits. There were some with myopic policies while the decisions of some others were coloured by rivalry and an obvious lack of concern for the common good.

Summing up, one may say that the Synod of Diamper, when viewed in its historical perspective, represents a stage that many other Christian communities too have gone through when encountering for the first time fellowships differing from them in origin and lifestyle. The fact that the entire Church of the St Thomas Christians came through the Synod of Diamper in one piece, that is, as one undivided, though humiliated Community, is itself a great achievement, especially if the Synod of Diamper is compared with similar events in the history of the other Catholic Oriental Churches, the Maronites excepting. The Community of the St Thomas Christians by maintaining itself one and whole fared better than their sister-Churches at times caustically labelled as *Uniates*, all of which in the ultimate analysis appear to be breakaway groups of dissimilar proportions from their respective mother Churches. However, the commercial interests and unconcealed power politics prevented this encounter between the disciples of Jesus from the East and the West from being an event of mutual edification in the spirit of the Gospel.

Istituto Storico Cappucino
CP 18382 Bravetta
00163 Roma, Italy

Benedict Vadakkekara, O.F.M. Cap.

K. J. John

MENEZES ON THE ROAD TO DIAMPER

The newly appointed Archbishop of Goa was Dom Alexis de Menezes, a man of strong character and proven ability. He arrived in India in 1595. He was firmly determined to shake down the fruits which had now been ripening for fully half a century and to make the Kerala Church an integral part of Rome. He instituted a secret enquiry about the faith and life of Mar Abraham through the Jesuit Fathers of Vaipicotta and found him guilty of heresy. The result of this enquiry was sent to Rome by Menezes.[α] Meanwhile stern orders were issued to all the Portuguese ports on the Indian Ocean that no Nestorian Bishop hailing from Mesopotamia and bound for Kerala should be allowed to proceed on his journey. Mar Abraham lost all hope of a Persian succession. In the circumstances he desired to have his successor in his own archdeacon George de Cruz and nominated him as the vicar of Angamaly.[β] Mar Abraham died in the year 1597, which marked the end of Persian succession in Kerala.

With the death of Mar Abraham the catholicization of the Nestorian Christians seemed to be free of impediments. In the first half of the sixteenth century the Catholic missionaries attempted to introduce the Latin liturgy and customs of the Roman Catholic Church amongst the Kerala Nestorians, but though they were able to obtain the collaboration of Mar Jacob, after his death, his successors Mar Joseph and Mar Abraham were not so enthusiastic about Roman Catholicism. At the death of Mar Joseph, Mar Abraham alone was holding the control over the Thomas Christians under the shadow of Portuguese Court of Inquisition. Though unwillingly, sometimes he introduced Catholic customs and practices in the Kerala Church, he cleverly evaded the Padroado jurisdiction of the Portuguese. He never cared to maintain any relationship with the Roman Catholic diocese of Cochin. The Thomas Christians were closely attached to this prelate from Mesopotamia and his instructions were the last word for

---

[α] Cyriac Thevarmannil, *Mar Abraham, the Archbishop of St. Thomas Christians in Malabar (1508-1597)*, Unpublished Ph.D. Thesis, Gregorian University, Rome, 1965, pp. 217-219.

[β] D. Ferroli, *The Jesuits in Malabar,* vol. I, Bangalore, 1939, p. 178.

Portrait of Archbishop Dom Alexis Menezes.
Reproduced from K. J. John, *The Road to Diamper,* Cochin, Kerala Latin Catholic History Association, 1999, frontispiece.

them. The concerted attempts of the Jesuits in the second half of the sixteenth century also failed to have any considerable success as we find that at the death of Mar Abraham the Thomas Christians of Angamaly were en masse adhering to the Archdeacon George and not to the ecclesiastical authority of the Archbishop of Goa. As long as Mar Abraham lived it was not easy for the Jesuits to bring these Christians under their cover and jurisdiction. Collaboration with Mar Abraham for catholicizing the Kerala Church became impossible as there was mutual suspicion. The Catholic missionaries were convinced that Mar Abraham was an heretic and a rebel to the Roman Church. Mar Abraham considered the Portuguese missionaries, especially the Jesuits, as helping the Archbishop of Goa to deprive the Kerala Christians of a Nestorian succession from Persia. It was this relationship with the Nestorian Church that the Portuguese were bent on bringing to an end and thus establishing the "One and Holy Roman Catholic Church" in Kerala. And with the arrival of Dom Menezes, an able and resolute man of commanding personality and in the prime of life, as the Archbishop of Goa, the catholicization of the entire Kerala Church became a reality.

Armed with the Padroado right and ecclesiastical authority granted by the Pope, the Archbishop of Goa was entitled to the spiritual leadership and governance of all the Indian Christians. To the Portuguese, the existence in Kerala of a Nestorian Church, Oriental in character and not subject to the Roman Pontiff and Portuguese hierarchy, and not conforming in practice to Roman Catholicism was an anomaly. To them the Church was one, holy, universal and Catholic with the Pope at its head. In the medieval context all the Churches which did not declare allegiance to the Pope were considered heretical. We have seen how the Nestorian bishops from Persia had reached Kerala in disguise knowingly or unknowingly ignoring the Padroado Jurisdiction. It could be seen that the cause of confrontations in the Kerala Church was the unauthorised entry of these Persian prelates and their craze for ecclesiastical power in Kerala. Fr. Antonio de Porto in a letter written in November 1557 addressed to the King of Portugal says:

> I have advised them [the bishops from Persia] with all the force I could muster, the reasons why they should not go to Kerala. I told them that it is irregular to enter and to attend to the spiritual needs of the folk of another bishopric, and that the Bishop of Goa is the Bishop of Malabar too and the whole of India, and of all the other parts of the Orient conquered

> by Your Majesty and no one without his permission could interfere with the Christians of these parts and that those who went to administer the sacraments to the Christians of Kerala without the permission of the bishop of Goa were thieves who did not enter the sheep-pen through the front door.[1]

The Bishop of Cochin and the Catholic missionaries exerted all means to bring Mar Abraham who was in Kerala for over thirty years, to the Catholic fold. They failed in their attempts despite threats and allurement. Until his very end he continued to stick to his Nestorian faith cleverly disguising himself as a Catholic in the eyes of the Portuguese. According to the contemporary Portuguese historian, Gouvea, Mar Abraham refused to accept the Catholic faith till his end.[2] What the Dominicans had failed to do with their early mission at Quilon, the Franciscans with their college at Cranganore and the Jesuits with their seminary at Vaipicotta, and the inquisition of Goa could not attain, Archbishop Menezes of Goa was now determined to do once and for all: to destroy every trace of Nestorian heresy and 'pagan' practices in the traditional Christian community of Kerala. He set out to do it with vehemence, intimidation and intrigue by exercising his ecclesiastical authority as Primate of the East to force the Kerala Christians to renounce forever their allegiance to the Nestorian Patriarch of Persia and submit to the authority of the Pope. Menezes was a man of great zeal and extraordinary commitment to his cause. He had the vision and boldness to conceive big plans and the determination and courage to execute them. To win lands and people for Roman Catholic Church and the King of Portugal was the ideal that motivated his Indian mission. Moreover, during this period the entry of the English and the Dutch, the religious and commercial rivals of the Portuguese, into the eastern seas had sent alarming waves to the Portuguese administration in India. Portugal, a nation of only one or two million people was scared of maintaining its authority in India without sufficient military power and probably they were keen to subjugate the robust Thomas Christians of Kerala who were excellent soldiers and to bring them under Portuguese control. Alexis

---

[1] The Portuguese text of the letter is given in Giuseppe Beltrami, *La chiesa caldea nel secolo dell'unione*, (*Orientalia Christiana*, vol 29, no. 83), Rome, 1933, pp. 40-43. An English translation of the letter in full by Fr. Heras can be found in *Examiner*, 19 Feb. 1938.

[2] Antonio de Gouvea, *Jornada do Arcebispo de Goa Dom Frey Aleixo Menezes...*, Coimbra, 1606; reprint Lisboa, 1988, pp. 64-65. See also Joseph Thekkedath, History of Christianity in India, vol. II, Bangalore, 1988, p. 56; Ferroli, op. cit., p. 175.

de Menezes born and brought up in a royal family of Lisbon and in the atmosphere of militant Counter Reformation in Europe was destined to realise Portugal's political and religious designs.

EARLY LIFE

Alexis de Menezes was born on 25 January 1559 in a noble family of Lisbon as the son of Dom Alexis de Menezes, a relative of King Sebastian and Dona Luiza de Noronha.[3] In his fifteenth year Menezes completed his early education and joined the Augustinian Monastery Nossa Senhora de Graca in Lisbon as a member of the Eremite Order of St. Augustine (24 February 1574) and received the name Fr. Alexis de Jesus. In 1578 he joined the prestigious University of Coimbra to study philosophy, logic and theology. After graduation he was appointed as the rector of Coimbra Academy and later served the monasteries of Santo Agostinho de Torres Vedras in Santarem and Nossa Senhora da Graca in Lisbon as the Prior. This young man soon distinguished himself as a brave and intelligent administrator among the members of the Augustinian Order. King Philip II of Spain nominated Alexis de Menezes to lead the Catholic Church in Asia Portuguesa, when, in 1593, Dom Mateus de Medina, the Archbishop of Goa, expired.[4] King Philip II was confident that the 35 year old Augustinian friar was capable of exercising even the viceregal power and to lead the ship of Catholic Church boldly and intelligently in the rough seas of the East infested with heresy. The young Menezes who dedicated himself to the cause of Christian life was unmindful of official positions in the Church hierarchy. This is very clearly reflected in one of the letters he had written to his uncle Dom Frei Agostinho de Jesus who was the Archbishop of Braga in North Portugal: "When His Majesty the king selected me from the confinement of my room

[3] For biographical details see Carlos Alonso, *Alejo de Menezes, O.S.A.. Arzobispo de Goa (1595-1612)* (Spanish) Valladolid, 1992, p. 13 ff; Idem, "Documentation inedita para since biografia de Fr. Alejo de Menezes, O.S.A., Arzobispo de Goa (1595-1612)" in *Analecta Augustiniana*, XXVII, 1964. Some useful details are available in Mons. Conego J. Augusto Ferreira, *Fastos Episcopaes da Igreja Primacial de Braga*, Tomo lll, Lisbon, 1932, pp. 114-115; see also *Encyclopedia Luso-Brasilieria de cultura*. vol. 13, p. 324; J. F. Raulin, Historiae Ecclesiae Malabaricae cum Diamperitana Synodo, Rome, 1745, d2-d3.

[4] During the period, Portugal was ruled by the Spanish Sovereign. For details of the Archbishops who administered Goa, see Paulino a S. Bartholomaeo, *India Orientalis Christiana*, Rome, 1794, pp. 31-44.

in the monastery for the highest post, to send me to distant lands, I presented a lot of excuses."[5]

But none of the excuses seems to have worked. Many high ranking people from the nobility of Lisbon persuaded him to accept the position. King Philip himself wrote to him in person on the 21 November 1594.[6] Not only did he recognise the extraordinary qualities of Menezes but also offered many additional facilities. It was stipulated that a sum of four thousand cruzados should be given to him for expenses in connection with the episcopal ordination and nine thousand cruzados as annuity from the royal coffers. He was also offered discretionary powers to appoint priests and missionaries in the Portuguese territories in the East, a power which was previously exercised by the Portuguese Viceroy. In addition to this it was also stipulated that all administrative decisions in 'Estado da India' would be taken only in consultation with Archbishop Alexis de Menezes.[7]

At last under great pressure and persuasion the young Dom Menezes agreed to become the Archbishop of Goa, and his episcopal ordination took place on 26 March 1595 at the Augustinian Monastery in Lisbon.[8] In the same year Menezes undertook the voyage to Goa in the ship Nossa Senhora da Vitoria (Our Lady of Victory) accompanied by Augustinian friars Cristovao do Espirito Santo, Diogo de Santana and Diogo da Conceicao (who was appointed as his Auxiliary Bishop but died on the way to Goa).[9] During this difficult voyage to India it was reported that they were stricken with a fatal epidemic

---

[5] Ms. 8a dated Goa, 23 December 1602, in the Archives of Conciliar Seminary of Braga (hereafter CSMS) in North Portugal. I was introduced to these unpublished letters by Prof. Dr. Jose Bacelar E. Oliveira S.J., who was the former Rector of the Catholic University of Lisbon, and who teaches in the Faculty of Philosophy in Braga. I could take copies of all these letters from the Conciliar Seminary. There are about 15 unpublished letters of Menezes written to his uncle Dom Agostinho de Jesus who was the Archbishop of Braga. After the accomplishment of his Indian Mission Menezes succeeded his uncle as the Archbishop of Braga. The letters of Menezes throw considerable light on hitherto unknown personal life of Dom Menezes. These manuscript letters are indexed in the Conciliar Seminary Archives as No. 42, fl. 342 to 407.

[6] Ms. 581., fol. 373[r] in ANTT Lisbon.

[7] Avelino de Jesus da Costa, in: *Congresso do Mundo Potugueses, VI*, tomo 1, Lisbon, 1940, p. 212.

[8] His appointment was confirmed by the Bull *Divina disponente* dated 13 February 1595. He was consecrated to the episcopal dignity by the Patriarch of Lisbon Dom Miguel de Castro. See Mons. Conego J. Augusto Ferreira, op. cit., p. 115; See also Carlos Alonso, op. cit., pp. 23-26.

[9] Carlos Alonso, op. cit., p. 30.

and only five among the 550 passengers were free from it.[10] Menezes devoted himself to nursing the sick and offered them help. He played the roles of friend and physician and everything that he stored for his personal use he shared with his fellow passengers. As a result not only did he fall sick but also become a debtor.[11]

In September 1595, when Menezes reached Goa a great reception was accorded to him by the Viceroy and a crowd thrilled with joy had collected at the entrance of the city.[12] As the Archbishop of Goa and Primate of the East there were many religious and political duties for him to perform. Menezes was also aware of the fact that the battleground of his Indian mission was Kerala. As such he tried to ameliorate the degenerated social conditions of his immediate surroundings in Goa and nearby places from the very beginning of his stay in India. His letters make it clear that the life Menezes saw in 'Portuguese India' in general and Goa in particular was very bad debased and deplorable. Missionaries of different orders were infested with groupism and rivalry and many among the secular priests were in jail.[13] Menezes saw that the standard of morality in the society was very low as there was no insistence on social discipline by the Portuguese authorities, civil or ecclesiastical, in their settlements. The life of common people was very miserable due to poverty and other social disabilities. In Goa and neighbouring islands about twenty thousand people were converted to Christianity by the Portuguese missionaries but they were not instructed in Catholic doctrines and their faith was superficial.[14]

The new Archbishop of Goa, unperturbed by the difficulties and adverse circumstances initiated several bold steps to lay the foundations of a strong Catholic life. As a result of untiring efforts Menezes was able to create among the warring priests of the Archdiocese a sense of unity and peace. In one of the letters to his uncle he laments:

> I had to face a number of problems in my reformative attempts. In spite of protests from the priests and internal quarrels, I could face the challenges and reach the goal. It was a great relief that I was able to root out the undesirable tendencies among the priests and missionary orders. I am keen to enforce strict discipline and am trying to issue strict orders in

[10] Avelino de Jesus da Costa, op. cit., p. 213.

[11] Ibid.

[12] Carlos Alonso, op. cit., p. 31.

[13] Ibid., pp. 32-33.

[14] CSMS letter 1a dated 23 December 1595 and 2a dated 18 December 1596.

that direction to everybody in my Metropolitan See and to find solutions to the rivalry among the religious orders. However, I am happy that I have succeeded in my attempts to settle the troubles.[15]

The four member commission of theologians appointed by the Archbishop to root out the immoralities and heresies among the faithful in the light of the decisions of the Council of Trent, was accorded royal sanction on 12 February 1597. In 1598 he founded a recluse house in Goa for orphan girls as per the orders of the King. The house when completed in 1605 could accommodate 100 to 150 orphan girls besides the managerial staff, servants and slaves.[16] It was named the Recluse House of Our Lady of Serra as the building was close to the church of Our Lady of Serra. Menezes also founded another recluse house named after St. Maria Magdalena for the fallen women.[17] There were instances of women leaving their Portuguese husbands due to cruelties. Many died at the hands of their husbands and some became widows. Menezes reported to the King about the debauchery practised by the Portuguese in Goa and the loose conduct of the ladies. He stated that some 52 women were killed at the hands of their husbands for the offence of adultery.[18] In 1599 Philip III granted permission for the establishment of a nunnery in Goa. It was dedicated to St. Monica. On 8 September 1607 some 16 to 18 women under prioress Isabel da Cruz took the solemn vows and received their religious habit from the hands of Archbishop Alexis de Menezes.[19] The establishment of these three houses for women gave a much-needed fillip to discipline and morality in the degenerated social milieu of Portuguese India.

The dynamism of the young Archbishop was endowed with the excellent qualities of humility, obedience, selflessness, poverty and endurance in hardships. His ardent love for the poor and destitute soon won a number of souls. He could create in the minds of the people strong waves of kindness and sympathy with the help of his

---

[15] CSMS letters 1a, 2a cited above and 9a dated 20 December 1603 (translation mine).

[16] A. Lourdinho Rodrigues, "The Recluse Houses of Goa," *Boltim do Instituto Menezes Braganca*, No. 106, Panaji, 1974, pp. 10-11.

[17] Ibid.

[18] Afonso de Figueiredo, *A Mulher nu India Portuguesa*, Nova Goa, 1933, pp. 87-88; See also Avelino de Jesus da Costa, op. cit., p. 215.

[19] A. E. Moniz, "Relacao Completa das Religiosas do Mosteiro de Mosteiro de Santa Monica de Goa" *Oriente Portuguese*, IX, Nova Goa, 1909, p. 178.

brilliant oratorical skills. His eloquence was excellent that people sat spellbound for hours. Among the people converted as a result of listening to his apostolic oration there was a young prince, who was the Ambassador of the Mongol king.[20] Menezes gave him his own name on the occasion of his baptism. He set apart one hour everyday for the common people and heard their confession. He found time to look after the needs of slaves and prisoners in the jail during Lent. On these occasions he used to give them some money also according to their need. With the objective of reforming the customs of the people in his vast See he convened in 1606 the fifth Provincial Council of Goa which was attended by bishops from Japan, Macao, Malacca, Cochin and Angamaly in addition to the superiors of all the religious orders in Portuguese India.[21] The marvellous result he achieved in his reformative attempts was because of his exemplary life, charity without limit and his strong will to implement Catholic discipline.[22]

To fight the miseries of the people in his metropolitan See Menezes sought the help of Fr. Luiz Laivao, S.J., and asked him to prepare the statistics of the helpless and the poor people and also of the fallen women in Portuguese India. He initiated steps to improve their lot, thereby laying the foundation of the tradition of social service of the Indian Catholic Church. It is seen that throughout his tenure he had given regular allowances to unemployed people and orphans who approached him. This was distributed by Fr. Laivao and Procurator of the Archbishop.[23] He was such a kind person that every day he invited twelve poor people to share his table.[24] While in Goa Menezes used to draw to him the poor and the orphaned. He states: "I did not have to disappoint even a single widow or a poor soldier or a helpless Christian who approached me.[25]

His annuity of 9000 cruzados was not enough to match his unbridled charity. He never let down the people who approached him and

---

[20] Cited by Avelino de Jesus da Costa from *Chancelaria Philip de II,* liv. 23, f1. 328, in op. cit., p. 215.

[21] Carlos Alonso, op. cit., p. 215.

[22] See the letters of the Viceroys of India for the years 1597, 1599, 1600 and 1609 cited by Casmiro Cristovao da Nazaret in *Mitras Lusitanas no Oriente*. XII, Lisbon; cf. Aveliono de Jesus da Costa, op. cit., p. 10.

[23] Avelino de Jesus da Costa, ibid., p. 216.

[24] This he mentions in a letter to his uncle in Braga. See CSMS letter 2a dated 18 December 1596.

[25] Ibid., and also see CSMS Letter dated 9 December 1597.

lived in his metropolitan palace as a poor man. In another letter dated 16 December 1600 he wrote:

> I am living in utter poverty. I have a lot of debts to pay off. There is no end to the demands of the destitute in this city, which I have to meet with urgency. Sometimes I will have to sell off myself to meet the needs of the poor in the city."[26]

To help the poor and the needy, on occasions he had to sell his valuable bedcovers and silver cutlery. As a result of his generosity the debts of the saintly Archbishop touched 45000 cruzados, which was far beyond his means.[27] His concern for the poor and the unfortunate in society was only one side of his luminous personality. While in Goa he was vigilantly looking forward to the proper time to embark upon disciplinary measures to correct the affairs in the Kerala Church which was infested with heresy. In the mean time Dom Menezes kept himself busy with visiting the Portuguese settlements in and around Goa and places like Chaul, Bassein, Daman, Diu, etc. for the purpose of enforcing discipline and order among the Portuguese and indigenous Christians living in those parts.[28] There was no end to the steps he initiated to spread the Catholic faith within the boundaries of his archbishopric which comprised areas of Asia and Africa. Having committed to provide support to mission centres in the Estado da India he extended all possible help to the Jesuits, Dominicans, Franciscans and Augustinians of his own Order. He provided all facilities to the missionaries for their vigorous apostolic work in Portuguese Asia. Menezes established several colleges, monasteries, convents and churches in west Asia and in India for the conversion, instruction and spiritual formation of the infidels and for the maintenance of Catholic Church. As the Primate of the East he sent missionary groups to Cochin-China, Bengal, Basarha, Persia, Socotora, Abyssinia, Mombasa etc. for proselytization work among the infidels and heretics.[29] It is no exaggeration to say that there were no places

[26] CSMS Letter dated 16 December 1602 (translation mine).

[27] Letter of the Viceroy of India for the year 1609 cited by Avelino de Jesus da Costa, op. cit., p. 216; see also the letter of Dom Alexis de Menezes to Philip II dated 21 March 1617, cited ibid.

[28] Carlos Alonso, op. cit., pp. 43-47.

[29] See Avelino de Jesus da Costa, op. cit., pp. 217-218; see also Carlos Alonso, op. cit., pp. 48-53. Menezes' concern for apostolic work in the Portuguese Asia is very much reflected in his letters. See CSMS Letter 5a dated 16 December 1600 and 7a dated 20 December 1601.

in 'Estado da India' which he or his emissaries on his behalf did not visit in search of lost sheep. In all these untiring efforts he exhibited apostolic fervour, prophet-like bravery and God infused vigour. He wrote to his uncle in Braga about the spirit of his prolonged journeys:

> As I am conscious about my duties I have visited several cities several times and I could baptise many infidels who listen to the call of Our Lord. Those who know the origin and growth of Christianity will understand the meaning of my prolonged journeys. My prime aim is to win the gentiles for Jesus and provide proper spiritual formation for them. During my latest journey, I baptised 700 souls in one parish, and in the twelve parishes of the Island of Salsette 1200 souls were baptised by my own hands and 7000 people were administered confirmation. This is how I work in the parishes. This provides me great satisfaction.[30]

JOURNEY TO KERALA

Menezes, who had let loose a tempest of reformatory activities in pursuance of the decisions of the Council of Trent in Goa as well as in the neighbouring islands and the other Portuguese colonies in the East, was particularly vigilant in the case of Kerala. We have mentioned the brief issued by Pope Clement VIII to the Archbishop of Goa directing an enquiry into Mar Abraham's life and the state of faith. It was found after enquiry that Mar Abraham was heretical and guilty of other lapses prima facie. The report prepared by Menezes was sent to Rome. On 16 February 1597 when Archbishop Menezes was making an apostolic visit to the Island of Daman he received intelligence of the death of Mar Abraham from the Portuguese Viceroy Mathias Albuquerque. Fearing the work on hand could not be postponed he decided to act immediately and by virtue of authority bestowed on him by another Papal brief of 21 January 1597[31] nominated the Jesuit Fr. Francis Ros, a scholar in Syriac, as the Vicar Apostolic of the vacant See of Angamaly. Besides, it was incumbent on him by right, as the Archbishop of Goa being the Primate of all the Orient, to look after the affairs of the vacant See. Actually, when Mar Abraham signed the decrees relating to the Archdiocese of Angamaly in the third Provincial Council of Goa in 1585, he had subjected himself to the Padroado jurisdiction of the Portuguese authorities and legally accepted the authority of the Archbishop of Goa over the See

[30] CSMS Letters 2a and 7a (translation mine).

[31] J. F. Raulin, op. cit., p. 60.

of Angamaly. Moreover, the Roman Pontiff through his Brief of 1597 entrusted Menezes with the government of the vacant See of Angamaly till the Holy See provided a bishop.[32]

Though nomination was made Menezes could not succeed immediately to consecrate Fr. Francis Ros, S.J., who had worked for twelve years as the Counsel of Mar Abraham. Archdeacon George de Cruz had already taken over the reigns of Angamaly at the death of Mar Abraham on his own. In May, when Menezes returned to Goa from Daman, the Councillors of Goa advised him not to dethrone archdeacon George in spite of the fact that Rome had stipulated otherwise.[33] Menezes had to accede to this request and appointed the archdeacon himself as the Administrator at Angamaly subject to certain conditions.[34] Fr. Francis Ros was appointed Rector at the Seminary of Vaipicotta and as the chief counsel of the archdeacon. Menezes stipulated that important decisions should not be taken without the permission of Fr. Ros and that the archdeacon should profess his faith in Roman Catholicism.[35] The clever archdeacon said that he would do so in four months' time from then, on Maundy Thursday of the year 1598.[36] The archdeacon expected the arrival of a Nestorian Bishop from Persia within that period. However, since the Portuguese controlled the ports of Kerala, it was not easy for any one from Persia to enter Kerala escaping the Portuguese vigilance. The restless archdeacon convened an assembly of his followers at the church of Angamaly and declared that he was not prepared to give up the faith of his fathers and that he would not accept a bishop from places outside Persia. The people assembled there took an oath that they would act only according to the wishes of their Archdeacon.[37] Antonio Gouvea, the contemporary Portuguese historian who visited Kerala during the period, asserts that the archdeacon declared in the church of Anga-

---

[32] The argument of Jonas Thaliath in his thesis on the Synod of Diamper that Menezes had no metropolitan rights over the see of Angamaly is unconvincing. The authority of Menezes was derived from the two apostolic briefs and padroado right. See for argument against Menezes, Jonas Thaliath, op. cit., Roma, 1958, pp. 51-62. See for arguments in favour of Menezes, J. F. Raulin, op. cit., ibid.

[33] Gouvea, *Jornada*, pp. 65-72.

[34] Avelino de Jesus da Costa, op. cit., pp. 225-226.

[35] Gouvea, *Jornada*, loc. cit.

[36] Jacob Kollaparambil, *The Archdeacon of All India*, Rome, 1972, pp. 90-100.

[37] ARSJ, Goa, Vol. 14, folio 357: Letter of Ros to the Jesuit General Fr. Aquaviva on 24 December 1597; See also Gouvea, *Jornada*, fol. 12, p. 66.

maly that his Church was founded by St. Thomas and that the Church of Rome founded by St. Peter had nothing to do with it.[38]

Determined to bring the heretics into the fold of Roman Catholicism at the opportune time and having failed in his negotiations with the archdeacon, Menezes assumed the roles of the Primate of the East, Metropolitan of the vacant See and of Apostolic delegate decided to visit Kerala for the finale in person.[39] He explained the scope of his visit to his uncle, the Archbishop of Braga, that the time had come to bring the Nestorians of Kerala to the Holy Roman Catholic Church and that he was keen to visit all the churches of Thomas Christians. He also stated that after his tour he would convoke a synod of all priests and representatives of these Christians to get their obedience to the Church of Rome.[40] The Viceroy and his advisors in Goa cautioned the Archbishop not to expose himself to such imminent danger. However, his answer to them was that his life was secure and that he had never merited enough to entitle him to the honour of being a martyr.[41]

In this background Menezes was commissioned by the Council of Goa to act as their envoy to the local rulers of Kerala and muster their support for the Portuguese. In particular they wanted him to suppress with the help of the Zamorin the growing power of Mohammed Kunhale Marakkar who was a constant threat to the Portuguese trade. Menezes collected articles worth 18000 pardaos to be presented to the native princes. The King of Portugal and the Viceroy gave 5000 and 3000 xerafins respectively for this purpose.[42]

On 27 September 1598 Menezes embarked at Goa on board a galley strongly armed and commanded by Dom Alvaro de Menezes.[43] He was accompanied by his confessor Fr. Braz de Santa Maria and Jorge de Castro (Jesuits).[44] During the journey he had a stopover at Kottakkal near Badagara the head quarters of Kunhale Marakkar. He was

---

[38] Ibid.

[39] See CSMS, 3a; Letter of Menezes dated 9 December 1597.

[40] Ibid., See also the letter dated 19 December 1596 of Menezes to Fabio Biondi, titular Patriarch of Jerusalem, in Beltrami. op. cit., p. 121.

[41] Gouvea, *Jornada*, fol. 12.

[42] Avelino de Jesus da Costa, op. cit., p. 226.

[43] Michael Geddes and Gouvea mention 27 December, while Avelino de Jesus da Costa and La Croze assert 26 September. The date given by Carlos Alonso is 28 December 1598.

[44] Avelino de Jesus da Costa, op. cit., p. 226.

received there by the whole of the Portuguese Armada, commanded by the Viceroy's brother, and was saluted with the guns and music of the fleet. After studying the political conditions Menezes convened a council of war where several plans were chalked out for the siege of the fortress of Kunhale Marakkar and for the elimination of Kunhale Marakkar with the help of Zamorin. Accordingly, a resolution was forwarded to the Council of State at Goa.[45] After completing the arrangements for the capture of the fortress, Menezes proceeded to Cannanore where he remained for sixteen days and then sailed direct to Cochin reaching there on the 1 February 1599.[46] He was given a rousing reception at the Santa Cruz Cathedral at Cochin by the Portuguese Captain Dom Antonio de Noronha and Dom Andre de Santa Maria and the nobles of the city of Cochin.[47]

Next day when the Magistrates of the city came to offer their respects to the Archbishop, he informed them of his determination of reducing the Thomas Christians to the obedience of Rome and to bring them all together to the Catholic fold before he returned to Goa and demanded their whole-hearted assistance in his Kerala mission, which they readily promised. As a first step the Metropolitan sent a request to the Archdeacon to come and speak with him at the fortress of Cochin. But having waited for several days without any response, Menezes concluded that the Archdeacon was scared enough to meet him at the Portuguese stronghold. But to allay his fears Menezes further sent him a letter of safe conduct with promise that he would not question him about anything that happened in the past. The perturbed Archdeacon, on receiving the second letter from the Metropolitan, soon convened a meeting of his followers to discuss and decide upon what was best to be done. This meeting came to the conclusion that it would not be wise to antagonise the Portuguese Archbishop and that the archdeacon should go and wait upon Dom Menezes who was a person of great authority. They feared that the Archbishop would stop their pepper trade with the Portuguese, on which they chiefly subsisted. They also realised that the local rulers including the king of Cochin were completely obliged to the Metro-

[45] Michael Geddes, op. cit., p. 53. See also O. K. Nambiar, *The Kunjalies, Admirals of Calicut*, Bombay, 1963, p. 119.

[46] Carlos Alonso, op. cit., p. 73.

[47] Ibid.

politan.[48] Prompted by the decision of this meeting Archdeacon George de Cruz and a few local priests accompanied by the contingent of three thousand armed Thomas Christians who were led by Christian Panikkars, reached the fortress of Cochin.[49] Dom Antonio Noronha, the Governor of Cochin received them and ushered the Archdeacon and a few representatives to the palace of the Archbishop. The archdeacon and the priests knelt before the Archbishop and kissed his apostolic ring before they started discussion with him.[50] It was agreed that a series of apostolic visits to the Churches of Thomas Christians would start on the following day beginning from Vaipicotta where the archdeacon and his priests had to meet him.[51]

Having made the necessary arrangements for his voyage through the backwaters of Cochin, Menezes and his cortege embarked on seven *tonees* (boats); and Roque de Mello Pereyra, who had been Governor of Malacca, accompanied him with two *tonees* more; and Joao Pereyra de Miranda, afterwards Governor of Cranganore, with another.[52] On his arrival at Vaipicotta the Metropolitan was conducted by the Jesuits and their scholars and Christians of the village to the church in procession. There he put on the mitre on his head and with the crosier in his hand gave them a long sermon.[53] His discourse was based on a sentence from the Gospel of St. John.[54] He began his spiritual crusade with the statement that the Nestorian bishops who came to Kerala from Babylonia were thieves, that they did not enter the sheepfold through the front door and that they were mere murderers of the folk.[55] He told them that the true pastors were

---

[48] Michael Geddes, op. cit., pp. 56-57

[49] Gouvea, *Jornada*, fol. 29, p. 97. *Panikkars* are master warriors who train young boys to arms in *Kalari* (gymnasia). These *Panikkars* were venerated as spiritual masters or gurus by their warrior disciples. There are *Nāyar Panikkars* and Christian *Panikkars* in Kerala's military heritage. Among the best known warrior preceptors were the *Malittas* of Mavelikkara, a family of Christian *Panikkars* who created their own net works of both Christian and Hindu trainee disciples.

[50] Gouvea, ibid, pp. 93-98.

[51] Ibid.

[52] Ibid., p. 99.

[53] A mitre is a head-dress, and a crosier is a staff surmounted by a cross and borne by a bishop on occasion of ceremony.

[54] Gouvea, *Jornada,* loc. cit: "Verily, verily I say unto you. He that entereth not by the door into the sheepfold, but climbeth up some other way, the same is a thief and a robber."

[55] Ibid.

the ones sent forth by the Roman Pontiff who was the Vicar of Christ on earth. The contemporary Portuguese historian Gouvea describes this sermon as very eloquent and full of devotional sentiments that it drew tears from those assembled in the church.[56]

After the sermon, Menezes appealed to the congregation to assemble next day in the church again so that he could administer the sacrament of confirmation. Gouvea describes that the entire Christian population of Vaipicotta assembled in the church for getting confirmed in the Catholic faith which was unknown to them.[57] The archdeacon had not yet made his appearance until two days after the arrival of the Metropolitan. But when he arrived Menezes did not show any displeasure for the lapse but explained to the archdeacon the course of actions he proposed to take for bringing the Nestorian Church of Kerala to the Catholic fold. During his stay at Vaipicotta, one evening Menezes while participating in the Syriac service noticed that they were praying for the Patriarch of Babylon as 'Universal Pastor' of this Church. On enquiry he was convinced that many errors and heretic teachings still remained in Syriac liturgy.[58] He was infuriated at the passive response of the Jesuits in this respect even at Vaipicotta where Syriac scholars were posted for the purpose. He told them that the Patriarch of Babylon was a Nestorian heretic and that he would not allow any one in his See to proclaim the heretic patriarch as the universal pastor of the Church.[59] He refused to listen for a moment the proposal of the Jesuits to compromise the matter with the Thomas Christians for the time being. Menezes was a man of different mettle and he remained inflexible. The next evening without declaring his intentions to anyone he convened a meeting of the Jesuits who ran the Seminary, the archdeacon and the local priests. He gave a brilliant speech at this meeting in which he declared that the Roman Pontiff was the only head of the Church on earth and that the Bishop of Babylon was a heretic and schismatic.[60] Then he dramatically pulled out of his pocket a sentence of excommunication, written in Latin, and commanded his secretary to read it aloud. When the secretary finished the reading, Menezes asked his interpreter to

---

[56] Ibid., 100

[57] Ibid.

[58] Michael Geddes, op. cit., p. 61.

[59] Ibid.

[60] Ibid.

explain it in Malayalam to those who did not understand Latin. Through this document he forbade all persons in the diocese of Angamaly to give in future the title of 'Universal Pastor' to the Patriarch of Babylon.[61]

When this document had been read out and interpreted, Menezes called upon the archdeacon and two senior priests of the Thomas Christians to sign it. The archdeacon was hesitant to comply with the demand, and on seeing this the Archbishop commanded to him: "Sign it Father, for the time has come to lay the axe to the root of the tree.[62] The archdeacon and the priests had no alternative but to obey the Metropolitan. Immediately the excommunication order was affixed to the gates of the Church. Gouvea records that this incident created a big furore.[63] The schismatic Christians of the village, when they came to hear of the incident, were greatly enraged. They ran to the seminary premises to wreak vengeance on Menezes who was determined to root out their religious customs and faith. The Jesuits told Menezes that the excommunication order was untimely and urged him to escape immediately in one of his boats beyond the reach of danger.[64] But Menezes paid no regard either to their remonstrances or their advice. He told them plainly that he was engaged in the cause of God and His Church and that he would defend it to the last.[65] He declared that he was not repentant on his action and that he would do it again if necessary. Instead of retreating to Cochin he was determined to go the following morning to North Parur, another important centre of Thomas Christians.

Parur, a few miles west of Vaipicotta, was the seat of the king of the locality and there lived a good number of Christians. Some time before, two Nestorian Christians of this town were converted to Roman Catholicism and received the names Dom Jorge da Cruz and Dom Joao da Cruz and were sent by the Portuguese to Rome in the time of Pope Gregory XIII, who paid them great honour, and granted them many indulgences to their church in Parur, claimed to have been established by St.Thomas, the Apostle.[66] But the Nestorians of

---

[61] Ibid.

[62] Gouvea, *Jornada*, pp. 101-102.

[63] Ibid.

[64] Michael Geddes, op. cit., pp. 62-63.

[65] Gouvea, *Jornada*, p. 103.

[66] Ibid.

Parur refused to accept the indulgences from the Roman Pontiff and the two native priests were forced to seek refuge among the Portuguese at Cranganore.[67] In spite of this prevailing hatred towards the Catholic faith, as per the agreement with their archdeacon, the Christians of Parur prepared great festivities for the reception of the Archbishop. But having heard of the happenings at Vaipicotta, they changed all their festive preparations and got ready with arms for a showdown.

Sensing that the Archdeacon had influenced the Christians of Parur through the back door, the Archbishop came out alone from the boat. There were only ten Christians and the archdeacon waiting for him at the jetty. Menezes gave them his cross to carry before him and followed them direct to the church. When he entered the church he found it full of men, armed with swords and lances, bows and muskets. Suddenly, he asked his guards who reached there by then to return to the boats and he retained two priests to assist him in the ceremonies he was about to perform.[68] Unperturbed by the hostile scene at the Parur church, he walked alone to the altar. Having put on his pontifical vestments and pronounced a benediction on the people, he made a powerful oration lasting for about an hour and a half, in which he stated that there was only one true Church and that was Roman Catholic; and that all Christians were under an indispensable obligation to submit themselves to the Roman Pontiff.[69] It is very clear that the motto of Menezes was 'one shepherd and one sheep-pen.' He believed that it was his bounden duty as the Metropolitan and Primate of the East to achieve this objective even at the cost of his life. No other consideration had prevented him from pursuing this path since he had come to the East as the watchdog of the reformative decrees of the Council of Trent.

When he had finished his sermon, he explained the sacrament of confirmation and appealed to the congregation to come forward to receive it. The Thomas Christians who had not so far heard the sacrament of confirmation cried out that it was an invention of the Portuguese to make them their slaves. When they started creating confusion in the church, Menezes rose up and advancing towards them, with the crozier in his hand and mitre on his head, declared:

---

[67] Ibid.

[68] Ibid., pp. 103-104.

[69] Michael Geddes, op. cit., p. 65.

> This is the true and Catholic faith which I preach to you... all true Christians admit this doctrine and I am ready to die for it. I shall not leave this country until I have established it with my blood or my words. If you want you can shed my blood. I am unarmed; I am not in a state to defend myself. The shepherd does not fight; he has no other function than to feed his sheep. If you thirst for the blood of your shepherd you can have it. You can pierce me with your spears. Let the sabres be stained with blood. Shoot me with guns if you wish. Let the spilling of my blood help you to accept my declaration of true faith. May you know that nobody would be prepared to be a martyr for untruth. It is only to ensure truth that one achieves martyrdom.[70]

Gouvea further records that after listening to the archbishop's bold oration the congregation began to disperse one by one from the church with a guilty conscience. The Archbishop was informed that the archdeacon had on the preceding night convened secretly the prominent Christians of Parur and instigated them to refuse any demand to renounce the Patriarch of Babylon. Menezes alluded to this publicly when he said that those who taught falsehood and heresy would hold the light in detestation and their nocturnal assemblies in obscure places.[71] He challenged such people to come forward to have an open debate with him. However, no one came forward to contradict the Archbishop openly. But the archdeacon rushed out of the church and picked about ten youngsters whom he presented to the Archbishop for administering the sacrament of confirmation. Menezes gladly confirmed them in Catholic faith but finding that no one else came forward returned to his boat angrily and proceeded to Alangad the next morning.[72] Gouvea states that there were two conspiracies hatched by the Thomas Christians of Parur against the life of Menezes.[73] Nothing could deter the zeal and determination of Menezes and he reached the church premises of Alangad for the accomplishment of his mission. On his arrival there he was received without any ceremony. A small number of people led him to the interior of the church which was found filled with household goods and women. These Christians sought refuge inside the church as a result of the war that had broken out between the rulers of Parur and Alangad. After having consoled the Christians for the losses they had al-

---

[70] Gouvea, *Jornada*, pp. 104-106 (translation mine).

[71] Michael Geddes, op. cit., p. 66.

[72] Portuguese corruption of Alangad is Mangate. It was the capital of a small principality near North Parur.

[73] Gouvea, op. cit., pp. 99-107.

ready sustained and given them his blessings, Menezes began to preach against the heresy in which they were brought up. Finally, he exhorted them to be obedient to the Church of Rome and to the Pope. But having intelligence report that a suicide squad was in pursuit of him from Parur, Menezes shortened his visit and went straight aboard his boat before dusk and proceeded to Chovvara where he reached on the following morning.[74]

When the Archbishop arrived for the apostolic visit to Chovvara he found the church closed, and there was no one to receive him. Being frightened of the consequences of not accompanying the prelate as promised, the archdeacon was hiding in a house at Chovvara and was resolved never to see His Lordship again. The Portuguese members in the entourage were tired of these humiliating experiences and they insisted on Menezes to retire to Cochin. Dom Menezes, the second command of the Portuguese in India was not dispirited and told them with all humility that nothing should turn him from his mission even though he were compelled to travel alone.[75] He retired all alone to his cabin and wrote a long letter to the archdeacon who was reported to be in the town. In the letter the Metropolitan made it clear that he would forget all past events and that he had no design of doing him any harm, and if he would but do him the favour to come and speak with him once more, he could certainly convince him of his errors and bring him to the fold of Catholic Church.[76] The letter was delivered the same night to the archdeacon, who accepted the invitation. Gouvea gives the details of the prolonged dogmatic discussion which the Archbishop had with the archdeacon and the local priests concerning the heretic nature of Nestorian faith and the holy nature of the Catholic faith founded on the Gospels.[77] At last it was decided that a diocesan synod should be convened to have a final settlement

---

[74] Ibid., p. 108. Gouvea refers to the word *amoucos* for suicide squad. The Malayalam term for the suicide squad is *chavettu pada*. *Pada* means army and *chaver* one who bound oneself to death. Such *amoucos* were common in Kerala during the Portuguese era. For Chovvara, Gouvea uses the Portuguese corruption *Chequree*, and this village was within the territory of the ruler of Cochin.

[75] Gouvea, loc. cit.

[76] Michael Geddes, op. cit., p. 68.

[77] See for details Gouvea, op. cit., pp. 108-111. See also James Hough, *The History of Christianity in India*, I, London, 1839, pp. 364-373.

concerning faith and life in the diocese of Angamaly. An agreement to this effect was signed by the archdeacon and the Archbishop.[78]

Immediately after this arrangement the Archbishop proceeded to the church at Kanjur in his boat, and the archdeacon by land. The Christians of Kanjur received the Metropolitan courteously. Menezes gave them a long sermon in which he highlighted the errors of Nestorius, and emphasised the supremacy of Roman Catholic faith. Soon the archdeacon retired to Chovvara with the permission of the Archbishop, probably as a sign of his disapproval of Menezes' long sermon against the faith of his fathers.[79] However, he did instruct his priests to receive the Archbishop with due honour.[80] The experience of the Archbishop at the five churches which he had already visited was not encouraging. In all these places the baffled archdeacon persuaded the Christians from behind to resist the spiritual demands of the Metropolitan and he was successful in his designs. The archbishop now decided to proceed southward where the influence of the archdeacon was negligible. On the Ist of March, he set sail for a castle near Cochin, where the Governor and the Bishop of the city met him.[81] After finalising his itinerary for the south and appraising them of his designs, Menezes proceeded to Porakkad where the King of the principality had been expecting him for some days.[82] He was welcomed at the church of the Thomas Christians of Porakkad with great demonstrations of joy as commanded by the ruler, who professed great friendship for the Portuguese. The following morning the Archbishop went to the church where he said mass and confirmed the whole congregation in the Catholic faith.

The next destination of Menezes was Quilon where he had to accomplish a political mission and from there he left for Cochin to conclude a treaty of friendship with the Zamorin.[83] From Cochin Menezes went direct to Molanthuruthy, an important town of the Tho-

---

78 Michael Geddes, op. cit., p. 70.

79 James Hough, op. cit., p. 374.

80 Tisserant, op. cit., p. 53.

81 Michael Geddes, op. cit., p. 71.

82 Gouvea, op. cit., p. 113. Gouvea uses 'Porcaa', a Portuguese corruption for Porakkad. The King of Porakkad in the local parlance was the King of Chembakassery.

83 This treaty of friendship between the Portuguese and the Zamorin was worked out by Menezes on his arrival in Kerala for the annihilation of Kunhale Marakkar, their common enemy. The treaty was signed at Vaipin.

mas Christians. Here also Menezes was received with great festivities by the native Christians. He ardently preached against heresy and administered the sacrament of confirmation to the whole congregation.[84] Slowly, Menezes was gaining popularity among the Kerala Christians. He tried his best to gain their good will by showing them benevolence and by giving alms liberally to the poor. His kindness and love for the poor had great impact on the people. But the archdeacon and his priests maintained their opposition to the Archbishop for officiating in their churches. He wrote to all the churches of Thomas Christians cautioning them against the activities of the prelate. Dom Menezes now thought of a strategy to wean the Christian folk away from the influence of the archdeacon and he had decided to ordain new priests from among the Thomas Christians at different places.[85] A decree was published in the whole of the Angamaly Archdiocese directing those who wished to be ordained to present themselves to the Metropolitan at Udayamperur (Diamper) on the Saturday before the approaching Palm Sunday.[86] The archdeacon opposed the move and again questioned the authority of the Metropolitan. The candidates for ordination were threatened with excommunication.[87] Menezes affirmed that nothing would hinder him from his apostolic actions and that he would exercise all acts of episcopal jurisdiction, in obedience to the briefs of the Roman Pontiff.[88] The archdeacon finding that the Archbishop was absolutely determined to ordain the candidates for priesthood tried to persuade him to ordain only the Latins.[89] The Archbishop informed him again that he would ordain both Latins and Syrians since his mission was to bring all Christians under one head.[90] On the appointed day Menezes ordained thirty-eight priests at Udayamperur.[91] The new priests denounced the Nestorian creed and professed that of Pope Pius IV. They swore allegiance to the Roman Pontiff and abjured the Nestorian Patriarch of

---

[84] Michael Geddes, op. cit., p.77.

[85] Gouvea, op. cit., p. 118-119.

[86] Michael Geddes, op. cit., p. 78

[87] Joseph Thekkedath, op. cit., p. 68.

[88] Michael Geddes, op. cit., p. 78.

[89] Geddes explains that by the Latins were meant the Portuguese and those Kerala Christians who were educated under the Jesuits and other Latin missionaries in their colleges.

[90] Michael Geddes, op. cit., p. 79.

[91] Joseph Thekkedath, op. cit., p. 68.

Babylon.[92] Thus Dom Menezes began to secure a number of persons of importance who remained faithful to the Roman Catholic Church in Kerala.

The Archbishop celebrated the Holy Week of Easter at Kadathuruthy.[93] On the way he visited several churches in the domains of the Queen of Pimenta (Vadakkumkoor).[94] He was received by the Christians courteously and from them he mustered support for his campaign against heresy. They all avowed that they accepted the Pope as the Supreme Pontiff of the Church. Gouvea has recorded that at Kadathuruthy two leaders of the community namely Itty Mathu Mappila and Itty Mani Mappila had made elaborate preparation for the reception of Dom Menezes, for his liturgical service during Easter and for the priestly ordination.[95] A choir had arrived from the Santa Cruz Cathedral in Cochin to add lustre to the Catholic liturgical service. In the main church of Kadathuruthy, Easter services were performed from Holy Wednesday, first in Latin and then in Syriac. The Archbishop's intention was to make it clear that his aim was to emphasise the supremacy of the Catholic Church and not to emphasise supremacy of either Latin or Syriac liturgy. The Thomas Christians openly acknowledged that the services of the Catholic Church far surpassed those of their own.[96] On Maundy Thursday when Menezes, robed in his pontificals, with the mitre on his head, washed the feet of the local priests and kissed them, the congregation burst into tears of joy.[97] When the adoration of the cross was performed on Good Friday, a local priest, who was the follower of the archdeacon, entered the church with a few armed men. The people did not like this. They caught hold of the priest and brought him before Dom Menezes. When he refused to apologize, he was mercilessly expelled from the church.[98] The Thomas Christians and their priests who had gathered there in large numbers declared Menezes as their shepherd. Many local priests threw themselves at his feet and reproached themselves

---

[92] Michael Geddes, op. cit., p. 79. See also James Hough, op. cit., pp. 391-392.

[93] Gouvea uses the Portuguese corruption Carturte for Kadathuruthy.

[94] Pimenta in Portuguese means pepper and the area under the Queen of Vadakkumkoor was rich in spices and hence the Portuguese historians described the ruler as the Queen of Pimenta.

[95] See Gouvea, op. cit., p. 126.

[96] James Hough, op. cit., p. 402.

[97] Gouvea, op. cit., pp. 126-127.

[98] Gouvea, loc. cit.

for their past resistance to his authority and openly renounced the heresy and supremacy of the Patriarch of Babylon.[99] On the Easter eve the Archbishop ordained a large number of priests at Kadathuruthy with the fullest cooperation of the local Christians. Thus did Menezes gain a considerable accession of strength among the Thomas Christians and equipped with added confidence for the successful conduct of the approaching Synod of Diamper. On the Easter Sunday Menezes was invited by the Christians to bless as their Metropolitan the customary *nercha* or love-feast. He spent the day going round the houses visiting the sick and the poor, speaking kindly to them and helping them with gifts of money, regretting at the same time that their own bishops had so much neglected this part of a pastor's duty.[100] With the conquest of Kadathuruthy, the task of Menezes became easier. As the church historian C. B. Firth observed:

> He [Menezes] went on his way, combining aggression with condescension, hectoring rulers and their officials if they obstructed him, calling them to his aid if the people were obstinate, almost always master of the situation, steadily extending his influences over clergy and people and building up support for his motto "One shepherd and One sheep-pen.[101]

The archdeacon remained at a distance doing his best to foment opposition among the people and local rulers but soon he realised that the situation was going out of hands. Sensing the tactics of the archdeacon, Menezes threatened to depose him and appoint in his place Thomas Kurian of Kuravilangad, a nephew of the former archdeacon George de Christo.[102]

The archdeacon continued to stir up the people against the Metropolitan and encouraged the suspicions of the King of Cochin and other rulers that the Portuguese were seeking to secure the allegiance of the Christians to Portugal in the name of religion. Realizing this Menezes went to the King of Cochin, spoke very harshly to him, without giving any opportunity for reply, insulted his gods and threatened him with hell.[103] The king swallowed the Archbishop's insults along

---

[99] James Hough, op. cit, pp. 407-408; See also Carlos Alonso, op. cit., pp. 87-90.

[100] Michael Geddes, op. cit., pp. 85-86.

[101] See Cyril Bruce Firth, *An Introduction to Indian Church History*, Madras, 1961, p. 86.

[102] Joseph Thekkedath, op. cit., p. 69.

[103] K. P. Padmanabha Menon, *The History of Cochin,* (Malayalam), Calicut, reprint, 1989, pp. 214-218; See also L. W. Brown, *The Indian Christians of St. Thomas,* Cambridge, 1956, p. 32.

with his own rage, and did what Menezes required of him. The archdeacon now feared that any further resistance by him might end up with his elimination from the scene. He therefore, decided to surrender to the Archbishop and politely informed him that "he had been overcome at last by the irresistible force of truth and was resolved to submit himself to the Roman Catholic faith entreating His Grace to pardon all the past errors of an ignorant son."[104]

Menezes visited many more churches, and the large congregations of Mulanthuruthy and Udayamperur declared complete allegiance to the Metropolitan. He conducted the third ordination service successfully at the church of Parur where he had been threatened with death at the beginning of his journey.[105] Most of the local rulers, having sensed the change of mind of the people, commanded their subjects to obey the Archbishop.[106] Having received the message of apology from the archdeacon, Dom Menezes informed him that he could not trust the archdeacon anymore before he had subscribed to the ten following conditions: 1) to condemn Nestorianism and to acknowledge Nestorius, Diodorus and Theodorus to be cursed heretics and that they are in hell for their errors; 2) to confess that there was but one Christian law; 3) to make the profession of faith as per the formula already sent to him from Goa; 4) to hand over all the books of the diocese to be amended or burnt; 5) to swear obedience to the Pope as St. Peter's successor and Christ's Vicar upon earth and the supreme head of all Christians; 6) to condemn the Patriarch of Babylonia as a Nestorian heretic and schismatic and to swear not to have any further relations with him; 7) to swear never to receive any bishop other than the one sent by the Pope and obey whomsoever be sent; 8) to swear to acknowledge the Archbishop Menezes as his superior as being made so by the Pope; 9) to circulate notice to convoke a diocesan synod in the place prescribed by Dom Menezes, to accept everything that would be settled there, and to convoke to it priests and representatives of laymen of the diocese; and 10) to accompany the Archbishop peaceably wheresoever he went in the same conveyance and without the armed guards.[107]

---

[104] Michael Geddes, op. cit., p. 94.

[105] Joseph Thekkedath, op. cit., p. 68.

[106] Michael Geddes, op cit., p. 92.

[107] Ibid., pp. 94-96; James Hough, op. cit., pp. 440-442; P. J. Podipara, op. cit., pp. 137-138; Ferroli, op. cit., I, p. 183.

Upon receipt of this message the archdeacon informed the Metropolitan that he was ready to accept all his commands and would wait upon him in the Jesuit College of Vaipicotta. Menezes was jubilant and they met first at the church of Vaipicotta where the archdeacon threw himself at the feet of the Archbishop with the words of the prodigal: "Father, I have sinned against heaven, and against thee, and am no more worthy to be called thy son. I do humbly beg pardon for all my errors which have been great."[108]

The Archbishop lifting him up and embracing him tenderly told him that all the past was forgiven and forgotten. Then the archdeacon knelt down before a crucifix and laying his hands upon Missal, swore by the ten articles stipulated by Dom Menezes as the profession of faith and finally signed the document.[109] It was decided that a diocesan synod will be convoked at Udayamperur on the 20 June 1599. Then a notice dated 11 May was issued signed both by the archdeacon commanding all priests and four representatives of the people from every church to be present at the synod.[110] After making these arrangements Dom Menezes retired to the Portuguese fort of Cranganore, where according to Gouvea, he completed without anybody's assistance the drafting of the decrees of the synod, from the notes he had taken about the heathen customs and abuses existing in the Kerala Church.[111] When the drafting was over, he had the decrees translated from Portuguese into Malayalam by Father Jacob of Palluruthy.[112]

On the 9 June, ten days before the synod began, Menezes reached Udayamperur, accompanied by six Jesuit scholars, his confessor and a few eminent local priests. He immediately constituted a *Junto* (secret conclave) of eight of the most popular and learned priests of Thomas Christians, before whom he laid the decrees for their opinion. At the discussion on decrees related manners and customs he invited four of the most prominent lay leaders to participate. After some debates some modifications were suggested, and finally the draft of the decrees was approved by the Junto.[113] It should be par-

---

108 Michael Geddes, ibid., p. 104.

109 Ibid., p. 105.

110 Ibid., p. 106.

111 Gouvea, op. cit., pp. 155-157.

112 Michael Geddes, op. cit., pp. 107-131/99; See also Jonas Thaliath, op. cit., p. 27.

113 Michael Geddes, ibid., p. 108.

ticularly noted that the synod was convoked and representatives were invited strictly in accordance with the traditions of the Kerala Church and giving due respect to the opinion of the archdeacon.

On 14 May the convening of the synod by Dom Alexis de Menezes, the Archbishop and Metropolitan of Goa, was published from Chanotta (Chendamangalam).[114] The synod was convoked at Udayamperoor, 20 June 1599 on the third Sunday after Pentecost.

Calicut University
P.B. No. 8
673635 Calicut
Kerala, India

K. J. John

[114] See Appendix II: "The Publication and Calling of the Synod" (pp. 206-210). Source: Michael Geddes, *The History of the Church of Malabar*, London, 1694, pp. 89-96.

Vincenzo Poggi, S.J.

Gesuiti e Diamper

Il Prof. Ernst Christoph Suttner ha scritto un articolo sui gesuiti e l'Oriente Cristiano che affronta il problema delle loro responsabilità nei confronti del sinodo di Diamper[1]. Egli ricorda che i gesuiti fin dalle loro origini incontrano i Cristiani di S. Tommaso.

> La Compagnia di Gesù, nata all'inizio dell'evo moderno e del colonialismo europeo, rese molti servizi alla Chiesa. I gesuiti furono spediti ai quattro punti cardinali. Con Francesco Saverio incontrarono fin dal 1541 la costa del Malabar[2].

L'incontro era animato dalle migliori intenzioni ma non poteva non rivelare una fatale conflittualità. Suttner ne individua la causa in una determinata concezione gesuitica che si scontra con la realtà dell'Oriente Cristiano.

> Tale incontro iniziò con ammirevole disponibilità e abnegazione. Ma produsse anche conflitti. Una causa dei conflitti, forse la principale, è da ricercarsi in una concezione ecclesiologica dalla quale Ignazio e i suoi erano guidati. Questa concezione, anche senza affiorare alla superficie della coscienza, era per molte generazioni di gesuiti il *Leitmotiv* di ogni loro piano di azione. [...] Chi professa un continuo esercizio del primato papale sull'ordinaria cura pastorale in qualunque parte del mondo, annette al dogma cattolico del primato del papa di sindacare ogni cosa e ovunque nella Chiesa; perciò bisogna tener presente in partenza che ovunque i gesuiti agiscano nell'Oriente cristiano, i conflitti sono inevitabili. Se dei religiosi, dalla concezione ecclesiale universalista, si sentono inviati sempre e ovunque al servizio ordinario della Chiesa, direttamente dal vescovo di Roma, cui soltanto sono tenuti a rendere conto, se hanno a che fare con Cristiani orientali, la cui ecclesiologia e concezione pastorale si basa sull'idea che l'una, santa, cattolica e apostolica Chiesa — per dirla con la costituzione sulla Chiesa del Vaticano II — si trova nelle singole Chiese e ne è costituita, per forza verranno in conflitto con loro[3].

---

[1] E. Ch. Suttner, "Die Jesuiten und der christliche Osten", *Stimmen der Zeit* 209 (luglio 1991) 461-476.

[2] Id., Ibidem, 461.

[3] Id., Ibidem, 461-462.

Ci sarebbe insomma una pregiudiziale insormontabile nei gesuiti per immedesimarsi con la "Christian way of life" dei Cristiani di S. Tommaso.

> Né l'arcivescovo di Goa, né i gesuiti erano disposti a capire usi e costumi siriaci. Le formulazioni dottrinali arcaiche a loro ignote, che avrebbero dovuto essere lette in un contesto del tutto alieno al pensiero e alle concezioni cristiane occidentali, erano per loro eretiche. Nella loro vita liturgica, tutto quanto non corrispondeva alla loro liturgia occidentale, li allarmava e li portava a giudicarlo superstizioso. D'altro canto consideravano un'imperdonabile lacuna che mancasse presso i Cristiani di San Tommaso quanto invece c'era nel loro rito d'occidente. Per essere sicuri che i preti dei Cristiani di S. Tommaso amministrassero correttamente i sacramenti della Chiesa fu tradotto infine il rituale latino in siriaco e si cercò di convincere il clero a servirsene. Preoccupato della purezza della fede il P. Francisco Ros compilò negli anni 1586-1587 una lista delle dottrine che suonavano offensive, anzi eretiche, a orecchie occidentali. Nel 1599 un sinodo condannò tali dottrine, rese obbligatorie le latinizzazioni rituali e inserì saldamente i Cristiani di S. Tommaso nelle strutture dell'arcivescovado di Goa e nel Padroado portoghese[4].

Tanto più ci interessa questa disanima del Suttner sul sinodo di Diamper in quanto egli ne traccia anche le conseguenze e le ripercussioni.

> Per tutto il tempo del dominio portoghese i vescovi dei Cristiani di S. Tommaso furono gesuiti che conservarono il loro rito latino. Il diritto orientale tradizionale di quei Cristiani e il loro rapporto con il Patriarca della Chiesa di Oriente fu interrotto. Dopo la metà del secolo XVII gli Olandesi subentrarono a Portoghesi e Spagnoli, che erano uniti sotto lo stesso monarca. Appartenendo alla Riforma gli Olandesi non sostennero più i missionari latini come avevano fatto gli Iberici. Fra i Cristiani locali si manifestò un movimento in favore del ritorno alle vecchie tradizioni e ne conseguì il primo grande scisma tra loro. Si dovette alla sostituzione dei Gesuiti con i Carmelitani se i Cristiani di S. Tommaso non si allontanarono in blocco, tutti dalla Chiesa Cattolica[5].

Ho citato Suttner perché non essendo gesuita è più libero d'esprimere francamente il suo pensiero circa la parte che hanno avuto a Diamper i gesuiti. E inoltre perché quanto lui scrive mi sembra meritevole di meditazione per i gesuiti che vogliano riflettere sulla storia della loro famiglia religiosa, storia sempre educativa, anche per non commettere gli errori dei precedenti confratelli. L'aver premesso le pagine di Suttner che cercano già la spiegazione dei fatti o l'*epoché*

---

[4] Id., Ibidem, 463.

[5] Id., Ibidem, 463-464.

del fenomeno, può darci una maggior lucidità e oggettività nell'affrontare storicamente la parte che hanno avuto i gesuiti a Diamper.

DE MENEZES, AGIOGRAFICO

Non si può negare che il sinodo di Diamper sia un caso di latinizzazione forzata dell'Oriente cristiano, quindi qualcosa di erroneo e penoso. Essendo io gesuita, è comprensibile che, per solidarietà con i miei confratelli, tenti, se possibile, di lavarli dalla macchia di aver provocato i mali conseguenti al sinodo di Diamper. Pur avendo sempre davanti agli occhi l'imparzialità aristotelica che diceva, "Amicus Plato, sed magis amica veritas".

Un primo elemento apologetico potrebbe essere quello di constatare che la responsabilità maggiore di quel sinodo non ce l'hanno i gesuiti, ma l'arcivescovo di Goa, Aleixo de Menezes. Fu lui infatti che lo volle e lo condusse a ritmo serrato in una settimana, dal 20 al 27 giugno 1599, anzi propriamente in cinque giorni, dato il solenne pontificale all'inizio e la processione alla fine, con tutta quella congerie di decreti che sorprende per esser stata redatta in tempo così breve. Joseph Wicki scrive che Menezes si è servito dei gesuiti come di strumenti, assumendosi la responsabilità del sinodo di Diamper[6]. E benché mi venisse spontanea questa prospettiva apologetica in favore della Compagnia di Gesù, per *legitima suspicione* di lasciarmi guidare da parzialità a causa dello "spirito di corpo" della Compagnia di Gesù cui appartengo, ho cercato conferme presso non gesuiti. L'ho già fatto premettendo le citazioni di Suttner. Ma ora ricorro ad altri autori che trattano di Diamper. Il primo è un noto studioso agostiniano specialista di missioni orientali del suo Ordine, il P. Carlos Alonso O.S.A.[7]. Egli aveva già scritto precedentemente vari saggi sulla figura dell'arcivescovo di Goa, Aleixo de Menezes[8]. Ma a conclusione delle

---

[6] J. Wicki S.J., "Die Synoden der Thomaschristen (auch Syromalabaren genannt) (1563-1603)", *Annuarium Historiae Conciliorum* 18/2 (1986) 334-447, qui 362-363.

[7] Carlos Alonso O.S.A., *Alejo de Meneses O.S.A. Arzobispo de Goa (1595-1612): Estudio biográfico*, Valladolid 1992.

[8] "Documentación inedita para una biografía de Fr. Alejo de Meneses,OSA, arzobispo de Goa (1595-1612", *Analecta Augustiniana* 27 (1964) 263-333; "Elección y consagración de Alejo de Meneses OSA como arzobispo de Goa", *Analecta Augustiniana* 49 (1986) 89-135; "La visitas ad limina de Alejo de Meneses OSA arzobispo de Goa y de Braga", *Archivo Augustiniano* 72 (1988) 39-74; "Vida del beato Gonzalo de Lagos por Alejo de Meneses OSA arzobispo de Goa", *Archivo Augustiniano* 72 (1988) 275-298.

ricerche su di lui, ha dedicato al personaggio un intero volume monografico nel 1992. Come si può vedere dal contenuto di quel volume, il sinodo di Diamper vi prende molto spazio e importanza. Alonso ha consultato seriamente le fonti (Antonio de Gouvea OSA, *Jornada do arcebispo de Goa Dom Frey Aleixo de Meneses, primas da India Oriental, religioso da Ordem de S. Agostinho, quando foy as serras do Malavar*, Coimbra 1606; Mansi, *Sacrorum Conciliorum nova et amplissima Collectio*, vol. 35, coll 1161-1368; *Bullarium Patronatus Portugalliae*, Olisiponae 1868-1878; *Subsidium ad Bullarium patronatus Portugalliae*, Allappe 1903 etc.[9]) senza trascurare gli archivi romani. Con vero *fair play*, quando Carlos Alonso ha saputo che studiavo la responsabilità gesuita a Diamper, ha rinunciato a trattarre lo stesso tema in altro simposio al quale era stato invitato a partecipare. Di riscontro devo riconoscermi molto debitore della sua monografia sul de Menezes. Tra l'altro vi ho trovato la lettera del Campori riportata dal Possevino, che implica senza scampo la corresponsabilità dei gesuiti.

Ora, questo libro di Alonso sulla vita e l'opera dell'arcivescovo di Goa, nella quale il sinodo di Diamper ha tanto rilievo, termina con un giudizio complessivo molto favorevole sull'opera del de Menezes quando era arcivescovo di Goa.

> Salvo meliori iudicio il bilancio finale della gestione pastorale dell'archidiocesi primaziale di Goa da parte di Aleixo de Menezes può essere qualificato come molto positivo[10].

Si può dissentire da tale giudizio. Secondo Carlos Alonso, l'arcivescovo primate di Goa, artefice del sinodo di Diamper, avrebbe anche ottenuto dal papa Aldobrandini, Clemente VIII, una solenne approva-

---

[9] Per la storia si devono tuttora consultare: M. Geddes, *The History of the Church of Malabar*, London 1694; I. F. Raulin, *Historia Ecclesiae Malabaricae cum Diamperitana Synodo*, Romae 1745; A. Silva Rego (ed.), *Documentaçao para a Historia das Missoês do Padroado Portugues do Oriente-India*, 12 vols Lisboa 1947-1958; J. Wicki S.J., "Die Synoden der Thomaschristen (auch Syromalabaren genannt) (1563-1603)", *Annuarium Historiae Conciliorum* 18/2 (1986) 334-447 ("Die Synode von Diamper 1599", 343-440); Id., *Documenta Indica* 18 vols. Romae 1948-1988; J. Tekkedath, *History of Christianity in India From the Middle of the XVIth Century to the End of the XVIIth Century*, Bangalore 1988. Recentemente alcune fonti sono state riedite: O. Bragança, *Actas do Sinodo de Diamper*, Lisboa 1987; A. de Gouvea, *Jornada do Arcebispo*, Lisboa 1988; Scaria Zacharia (ed.),*The Acts and Decrees of the Synod of Diamper 1599*, (in inglese e in malayalam) Edamattam 1994.

[10] Carlos Alonso O.S.A., *Alejo de Meneses O.S.A. Arzobspo de Goa (1595-1612) Estudio biográfico*, Valladolid 1992, p. 289.

zione del sinodo con il breve *Divinam Dei omnipotentis Providentiam* del 19 maggio 1601. Jonas Thaliath confuta tale opinione[11].

Penso che João Paulo Oliveira e Costa inserirebbe la monografia di Carlos Alonso, su de Menezes, nella prima categoria degli scritti che affrontano la storia dei rapporti fra Portoghesi e Cristiani di San Tommaso, come fa del resto per l'illustre storico da Silva Rego. Per quella categoria di storici, i primi Portoghesi sbarcati in India

> considerarono eretica la cristianità locale e svolsero un'azione programmata che avrà la sua naturale conclusione nell'intervento di Aleixo de Menezes nel 1599. Esempio tipico di tale approccio storico è quello di A. de Silva Rego (*Historia das Missoês do Padroado Portugues de Oriente – India*, Lisboa 1949) che, nella prospettiva eurocentrica della Chiesa postridentina, vede naturale e positiva la latinizzazione dei Cristiani di San Tommaso[12].

Tuttavia lo stesso Oliveira e Costa rifiuta l'approccio storico opposto, che mostra

> la comunità malabarese solo come vittima di un'acculturazione violenta della quale sono corresponsabili tutti i Portoghesi venuti in India[13].

Anche Giuseppe Beltrami, nel suo libro tuttora utile, *La Chiesa caldea nel secolo dell'unione*, lascia la maggiore responsabilità del sinodo a de Menezes. "Una sola voce — scrive — si leva a domandare la nomina di un vescovo latino: è quella del de Menezes. Mentre con occhio più sereno, nonostante il controllo della polizia portoghese, vedeva le cose il gesuita P. Antonio de Monserrate, il quale scriveva al Padre Generale Mercuriano [ancora nel 1579, benché Beltrami, a torto, voglia ritardare quella data]:

> Soprattutto mi pare che sarebbe molto opportuno che Sua Santità inviasse un nunzio, il quale, prendendo saldamente in mano la situazione della cristianità, ordini quanto reputi di maggior servizio di Nostro Signore e in specie riguardo alla dipendenza immediata da Sua Santità o dal Patriarca di Siria; se i vescovi della Sierra debbano essere suffraganei dell'arcivescovo di Goa, tenuti alla convocazione di concili provinciali perché, in ambedue le alternative bisogna riflettere su molte cose che non si possono scrivere. Comunque converrebbe che questo nunzio fosse straniero e non portoghese e venisse per la via di Ormuz perché, se fosse portoghese e venisse per la via di Portogallo ne arguiranno, sia i cristiani

---

[11] J. Thaliath, *The Synod of Diamper*, Roma 1958, 118-127.

[12] J. P. Oliveira e Costa, "Os Portugueses e a cristandade siro-malabar (1498-1530)", *Studia*, Lisboa 52 (1994) 121-178, qui 123-124

[13] J. P. Oliveira e Costa, "Os Portugueses e a cristandade siro-malabar (1498-1530)", *Studia*, Lisboa 52 (1994) 124.

che i cassanari, l'arcivescovo [Mar Abraham] e i pagani che i portoghesi vogliono impadronirsi della Sierra e così non si otterrà nulla di buono. Ma se venisse per l'altra via, benché mandato da Roma e lo sapessero, lo riceveranno meglio e con venerazione, potendosi poi lui muovere a suo piacere. E quanto al togliere la giurisdizione al Patriarca di Oriente, Sua Santità potrà assegnargliene un'altra, in diverso territorio, più vicino a Babilonia e alla Siria[14].

Beltrami aggiunge in nota:

Questa lettera fu pubblicata in inglese nel *Catholic Herald of India* del 30 gennaio 1924 e poi da Bernard of St. Thomas[15], e di qui l'abbiamo tolta e tradotta[16].

Beltrami dubita della data della lettera e vorrebbe ritardarla di quasi vent'anni al 1597. Ma l'edizione del Wicki, venuta dopo, la assegna senza esitazione al 16 gennaio 1579[17]. Il P. A. Gille che per primo pubblicò la lettera, fa seguire questo commento:

Ecco quanto uno spagnolo e un gesuita scrive, nonostante la sorveglianza della polizia portoghese; ma il suo parere cadde invano. E per più di tre secoli i missionari europei continuarono a calpestare, offendendo e contristando i poveri Siriani coi loro vescovi latini. Finché Leone XIII, ne ebbe abbastanza e, nonostante una forte opposizione, nominò tre vescovi indiani di rito siriaco[18].

Aggiungo a conferma che la lettera è del 1579 e a escluderne la datazione al 1597, che P. Antonio de Monserrate lascia Goa l'anno 1589 per recarsi in Etiopia insieme con il confratello P. Pedro Paez. Durante quel viaggio e precisamente il 14 febbraio 1590 i due sono catturati da pirati musulmani e portati in Arabia in attesa del pagamento del riscatto. Le loro peripezie e le loro sofferenze sono narrate dal P. Paez nei capitoli 15-21 della sua *Historia de Ethiopia*, edita da Camillo Beccari nella monumentale raccolta, *Rerum Aethiopicarum scriptores occidentales inediti.* Riscatto e liberazione avvennero soltanto sei anni dopo la cattura e il de Monserrate stremato dalle fatiche, non si

---

[14] G. Beltrami, *La Chiesa caldea nel secolo dell'unione,* (=Orientalia Chrstiana N. 83) (Romae, Januario-martio 1933) p. 130.

[15] Bernard of St. Thomas, *A Brief Sketch of the History of St. Thomas Christians,* Trichinopoly 1924,48.

[16] G. Beltrami, *La Chiesa caldea nel secolo dell'unione*, op. cit. nota 93, p. 130.

[17] J. Wicki S.J., *Documenta Indica* XI, Doc. 65, pp. 505-528, qui 527-528; Id., "Die Synoden...", art. cit., 433.

[18] G. Beltrami, *La Chiesa Caldea nel secolo dell'Unione*, op. cit., p. 130.

riprende più completamente e il catalogo geuita del 1597 nota che ormai non fa che ascoltare le confessioni. Muore l'anno 1600[19].

De Menezes politico

Un altro studio sul sinodo di Diamper, è uscito l'anno 1998 su una rivista francese. È un saggio di taglio socio-culturale[20]. Anche in quello il protagonista quasi esclusivo è il de Menezes. L'Autore, Sanjay Subrahmanyam, come Carlos Alonso, gli attribuisce la più grande responsabilità, benché sia molto meno elogiativo nei confronti del de Menezes di quanto non lo sia Alonso:

> Fra i grandi attori della storia dell'India portoghese alla fine del secolo XVI l'arcivescovo agostiniano di Goa dal 1595 al 1612 portò il pesante fardello di avere orchestrato il celebre sinodo di Diamper (Udayamperur) nel Kerala centrale, fra il 20 e il 27 giugno 1599[21].

Secondo Subrahmanyam la buona accoglienza che i Cristiani del Kerala fanno ai portoghesi si basa sulla speranza di trovare in loro dei difensori dai musulmani e dagli indù. Quanto al rapporto fra le due cristianità lusitana e indiana si tratterebbe di un confronto piuttosto che di un conflitto.

Infatti il rapporto fra Cristiani di S. Tommaso e Portoghesi rimarrebbe piuttosto "economico". Essi privilegiano i Portoghesi nel commercio ma non intendono sottomettersi a loro. Verso la metà del secolo XVI la situazione cambia quando ci sono in Mesopotamia due gerarchie ecclesiastiche, una cattolica e un'altra non cattolica e arrivano in India vescovi dall'una o dell'altra. I Portoghesi guardano con sospetto questi vescovi sirofoni e sono piuttosto duri con Mar Joseph e con Mar Abraham. Nel 1560 a Goa, divenuta sede archiepiscopale, s'instaura l'inquisizione. Uno dei più severi arcivescovi è il domenicano Jorge Temudo, seguito nella stessa linea dai successori, pure domenicani, Henrique de Tavora e Vicente de Fonseca. Tra gli altri

---

[19] Cfr R. B. Serjeant and C. F. Beckinghan, "A Journey by two Jesuits from Dhufār to San'ā in 1590", R. B. Serjeant, *Studies in Arabian History and Civilisation*, London 1981, pp. 194-207. J. Wicki, *Documenta Indica* XVIII, 844. J. Fejér, *Defuncti primi saeculi S.I. 1540-1640*, Romae 1982, 151.

[20] Sanjay Subrahmanyan, "Dom Frei Aleixo de Meneses (1559-1617) et l'échec des tentatives d'indigénisation du Christianisme en Inde", *Archives de Sciences sociales des Religions* (1998) 21-42.

[21] Subrahmanyan, "Dom Frei Aleixo de Meneses (1559-1617) et l'échec des tentatives d'indigénisation du Christianisme en Inde", *Archives de Sciences sociales des Religions* (1998) 21-22.

religiosi, i francescani sono latinizzanti e ci sarebbero, sempre secondo Subrahmanyam, due categorie di gesuiti, i *severi* e i *flessibili*. Il "nocciolo duro" però sarebbe rappresentato da domenicani e agostiniani, soprattutto quando sono più strettamente legati allo *estado da India*. Subrahmanyam, che lamenta nelle biografie di personaggi ecclesiastici come de Menezes una prospettiva troppo agiografica, (sembra alludere velatamente agli studi biografici su Menezes scritti da Alonso, benché non citi esplicitamente la monografia pubblicata nel 1992) scopre nella corrispondenza del de Menezes preoccupazioni nepotistiche, di gloria umana e di carriera politica. Alla morte di Mar Abraham nel 1597 i Portoghesi si preoccupano che non giunga un altro vescovo dalla Caldea, dalla Persia ovvero dai territori dove si parla l'aramaico. Subrahmanyam cita una lettera di Menezes di quell'anno.

> Questi malabaresi sono ottimi a combattere e molto obbedienti al loro vescovo. Se accettano un vescovo latino avremo a disposizione 50.000 soldati già addestrati nell'uso delle armi da fuoco[22].

Subrahamanyam cita pure altre lettere di Menezes[23]. In una di esse trova un'affermazione sul diverso approccio dei portoghesi con i cristiani orientali e con i non-cristiani. In quella lettera de Menezes scrive che

> i vescovi "armeni" provenienti da Babilonia sono eretici, scismatici, nostri peggiori nemici e ci detestano più che non lo facciano gli stessi infedeli[24].

In base a questi principi de Menezes pianifica la sua strategia con i Cristiani di S. Tommaso. Affinché i *cassanar* o preti locali non gli muovano guerra, fa tre ordinazioni collettive alle quali ammette parecchi di loro. Minaccia di scomunica chi è sospetto di eresia. Gli effetti del sinodo sono noti. I Cristiani del Kerala rompono le relazioni con la Mesopotamia e accettano un vescovo latino. Cinquant'anni dopo, quando l'arcidiacono invita un vescovo sirofono, si hanno i primi sussulti della rivolta. Tuttavia Subrahamanyam rifiuta di formulare il bilancio di Diamper in termini esclusivamente negativi.

---

[22] Id. Ibidem, p. 37. Cfr C. Alonso, *Alejo de Meneses O.S.A.*, Valladolid 1992, 67.

[23] Arthur Beylerian, "Cinq lettres inédites de D. Frei Aleixo de Meneses, Archevêque de Goa", *Arquivos do Centro Cultural Portugues*, vol. VIII, 1974, 582-587. Erano già edite da B.J. Senna Freitas nel 1909, come rammenta Wicki, "Die Synoden...", 344 nota 20.

[24] Subrahmanyam, art. cit., p. 38.

Diamper per un verso è l'insuccesso dell'inculturazione, in quanto la Chiesa latina e occidentale riesce apparentemente a imporre la sua concezione nei comportamenti e negli aspetti socioreligiosi. Ma questo processo è abbastanza spiegabile in termini di rapporto di forze fra Padroado e Cristiani del Kerala. A differenza di quanto avviene nel Maduré dove i gesuiti operano in una sfera politica nella quale i Portoghesi sono marginali, nel Kerala i preti latini sono rappresentanti di un potere politico non trascurabile. Accettano il compromesso di un rapido diffondersi dell'occidentalizzazione, senza che si verifichi una vera indigenizzazione delle pratiche religiose importate dall'Europa. Anche la politica lo dimostra. Quando gli Olandesi attaccano Kollam, Cannanore e le fortezze portoghesi di Cochin, i Cristiani del Kerala non prendono le difese dei Portoghesi, ma si tengono fuori dal conflitto.

Padroado

Anche tenendo presente la politica portoghese, si è tentati di gettare su quella la responsabilità degli errori commessi a Diamper. Il sinodo di Diamper si è svolto nel contesto del Padroado portoghese e non dimentichiamo che la Congregazione di Propaganda Fide, insediata saldamente a partire dal 1622, cerca appunto di ovviare ai pericoli del Padroado. Anzi, la Congregatio de Propaganda Fide era stata preceduta da tre Congregazioni che la precorrevano e precisamente dalla *Congregatio de rebus Graecorum*, cui era succeduta la *Congregatio super formatione Graecorum*, poi sostituita dalla *Congregatio super negotiis sanctae fidei et religionis catholicae*. A. Castellucci ha scritto decenni fa un saggio[25] in cui si occupa tra l'altro di una delle congregazioni che avevano preceduto Propaganda e i cui atti si riferiscono al sinodo di Diamper:

> Dai cardinali della congregazione sotto Clemente VIII furono sottoposte ad esame per essere approvate le costituzioni dei sinodi a cominciare da quello di Diamper[26].

In appendice al suo studio Castellucci riporta brani dagli *Acta Congregationis super negotiis Sanctae Fidei et Religionis Catholicae* dei

---

[25] A. Castellucci, "Il risveglio dell'attività missionaria e le prime origini della S.C. de propaganda fide", in *Le Conferenze al Laterano*, marzo-aprile 1923, Roma 1924, pp. 117-254.

[26] Id., Ibidem, p. 194.

giorni fra il 10 e il 17 agosto 1600 conservati nell'Archivio di Propaganda. Vi figura appunto la

> Relatione delli cristiani di S. Tommaso del rito caldeo redotti all'obbedienza della Chiesa Romana l'anno del 1599 nell'India Orientale nei regni della Serra.

Vi si legge di uno scritto di Menezes al papa e del proposito di inviare gli atti sinodali di Diamper.

> L'arcivescovo di Goa ha scritto a sua Santità una lettera sopra questa materia e l'informa dello stato di quella Chiesa e ha ancora mandato il detto concilio che adesso si sta traducendo in latino et finito si darà a Sua Santità[27].

Questo documento che Castellucci ha segnalato e in parte riprodotto è stato stampato integralmente da Beltrami[28].

De Menezes è tipico rappresentante del Padroado. Egli, che al battesimo era Pietro de Menezes, aveva cambiato nome in Alessio quando si era fatto agostiniano in ricordo di suo padre Alessio, figlio a sua volta di Dom Pietro de Menezes, conte di Castanhede e nipote del governatore dell'India portoghese, Lopo Soares de Albergaria. Il padre dell'agostiniano, gentiluomo di corte al servizio del re, ebbe altissimi incarichi in Africa e in India e, infine, ricevette il delicato compito di negoziare il matrimonio di Filippo II di Spagna con la principessa Maria di Portogallo, cosi da unire, dal 1580 al 1598, le due corone sul capo di Filippo II. Del resto suo figlio, frate agostiniano, predicatore regio e arcivescovo di Goa, fu in seguito governatore dell'India. Fu anche proposto come viceré dello *estado da India* e la sua candidatura fallì soltanto perché "ritenuto disdicevole al suo stato di arcivescovo di brandire la spada e perché avrebbe fatto credere ai musulmani e ai gentili che sua maestà non avesse più condottieri laici per guerreggiare"[29]. Fu richiamato in patria per divenire arcivescovo di Braga. Filippo III lo nominò viceré del Portogallo. De Menezes presiedette negli ultimi due anni di vita il consiglio della nazione portoghese.

---

27 Id. Ibidem, p. 228.

28 G. Beltrami, *La Chiesa caldea nel secolo dell'unione*, op. cit. doc. XXXII, pp. 257-263.

29 Subrahmanyan, art. cit., p. 32.

RESPONSABILITÀ GESUITA

Un altro argomento a sgravio dei gesuiti. Sono loro a insistere perché l'arcidiacono *sede vacante* assuma la gestione ordinaria della Chiesa[30].

Altro punto a favore dei gesuiti: Il P. Alessandro Valignano esorta Mar Abraham a recarsi al concilio di Goa nel 1585, promettendogli di riportarlo sano e salvo alla Serra e il gesuita P. Pacheco gli ottiene una pensione regia di 400 crusados[31].

Invece il 15 dicembre 1593 il P. Abraham De Georgiis S.J., che sarà ucciso in Etiopia nel 1595, descrive al P. Acquaviva la sua preoccupazione per le idee che circolano fra i Cristiani di S. Tommaso:

> Per loro Cristo è soltanto uomo, la passione di Cristo contraddicendo la sua divinità, e Maria non è la Madre di Dio. La legge dell'apostolo Tommaso è diversa dalla legge dell'apostolo Pietro. Mar Abraham che regge l'archidiocesi di Angamale la fa da papa e da patriarca nel suo territorio[32].

Questo gesuita Abraham De Georgis, maronita, conoscitore del siriaco, fa accuse simili a quelle che Ros espone gli anni 1586-1587 nel *De erroribus Nestorianorum qui in hac India orientali versantur*[33]. Con tutto ciò, propone un vescovo sirofono, che potrebbe essere della sua Chiesa di origine, cioè Maronita[34]. La campagna accusatoria del Ros e del De Georgis spiega come mai un Breve di papa Clemente VIII del 27 gennaio 1595 raccomandi all'arcivescovo di Goa di esaminare accuratamente la vita e la dottrina di Mar Abraham. E ignorando il precedente documento che, in caso di vacanza della sede, costituiva amministratore l'arcidiacono, il papa nel Breve del 21 gennaio 1597 progetta la nomina di un vicario apostolico "di rito latino che conosca se possibile il caldeo o il siriaco" mentre vieta che il futuro arcivescovo sia eletto sinodalmente, esigendo invece che sia di nomina papale[35].

---

30 Cfr J. Kollaparambil, *The Archdeacon of All-India: Historic-Juridical Study,* Rome 1972.

31 Ferroli, *The Jesuits in Malabar*, vol. I, 171.

32 Ferroli, *The Jesuits in Malabar*, I 173-174; Beltrami, op. cit., 113-114.

33 *De Erroribus Nestorianorum qui in hac India Orientali versantur auctore Francisco Roz S.I.*. Inédit latin-syriaque de la fin de 1586 ou du début de 1587, retrouvé par le P. Castets S.J., annoté par le P. I. Hausherr S.J. (= Orientalia Christiana N. 40.) Romae 1928.

34 Wicki, "Die Synoden...", 428. Id., *Dcumenta Indica* XVI (1984) 559-567.

35 Ferroli, *The Jesuits in Malabar*, I, 174-175.

L'ARCIDIACONO

Difatti, prima della sua morte, avvenuta il 3 gennaio 1597, Mar Abraham aveva designato l'arcidiacono Giorgio di Cristo come Vicario dei Cristiani di San Tommaso. Un Breve papale del 21 gennaio di quell'anno, senza ancora sapere di quella morte, nomina Vicario il gesuita Francisco Ros. La notizia provoca reazioni popolari e gli stessi gesuiti fanno opera di persuasione presso l'arcivescovo, che nomina vicario il nuovo arcidiacono Giorgio della Croce. Contemporaneamente de Menezes designa i gesuiti di Vaipicotta, i Padri Francisco Ros, e Jorge de Castro, consiglieri dell'arcidiacono. Tuttavia l'arcidiacono non vuole saperne di consiglieri latini e rifiuta di fare la professione di fede tridentina davanti al P. de Castro rettore di Vaipicotta. Dice anzi ai cassanar che devono obbedire soltanto a lui e ai vescovi che arrivino da Babilonia. De Menezes è pronto a recarsi ad Angamale. L'arcidiacono prende tempo dicendo che non vuole fare la professione di fede davanti a gesuiti. L'arcivescovo designa un teologo francescano a ricevere la professione e questi la riceve in forma privata. De Menezes informato intima all'arcidiacono di professare un'altra volta. Quegli accetta, ma insiste nel dire che de Menezes è metropolita dei Latini dell'India. Allora, de Menezes è informato della situazione dal visitatore gesuita e ne è richiesta la presenza dal Rettore di Vaipicotta. Menezes decide di recarsi di persona nel Malabar.

> Sembrò opportuno al Padre Visitatore d'informare in Goa il Viceré e l'arcivescovo di quanto avveniva e io stesso feci in modo che Sua Signoria l'Arcivescovo venisse di persona a riformare questa Cristianità[36].

L'arcidiacono deve riceverlo a Cochin, ove de Menezes è arrivato nel febbraio 1599. Lo attende con una schiera di giovani bellicosi, come un generale a capo del suo esercito. De Menezes è buon diplomatico. Non vuole scontri frontali e si ritira a Vaipicotta dove incontra finalmente l'arcidiacono, riuscendo a placarlo senza far concessioni, anzi proibendo la recita delle ore canoniche nelle quali i Cristiani locali pregano per il patriarca nestoriano senza menzionare affatto il papa. De Menezes ordina una quarantina di nuovi sacerdoti contro la volontà dell'arcidiacono che teme defezioni nel suo partito.

---

[36] P. Giorgio de Castro al Generale Aquaviva, il 22 dicembre 1599. ARSI, Goa 14, f. 421. Cfr. J. Kollaparambil, *Archdeacon of All-India*, 102. A. De Gouvea, *Jornada do Arcebispo de Goa Dom Frey Aleixo de Menezes Primaz da India Oriental*, Coimbra 1606, ff. 13-15. Ferroli, *The Jesuits in Malabar*, I, 175-176; Wicki, "Die Synoden...", 358-359. Si veda più oltre e nell'Appendice III la lettera di Giovanni Maria Campori del 25 nov. 1599.

De Menezes celebra l'Eucaristia davanti al popolo con la maggiore solennità possibile. Sembra a un certo punto che l'arcidiacono sia al limite della sopportazione e voglia addirittura lanciare la scomunica a de Menezes. Ma il raja di Cochin, nel timore di perdere i vantaggi del commercio con i Portoghesi, fa da paciere tra i due. E de Meneses ne approfitta per lanciare un *ultimatum* all'arcidiacono: Abiurare la dottrina di Nestorio; dichiarare che la legge di Tommaso e la legge di Pietro sono identiche, professare la stessa formula di fede che ha emesso quando è stato nominato vicario, riconoscere il Papa quale capo supremo di tutta la Chiesa; sconfessare il patriarca nestoriano, non ricevere vescovi che non siano nominati dal papa, riconoscere il Primate di Goa come superiore, partecipare al sinodo, accompagnare senza armi e senza soldati il metropolita in visita pastorale[37].

SINODO = "RIDUZIONE"

Il gesuita Andrea Buccerio scrive dal Malabar il 14 dicembre 1599 manifestando un'immediata reazione entusiastica al sinodo di Diamper. Tra l'altro, nella sua lettera la parola "riduzione" non ha l'accezione tecnica più famosa delle "riduzioni gesuitiche" del Paraguai e di altri territori dell'America Latina, dove gli indios occidentali venivano sedentarizzati e cristianizzati. Ma in questa lettera del Buccerio e nella lettera di Giovanni Maria Campori del 5 gennaio 1998 che riportiamo più avanti, ha invece il senso di "riduzione all'ovile di Pietro" e viene in tale accezione applicata ai Cristiani di S. Tommaso, così pure nel testo citato nella nota 27 sopra. Ci piacerebbe approfondire il paragone fra le due accezioni del termine. Ma lasciamo ad altra sede questo confronto filologico-storico.

> Una delle principali cause de servicio del Signore che la Compagnia ha estendido in queste parti dell'India è la reduttione dei Christiani antiqui che per quelle parti ha del beato Santo Tommaso Apostolo, i quali sono da ottanta mil o più e benché siano per l'ordinario fermi nella fede di nostro Signor Jesu Cristo al suo modo, e molto observanti dei suoi riti antiqui et se stimano a honor esser tali, per esser ciò ancor quanto adiante dei gentili molto stimati in genere di nobiltà, tuttavia come quelli che furono ordinati da prelati venuti per via del Patriarca de Babilonia, e schismatici, *in multis errabant a vera fide,* non riconoscevano per capo della Chiesa il Papa di Roma, ma detenevano per tale a detto patriarca e il che di ciò seguitava, tenevano et adoravano l'empio Nestorio e altri heretici per santi, e molti veri santi per heretici como Cirillo [d'Alessandria]

[37] Ferroli, *The Jesuits in Malabar*, I, 184; Wicki, "Die Synoden...", 359-363.

ecc. e le heresie di Nestorio erano tenute per verità e d'alcun altre che più assai contradicono Cristo Nostro Signore, come della virginità della Vergine sua Madre e dell'immagini. Per liberarli da quelli errori la Compagnia ha molti anni fece un seminario de clerici di quella natione, alcune legue per la serra dentro de Cochin, dove ha ensinhati [formati] molti sacerdoti cattolici, i quali col sapere il soriano e latino insieme, sono rimasti capaci che la Scrittura nostra e loro he l'istessa e solo la lingua è diversa, i nostri Padri molto dotti nella lingua soriana e malavar con le prediche, e sermoni ai Cristiani pouco a pouco han fatti capaci dell'istesso, e che la fede e la legge tutta è una, ma che essi con la contagion di Babilonia andavano errati. Andando li nostri in queste occupazioni e in questi desiderij, mosser l'animo a dietro l'arcivescovo Soriano e con l'accordo che s'è tenuto, non è venuto da Babilonia successore, ma rimane il carrego all'Arcivescovo di Goa Dom Alessio de Meneses, il quale per nobilissimo che sia, tiene più de santità e zelo che de nobiltà e in quest'anno a molti dei nostri è venuto in persona, e accompagnato da noi ha visitato detta cristianità e dopo molte difficoltà ha ottenuto quello che da tanto tempo se desiderò, l'arcidiacono che adesso governava e gli altri chierici e li principali d'ogni hā [casa?] di detta cristianità ajontati [riuniti] in numero di 800 in sinodo provinciale in presentia di detto Arcivescovo e dei nostri se soggettarono alla Chiesa Romana, fecero la professione della vera fede cattolica e anatematizzarono del patriarca de Babilonia e de tutte le heresie contrarie a detta fede cattolica, e receverono l'Arcivescovo per suo prelato e jurarono de recever ogn'altro che dal sommo Pontefice Romano sarà mandato. Nell'istesso sinodo se buttarono tutti gli abusi e riti incogniti [non riconosciuti] e se ordinò la maniera come per l'avenire se hanno de governar. A tutte le chiese se pose il suo vigario e se reservano e se facciano molte residenze della Compagnia in diverse parti di quella christianità. Li libri tutti furono presentati all'Arcivescovo, e emendati per il P. Francisco Ros aragonese prefetto della lingua e maestro del Seminario, ajudado dal fratello Joan Maria [Campori] lucchese che arrivando all'Indie, subito fu mandato ad aprendere detta lingua e sta molto approfittato in quella, che me dice he facile e che in due anni se podra ben saper. Questo fratello venendo a Coulam col signor Arcivescovo, dove anco ha molte chiese di quelli cristiani, me mostrò hum quinterno de heresie molto diaboliche, che in detti libri stavano. Nostro Signore sarà servito che a quei buoni principi risponda il progresso che se attende e in grande parte depende dal prelato che di Roma ha da venir[...][38].

Il gesuita Ros, primo vescovo latino

Ho detto che l'iniziativa di un vescovo di Angamale di rito latino sarebbe partita dall'arcivescovo di Goa, de Menezes. Ma il P. Jorge de

---

[38] A. Buccerio S.J., Lettera dal Malabar, 14 dic. 1599. ARSI, Goa 14, f. 414.

Castro, rettore del Collegio di Vaipicotta scrive al P. Generale il 22 dicembre 1597:

> Sono già due anni [...] che la Signoria Vs scrive a Sua Maestà che conviene il prelato sia della Compagnia oppure sia lo stesso de Menezes rinunciando a Goa, come sembra che lui stesso desideri. Ma ho sentito che si fa il nome di P. Francisco Ros, grazie alle lingue che conosce. Mi sembra tuttavia opportuno ricordare a V.P. che questo Padre è limitato in fatto di talento e manca di esperienza di governo, è di spirito piuttosto singolare e bizzarro. Ho paura che crei problemi ai Nostri non appena elevato a dignità. Chiunque venga dal Portogallo sarà più rispettato e meglio dotato di lui[39].

Il P. Ros[40] diviene vescovo di Angamale nel 1600, quando cioè il sinodo di Diamper è stato celebrato. Nel sinodo ha collaborato con l'arcivescovo de Menezes come consigliere. Francisco Ros esprime così al Generale dei gesuiti le sue reazioni quando sa di essere destinato al vescovado:

> Molto Revdo Padre nostro in Christo, Pax Christi, L'anno scorso ho ricevuto una lettera di Vostra Paternità molto lontana dai miei intenti e dai miei lavori, con la quale non poco fui turbato vedendo che facevano nocchiero uno come me che non ha mai saputo remare in un mare tempestoso e pieno di pirati. Per la qual cosa non riuscendo a decidermi ad accettare quell'incarico, resistetti confidando che l'obbedienza non poteva comandarmelo. Ma il Padre Visitatore consultati i padri me lo ordinò per iscritto in forza di santa obbedienza, e io accettai se sua Paternità me lo comandava, vista la necessità di questa Chiesa.[...] presi la croce e andai a Goa[41].

Nella lettera al P. Generale il 28 gennaio 1601 Ros non parla di Diamper ma enumera tre problemi: a) è una *diminutio capitis* la retrocessione dell'archidiocesi di Angamale al rango di semplice diocesi, oltre la subordinazione all'archidiocesi di Goa, b) il vescovo ha bisogno di speciali facoltà dal momento che i Cristiani di S. Tommaso non hanno l'abitudine di ricorrere alla Santa Sede e non lo faranno in nessun caso; c) bisogna trasferire la sede della diocesi da Angamale a Cranganor[42].

---

[39] C. Alonso O.S.A., *Alejo de Meneses O.S.A. Arzobspo de Goa (1595-1612): Estudio biográfico*, Valladolid 1992, 164-165.

[40] Angel Santos Hernandez S.J., "Francisco Ros S.I. Arzobispo de Cranganor, primer obispo jesuita de la India", *Missionalia Hispanica* 5 (1948) 325-393; 6 (1949) 79-142.

[41] ARSI, Goa 15 ff. 30^r-31^v.

[42] C. Alonso O.S.A., *Alejo de Meneses O.S.A. Arzobispo de Goa (1595-1612): Estudio biográfico*, Valladolid 1992, 169.

È comprensibile che la retrocessione dell'archidiocesi di Angamale al grado di semplice diocesi non sia accolta favorevolmente. Infatti i Cristiani del luogo si domandano come mai una Chiesa fondata da un Apostolo e più antica di quella di Goa debba sottomettersi a Goa e si domandano pure come il prelato di Angamale abbia soltanto il titolo di vescovo mentre i suoi predecessori avevano quello di arcivescovo[43]. Di fatto il contenzioso per ricuperare il titolo di arcivescovado incomincia ben presto fin dall'inverno 1601, con lettere dell'archidiacono[44], del capitolo diocesano, del clero e del popolo[45].

Ma consideriamo l'atteggiamento del Ros riguardo al sinodo di Diamper. Sembra quasi che egli non sia d'accordo con l'arcivescovo de Menezes che lo ha indetto e vi ha presieduto. Apparentemente ne prende le distanze e non vi si riconosce quanto alla responsabilità. Ciò apparirebbe da quanto Ros scrive sull'approvazione papale del sinodo di Diamper che de Menezes vuole ottenere. In lettera al P. Generale Claudio Acquaviva del 20 novembre 1603, il vescovo Ros dichiara:

> Il Signor Arcivescovo mi mandò a chiedere le firme del sinodo per inviarle a Sua Santità in vista della conferma. Le ho mandate avvertendo lo stesso Signor Arcivescovo che se Sua Santità conferma quel Sinodo, mette conseguentemente in stato di peccato mortale tutti questi Cristiani che certamente non osserveranno i canoni di quel sinodo. Infatti, per essere sinceri, alcuni di quei canoni del sinodo li ha fatti lo stesso arcivescovo dopo la celebrazione del sinodo e nessuno di quei canoni è stato presentato per eventuali critiche, come si dovrebbe in un sinodo, perché in quel sinodo si sono proposte soltanto regole direttive e prescrizioni, senza cura della comprensione e discussione, come possiamo testimoniare io e i Padri che comprendiamo la lingua[...]. Ecco cosa è avvenuto nel sinodo, come ho fatto notare al Signor Arcivescovo di Goa[46].

Il vescovo Ros rinnega ancora più esplicitamente il sinodo di Diamper scrivendo all'assistente gesuita P. Juan Alvarez il 27 dicembre 1603:

> Ho sentito che l'Arcivescovo di Goa vuole mandare a Roma gli atti del Sinodo che ha celebrato in Diamper quando ha soggiornato in questa terra. E siccome non è stato un vero sinodo perché non si volle dare alcun

---

[43] Alonso, *Alejo de Meneses O.S.A. Arzobspo de Goa (1595-1612)*, op. cit., 170.

[44] Scritta il 20 dicembre 1601. Cfr G. Beltrami, *La Chiesa caldea nel secolo dell'unione*, op. cit. doc. XXIII, 263-267.

[45] Alonso, *Alejo de Meneses O.S.A. Arzobispo de Goa (1595-1612)*, op. cit., 171.

[46] Archivum Romanum Societais Iesu (= ARSI) Goa vol. 15, fol. 155^{r-v}. Alonso, *Alejo de Meneses O.S.A. Arzobispo de Goa (1595-1612)* 173.

ascolto, né i Cristiani si formarono alcuna idea di quanto si trattava, e se hanno firmato lo hanno fatto per mia insistenza, non conviene affatto presentarlo a Sua Santità, infatti alcune cose sono insostenibili e i Cristiani non ne seppero nulla, anzi lo stesso arcivescovo ha redatto alcuni canoni dopo la chiusura del sinodo e all'insaputa dei sinodali[47].

Che non fosse soddisfatto del sinodo di Diamper Ros lo dimostrò anche con il nuovo sinodo che celebrò poco tempo dopo, nel 1603. Purtroppo gli atti di quel sinodo sono andati perduti. Ne restano solo gli statuti redatti dal Ros in base ai canoni che ci rimangono ignoti[48].

D'altra parte l'anno seguente 1604, la Relazione della Serra, le cui ultime sei righe sono autografe di Ros, mentre per la maggior parte ha la calligrafia di Giovanni Maria Campori S.J.[49]. espone i fatti di Diamper in una prospettiva di consenso e di approvazione. Queste contraddizioni del Ros confermerebbero il monito di P. Jorge de Castro, che Padre Ros non era per il governo, essendo uomo "singolare e bizzarro"? Quel documento, menzionato da molti, edito in minima parte da Gregorio M. Antâo[50] e dal prof. J. Kollaparambil[51], è riferito integralmente, in appendice. Qui ne traduciamo il passo su contesto e storia del sinodo di Diamper.

In seguito, nell'anno 1584, si aprì in Vaypicotta, per ordine del padre Alessandro Valignano un seminario per i ragazzi cristiani di San Tommaso, il quale essendo ubicato nella Serra e grazie anche all'industria e al molto lavoro del padre Giorgio de Castro della Compagnia di Gesù, fu accetto ai Cristiani di San Tommaso e subito vi insegnarono i padri della Compagnia le due lingue latina e caldea. Era l'epoca di Mar Abraham e dopo di lui della celebrazione del concilio nel quale vennero messe in ordine molte cose di questa Chiesa. Era infatti venuto l'arcivescovo Don Alessio de Menezes, inviato da sua Santità a visitare i Cristiani di S. Tommaso. Arrivò a Cochim il 2 febbraio del 1599 e lo ricevettero come legittimo prelato l'arcidiacono Giorgio e i notabili dei Cristiani della Serra. Fu accolto con entusiasmo anche perché si esponeva coraggiosamente a rischi. Profondendo con munifica generosità molto denaro in doni, restauri di chiese e opere pie, convocò il Sinodo di Diamper il 22 di giugno 1599, nel

---

47 ARSI, Goa, vol. 15, fol 178^{r-v}.

48 Wicki, "Die Synoden...", 442.

49 Che il MS British Libray Add. 9853, ff. 85-99^{r} sia in gran parte autografo di G. M. Campori S.J. lo afferma J. Kollaparambil introducendone una parziale edizione in *Historical Sources on the Knanites*, Kottayam 1986, 13.

50 Gregorio Magno Antâo, *De Synodi Diamperitani Natura atque Decretis*, Dissertatio ad lauream in Fac. Iuris Canonici P. U. Gregorianae, Goa 1952, Documentum XX pp. 174-177.

51 J. Kollaparambil, *Historical Sources on the Knainites*, Kottayam 1986, Doc. VIII, 13-20.

quale regolarizzò le strutture e la vita di questa Chiesa, costituendo parroci per tutte le 75 curazie, per le quali sua maesta il re provvede ogni anno, attraverso l'arcidiacono, la somma di duemila serafini, oltre il vino da messa. Fu una visita faticosa volendo il prelato recarsi di persona nella maggior parte delle chiese della Serra, ma molto fruttuosa per la simpatia che suscitò nella gente, e l'approvazione incondizionata di tutto il suo operato, benché all'inizio ci fosse un po' di ostilità da parte dell'arcidiacono e dei suoi seguaci, superata però dalla dolcezza e dalla prudenza del prelato. A lui i padri della Compagnia di Gesù mostrarono vari libri caldei eretici che erano riusciti a emendare. Gli manifestarono le difficoltà spirituali della popolazione che aveva bisogno di assistenza pastorale: Il prelato inviò allora dei pastori in luoghi remoti e gesuiti che raggiungessero zone montuose e isolate ove, affrontando rischi e pericoli, battezzassero e costruissero chiese. Provvide pure il prelato queste chiese di immagini, di retabli e di paramenti, di cui erano povere. Amministrò il sacramento della confermazione nella maggior parte del territorio. Ordinò sacerdoti alcuni giovani e sanò situazioni manchevoli in fatto di ordine sacro a causa dell'ignoranza crassa di Mar Abraham. Finalmente dette struttura e dignità di Chiesa a questa cristianità e, a mio giudizio, cosa ammirevole, convinse di anatema, a voce di popolo, il patriarca di Babilonia quale eretico nestoriano, il quale prima era eguagliato al sommo Pontefice. E fece menzionare apertamente nelle pubbliche orazioni il nome del papa come capo di tutta la Chiesa, togliendo invece il nome del patriarca nestoriano come prima facevano. In tal modo spalancò al bene le porte di questa Chiesa. Perciò i Padri della Compagnia che abitano nella Serra sono ora liberi e senza impedimento nel lavorare a vantaggio di questa Chiesa, a gloria di Dio e a salvezza delle anime[52].

GIOVANNI MARIA CAMPORI S.J.

Ros non è comunque il solo gesuita a esprimere riserve sul sinodo di Diamper. Un altro che al tempo del sinodo di Diamper stava studiando per il sacerdozio, il P. Giovanni Maria Campori, scrive all'assistente portoghese in Roma ai primi di gennaio 1604:

> Non posso far a meno di segnalare una cosa di grande importanza: Quando l'arcivescovo di Goa venne a visitare la Serra e celebrò un concilio, non ne ebbe, a dire il vero l'ordine e il carattere, dal momento che aggiungeva a suo piacere, perfino a cose fatte, disposizioni che non si lessero nemmeno in pubblico o furono lette con tale fretta e confusione che i presenti non poterono, non dico approvarle, ma nemmeno capirle[53].

---

[52] Originale portoghese in British Library, Ms. Add 9853, ff. 93^{v}-94^{r}. Nostra versione italiana. Si veda nell'Appendice IV il testo originale con traduzione inglese.

[53] Alonso, *Alejo de Meneses O.S.A. Arzobspo de Goa (1595-1612)*, 174.

Mi piace soffermarmi su questo gesuita italiano perché la sua testimonianza dimostra che non si può comunque assolvere i gesuiti a Diamper. Giovanni Maria Campori nasce a Corsagna in provincia di Lucca nel 1574. Entra nella Compagnia nel 1592. Il P. Generale Claudio Acquaviva lo invia in India prima ancora del sacerdozio e gli raccomanda di tenerlo informato con frequenti lettere. Dopo essersi dedicato allo studio del siriaco, si consacra all'apprendimento della lingua malayalam. Divenuto sacerdote è scelto come segretario dell'arcivescovo Ros. È trovato morto inaspettatamente nel suo letto, a Cranganore, all'età di 47 anni, l'8 novembre 1621. Campori scrive all'Aquaviva il 5 gennaio 1598:

Molto Revdo Padre Generale, Pax Christi, È piaciuto alla provvidenza del buon Giesù adempirmi un desiderio che egli medesimo mi haveva inspirato, di andare in qualche paese dove se bene per adesso non sono atto per travagliar nella conversione dell'anime, almeno mentre acciò mi apparecchi con studi di lettere e di lingue, non mi mancasse pericolo di patire per amor di nostro Signore. Il P. Visitatore due dì anti di partire mi avvisò ch'io fossi con lui senza dirmi dove ed arrivati in Cocin mi mandò in questa residenza di Vaipicotta tra li Cristiani di S. Thomé justa di queste montagne di Malavar e soggetta al re di Coccin, dove se bene non habbiamo molta materia di conversioni, non ci manca però di reducioni all'ovile di S. Pietro. Di questa Christianità non mancherò sempre di dar avviso a vostra Paternità per compire al santo obbligo che mi impose costì; e per procurar il bene di questi Christiani quanto posso. Mi trovo qua tanto consolato che non lo posso explicare, perché vedo questa gente con tanta semplicità, tanto capace delle cose di Dio, e tanto devota che certo credo se havessero pastori che con erbe salutifere le pascolassero, tenendoli en tanta reverenza come tengono, fariano mille gradini nello spirito, donde per lo contrario, havendo havuto insino adesso cassanarii, stanno pieni di superstizioni e ignoranze, dalle quali vanno ogni giorno li nostri tirandoli e spero che si farà grandissimo frutto se non saremo impediti dal buon zelo, *sed non secundum scientiam* di altri che vanno subseminando zizzanie. *Sed maior est Deus corde magno.* Vostra Paternità mi intenderà per una [lettera] del P. Stefano de Brito superiore in questa Casa. Non posso fare per l'amore che già tengo concepito a queste anime di non pregare con tutto il cuore Vostra Paternità per le viscere di quel dolcissimo Iddio che pose l'anima sua per queste pecorelle e per le affezioni e devozione particolare che tiene al glorioso S. Thomaso Apostolo che procuri di remediare a questi pericoli, e favorire con tutte le sue grazie queste piante apostoliche/acciò che piantate da S. Thomaso irrigate per mezzo di Vostra Paternità e di noi altri suoi figli con l'incremento che Nostro Signore va promettendo possino dare quel frutto che a maggior gloria di Dio tutti desideriamo. Alli suoi santi sacrificij e orazioni caldissimamente mi raccomando, perché possa meritare quello che con un'aria tesa ci minacciò l'antivigilia di Natale un Naire gentile per che prohibirono li Padri certe cerimonie che al demonio alcuni gentili facevano vicino alla nostra chiesa [...] Di Vaipicotta alli 5 gennaio 1598 di V P servo e figlio in Xto Jesu Gio: Maria Campori[54].

Un'altra lettera del Campori al Padre Generale Claudio Acquaviva, del 2 dicembre 1599 indica chiararamente la strategia di "restituire questi Christiani alla purità anticha della fede e della vera dottrina e costumi". Quanto ai testi siriaci dei Cristiani di S. Tommaso, il Campori che conosce il siriaco, annuncia che andrà "per emendare molti libri che, per la fretta che aveva il signor arcivescovo di Goa, non si potevano corregere".

Molto Reverendo in Xto Padre, La grazia dello Spirito Santo, la charità di Gesù Cristo, l'amore della Vergine Madre di Dio sia con tutti. Amen. Se bene dalle lettere annue e dal Padre Alberto Laertij intenderà Vostra Paternità il copioso frutto, quale han raccolto quest'anno gli operarij di questo campo dico della Christianità che chiamano di S. Thomaso, in questi monti del Malavare, e qualmente il benignissimo Padre dalla persecuzione nata contra li figlioli di questa sua minima Compagnia, sapientissimamente cavò l'universale riduttione di 80.000 anime al grembo della santa Chiesa Romana; con tutto ciò mi è parso bene soddisfare a quello che Vostra Paternità mi [co]mandò [cioè di tenerlo informato], con questa [lettera]; nella quale solamente gli dirò il grandissimo contento che gode l'anima mia in vedere che Nostro Signore è stato servito di chiamarmi a questa vigna nella cultivatione della qual tanto si serve a Sua Divina Maestà e alla mia dolcissima madre religione per che si bene il principal frutto che qui si ottiene è il restituire questi Christiani alla purità anticha della fede e della vera dottrina e costumi con tutto ciò speriamo nella misericordia del Signore, Padre delle misericordie, e Dio di tutte le consolationi, che aprirà in questo Malavare una grandissima porta alla generale conversione di tutta questa gentilità, il che è tanto facile alla sua infinita potentia. e già ce ne va dando alcuna mostra, come intenderà Vostra Paternità dalle lettere del P. Francisco Ros, il quale come credo le darà notizia della conversione di un parente del Rei di Calicut, e di un altra signora principalissima nell'istesso regno e se Nostro Signore apre gli occhi ad uno di questi principi malavari, si spera che facilissimamente tutti abbracceranno la nostra santa fede. Insino adesso mi sono occupato per mandato dell'obbedientia nella lingua caldea, da qui per diante mi impiegherò nella malavare, per poter meglio con questi due talenti travagliare per sua maggior gloria. Fra sette o otto giorni anderò con il P. Rettore discorrendo per alcuni castelli que[sic] restavano /per emendar molti libri, che per la fretta che aveva il signor arcivescovo di Goa, non si potevano corregere. Prego Vostra Paternità che ci faccia charità di mandare altri libri suriani principalmente della Sacra Scrittura perché in tutta questa diocesi non si ritrova una biblia intera suriana. E

---

[54] ARSI, Goa 14, 359^{r-v}.

con questa finale alli Santi sacificij e orationi di Vostra Paternità infinitamente mi raccomando, pregandola che con quell'amore particolare con il quali il Signore mi amò oltre ogni mio merito mi mandi la sua beneditione. Dal Collegio di santa † (Croce) alli due de dicembre 1599[55].

Ma dello stesso Campori vogliamo riferire la lettera del 25 novembre 1599. È riportata in latino sotto la voce "Diamperiense Concilium Provinciale habitum anno 1599" da Antonio Possevino S.J. in *Apparatus sacer ad Scriptores veteris et novi Testamenti Eorum Interpretes. Synodos etc. Tomus primus.* Tratta specificamente del sinodo di Diamper e del contributo che i gesuiti gli hanno dato. Le primissime righe, del Possevino, introducono la testimonianza del protagonista, Giovanni Maria Campori S.J.

Quel sinodo provinciale fu celebrato l'anno 1599 dall'arcivescovo di Goa, a Diamper che si trova in Asia, presso la città detta di S. Tommaso. Quel sinodo non ha inaugurato la fede cattolica, ma l'ha portata a compimento, restituendole tutto quanto appartiene alla disciplina ecclesiastica. E affinché ciò si comprenda facilmente, giova che uno dei testimoni che vi ha assistito dall'inizio alla fine, ne scriva ai Nostri. Ed ecco cosa ne scrive:[56]

L'arcidiacono gradatamente si esime dall'obbedire all'arcivescovo, rifiuta di accompagnarlo, riceve coloro che l'arcivescovo ha scomunicato, non toglie la menzione del nome del patriarca; e protesta in molte maniere che sanno di empietà. Pochi giorni dopo l'arcivescovo indice il solenne conferimento degli Ordini sacri. L'arcidiacono si sforza di impedire quel grande aumento di potere, incute timore negli ordinandi e nei loro parenti, ma invano. Il sabato prima della Domenica di Passione l'arcivescovo promuove molti agli ordini sacri, mentre quanti partecipano alla liturgia, tutti lodano le sacre cerimonie della Chiesa Romana. Dopo le quali l'arcivescovo si reca a *Carturte* [Kaduthuruthy] per celebrarvi i riti della Setttimana Santa. Con solenne cerimonia benedice le palme, il giovedì santo *in Coena Domini* consacra il crisma; lava con lacrime e acqua i piedi di dodici sacerdoti. E ripone il sacro Corpo di Cristo come nel sepolcro. L'azione dello Spirito Santo aggiunge vigore alle sacre cerimonie, una grande folla di gente è mossa da Dio al cospetto dei divini misteri, i cuori impietriti s'inteneriscono e si spezzano, sgorgano lacrime dal ciglio, gli occhi che non si inumidiscono sono reputati sacrileghi, tutti gridano, mescolando voci e lacrime: Questi è il nostro Pastore, noi siamo le sue pecorelle, vogliamo accoglierlo e ascoltare la sua voce. I mercenarii di Babilonia, i lupi rapaci se ne vadano in perdizione, s'allontanino da noi gli operatori di iniquità, perché Dio ha voluto essere con noi munifico;

---

55 ARSI Goa 14, 405^{r-v}.

56 Ant. Possevini Societatis Iesu, *Apparatus Sacer ad Scriptores veteris et novi Testamenti. Eorum Interpretes, Synodos etc., Tribus Tomis distinctus. Tomus Primus,* Venetiis MDCVI, 392.

siamo figli della Chiesa di Roma che confessiamo capo e maestra di tutte le Chiese. E tali convinzioni già possedute nel cuore erano confessate con la bocca e con gli occhi a loro salvezza. Quale fosse allora la gioia dell'arcivescovo, quali i suoi sentimenti, dichiaravano gli impeti di lacrime che riempivano di gioia la città di Dio. Nel giorno poi sacrosanto della Resurrezione si svolse una processione in pompa magna. Il P. Francesco Ros, tenne al popolo una toccante predica, con tale frutto che se ancora ci fosse stata una goccia di veleno, anche quella avrebbe cacciata del tutto, e l'intera società sarebbe risorta con Cristo alla vera vita della fede cattolica. E l'arcivescovo con massimo frutto ritornò all'idea che se l'arcidiacono non avesse voluto obbedire dovrebbe esser deposto e sostituito con un altro. Perciò gli inviò una lettera ammonendolo a ritrattarsi e, a certe condizioni, a recarsi entro sei giorni a Vaipicotta, altrimenti sarebbe considerato eretico pertinace e pubblico. Questi, preso dal timore, risponde di accettare le condizioni e di essere pronto ad obbedirlo in tutto. Frattanto chiede per lettera al Padre Fr. Ros di recarsi dove lo stesso arcivescovo aspetterebbe l'arcidiacono pentito. Ros, quale padre dai sentimenti paterni esorta l'arcidacono e lo scongiura perché ponga fine agli scandali, abbia pietà della sua anima, consideri a quali pericoli si esponga, riconosca invece la clemenza del vescovo, la sua disponibilità, non abusi della pazienza divina che lo chiama a penitenza; non ponga la sua speranza nella forza del braccio, ricordi, lui che ha confidato nel loro aiuto che i Re sono infedeli e non lo sosterrebbero in futuro. Fu vinto finalmente sia dalle parole del Padre, sia dal timore e si diresse verso l'arcivescovo. Quegli allora come genitore misericordioso abbraccia il figliol prodigo e gli concede il perdono, donandogli una croce preziosissima in segno di affetto e promette qualcosa di più grande se persista nel buon volere[57].

Ecco allora come il Campori descrive il vero e proprio sinodo di Diamper. È il pieno trionfalismo della cultura romano-cattolica.

Il giorno seguente l'arcivescovo indice nella Chiesa il concilio provinciale per estirpare le eresie, per correggere i costumi, espellere le superstizioni, e regolare ogni cosa spettante al culto divino. Tutti gli ecclesiastici sono convocati per lettera, oltre a quattro notabili per ogni villaggio. Con gioia universale e consenso comune lo celebrano nella città di Diamper, dove anatematizzano le eresie, i loro capi, i seguaci e specialmente il patriarca di Babilonia. Mentre riconoscono il Romano Pontefice come Vicario di Cristo e capo della Chiesa e promettono a lui obbedienza: obbligandosi con giuramento a non ricever alcun vescovo se non inviato dalla Santa Sede. Alla fine sono costituiti parroci per ogni chiesa, cosa nuova per questa diocesi. A loro sostentamento lo stesso arcivescovo assegna dalle sue rendite annualmente mille monete d'oro. Il pio pastore ha speso in questa visita circa sedici mila pezzi d'oro. Ma il frutto è mille volte tanto[58].

---

[57] Id., Ibidem, 392-393. Cfr Appendix III, Introduzione di Possevino + nn. 1-5.

[58] Id., Ibidem, 393. Cfr Appendix III, nn. 6-7.

Viene quindi il dopo-sinodo con tutte le conseguenze della vittoria romana.

> Concluso il sinodo, l'arcivescovo inizia la visita di tutta la diocesi perché siano mandati ad esecuzione i canoni legittimamente redatti nel concilio. Quindi parte alla volta di Angamale [metropoli della diocesi e sede del vescovo] dove è ricevuto trionfalmente. Il terreno è ricoperto di candidi lini, di fiori e di fronde. Lo precedono circa trecento notabili in festa, lo seguono altri i quali giostrano le loro armi con la massima rapidità. Un'immensa moltitudine di gente batte le mani, canta, percuote timpani, dà fiato a trombe, riempie l'aria di acclamazioni, né mancano le armi da fuoco per manifestare con gli spari la gioia per l'arrivo di tanto personaggio. Questi conferisce al massimo numero di uomini il sacramento della cresima. I sacerdoti assenti al concilio fanno ora pubblica abiura delle eresie e della soggezione al patriarca. Promettono di obbedire al Romano pontefice, così come nel concilio è stato stabilito[59].

E a questo trionfo della concezione cattolica romana il gesuita Campori è fiero di aver personalmente contribuito quale figlio di Ignazio di Loyola. Purtroppo tanto zelo per la causa di Roma suscita giustificate reazioni, non solo dei Cristiani Orientali che si sono occupati negli ultimi tempi del sinodo di Diamper, ma anche della scienza la quale, come scriveva a ragione il siriacista Jean-Baptiste Chabot, si indigna del rogo di manoscritti siriaci insostituibili "La destruction des exemplaires qui ont péri est donc regrettable"[60].

> Frattanto il P. Francesco Ros e io ci occupiamo dell'esame dei libri, distruggendo, smembrando, gettando nel fuoco volumi interi, senza che io riesca a esprimere con quanta gioia lo facciamo. Abbiamo impiegato dodici interi giorni in questo lavoro. Tutti i volumi del precedente vescovo e di sacerdoti li abbiamo restituiti alla purezza cattolica o li abbiamo dati alle fiamme. Tutti ritenevano che quest'opera di bonifica fosse miracolosa. Infatti prima erano così attaccati a quei libri che non ci permettevano neppure di aprirli. Adesso invece lasciano senza difficoltà che noi li cancelliamo, li smembriamo e perfino li bruciamo totalmente[61].

Se de Menezes campeggia come principale responsabile, i gesuiti si sforzano di servirlo nella sua strategia acculturante. Traducono dal

---

[59] Id., Ibidem, 393. Cfr Appendix III, nn. 8-10.

[60] J.-B. Chabot, "L'Autodafé des livres syriaques du Malabar", *Florilegium ou Recueil de Travaux dédiés à Melchior de Vogüé*, Paris 1909, 613-623; Geevarghese Chediath, "The Syriac Manuscripts Burned by Order of the Synod of Diamper (1599)", R. Lavenant S.J. (Ed.), *V Symposium Syriacum 1988*, (= OCA 236) Rome 1990, 409-422.

[61] Ant. Possevini Societatis Iesu, *Apparatus Sacer ad Scriptores veteris et novi Testamenti. Eorum Interpretes, Synodos etc., Tribus Tomis distinctus. Tomus Primus*, Venetiis MDCVI, 393. Cfr Appendix III, n. 11.

latino in siraco, perché patristica, liturgia, pastorale abbiano presso i Cristiani di S. Tommaso l'impronta latina.

L'arcivescovo continua la visita, come attesta lui stesso, con la massima soavità. Dovunque è ricevuto come buon pastore e ne esercita l'ufficio. Cresima, battezza, caccia le concubine dei sacerdoti sposati; vestito di paramenti pontificali insegna con massimo frutto la dottrina cristiana ai bambini e alle bambine, servendosi come interpreti degli alunni del nostro seminario, predica quotidianamente, sempre elargendo elemosine ai poveri. I re del Malabar accorrono a vedere questo alto personaggio che tratta con tanta umiltà le sue pecorelle. Lui stesso stabilisce quanto è necessario al bene della Chiesa, e procura le cotte, l'astuccio per conservare il crisma, l'altare consacrato, le vesti necessarie alla messa, per ogni singola chiesa. Fa tradurre al p. Francesco Ros dal latino in siriaco l'ordo del battesimo, dell'unzione degli infermi, della celebrazione delle nozze e lo consegna ai singoli parroci insieme con la dottrina cristiana in lingua malabarica[62].

È una "Chiesa diversa" che si ottiene con questi sforzi ai quali partecipano sia pure in sott'ordine i gesuiti, ma con tanto zelo che di tutto il bene operato "ne sono autori essi stessi"! È la ammissione pubblica di corresponsabilità gesuita a Diamper. Lo proclamano senza mezzi termini. I gesuiti sono "partecipi di tutto attraverso il consiglio, lo zelo, il lavoro anzi, per meglio dire ne sono autori loro stessi".

Dovunque noi esaminiamo i libri, li purghiamo con la massima cura, tanto che si direbbe una Chiesa diversa. Infatti adesso risuona ovunque il nome del pontefice romano, di Agostino, di Gerolamo, di Ambrogio e degli altri santi che la Chiesa cattolica venera e di cui si ascoltano i santissimi nomi. Tace ora Nestorio e tace la bocca svergognata degli altri eretici. Adesso è più frequente l'uso dei sacramenti secondo la tradizione della Chiesa di Roma e il campo del Signore promette ovunque la massima fecondità nella messe. Sarebbe troppo vasto scrivere detagliatamente di tutto. I Padri della Compagnia, guidati dall'amore per la salvezza del prossimo, divorati da zelo indefesso, guidano l'arcivescovo, e gli danno suggerimenti, partecipi di tutto attraverso il consiglio, lo zelo, il lavoro anzi, per meglio dire, ne sono autori loro stessi! L' arcivescovo riconosce la nostra opera, proclama a tutti la nostra diligenza, loda l'istituto della Compagnia. Ve lo dice Giovanni Maria Campori, S.J. del collegio della Compagnia in Vaipicotta nell'India orientale 28 nov 1599 che aggiunge pure di quanti errori fossero pieni quei libri nestoriani come testimoniano gli altri suoi scritti che stanno già presso di noi[63].

---

[62] Id., Ibidem, 393-394. Cfr Appendix III, nn. 12-13.

[63] Id., Ibidem, 394. Cfr Appendix III, nn. 13-15 + Colofone.

Wicki ricorda come Gouvea sia indotto a scrivere la *Jornada* per riparare all'imperdonabile lacuna del vistatore gesuita Nicolau Pimenta che in una sua lettera attribuisce ai soli gesuiti il merito di Diamper ignorando Menezes[64].

Paragone con De Nobili

Ho voluto riferire questo testo di un giovane gesuita, appena venticinquenne e non ancora sacerdote. Scriveva senza malizia e senza secondi fini lasciandoci la testimonianza spontanea e disarmante di quanto abbiano fatto i gesuiti nel sinodo e attorno al sinodo del quale, come Campori afferma "ne sono autori loro stessi". Non si può quindi assolvere i gesuiti per non aver commesso il fatto. Semmai ci si può chiedere come mai essi abbiano commesso un errore di tattica così grave proprio nel tempo in cui con de Nobili e con Ricci realizzano una inculturazione saggia e coraggiosa? Non soltanto Subrahmanyan, ma anche Suttner nell'articolo citato all'inizio si pone lo stesso problema.

> Quello che abbiamo dovuto riferire del Malabar [...], avviene contemporaneamente a quella strategia di adattamento della vita cristiana alla cultura dell'India, alla cui guida sta Roberto de Nobili. Anzi nell'Asia Orientale dei secoli XV-XVII quella strategia dell'adattamento era caratterisica della maggioranza dei gesuiti, pensiamo a Matteo Ricci e Adam Schall. Alessandro Valignano che era provinciale dell'India al tempo delle accuse di eresia rivolte da Ros ai Cristiani di S. Tommaso era molto aperto riguardo all'apostolato *ad gentes*. Come poteva la stessa autorità alla testa della missione di Goa dirigere due opposte politiche della caccia alle eresie e della tolleranza dei riti locali?[65].

> C'è però un'essenziale differenza. [...] Ai non cristiani [... i gesuiti] concedevano un certo adattamento. Lo scopo era di vestire all'indiana, alla cinese o alla giapponese il cristianesimo locale. Il problema era del tutto diverso nei confronti dei Cristiani di San Tommaso[...]. Il loro Cristianesimo non era venuto dall'occidente e neppure attraverso la storia del pensiero greco-latino. Non si trattava di modifiche secondarie. Presso i Cristiani di San Tommaso [...] i gesuiti trovarono delle maniere tradizionali di essere cristiani basate su una concezione ecclesiologica cui era aliena la soggezione diretta al vescovo di Roma e perciò non potevano conciliarle con il proprio patrimonio latino-occidentale. Ciò era impossibile a latini del secolo XVII, convinti della *praestantia ritus latini*. che sarà espressa

[64] Wicki, "Die Synoden...", 358.

[65] E. Ch. Suttner, "Die Jesuiten und der christliche Osten", *Stimmen der Zeit* 209 (1991) 466.

da Benedetto XIV nell'enciclica *Etsi pastoralis* del 1742 [...] Il gesuita W. de Vries esplicita la concezione di Benedetto XIV e conseguentemente dei gesuiti in Malabar. [...] La *praestantia* ovvero la superiorità del rito latino nei confronti di tutti gli altri riti della Chiesa è un assioma che regge tutta la sua politica nei confronti dell'Oriente cristiano. Questa superiorità si basa sull'essere il rito della santa Chiesa di Roma, la madre e la maestra di tutte le Chiese. Perfino i riti greci sorti indipendentemente dalla Chiesa di Roma e sottratti dopo lo scisma alla sorveglianza romana sono guardati con sospetto da Benedetto XIV come pure da alcuni suoi predecessori. [...] Dice infatti lo stesso papa nella costituzione *Allatae sunt* "La sede apostolica accertando che un rito pericoloso o disdicevole si è infiltrato nelle Chiese di Oriente, lo condanna, lo rigetta e proibisce. La S. Sede non ha mai cessato di proibire singoli riti ai Greci pure di uso inveterato, ogni volta che ha dovuto constatare che erano dannosi, cattivi o potevano diventarlo"[66].

Mi piace constatare come Suttner non manchi di citare il gesuita Wilhelm de Vries, del Pontificio Istituto Orientale, preoccupato di un aggiornamento dell'esercizio del primato del papa. Come è stato affermato da Subrahmanyam riguardo al sinodo di Diamper, che si davano tra gli stessi gesuiti dei *severi* e dei *flessibili*, forse si può sfumare la tesi del Suttner che i gesuiti non potevano avere altro atteggiamento che quello avuto. In realtà la tesi di Suttner è troppo "cartesiana" per accontentare completamente lo storico. Chissà cosa avrebbe detto dell'articolo del Suttner il P. Josef Wicki S.J., uno dei maggiori competenti, editore dei diciotto volumi di *Documenta Indica* e autore di saggi sui sinodi di Malabar (1583-1603) e sulla canonicità del sinodo di Diamper[67]. Purtroppo quei volumi di documenti si arrestano proprio alla soglia del sinodo. Bisogna continuare il lavoro del Wicki. Solo un indagine completa sui documenti di prima mano può approfondire ulteriormente la questione della responsabilità gesuita a Diamper. Suttner paragona a ragione l'attività gesuita presso i Cristiani di S. Tommaso con quella dei gesuiti in Etiopia. L'approccio è simile e le cause degli insuccessi sono le stesse. Ma come è storicamente errato rilevare soltanto colpe dei gesuiti nei confronti dei Cristiani d'Etiopia, così è altrettanto parziale e incompleto presentare Diamper soltanto come frutto di errori gesuiti. Secondo Joâo Paulo Oliveira e Costa, verso gli anni trenta del secolo XVI,

---

[66] Id., Ibidem, 466-467.

[67] J. Wicki, "Die Synode von Diamper in Malabar (1599) und ihre Beurteilung (1600-1975)", *Ann Hist Concil* 9 (1977) 190-205; Idem, "Die Synoden der Thomaschristen (auch Syromalabaren genannt) (1583-1603) *Ann Hist Conc* 18 (1986) 337-447.

prese a intensificarsi un rapporto fra Portoghesi e Cristiani di San Tommaso che permetteva il realizzarsi di posizioni moderate che prevedevano l'appoggio esplicito del più alto dignitario della Chiesa siro-malabarese, a un graduale adattamento ai costumi occidentali [...]. Si sarebbe trattato di un avvicinamento reciproco senza misure radicali come quelle di Diamper o il rogo dei libri eretici legato a quel sinodo[...]. Fu invece il comportamento dei dignitari del Regno e di molti membri del clero a deludere gli Indiani. Infatti nel 1556 l'arrivo del vescovo caldeo Mar Abraham riempì di gioia la comunità malabarese, mentre spinse i Portoghesi a reagire con autoritarismo anche contro le disposizioni del Re[68].

Comunque, insieme al testo latino della lettera del Campori che afferma decisamente la corresponsabilità dei gesuiti, ritengo necessario dare alle stampe anche tutta la *Relaçâo sobre a Serra* redatta l'anno 1604, di cui soltanto pochi brani sono stati finora pubblicati. In quella appaiono tanti elementi positivi di zelo, di interesse per la cristianità locale, di studio della sua lingua sacra il siriaco e della sua lingua viva, il malayalam, di ricerche sulla storia della comunità fin dalla sua nascita, che l'accusa di colpevolezza rivolta senza discriminazione ai Ros, ai Campori, ai Laerzio, ai Fenicio e ai Toscano, apre la strada perlomeno a molte attenuanti, se non alla loro assoluzione. Secondo Wicki, Ros avrebbe impedito, con la sua competenza in siriaco e in malayalam, la totale latinizzazione dei Cristiani malabaresi[69]. *La Relaçâo sobre a Serra* documenta questa linea di condotta:

Nell'anno 1541 i religiosi di San Francesco aprirono un seminario a Cranganore nel quale insegnavano latino e buoni costumi a ragazzi cristiani di S. Tommaso che entravano in quel seminario e vi si formavano su ottime basi educative. In seguito però, siccome distoglievano questi cassanari dal celebrare col pane lievitato e li persuadevano a mangiare pesce in giorno di digiuno e altre simili cose che a loro dispiacevano e siccome i sacerdoti latini che i detti padri formavano imponevano rigorosamente cose di nessuna importanza per la salvezza, per esempio dissuadendo dalle antiche abitudini nei giorni di digiuno, anzi obbligando a cominciare la quaresima il mercoledì delle ceneri e proibendo le riunioni in chiesa a mangiare insieme pane benedetto, come abbiamo menzionato. Per il loro attaccamento alla tradizione i Cristiani di San Tommaso si dispiacquero e si allontanarono, perché i sacerdoti che i religiosi formavano erano di rito latino e pretendevano cambiare i loro costumi, tanto che quei sacerdoti non trovarono posto nella Serra. Dimodoche il detto seminario di Cranganore rimase fino ad oggi seminario del vescovado di Cochim, senza che un solo rimanesse nella Serra, come è risaputo [...] In seguito, nell'anno

---

68 J. P. Oliveira e Costa, "Os Portugueses e a cristandade siro-malabar (1498-1530)", *Studia*, Lisboa 52 (1994) 121-178, qui 168-169.

69 Wicki, "Die Synoden...", 429-432.

1584, si aprì in Vaypicotta, per ordine del padre Alessandro Valignano un seminario per i ragazzi cristiani di San Tommaso, il quale essendo ubicato nella Serra e grazie anche all'industria e al molto lavoro del padre Giorgio de Castro della Compagnia di Gesù, fu accetto ai Cristiani di San Tommaso e subito vi insegnarono i padri della Compagnia le due lingue latina e caldea[70].

Anche la *Relatione delli christiani di S. Tomaso* redatta dal P. Alberto Laertio S.J. nell'anno 1600 si esprime in questo senso riguardo ai Cristiani di S. Tommaso

3. Né si pensi che se gli potrà levare in alcun tempo la lingua caldea e introdurli nella latina, perché è impossibile, havendola loro sempre usata, ed è tanta l'affettione che ci portano che questa saria causa di gran rumore tra loro, et si esporria a pericolo evidente di perderli tutti.

6. Pare anco necessario che il vescovo hora di nuovo consacrato, ancorché lui sia latino, possa celebrare in caldeo le Messe et offici divini, poiché è vescovo de' sacerdoti del rito caldeo, et loro hanno da aiutare nelle Messe e offici pontificali, ché altrimenti non potria fare le loro feste [...] né saria da loro havuto per vescovo, né amato, né obbedito etc. [...] anzi questo medesimo ancora si desidera che si conceda alli padri della Compagnia che hanno fra loro e sanno il caldeo, perché con ciò saranno da loro molto più amati et faranno maggior frutto[71].

Non possiamo dimenticare le pagine dolorose del passato, ma dobbiamo trarne insegnamento. Perché non avrebbe potuto attuarsi proprio quanto il P. de Giorgiis deprecava come blasfemo, cioè che quella Cristianità mantenesse la sua autonomia e la sua dipendenza immediata da un patriarca orientale. Alcuni gesuiti e anche non gesuiti hanno creduto allora impossibile quella soluzione. Ma altri gesuiti non la escludevano come appare dalla lettera citata del P. Antonio de Monserrate S.J. Egli infatti, scrivendo da Cochin il 12 gennaio 1579 al Padre Generale Everardo Mercuriano, sintetizza così le possibili alternative per la Chiesa siro-malabarese: "o dipendere immediatamente dal Papa; oppure dipendere mediatamente dal Papa e immediatamente dal Patriarca di Siria; o, altrimenti, dipendere immediatamente dall'arcivescovo di Goa e mediatamente dal Papa"[72].

---

[70] Originale portoghese in British Library, Ms. Add 9853, f. 93^{v}. Nostra versione italiana. Cfr Appendix III, nn. 23-24.

[71] Alberto Laertio S.J., *Relatione delli christiani di S. Tomaso.* Doc. XXXII in G. Beltrami, *La Chiesa Caldea nel secolo dell'Unione*, OC N. 83 (Romae, Januario-martio 1933) pp. 260-262.

[72] G. Beltrami, *La Chiesa caldea nel secolo dell'unione,* OC N. 83 (Romae, Januario-martio 1933) p. 130. Questo documento è stato edito integralmente nell'originale portoghese da J. Wicki, *Documenta Indica*, XI, 505-528, qui 528.

L'alternativa consacrata a Diamper è la dipendenza immediata dall'arcivescovo di Goa. Tuttavia, secondo il gesuita de Monserrate, la stessa dipendenza immediata dal Patriarca caldeo era degna di considerazione. Del resto, apparirebbe da quanto ho scritto, che una prima reazione entusiasta di gesuiti al sinodo di Diamper, venisse subito dopo seguita da critiche di alcuni di loro, per esempio di Ros e di Campori, sulla maniera in cui il sinodo era stato condotto e dei pesi eccessivi che aveva gettato sulle spalle dei Cristiani di San Tommaso. Il Ros se ne sarebbe reso conto ben presto, una volta divenuto vescovo di quei Cristiani.

Pontificio Istituto Orientale
Piazza S. Maria Maggiore, 7
00185 Roma

Vincenzo Poggi, S.J.

George Nedungatt, S.J.

THE SYNOD OF DIAMPER AND THE UNION OF BREST A COMPARISON

The Synod of Diamper (1599) was held in the Thomaschristian Church of Malabar just three years after the Union of Brest (1595-1596) of the Ruthenian Church. Though these two events were not historically related, they have some remarkable similarities as well as some significant differences. While Brest was indeed a union synod, Diamper was not. However, the latter, too, is often seen or presented as if it were a union synod. A comparison between the two can shed light on this question and help us evaluate the significance of these two ecclesial events that took place at the close of the convulsed sixteenth century. Obviously, in a short communication like this all that can and need be attempted is a short sketch with a minimum of essential bibliography.[1]

1. THE UNION OF BREST (1595-1596)

The Union of Brest did not come about overnight, it was long in remote preparation and had a few antecedents. With the hope of obtaining western military help against the forces of the Mongols or Tartars, King Daniil of Galizia (1240-1264) and Volinia, had entered into union with the Roman Church and was crowned king of Rus' in 1253. Freed from the Mongol yoke in the second half of the fourteenth century, and with the state capital shifted from Kiev to Vilna, a large section of the clergy and people were open to the Western culture. Most of Ukraine came under Catholic Lithuania in the fourteenth century. Though a union with the See of Rome was then brought about at the Council of Florence (1439) by Metropolitan Isidore of Kiev, it was short-lived. However, the seeds of union had been sowed. After several intermittent attempts, under the Polish domination and as a result of Jesuit activity, a fresh union between

[1] For a more ample treatment and bibliography, see Bernard Dupuy, "L'Union de Brest jugée avec le recul de temps, *Istina* 25 (1990) 17-49; *Analecta Ordinis S. Basilii Magni* 15 (1996) 1-459 (various articles); bibliography, pp. 521-551.

Rome and Kiev was effected at Brest (1595-1596), where the Ruthenian hierarchy of Ukraine and Bielorussia ratified the deed.[2]

The Union of Brest was primarily the initiative of the Ruthenian hierarchy itself. The opponents and detractors of this Union have misrepresented it as an imposition of the king of Poland, yielding to the pressures of the papacy and/or of the Jesuits. So, too, the Synod of Diamper has often been misrepresented as a union synod. The fact is that the Ruthenian bishops themselves took the first steps in view of the several advantages they saw in union with Rome.[3] Ecclesial communion was still understood in the East to be communion with, in, and through a patriarchate, as in the first millennium, and the Ruthenian bishops knew that only through association with a patriarchal centre would their Church have a standing and be able to make progress in the rather decadent conditions of their Church. They could possibly consider three such centres: Moscow, Constantinople, and Rome. In 1589 the Patriarchate of Moscow had been established, but it was feared that hierarchical communion with Moscow could have negative political repercussions leading to absorption and the loss of even lawful autonomy. Secondly, there was Constantinople, which, however, was struggling to survive under the Turkish yoke, and therefore not much help could be hoped for from such a weak centre. So the bishops unanimously turned to Rome. In a Provincial Synod held in June 1595 they drafted certain Articles as "guarantees" by the Holy Apostolic Roman See that their Eastern traditions, like communion under both species and married clergy, would be maintained and that their Church life uplifted and promoted. In general, their Eastern rite was to be treated on a parity with the Latin rite. They delegated two bishops to take their request of union to Rome. Their letter to the pope was signed by all the eight members of the hierarchy of the Kievan Church. In Rome, the two delegates made the Profession of Faith in the name of the entire Ruthenian hierarchy: The formula used contained the addition of the *filioque* to the Nicene-Constantinopolitan Creed, though in the Articles the bishops had affirmed the procession of the Holy Spirit "from

---

[2] Oscar Halecki, *From Florence to Brest*, (Sacrum Poloniae Millennium, 5), Rome, 1958; reimpression, Hamden, Conn., Ed. Archon Books, 1968.

[3] Sophia Senyk, "L'unione di Brest," in *Storia religiosa russa*, ed. Luciano Vaccaro, Gazzada, La Casa di Matriona, 1984, pp. 97-111, at p. 105; idem, "Vicissitudes de l'Union de Brest au XVII° siècle," *Irénikon* 65 (1992) 462-487; idem, "The Background of the Union of Brest," *Analecta Ordinis S. Basilii Magni* 15 (1996) 103-144.

the Father through the Son," according to the ecumenically agreed formula of the Council of Florence. The use of the former formula did not mean the exclusion of the latter, which they could still use. The union was approved by Pope Clement VIII with the apostolic constitution *Magnus Dominus et laudabilis* issued on the same day, 23 December 1595. And the union was ratified on 8 October 1596 in the Provincial Synod of Brest in the presence of three papal representatives and three representatives of the king of Poland, all of whom were officials of Lithuania. Its decree was signed by Metropolitan Michael Rahoza, five bishops, and three archimandrites. But the synod was surely attended also by the lower clergy and several lay Prominences. In opposition to this union synod, a counter synod was organized by Prince Constantine Ostroz'kyj, which was attended by two bishops, some abbots, some members of the clergy and a few prominent laymen.

It may be noted here that the role of laymen in Church affairs was strong in the Ruthenian Church as it was also in the Thomaschristian Church. Many prominent nobles used to be present in Ruthenian synods and at the election of Church officials. If in the Ruthenian Church this was due chiefly to mounting Protestant influence, which sought to control the Church, in the Thomaschristian Church it was due chiefly to the fact that the East Syrian bishops, who nominally governed the Thomaschristians, actually exercised only the power of orders and not, as a rule, the power of governance.[4]

There is another similarity between these two Churches, namely the rule by foreign bishops. The historically known hierarchy of the Thomaschristian Church consisted of East Syrian bishops till the end of the sixteenth century, save for one or two almost accidental exceptions. So, too, in the Ruthenian Church (called also the Church of Rus' centred on Kiev) till the invasion of the Mongols, all the twenty-three metropolitans (except two: Hilarion [1051-1054] and Kliment Smoljatic [1147-1155]) and not a few bishops had been Greeks.[5]

---

[4] George Nedungatt, *Laity and Church Temporalities: Appraisal of a Tradition,* (Dharmaram Canonical Studies, 1), Bangalore, Dharmaram Publications, 2000, pp. 118-123, 459.

[5] Jan Krajcar, "Quadro storico generale," in *Storia religiosa russa*, ed. Luciano Vaccaro, Gazzada, La Casa di Matriona, 1984, pp. 27-46, at p. 31.

2. Diamper Not A Union Synod

Whereas Brest was clearly a union synod, Diamper was quite different, since union with the Holy Apostolic See of Rome already existed since 1553 when Patriarch John Sulaqa made his Profession of Faith before Pope Julius III. When Archbishop Menezes of Goa had the synod convoked at Diamper through the Archdeacon with a threat of excommunication to all priests in case of failure to attend, which Church did he mean to excommunicate from, Catholic or Nestorian? To pose the very question is to discredit the legend about Diamper being a union synod. "The Synod of Diamper was not the inauguration of the Catholic faith but its completion, investing it with all that pertains to ecclesiastical discipline," so wrote on 28 November 1599 Giovanni Campori, S.J., a participant in the synod and a protagonist in the auto-da-fé of books that followed the synod.[6] It is true that not all the practical consequences of the Catholic communion hierarchically initiated and solemnised in 1553 had yet been fully drawn and applied, at least as the Westerners would have wanted. In particular, Sulaqa's promise to receive and carry out the decrees of the Council of Trent had remained almost a dead letter, which can easily be understood in the tumultuous sequel in and around the Babylonian Patriarchate. Moreover, the "Nestorian" books in Malabar had not been "corrected," according to the theological criteria and canonical norms of the Catholic censures. The neglect could not be simply faulted on Mar Abraham's, given his own convictions about the orthodoxy of his faith. From his point of view, it was his right and duty to resist the pretensions of the would-be correctors. This we can appreciate today, at least from hindsight, on the basis of Vatican II (OE 3, 5, and 6), and the papal-patriarchal Common Declaration of 1994.

Church divisions followed upon the wake of both Brest and Diamper sooner or later. The Union of Brest was opposed by a section of the clergy as well as by some of the prominent laity who had the support of Prince Ostroz'kyj. As was mentioned earlier, they held a counter synod headed by Bishop Balaban of L'viv, and Bishop Kopystenkyj of Przemysl and Archimandrite Nykyfor of the Kiev Lavra. This counter synod was dynamized by the arrival of a monk called Nicephorus claiming extraordinary powers delegated by the Patriarch

[6] Antonio Possevino, *Apparatus sacer ad scriptores Novi et Veteris Testamenti, etc.*, 3 tomes, Venice, 1906, tom. I, 392-394. (See Appendix III).

of Constantinople Jeremias II. More will be said below about Nicephorus. "To judge from the signatures of its decree, ten other monastic superiors and twenty-five members of the diocesan clergy attended. The lay delegation numbered twenty-two nobles and thirty-five burghers, with delegates of brotherhoods among the latter" and some others.[7] Attempts at reconciliation of the two factions failed. Nicephorus and the counter synod excommunicated the hierarchs who ratified the Union of Brest, and in turn the synod excommunicated Nicephorus, Balaban, Kopystenskyj and Tur. Thus the union with Rome was brought about at the cost of Church division, which then hardened into conflict and hostility. Josaphat Kuncevič, Archbishop of Polock, was killed in a tumult in 1623 and became a martyr of union. There were also exchanges of virulently polemical publications. However, efforts at reconciling the two parties and to bring them together to a common synod were never given up. The hope of such a reunion of the Catholic and Orthodox Ruthenians only ceased when in 1654 Kiev and the Eastern Ukraine came under the imperial sovereignty of Moscow. In the Western Ukraine efforts at union with Rome continued. They succeeded with the Orthodox eparchies of Przemysl in 1692, of L'viv in 1700, and of Luc'k in 1702. "The bishops of these eparchies, taught by the divisive corollary of Brest, took much time to prepare their clergy and other faithful before proclaiming the union, so that these successive unions after Brest were peacefully accepted by all."[8]

But at the Union of Brest itself the bishops had failed to prepare the faithful for the union, taking it almost for granted that the sheep would simply follow the shepherds. As Professor Sophia Senyk pointedly observes,

> The bishops who concluded the union, for all their concern with concrete pastoral problems, failed to grasp the implications of the most important developments of their times: the rise of a well-organized laity in the brotherhoods and the role of the printing press in forming opinion. Their shortsightedness in that respect led them to neglect the preparation of the laity and even the clergy in building up a climate favourable to the union.[9]

---

[7] Sophia Senyk, "The Background of the Union of Brest," *Analecta Ordinis S. Basilii Magni* 15 (1996) 103-144, at p. 143.

[8] Sophia Senyk, "L'unione di Brest," art. cit., p. 111.

[9] Sophia Senyk, "The Background of the Union of Brest," art. cit., p. 144.

3. Brest Not Like Diamper

Unlike Brest, Diamper did not issue immediately into a rupture of the Thomaschristian community, much less did it break up into two warring groups. This would probably have happened if the Thomaschristian Church had been divided into several dioceses or eparchies each governed by a bishop. Moreover, Mar Abraham, the single bishop of the Chaldean "monarchy," was dead since two years. Nevertheless, the seeds of a future division were sown already at Diamper and they would sprout and explode as a revolution in what is known as the Coonan Cross Oath in 1653. This oath was a public protest against the overbearing local Latin hierarchy, not a schism against the pope, nor a disclaimer of the Society of Jesus as such, as the matter is sometimes presented in certain writings.[10] The protest and oath of "ecclesial disobedience," a distant prototype of Mahatma Gandhi's civil disobedience, was occasioned by the high-handed rule of Archbishop Francis Garcia, S.J., who was supported by some (not all) of the Jesuits of the College of Holy Cross, Vaipicotta, but it was not against the Society of Jesus as an institution. In fact the Syro-Malabar priests would later request for a European Jesuit bishop when they gathered in a general meeting (23-26 May 1876) at Mannanam on the occasion of the visitation of the Apostolic Delegate Leo Meurin, S.J., the Vicar Apostolic of Bombay. The Jesuits were active both at Brest and at Diamper, and the role they played was not without its lights and shades.

Long after the Union of Brest, soon after the First World War, an autocephalous Ukrainian Orthodox Church was proclaimed in 1921 when in a special Church assembly Archpriest Vasyl Lypkivsky was "ordained" Metropolitan of Kiev and of All Ukraine by the laying-on-of-hands by the priests and the laypeople present. This "ordination" by a group of priests had a surprising parallel already in the Thomaschristian Church history, namely in the "episcopal ordination" of Mar Thoma I by the laying-on-of-hands by twelve priests after the Coonan Cross Oath of 1653.

---

[10] Among the many works which, following secondary sources, qualify the Coonan Cross Oath as "an oath to submit no longer to the authority of Rome," may be mentioned the otherwise very useful and informative book of Ronald Roberson, *The Eastern Christian Churches: A Brief Survey*, Rome, Edizioni Orientalia Christiana, 6 ed., 1999, p. 37. For an appraisal of the Coonan Cross oath as the Thomaschristians meant it, see George Nedungatt, *The Spirituality of the Syro-Malabar Church* (St. Thomas Academy for Research, Documentation 13), Alwaye, STAR Publication, 1989, pp. 24-29.

We have already drawn attention to the strong lay participation in Church life both at Brest and Diamper. This feature of the Thomaschristian community struck the Western missionaries so that they called it a "Christian republic." In the Ukraininian Church it merited the designation *Sobornopravna* or "Conciliar Church." The prominent lay element in Church life is marked in both the cases with light and shade. The laity's voice was not a universal suffrage but the voice of the Prominences. At Brest and in the Ukrainian Church traditionally, "the people who had any voice were the privileged few, more in some countries, fewer in others, but never the mass of the people."[11] In 1930, under Soviet pressure the "Conciliar Church" declared its own integration into the Russian Orthodox Church. Likewise, among the Thomaschristians the lay element that really counted was the voice of the rich few, not the people in the "democratic" sense. The lay element in this sense has a more decisive voice among the breakaway group, which became the Syro-Orthodox Church, so much so Church governance is not seldom piloted or comes to a standstill for the numerical superiority of the lay vote, especially in matters of the administration of church temporalities.

4. Common or Parallel Features

The situation of the Kievan Church (alias Ruthenian Church, Ukrainian Church) before the Union of Brest and that of the Church of Malabar before the Synod of Diamper were much similar from the point of view of the decadence of Church life. The cultural life of the two Churches was on the whole very low, and the standard of clerical formation mediocre. Decadence and stagnation marked their common denominator with several ills afflicting Church life.

A curious parallel between Brest and Diamper is the presence at both of a delegate claiming extraordinary powers from a higher authority: Nicephorus and Menezes. The latter conducted a diocesan synod at Diamper *sede vacante,* which was therefore unauthorised and *ultra vires*, as is shown in the study of Paul Pallath in this volume. As for Nicephorus, he was a monk who had attracted attention in 1995 by his political activities in Moldavia, and was put in prison;

[11] Sophia Senyk, "The Union of Brest: An Evaluation," in Bert Groen and Wil van den Bercken, eds, *Four Hundred Years Union of Brest (1596-1996): A Critical Re-evaluation,* (Eastern Christian Studies, 1), Louvain, Peeters, 1998, pp. 1-16, at p. 11. This book contains the papers presented at a 1996 Congress on the Union of Brest.

he then escaped and reached the court of prince Constantine Ostrozkyj. The following short description of this mysterious figure may be left to historian Senyk, whom we have already cited several times.

> He produced a document of November 1592, by which Patriarch Jeremias II of Constantinople ... named Nicephorus his protosyncellus (that is vicar or delegate) and endowed him with extensive and extraordinary authority in ecclesiastical matters. This document was issued in general terms and made no specific reference to the Ruthenian Church. Later Nicephorus was to claim that Jeremias II had written to him in September 1595, charging him to go to Ruthenian lands, but could not produce the letter. In any case, Jeremias II died in late 1595, hence any powers granted Nicephorus ceased (unless they were renewed by Jeremias' successors, something Nicephorus himsef never claimed). ...
>
> Even his supporters would have liked some more reliable proof than the document of 1592 for his authority to intervene; after all Nicephorus was not even a priest, yet he claimed the power to correct and depose bishops. After some debate, however, the Orthodox assembly accepted his credentials. ...
>
> The authorization given to Nicephorus by Jeremias is itself of doubtful validity and after Jeremias' death had no further force.[12]

Like Nicephorus at Brest, so too Menezes at Diamper claimed high-flown powers, not backed up with due testimonials, thus putting a question mark on the validity of the Synod of Diamper itself.

Another feature common to both Brest and Diamper was the presence and role of the Jesuits and the impact of the galvanising axiom, "No salvation outside the Church." The dynamism of the Jesuit missionaries both in Malabar[13] and in Ukraine,[14] but also elsewhere, was chiefly due to their desire to ensure the salvation of souls, although other secondary motives were not absent. Professor Sophia Senyk has rightly stressed the motive behind the Jesuit initiative and onslaught in Ukraine, highlighting the fact that what moved them into action was not merely the defence of the Ukrainian Christians from Protestant influence but concern for their eternal salvation.[15] The Council of Florence (1438-1452) had taught that people (pagans, Jews, heretics and schismatics) "who did not join the Catholic Church before

---

[12] Sophia Senyk, "The Background of the Union of Brest," art. cit., p. 142.

[13] For the role of the Jesuits at Diamper see the study of Vincenzo Poggi in this volume.

[14] For the role of the Jesuits at Brest see Jan Krajcar, "Jesuits and the Genesis of the Union of Brest," *Orientalia Christian Periodica* 44 (1978) 131-153.

[15] Sophia Senyk, "The Union of Brest: An Evaluation," p. 11.

the end of their lives" would go straight into hell. Antonio Possevino, S.J. (in certain respects the counterpart of Alessandro Valignano, S.J., who was the Jesuit Visitor to the Asian Missions), wrote in his *Moscovia:* "The fundamental and greatest error of the Greeks and the Ruthenians is that they believe that they can be saved outside the Roman Catholic Church." And "by their preaching and especially through their schools the Jesuits were soon converting numbers of Ruthenians to the Roman Catholic Church. Such conversions were often brought about by ridiculing Eastern traditions and rites."[16]

Except in rare cases like Roberto De Nobili, the situation on the Indian front was not dissimilar. As Joseph Wicki rightly points out "To expect of a Latin in that epoch much understanding for the Eastern traditions and rites would be to betray complete ignorance of the historical circumstances."[17] At Diamper, Menezes repeated several times that his intention was "only to show them the way of their salvation without obstacles."[18] In a "letter of edification" addressed to his fellow Jesuits five months after the Synod of Diamper, Giovanni Campori wrote: "The Fathers of our Society moved by the love for the salvation of neighbours, and devoured by untiring zeal, worked in collaboration with the Archbishop, or better as protagonists, taking him to different places and bringing him back, always ready with advice and the spirit of enterprise."[19] Indeed, the moving motto was "*extra Ecclesiam nulla salus,*" in which "Church" was understood as identical with the Roman Catholic Church in a reversible identity (Church = Roman Catholic Church = Church), a lesson that the sixteenth century Catholic missionary expansion had succeeded in passing on to some other Churches as well. Hence in the Profession of Faith signed by the first Catholic Chaldean Patriarch Mar John Sulaqa on his reception into the Catholic Church, we read: "I believe so strongly the unity of the Church and its gathering together, that I confess that no one outside the said Catholic Church can have a

---

[16] Ibid., p. 2.

[17] Josef Wicki, "Die Synoden der Thomaschristen (auch Syromalabaren genannt) (1583-1603)," *Annuarium Historiae Conciliorum* 18/2 (1986) 333-447, at p. 444.

[18] Francis Ros' letter of 20 November 1603 cited by Jonas Thaliath, *The Synod of Diamper,* (Orientalia Christiana Analecta 152), Rome, Pontifical Oriental Institute, 1958, p. 138.

[19] Antonio Possevino, *Apparatus sacer ad scriptores Novi et Veteris Testamenti, etc.*, 3 tomes, Venice, 1906, tom. I, 392-394. (See Appendix III).

share in eternal life."[20] Neither Brest nor Diamper, nor the zeal of the Western missionaries in India like St Francis Xavier or Menezes (however much these two men differed in mindset and character) can be correctly and fully understood and appraised without taking into account this overarching ecclesiological and missiological *Zeitgeist*.

Brest and Diamper have marked respectively the history and physiognomy of the Ukrainian Church and of the Thomaschristian Church, for better or for worse. Today, numerically, these two Churches are the first and the second largest Eastern Catholic Churches. And in hierarchical constitution, both are Major Archiepiscopal Churches among the twenty-one Eastern Catholic Churches. While the Ukrainian Catholic Church is a so-called *uniate* Church that issued from the Union of Brest, the Syro-Malabar Church is not a uniate Church that issued from the Synod of Diamper, in spite of the Portuguese propaganda to the contrary and the refrain of certain Indian writers.

According to the common understanding of a "uniate Church" it has two notes: first, it came into communion with the Catholic Church through the proselytising work of Latin missionaries; second, this union was effected by breaking loose from an Orthodox counterpart or Mother Church, and thus causing a Church division. These two notes do not apply to the Thomaschristian Church. The second note applies to the Chaldean Church, but not the first. Incidentally, in the context of Church divisions, the martyr of union Patriarch John Zulaqa compares with the Ruthenian martyr of union, Archbishop Josaphat (Saint).

Since the terms "uniate Church" and "uniatism" are often associated with the Union of Brest as well as the Synod of Diamper, without distinction, and "uniatism" has "many powerful enemies and calumniators," the following critical observations of Robert Taft on the subject of "Uniatism" may be cited here.

> I place "Uniatism" in quotation marks because it has evolved today into what many consider (and some deliberately use as) a pejorative term of contempt, like the epithet "papist" for "Catholic," despite the fact that historically, Christians of the Byzantine tradition in union with Rome once used it of themselves. Other names like "Greek Catholic," "Byzantine

[20] "Ecclesiae unitatem et congregationem tamvalde credo, ut nullos extra dictam Ecclesiam Catholicam existentes aeternae vitae participes fieri posse confiteor" — Samuel Giamil, *Genuinæ Relationes inter Sedem Apostolicam et Assyrorum Orientalium seu Chaldæorum Ecclesiam*, Roma, Loescher, 1902, pp. 15-23. (See Appendix I, 6 L).

Catholic," "Ukrainian Catholic," have like everything else, their origins and particular history. But history apart, to use "Uniate" as a name for Eastern Catholics can be gratuitously offensive.[21]

Union or communion with Rome involved also latinization of both the Ukrainian Church and the Syro-Malabar Church. This has been shown for the Ukrainian Church by Sophia Senyk in an article[22] and for the Thomaschristian Church, among others, by Jacob Kollaparambil and Jacob Vellian with their studies included in the present volume. Latinization has served to create or perpetuate for both these Churches the popular image of a "Uniate" Church. Moreover, Church divisions have followed remotely or closely upon the Synod of Diamper and the Union of Brest. And in referring to them "confessional paranoia often replaces rational discourse." In sharp contrast is "the well-informed, balanced and objective view of a historian, Ambroise Jobert":

> The Union of Brest is not the work of Polish or Roman policies. The Ruthenian bishops, irritated by the reforms of [Constantinopolitan patriarch] Jeremias II, requested it, the Polish court decided, not without hesitation, to risk it, and Rome received the Ruthenians into union without making any precise commitments in their regard.[23]

Finally, in both these Churches we can, moreover, note splinter groups splitting again often on financial disputes involving the hierarchy, and the resistance of the laity to episcopal supervision over Church temporalities, etc.[24]

CONCLUSION

To summarise and conclude: While with the Union of Brest a section of the Byzantine Orthodox who were living in the two territories of Ukraine and Bielorussia (and who would later be called Ruthenians/Ukraininas) entered into communion with the See of Rome, there

---

[21] Robert Taft, "Reflections on 'Uniatism' in the Light of Some Recent Books," *Orientalia Christiana Periodica* 65 (1999) 153-184, at p. 153.

[22] Sophia Senyk, "The Ukrainian Church and Latinization," *Orientalia Christiana Periodica* 56 (1990) 165-187.

[23] Ambroise Jobert, *De Luther à Mohila. La Pologne dans la crise de la Chrétienté, 1517-1648* (Collection historique de l'Institut d'études slaves, Paris 1974), 343, cited by Taft, art. cit. p. 155.

[24] George Nedungatt, *Laity and Church Temporalities: Appraisal of a Tradition,* Dharmaram Canonical Studies, 1), Bangalore, Dharmaram Publications, 2000, pp. 191-197.

was no such union at Diamper. Union had already taken place in 1553 officially at the patriarchal level in the Chaldean Church, which thus became a "uniate Church." In the sixteenth century, the Thomaschristian Church was an ecclesiastical province of the Chaldean Church in as much it was one of its Metropolitan Churches; consequently the union was effected not at Diamper in 1599 but half a century earlier in Rome in 1553. This undermines the Portuguese claim of having won over the Thomaschristians of Malabar to the Catholic Church in a union synod. At the time of the Synod of Diamper the Thomaschristians along with their Chaldean brethren professed the same orthodox faith as did the Portuguese Christians — that the Thomaschristians knew, and the Chaldeans knew, and some Jesuits knew. And we, too, know it today if only on the basis of the 1994 papal-patriarchal Common Declaration.[25] But Menezes did not.

The "correction" of books and the bonfire of "heretical works" that followed the Synod of Diamper served to revamp the Portuguese claim of having held a union synod and "reduced" the Thomaschristians of Malabar to the Catholic faith and brought them into obedience to the Roman Pontiff. But in the light of the historical evidence this claim sounds hollow propaganda and service to empire building. Elsewhere where the Latin missionaries could not lean on the military support of an imperial power as in Moscovia of Ivan IV, there was no union synod or "correction" of books or auto-da-fé. Ultimately, what made the difference between the union efforts of Antonio Possevino, S.J., in Moscovia in 1582[26] and those of Alexis Menezes in Malabar, O.S.A., in 1599 was power. If power had been wielded from the East rather than from the West (as happened during the reign of the Byzantine Emperor Justinian I, or with the Muslim conquest, or under the Turkish domination), one can only speculate if the "union" and the "correction" would have taken place in the reverse direction! This hermeneutical hypothesis helps at least to redefine the Menezian claim to have held a union synod at Diamper.

Pontifical Oriental Institute, Rome

George Nedungatt, S.J.

---

[25] *Acta Apostolicæ Sedis* 87 July (1995) 685-687. (See Appendix V).

[26] S. Polčin, *Une tentative d'Union au XVIe siècle: La mission religieuse du P. Antoine Possevin en Moscovie (1581-1582)*, Roma, 1957; H. F. Graham, *The Moscovia of Antonio Possevino, S.J.*, Pittsburgh 1977.

Jacob Kollaparambil

THE IMPACT OF THE SYNOD OF DIAMPER ON THE ECCLESIAL IDENTITY OF THE ST THOMAS CHRISTIANS

The Synod of Diamper (1599) was a historical event which had drastic, lasting, disastrous and subverting consequences upon the ecclesial life of the St Thomas Christians so as to shake the very foundations of this Church. These consequences, however, were not the result of a single strike or blow of the Synod of Diamper. They gradually evolved and reached a culmination. The latinising policy and process had been there from the first encounter of the Portuguese with the St Thomas Christian Church early in the sixteenth century. The Synod of Diamper was but a legalising camouflage, seal and stamp placed on that policy and process. Archbishop Alexis de Menezes of Goa, the main protagonist of this Synod, outdid all others in his zeal, even going to excesses.[1] To understand the consequences of this Synod we have to view them in their historical perspective. And so in the course of this paper, we shall examine how the latinising process had gradually evolved before the Synod of Diamper and was pursued afterwards.

The Portuguese had come to India at the dawn of the sixteenth century with the expectation to find a strong Church supported by Prester John, that legendary and powerful Christian monarch of the East, who hand in hand with the Western Christendom might liberate the Holy Land! The Portuguese were disillusioned of that rosy hope at their very first encounter with the St Thomas Christians. What they found in the St Thomas Christians was the only organized Christian community in India, ready to accept their offer of the protection of the King of Portugal, and to hand over the scepter of an already extinct royal dynasty of Villarvattam on 19 December 1502.

These Indian Christians, however, possessed considerable military strength, which the Portuguese hoped to harness and put to good use

[1] Some of the Jesuits themselves who collaborated closely with Dom Menezes for the Synod of Diamper, namely Bishop Francis Ros, Fr John Campori and Fr Albert Laerzio, wrote later in 1603/1604 about such excesses committed by Menezes with regard to the Synod of Diamper. See relevant texts cited in J. Thaliath, *The Synod of Diamper*: OCA 152 (Rome 1958) 130-136.

in their struggle against the Moors. They were producers and handlers of pepper and other spices of export, and hence friendship with them could serve the Portuguese economic and commercial interests while ending the Moorish monopoly of the spice trade with India. These were issues which the Portuguese colonial officials and missionaries in India used to write about to their superiors as the benefits to be derived from contact with the St Thomas Christians.

The Portuguese knew that the St Thomas Christians belonged to a different *sui juris* Church (if we may use a modern term), forming part of the East Syrian Church. Their liturgy, theology, spirituality and discipline were according to the East Syrian tradition, albeit with some inculturation on the Indian soil. In an age when the Western Church had little of ecumenism and more of polemics with the Eastern Churches, the Portuguese missionaries, educated and formed in the Western ecclesial tradition, applied their own categories and labelled as "Nestorian" the St Thomas Christians of India. At that time theological reflection, of course, had not progressed to the level of today. The question whether Nestorius was a Nestorian was hardly raised then. Today we know that the dyophysite Christology of the Antiochene School adopted by the East Syrian Church was essentially the same as the Chalcedonian formula accepted and interpreted by the Roman Church, differing only in terminology: so it has been officially stated in a recent joint declaration of Pope John Paul II and the Assyrian Patriarch Dinkha IV.

In an age of heresy hunting, the Portuguese suspected heresy and schism in everything that was different from what they were used to. In their zeal for souls, they wanted to bring the St Thomas Christians into complete uniformity with the Western Church. A perfect union might better serve the Portuguese temporal interests, too. Hence, they set forth as their objective the reform of the St Thomas Christians by reducing them to the Latin rite. A thorough latinising programme was planned and launched.

Among the many obstacles to be overcome, the following were to be specially noted:

1. The centuries-old hierarchical dependence of the St Thomas Christians on the East Syrian Church;

2. The presence of the East Syrian bishops whom the St Thomas Christians loved, respected and obeyed;

3. The indigenous clergy educated and formed in the essentially East Syrian and yet inculturated liturgy, spirituality, theology and discipline;

4. The East Syrian ecclesiastical books in use among the St Thomas Christians;

5. The believing and practising Christian community having their own liturgical, theological and spiritual traditions, as well as their own system of governance and discipline.

In order to overcome these obstacles the Portuguese elaborated a well articulated scheme, which they applied with zeal and persistence.

I. SEVERING OF THE HIERARCHICAL RELATIONS WITH THE EAST SYRIAN CHURCH

First of all, the Portuguese missionaries knew that the first move to be made in order to reform and latinise the St Thomas Christians was to sever their hierarchical link with the East Syrian Patriarch and to let no Oriental bishop reach Malabar any more. They, therefore, invoked the *Padroado* rights of the King of Portugal to present the candidates to be appointed bishops for Portugal and her overseas colonies. In 1517, a Portuguese missionary by name Alvaro Penteado advised the King of Portugal to let the St Thomas Christians elect one of their priests as bishop, whom the King might then confirm and support.[2] From the time the popes began nominating the candidates presented by the King of Portugal as bishops for the Padroado See of Goa and later of Cochin, the missionaries claimed that those bishops had jurisdiction also over the St Thomas Christians,[3] although these Christians actually lived outside the territory which was under the effective control of the Portuguese colonial power. Simultaneously, the missionaries did also petition the King of Portugal, and he favourably responded ordering the colonial officials to let no Oriental

[2] Letter of Fr Alvaro Penteado to the King of Portugal in 1517; Arquivo Nacional da Torre do Tombo, Lisbon (ANTT) *CVR No. 164*: A. da Silva Rego, *Documentaçâo ... India*, 3 (Lisbon 1950) 550-551.

[3] See the letter of Fr Antonio do Porto, OFM, to the King of Portugal on 20-11-1557: A. da Silva Rego, *Documentaçâo ... India*, 6 (Rome 1960) 325. Bishop Ambrosius Butigeg, OP, the Apostolic Nuncio for the Chaldean nation, refuted such arguments of the Portuguese missionaries: see *As Gavetas da Torre do Tombo*, published by Centro de Estudios Historicos Ultramarinos, 5 (Lisbon 1965) 37.

bishop reach Malabar, and to expel at once any one who might enter India eluding the Portuguese port authorities.[4]

However, ever since Mar John Sulaqa of the East Syrian Church made a formal union with the Holy See of Rome in 1553 giving origin to a line of the East Syrian Patriarchs in the Catholic communion, the popes had repeatedly recognized and confirmed the right of these Patriarchs to appoint bishops for the St Thomas Christians of India.[5] And, as advised by Pope Pius IV in 1565, Patriarch Mar Abdiso bifurcated the Church of Malabar and appointed Metropolitan Mar Abraham to the See of Angamaly and Mar Joseph as the metropolitan of the other part. Mar Abraham was named the Superior of all the bishops and metropolitans *(Rabba d'Kolhon Apeskope u Metrapolite*) in India.[6] The Patriarchal Synod elected Archdeacon George of Christ as bishop of Palayur and suffragan to Mar Abraham. Mar Abraham was authorized to do whatever was necessary for the Indian Church including the election and ordination of bishops.[7] In effect, Patriarch Mar Abdiso conferred super metropolitan authority and autonomy on Mar Abraham, as the head of the Indian Church.

And yet, in spite of the letters of Pope Pius IV to the Archbishop of Goa and to the Bishop of Cochin in favour of Mar Abraham, the Portuguese detained Mar Abraham and kept him in their custody for about two years. In 1575, the Second Provincial Council of Goa decreed (Session III, decree 1) that the St Thomas Christians should be governed by bishops nominated by the King of Portugal and not by the East Syrian Patriarch; or at least Mar Abraham (sent by the pa-

---

[4] See the order dated 6-3-1563: J. Wicki, *Documenta Indica*, 6 (1960) 11-14. The Jesuits had requested for such an order: See *Documenta Indica*, 4 (1956) 230; 5 (1958) 651, 655.

[5] See the letters written by Pope Pius IV in favour of Mar Joseph and Mar Abraham in 1564/5, addressed to Patriarch Mar Abdiso, to the Archbishop of Goa and to the Bishop of Cochin: S. Giamil, *Genuinae relationes inter sedem apostolicam et Assyriorum Orientalium seu Chaldaeorum ecclesiam* (Romae 1902) 69-73.

[6] Mar Abdiso's letter to the Archbishop of Goa on 24-8-1567. The original in Syriac is preserved in ARSI, *Gallia 95-1*, f. 197. See facsimile in J. Wicki, *Documenta Indica*, 11 (1970) p. 41*; Italian translation in A. Rabbath, *Documents inédits pour servir a l'histoire du Christianisme en Orient* II (Paris, Leipzig 1910) 432-434.

[7] See Mar Abdiso's decree dated 25-8-1567, nominating Archdeacon George of Christ as Bishop of Palayur: Portuguese translation in ARSI, *Goa 10-II*, f. 463: J. Wicki, *Documenta Indica*, 7 (1962) 703-705.

triarch) should attend the future Padroado Provincial Councils of Goa.[8]

Then the Jesuits took the lead in devising a cunning and dissembling strategy not to speak openly of subtracting the St Thomas Christians from the East Syrian jurisdiction. They suggested to the pope to appoint, with the "knowledge" (that is, consent) of the East Syrian Patriarch, an East Syrian (educated in Rome) or a Malabarian (e.g. Archdeacon George of Christ) as bishop, who should work with the Jesuits to reduce the St Thomas Christians to the Latin rite. In approving this plan, however, the Jesuit General completely ignored what had been suggested regarding the role of the East Syrian Patriarch.[9]

The Third Provincial Council of Goa in 1585, which was attended also by Mar Abraham and by several Jesuits, in its third session decreed that no one was to be received as the bishop of the St Thomas Christians unless his letters of appointment by His Holiness the Pope, or by his Catholic Patriarch in communion with the Roman Church, was first presented to the Archbishop of Goa, the Primate of India.[10]

The Provincial Congregation of the Jesuits held at Goa in 1588 offered the suggestion that the King of Portugal might seek from the Patriarch of Alexandria (?) the right to nominate bishops to the Church of the St Thomas Christians. But the reply of the Jesuit General was that he would propose a Latin bishop and it was not necessary to seek the consent of the Alexandrian Patriarch.[11]

In 1594, the Jesuits assured Mar Abraham that they would try to get Archdeacon George of the Cross appointed metropolitan to succeed Mar Abraham. In order not to appear "perfidious" (*foedifragi*) the Provincial Congregation of the Jesuits in 1594 did actually recommend to the Jesuit General to propose Archdeacon George, although he was "somewhat immature," as Mar Abraham's successor.[12] But the Jesuit Curia did just the contrary: in a memorial presented to the pope in 1596, the suggestion made was that not an East Syrian

---

[8] Paiva Manso, *Bullarium Patronatus Portugalliae Regum,* Appendix I (Lisbon 1872) 51.

[9] The First Provincial Congregation of the Jesuits at Goa in 1575: J. Wicki, *Documenta Indica,* 10 (1968) 268, 333-334. See J. Kollaparambil, *The St Thomas Christians' Revolution in 1653* (Kottayam 1981) 27, fn.60.

[10] Paiva Manso, *op. cit.,* 73-76.

[11] J. Wicki, *Documenta Indica,* 15 (1981) 24.

[12] J. Wicki, *Documenta Indica,* 16 (1984) 562-563.

but a Portuguese might be presented by the King of Portugal and appointed by the pope as successor to Mar Abraham.[13] The Jesuit General wrote in reply that since no suitable indigenous candidate was found, and great deliberation was required before nominating someone belonging to the Latin rite, no decision had yet been made by the pope.[14]

Subsequently, when the need did arise after the death of Mar Abraham to appoint his successor and the matter was dealt with in all seriousness in November/December 1599, Fr Francis Ros, S.J., was nominated Bishop of Angamaly by the Pope of Rome upon the proposal of the Jesuit Curia, without even consulting the Patriarch of the East Syrian Church.

In the meantime, the Synod of Diamper was celebrated in June 1599. Archbishop Menezes demanded that Archdeacon George of the Cross make the profession of faith and abjure the Patriarch of Babylon as a Nestorian heretic and schismatic.[15] And then the Synod as a whole was called upon to do the same, thus severing all hierarchical relations of the St Thomas Christian Church with the East Syrian Church, and promising to accept any bishop directly appointed by the Roman Pontiff, independently of the Babylonian Patriarch.[16] Besides, the Synod of Diamper in session III, decree 8, condemned the practice of calling the Patriarch of Babylon "the Universal Pastor and Head of the Catholic Church," since this title is due only to the Most Holy Father, the Bishop of Rome, whereas the Patriarch of Babylon was "a Nestorian and schismatic out of the obedience of the Holy Roman Church ... and excommunicated and accursed ... wherefore this bishopric ... upon pain of damnation, shall not from henceforward have any manner of dependence upon the said Patriarch of

---

[13] ARSI, *Goa 33*, f. 153.

[14] J. Wicki, *Documenta Indica*, 16 (1984) 651-652.

[15] At the first time when Archbishop Menezes insisted that the Patriarch of Babylon should not be commemorated as the universal pastor, but must be regarded as a Nestorian heretic, excommunicated from the Roman Church ... and got a document to that effect signed by the Archdeacon at Vaipicotta, the people there protested, "More than 1200 years we have been governed by the Patriarch." See A. Gouvea, *Jornada do Arcebispo de goa...* (Coimbra 1606) f. 30r; J. Hough, *the History of Christianity in India*, 1 (London 1839) 347. Session V, section II, decree 1 of the Synod of Diamper also speaks of the 1200 years of government by the Babylonian Bishops over the St Thomas Christian Church: *Ibid,* 2, 583.

[16] A. Gouvea, *Jornada do Arcebispo de Goa* ... (Coimbra 1606) ff. 52, 65; J. Hough, *op.cit,* 2, 523.

Babylon." Thus the Synod prohibited all, under the precept of obedience and pain of excommunication *ipso facto* incurred, to name the Patriarch of Babylon, even without the false title of Universal Pastor, in the Holy Sacrifice of the Mass or in the divine office.

Here we may note that the patriarch whom the St Thomas Christians were naming in the Holy Mass was Mar Simon,[17] who was in communion with the Holy See of Rome, and not Mar Elias, the Nestorian patriarch of the traditional line. However, Menezes, a Roman Catholic Archbishop, forced a Christian community of another *sui juris* Church to reject their Catholic patriarch as a heretic and schismatic. Surely this was not a light matter. But heresy was an easily chargeable crime in those days. And the *fidalgo* statesman in Dom Menezes had a clearly articulated ulterior motive for severing the hierarchical relation of the St Thomas Christians with their East Syrian patriarch albeit under the etiquette of orthodoxy: to bring under a Latin bishop the St Thomas Christians, who were the best warriors in Malabar and extremely obedient to their bishops, and thereby to ensure the military service of a fifty to sixty thousand strong army for the Portuguese colonial state in India.[18]

The East Syrian Catholic Patriarch Mar Denha Simon IX (1581-1600) or his successor Mar Simon X (1600-1636), however, did not effectively react to this affront to their good name and jurisdiction, probably because in their Mesopotamian home-region these Catholic

---

[17] The participants in the Synod of Diamper after the official acts of the first day were lamenting, "Tomorrow we will have to finish for ever with our Patriarch of Babylon, who governed us for so many years. No more shall we be naming, as we used to, in the Divine Office and in the Holy Mass Mar Simon" (so was called the Patriarch who was then governing them): A. Gouvea, *Jornada do Arcebispo de Goa ...* (Coimbra 1606) f. 64v.

[18] See the letter of Dom Menezes to Dom Agustin de Castro, Archbishop of Braga on 9-12-1597: Arquivo Ultramar, Lisboa, *India,* Caixa 1: "... e dahi me hei de hir envernar a Christandade da Serra de S. Tome, pera ver, se posso reduzir quella Christandade a obediencia da Igreja Romana, ... aqual tambem he muy importante para o bem temporal deste estado, porque como estes sâo Malavares, que he a milhor gente de peleja, e mais belicoza destas partes, e sejâo por estremo obedientes a seus Bispos, tomando Bispo nosso da Igreja latina ficâo os milhores em sincoenta, ou sesenta mil homens de peleja versados em espinguardas, seguros pella christandade, e por este estado todas as vezes, que os infiéis moverem guerra contra elle...": A. Beylerian, "Cinq lettres inédits de D. Frei Aleixo de Meneses, Archevêque de Goa," *Arquivos do Centro Cultural Português,* vol. 8 (Paris 1974) 582-583. See also A. Alonso, *Aleijo de Meneses, O.S.A., Arzobispo de Goa* (Valladolid 1992) 67; S. Subrahmanyam, "Dom Frei Aleixo de Meneses (1559-1617) et l'échec des tentatives d'indigénisation du Christianisme en Inde," *Archives de Sciences sociales des Religions,* 103 (1998) 37.

patriarchs had declined very much in authority, power and number of subjects *vis-a-vis* the Nestorian Patriarch Mar Elias VII (1591-1617) who, on the other hand, was then dealing with the Holy See of Rome for union.[19]

The synodal act at Diamper, however, had not influenced the pope in appointing Bishop Francis Ros, because the news about the Synod of Diamper could not have reached Rome before the papal act, nor was any reference made to the Synod of Diamper in the consistorial acts of 5 and 15 November, and of 20 December 1599.[20] The papal nomination was, therefore, the culmination of the latinising policy and process which the Portuguese missionaries had initiated early in the sixteenth century, and had actively promoted all through.

The promise under oath made by the St Thomas Christians at the Synod of Diamper to break all relations with the East Syrian Patriarch made it all the more easy for Bishop Francis Ros and his successors to demand their total obedience and submission.

With the appointment of Bishop Ros the see of Angamaly was reduced to a simple diocese and made suffragan to the Portuguese Padroado Latin Archdiocese of Goa. Eight months after the appointment of Bishop Ros, the Padroado rights of the King of Portugal was extended also over the see of Angamaly of the St Thomas Christians.[21]

Later, however, on repeated complaints to the Holy See by the St Thomas Christians, the metropolitan status of the see of Angamaly was restored in 1608.[22] And on the insistence of Archbishop Francis Ros, a limited exclusive territory also was assigned to the See of Angamaly-Cranganore, which thereby became circumscribed as part of a single Padroado hierarchy in India; thus losing All-India jurisdiction as well as the autonomy of a *sui juris* Church.

---

[19] "Denha Simon ... factus Patriarcha, nec aetate neque doctrina idoneus tanto muneri ... secesserat ad fines Persidis, potentiae cedens Patriarchae Babylonis. Quo loco etiam hodie manet eius successor Simon ... existimatione ac numero subiectorum ... praedecessoribus longè inferior." P. Stroza, *De Dogmatibus Chaldaeorum Disputatio,* (Romae 1617) f. a. 6v.

[20] See ASV, *Acta Consistorialia Miscellanea,* vol. 16, f. 111; vol. 23, ff. 69-70; vol. 30, ff. 168-169; vol. 37, f. 147; vol. 53, f. 277; *Acta Vicecancellari*, vol. 14, f. 133.

[21] The Apostolic Brief *"In Supremo Militantis"* dated 4-8-1600 by Pope Clement VIII; see *Bullarium Patronatus Portugalliae Regum, I* (Lisbon 1868) 260-261 or *Corpo Diplomatico Portuguez, XII* (Lisbon 1902) 80-82.

[22] By the Apostolic Brief *"Romanus Pontifex"* dated 22-12-1608; ASV, *Sec. Brev. Ap.*, 612, ff. 149-150; *Bullarium Patronatus Portugalliae Regum* II (Lisbon 1870) 8-9.

Thus Angamaly-Cranganore became a metropolitan see without any suffragan just like all the other Padroado sees in India and the Far East, such as Goa, Cochin, Mylapur, Macau, Malaca, etc. Under the hierarch of Angamaly-Cranganore there were two communities, the syro-Oriental St Thomas Christians and the Latin rite Christians within the exclusive territory assigned to the See. Similarly, a minority community of the St Thomas Christians existed under the territorial jurisdiction of the Latin Bishop of Cochin. Hence after the St Thomas Christians were brought under the Latin hierarchy, *de facto* there existed only one *sui juris* Church and one single jurisdiction in India; and it was Latin. The Church of the St Thomas Christians practically lost its hierarchical autonomy. Thus it continued for about three centuries, until the hierarchical autonomy was restored in 1887, albeit in the minimal grade of two vicariates apostolic, namely of Trichur and Kottayam. It would take another century before regaining the former super metropolitan grade translated into the present Major Archiepiscopal Church of Ernakulam-Angamaly.

II. Induced by the Missionaries, the East Syrian Bishops Introduced Some Latin Practices Among the St Thomas Christians

Although the missionaries had long wanted to get rid of the East Syrian Bishops, these were among the St Thomas Christians all through the sixteenth century except for short intervals (1552-1556, 1563, 1568-1570). These Christians loved, respected and obeyed their East Syrian bishops, and accepted their teaching without questioning. Anything said against the bishops was considered a lie. These Christians were so loyal, that thousands would even risk their lives in defence of their bishops.[23] Hence, not to estrange the Christians, the Portuguese missionaries had to put up with those East Syrian bishops who happened to be in Malabar. But to achieve their goals the missionaries coerced the bishops to introduce some Latin practices among the St Thomas Christians by cajoling them with economic baits or by threatening them with deportation.

---

[23] For example, in 1557, when the King of Vadakkankur in collusion with the Portuguese wanted to take Metropolitan Mar Abraham under custody, over two thousand St Thomas Christians declared themselves *amocos* (suicide squads) for their bishop, and successfully defended and freed him, although it cost them dearly having had to forfeit a good part of their properties: cf. Fr Melchior Carneiro's letter dated December 24, 1557: J. Wicki, *Documenta Indica,* 3 (1954) 800-801.

a) Under such pressure, Mar Jacob († 1552) encouraged the Christians to establish common cemeteries close to the churches, changing their practice of burying the dead in their own private properties.[24] Churches began to be constructed in the western architectural style with façade and tower so that they might look different from the Hindu temples built in the Kerala architectural style.[25]

Formerly, the St Thomas Christians were used to making only general confession, confessing their sins together to God in a community celebration, in an intoned voice.[26] Mar Jacob introduced private confession among the St Thomas Christians, using the formula of absolution from the *Rituale Romanum* translated into Syriac. Mar Joseph later made some improvements over Mar Jacob's translation.[27] Mar Joseph and Mar Elias had to celebrate the Holy Eucharist in the Latin rite, while they were among the Portuguese at Goa and Baçain in 1556-1557.[28]

(b) Mar Joseph († 1569) introduced the Latin vestments, Portuguese wine and unleavened bread for the Eucharistic celebration.[29] He translated the words of the institution from the Latin Missal and inserted it into the Malabar liturgy, adding, however, a few extra words.[30] The same bishop translated also the formula for the anointing of the sick ("Extreme Unction") from Latin into Syriac, and it came into use replacing the traditional practice of blessing the sick after placing on them some biblical verses written on palm-leaves or paper.[31] In the East Syrian Pontifical copied by Mar Joseph, he prescribed severe punishments for those who broke the seal of confessional, and forbade hearing confession without a confessional.[32]

(c) With the help of the Jesuits of the Vaipicotta Seminary Mar Abraham († 1597) translated the text of the Sacrament of the Holy

---

[24] Report of Fr Dionysio, SJ in 1578: J. Wicki, *Documenta Indica*, 11 (1970) 140.

[25] Fr Lourenco de Goes to the King of Portugal on 28-12-1536: A. da Silva Rego, *Documentaçâo ... India*, 2, 244.

[26] See Fr Alvaro Penteado's letter in 1517: ANTT, *CVR No. 164*: A. da Silva Rego, *Documentaçâo ... India*, vol. 3 (Lisbon 1950) 548.

[27] See Report of bishop Ros in 1604; British Library, *MS. add 9853*, f. 92 (see Appendix IV).

[28] See Letter of Fr A. do Porto in 1557: A. da Silva Rego, *op.cit.*, 6, 324.

[29] See Report of Bishop Ros in 1604; op. cit.

[30] *Ibid.*, f. 91; See also *Vat. Syr. 66*, f. 101.

[31] Report of Bishop Ros in 1604, *loc. cit*, f. 92 and P. J. Podipara, *The St Thomas Christians*, (Bombay 1970) 88-89. See *Documenta Indica* 17, pp. 408, 410.

[32] *Vat. Syr. 45*, ff. 172-173.

Myron (Confirmation) from Latin into Syriac. However, he ministered it as a rite separate from Baptism only for the *Ordinandi*.[33] Persuaded by the Jesuit Visitor Father Alessandro Valignano, Mar Abraham convoked a Synod at Angamaly in 1583. In this synod it was decided, (a) to accept the Gregorian Calendar and to celebrate the feasts according to it and on the same day as in the Latin Church, (b) to make annual Confession and Communion obligatory for all who attained the age of discretion (14 for boys, 12 for girls), (c) to issue the faculty to hear confession only to those priests who had sufficient knowledge about reserved cases and censures, (d) to declare Sacred Order as an impediment to Matrimony and to censure any one in Holy Orders attempting marriage with an *ipso facto* excommunication and suspension until he separated himself from the woman.[34]

In 1585, the Third Provincial Council of Goa legislated for the St Thomas Christian Church and decreed Marriage to be an impediment for Holy Orders, and applied also the Tridentine norms regarding the canonical minimum age for Ordinations (22 for subdeacons, 23 for deacons and 25 for presbyter).[35] Mar Abraham forbade the married priests to preside over Eucharistic celebration. The Council decreed also that the Latin Pontifical, Ritual, Missal and Breviary might be translated into Syriac for use in the Malabar Church.

In 1587/1588, finding fault with the East Syrian Pontifical, which did not contain the rite for the anointing of hands and the tradition of instruments for the priestly ordination, Fr Ros made a Syriac translation of the Latin Pontifical and compelled Mar Abraham to use it for re-ordaining all his priests.[36] Subsequently, for the administration of all the sacraments the priests of the St Thomas Christians were forced to use a Syriac translation of the *Rituale Romanum* prepared by Fr Ros. Only the Liturgy of the Eucharist and the Liturgy of the Hours were left in the original Syriac, although disfigured with many

---

[33] Report of Bishop Ros in 1604, *loc. cit.*, f. 91.

[34] Fr Jerome Rebello on 20-1-1584: J. Wicki, *Documenta Indica*, 13 (1975) 499.

[35] See Session III, decree 3: *Bullarium Patronatus Portugalliae Regum, Appendix I*, 73-74.

[36] See Letters of Fr Ros to the Jesuit General on 6-1-1587: ARSI, *Goa 13*, f. 334; of Fr Albert Laerzio to the Jesuit General on 22-11-1588; ARSI, *Goa 47*, f. 335; of Fr Jerome Xavier to the Jesuit General on 8-1-1590: ARSI, *Goa 14*, f. 1. The relevant texts are cited in J. Kollaparambil, *The St Thomas Christians' Revolution in 1653* (Kottayam 1981) 31, fn. 72.

corrections and Latin interpolations.[37] Mar Abraham permitted Holy Communion under the species of bread only.[38]

III. The Charter of Priestly Formation for Indigenous Missionaries Imposed on the St Thomas Christians

Another means adopted to latinise the St Thomas Christians was to replace the native clergy, educated and formed in the East Syrian ecclesial system, with others educated and formed in the Latin discipline. Already in the 1530's the Portuguese missionaries had given clerical formation to some St Thomas Christian young men at the Franciscan monastery in Cochin. A few were sent to Coimbra University in Portugal. In 1541, Fr Vincent de Lagos, a Franciscan, started the St James College at Cranganore and by 1549, when St Francis Xavier visited that College, out of about 100 students on the rolls more than 80 were St Thomas Christians. The College in fact offered good courses in ecclesiastical sciences. Some of the graduates excelled as linguists, artists or theologians. However, none of them was admitted to serve in the churches of the St Thomas Christians, because they, having been formed in the rites and customs of the Latin Church, began to insist that the St Thomas Christians should accept the Latin rite. They, therefore, ended up as missionaries in the Latin Diocese of Cochin.[39]

After starting their mission for the St Thomas Christians in 1577, the Jesuits conceived the idea of running a seminary as the best means to 'reduce' the St Thomas Christians to the Latin rite and usages. Shrewdly dissembling and concealing their real intentions,[40] they got permission from Mar Abraham to run a seminary for the St

---

[37] The Report of Bishop Ros in 1604, *loc. cit.*, f. 92; Fr Laerzio's letter on 22-11-1588: ARSI, *Goa 47*, f. 335; Fr Crasto in 1595: ARSI, *Goa 32*, f. 535. The relevant texts are cited in J. Kollaparambil, *op. cit*, p. 31, fn. 73. Even the Latin Mass was to be translated into Syriac for use by the St Thomas Christian priests (see Session III Art. 7 of the Third Provincial Council of Goa in 1585 and also Session V, Section II, decree 4 of the Synod of Diamper). Ros had translated the Latin Breviary into Syriac: a copy is kept in the Bibliotheca de Ajuda in Lisbon: see J. Wicki, *Documenta Indica,* 11 (1970) 845, fn. 65.

[38] See The Jesuits' annual letter in 1578: J. Wicki, *Documenta Indica,* 11 (1970) 288.

[39] The Report of Bishop Ros in 1604: *loc. cit.*, f. 93.

[40] See Fr Valignano's letters: J. Wicki, *Documenta Indica,* 10 (1968) 882-884; vol. 13 p. 430; p. 59. See the relevant passages cited in J. Kollaparambil, *op. cit.*, 32-33, fn. 80.

Thomas Christians at Vaipicotta. They started it in 1587 with a royal subsidy from Portugal. Father Ros was on the staff to teach Syriac, but the formation was in the Latin rite, and Metropolitan Mar Abraham did not like it. There was disagreement as to what discipline (Latin or Oriental) should be followed in the Seminary with regard to fasting, abstinence, liturgy of the hours, etc. The question was referred to Rome, proposing that Syriac should not be taught any more and that all should conform to the Latin rite. The Holy See's answer was an emphatic No, directing the missionaries to work harder for the preservation of Syriac, correcting only the errors and abuses, if any. The strong argument was that variety made the Church beautiful.[41] The Synod of Diamper in Session VII, section I, decree 1, made the knowledge of Syriac as one of the requirements for the reception of the Holy Orders by the St Thomas Christians.

According to a policy adopted in the Second Provincial Congregation of the Jesuits at Goa in 1583, the seminary courses for the natives were limited to the teaching of Latin and "Casus Conscientiae," without even an introduction to philosophy or theology or culture or higher arts. It was further decided that the seminarians of Malabar should not learn Portuguese, lest they should be tempted to leave the Serra and imitate the Portuguese in their enclaves.

The charter of education adopted for the education of the indigenous seminarians was, of course, adapted to the purpose for which the missionaries wanted to have indigenous clergy. Indigenous seminarians were meant to serve the missionaries as translators in their ministry of preaching. The indigenous priests were to remain as subordinates of the missionaries. They could, moreover, relieve the missionaries of the inconveniences of having to reside in remote, isolated missions, thus letting them enjoy the comforts and the security of the Colleges. Over these native subalterns they could exercise the powers of a Vicar General to appoint, transfer, punish or even to imprison them![42]

The Malabarians showed apathy for Latin, and so it was dropped from the curriculum of the Vaipicotta Seminary. The result was fore-

---

[41] See the report of Fr Salvador Machado in 1656: ARSI, *Goa 50*, f. 241. Bishop Ros wrote that Fr Laerzio brought the Holy See's instruction in 1602: ARSI, *Goa 15*, f. 178.

[42] The resolution of the Provincial Congregation of the Jesuits in 1583: ARSI, *Congr. 95*, ff. 171-172; J. Wicki, *Documenta Indica*, 13 (1975) 332-333. The relevant text is cited in J. Kollaparambil, *op. cit.*, 34-35, fn. 86.

seeable. With a teaching staff not very proficient in the language of the student body, and the students having no knowledge of the languages in which the teachers were at their best, the seminary could not offer very much in-depth study in any subject. Hence the Vaipicotta Seminary marked only a small change from the traditional *Malpan* System to a low quality seminary training in the Western tradition and mentality. The products could not be rated high by the standards of either tradition.

IV. THE AUTODAFÉ OF THE SYRIAC MSS ORDERED BY THE SYNOD OF DIAMPER: A DISASTER FOR THE ORIENTAL ECCLESIAL TRADITION OF THE ST THOMAS CHRISTIANS

The ecclesiastical language of the St Thomas Christians was Eastern Syriac, and all their ecclesiastical books — biblical, liturgical, spiritual, canonical, theological, patristic, hagiographical, historical, etc. — were written in that language. The bishops and priests were using them for the liturgy as well as for the education of the clergy and the laity. The early Portuguese missionaries did not know Syriac, but they suspected that those books contained heretical doctrines of the Nestorians.

Accused as a Nestorian heretic and for simony by Bishop George Temudo, OP of Cochin and indicted by Pope Pius V, Mar Joseph went to Rome in 1568. He took with him eighteen Syriac MSS of ecclesiastical books, probably to prove his orthodoxy. After he died at Rome in 1569, those MSS became part of the first collection of the Syriac MSS of the Vatican Library. They included a complete set of the books of the Bible (*Vat. Syr.* 2, 3, 4, 17, and 22); Pontificals, Missals and Rituals (*Vat. Syr.* 45, 46, 66); sets of the Liturgy of the Hours (*Vat. Syr.* 62, 85, 86, 87, 88, 99); other liturgical texts and ecclesiastical calendar (*Vat. Syr.* 65); Nomocanon of Abdiso (*Vat. Syr.* 128); homilies and devotional hymns (*Vat. Syr.* 186, 188). Some of these manuscripts included also texts of theological or catechetical reflexions and narrations of historical events.

In 1585, the Third Provincial Council of Goa nominated Fr Francis Ros, SJ, as companion and aid to Mar Abraham in reforming the Malabar Church, specially to examine the Syriac books in use among the St Thomas Christians and to correct the Nestorian errors they contained. Fr Ros began learning Syriac from the priests who had accompanied Mar Abraham to the Provincial Council of Goa. Eventually, he acquired a good command of Syriac and zealously fulfilled his duty. On the errors contained in the Syriac books he wrote two reports:

(1) In 1587: *De Erroribus Nestorianorum qui in hac India Orientali Versantur*.[43]

(2) In 1593: *Enformaçâo do Prelado da Serra*.[44]

With regard to the Syriac Bible in Malabar, he noticed that it was not fully concordant with the Latin Vulgata. It did not have Esther, Tobias, and Wisdom in OT; and 2Pet, 2Jn, 3Jn, Jude, and Revelation were wanting in NT. Differences were noticed in Mt 6:13; Lk 6:35, 10:1; Jn 7:53-8:11; Acts 20:28; Phil 2:6; 1Jn 3:16, 4:3, 5:7, etc. Fr Ros interpreted all these differences as changes introduced purposely by the Nestorians to justify their heretical teaching. In fact, they were some of the particularities of the *Psitha* version of the Bible that was in use in the Syriac speaking Churches.

In his first report (*De Erroribus Nestorianorum*) Ros culled and put together more than thirty texts from the books of the Liturgy of the Hours as examples of Nestorian formulae. He mentioned also several other books by name which contained Nestorian heretical teachings. He complained that, although Mar Abraham had promised at the Provincial Council of Goa (1585) to expunge all Nestorian heretical texts from the ecclesiastical books in use among the St Thomas Christians, he did not care to do so. Ros, therefore, suggested that Mar Abraham, was suspect of heresy, and should be accused before the Supreme Pontiff and degraded and deposed from his Archiepiscopal See.

The St Thomas Christians had defined their ecclesial identity as consisting in the "Law of Thomas," which was distinct from "the Law of Peter" of the Portuguese. Already in 1516, at the suggestion by Fr Alvaro Penteado that the St Thomas Christians ought to change their ecclesial customs accepting the Latin practices instead, they had responded, "As there were twelve Apostles, so did they establish twelve customs."[45] Later Mar Abraham gave expression to the same concept in the terms of "Law of Thomas" in juxtaposition to "Law of

---

[43] ARSI, *Goa 50*, ff. 198-214: I. Hausherr, ed., "*De Erroribus Nestorianorum* ...," in *Orientalia Christiana*, IX/1, No. 40 (1928) 1-40.

[44] ARSI, *Goa 32-I*, ff. 525-528 (Spanish), ff. 529-532 (Portuguese): Edn J. Wicki, *Documenta Indica*, 16 (Romae 1984) 1029-1039. See Appendix II.

[45] "asy como forâo doze apostllos, fizerâo doze costumes.": A. da Silva Rego, *Documentaçâo ... India*, 3 (Lisbon 1950) 550.

Peter." Father Ros, however, found fault with a "Law of Thomas" posing as distinct from "Law of Peter" and as defining the ecclesial identity of the St Thomas Christians.[46] Of course, according to the then accepted ecclesiology of the Portuguese, there was no place in the Catholic Church for a *sui juris* Church with a distinct ecclesial identity. On the other hand, the St Thomas Christians were showing the spirit of a communion ecclesiology in their relations with the Portuguese.

The two works *De Erroribus Nestorianorum* and *Enformaçâo do Prelado da Serra* by Father Ros were certainly the main sources on which the Synod of Diamper based its treatise on the Nestorian heresy and errors. Session III, decrees 2 and 3 enumerated the defects of the Syriac Bible and asked Fr Ros to translate into Syriac from the Latin Vulgata those books that were wanting in the Syriac Bible. Besides, the passages that were not concordant with the Latin Vulgate were to be corrected.

Session III, decrees 4-10 of the Synod of Diamper condemned several heretical doctrines contained in the Syriac books as well as the practice of honouring the Nestorian saints. In decree No. 7 the Synod judged that the making of a distinction between the Law of Thomas and the Law of Peter was a manifest error, clear schism and heresy and, therefore, it commanded that all the parish priests and preachers should instruct the faithful often about it. Decree No. 14 proscribed twenty-one Syriac books mentioned by their names with short descriptions of their contents. This decree forbade all, in virtue of obedience and under pain of excommunication to be incurred *ipso facto*, to keep, translate, read or hear others read these proscribed books.

Decree 15 points out the errors found in liturgical books. Those MSS which were needed for the liturgical services were allowed to be kept after expurgating them of Nestorian heresy, until corrected books would be printed and supplied to the churches. However, the entire Liturgy of the Hours of Advent and Nativity and of the feasts of the Nestorian saints were to be torn off the MSS and burned. Decree 16 ordered that all Syriac MSS must be handed over to Archbishop Menezes or to his deputy on visit to the churches. He would decide

[46] Cf. I. Hausherr, op. cit., p. 34; F. Ros, *Enformaçâo do Prelado da Serra* in J. Wicki, *Documenta Indica,* 16 (1984) 1038. See Appendix II.

what to do with them, whether to correct them or expunge the errors or simply burn them.

Accordingly, after the Synod of Diamper Don Menezes made official visits to some churches. In every church, in the presence of the people, himself dressed in pontificals, Menezes performed a solemn ceremony of burning the Syriac MSS collected from the place in a bonfire kindled in the church yard. After Menezes left Malabar, Fathers Francis Ros and Stephen Brito continued these visits to the churches. And they, too, performed the ceremony of burning the Syriac books.

In these auto-da-fé of Syriac books, as J. B. Chabot calls this act of vandalism,[47] perished many Syriac MSS of the St Thomas Christians. Only the Liturgy of the Eucharist and a two weeks cycle of ordinary ferial Liturgy of the Hours *(Kaskol)* were saved in the original Syriac, albeit much disfigured with Latin interpolations.

To our knowledge, only a few Syriac MSS which were in Malabar at the time of the Synod of Diamper have survived the auto-da-fé and come down to our own times: eg., (1 & 2) BNP (National Library of Paris) *MS. Or. 24* and *Ms. Or. 25* (Liturgy of the Hours); (3) Library of the Assyrian Church of the East, Trichur, *MS. 26* according to the numeration of Van der Ploeg (Liturgy of the Hours); (4) Metropolitan Library of Ernakulam, *MS. No. L22* (Nomocanon of Abdiso: the personal copy of Mar Abraham); (5) Library of Mar Ivanios College, Trivandrum, *E.S. MS. Ac. No. 3842, Call No.198* (The Gospels).

Most of the twenty-one proscribed books (Session III, decree 14), whose MSS in Malabar perished in the auto-da-fé, however, have survived in copies extant in the libraries of Europe and the Middle East. The real material loss caused by the burning of the Syriac MSS in Malabar, therefore, was the loss of the historical notes that might have been recorded in their colophons or on the blank folios usually left at the end of the MSS.

The loss of the Syriac MSS, however, caused an irreparable damage to the Oriental ecclesial traditions of this Church. The Syriac books had been the monuments of the theological, spiritual, liturgical, and disciplinary traditions of the St Thomas Christians. They were the sources also of the ecclesiastical sciences imparted to the clergy in the course of their education and formation. With the burn-

---

[47] J.B. Chabot, *"L'Autodafé des livres Syriaques du Malabar,"* in *Florilegum ou recueil de travaux d'érudition dédiés à M.le Marquis Melchior de Vogüé ...* (Paris 1909) 613-623.

ing of the Syriac MSS, therefore, the Oriental theological traditions of this Church also were laid to rest. Will they be revived through the modern efforts to restore the Oriental identity of the St Thomas Christians?

The clerics receiving their formation at the Vaipicotta Seminary had no use for those theological or patristic volumes of the Syriac tradition. For, as shown above, theirs was a watered down clerical formation of low quality in the Latin theological tradition. Thus the burning of the Syriac MSS along with the Vaipicotta Seminary formation dealt a deadly blow to the Oriental theological traditions of the Church of the St Thomas Christians making their clergy drift into a theological mediocrity and inferiority in knowledge and competence in the ecclesiastical sciences through the centuries to follow.

V. The Infra-Episcopal Organs of Church Administration

(a) The married clergy: Ordinarily the clergy of the St Thomas Christians were married. Father, sons and grandsons, ministering as priests at the same church were not rare cases. In the first half of the sixteenth century, after the Portuguese got effective control over Cranganore, Cochin, Quilon, etc., their missionaries began forbidding the St Thomas Christian married priests to exercise priestly ministry and to celebrate the East Syrian liturgy in those places.

In 1583, the Jesuit Visitor Fr Alessandro Vilignano persuaded Mar Abraham to convoke a synod at Angamaly. That Synod declared that Holy Orders was an impediment to marriage, and censured anyone in Holy Orders who attempted marriage with an *ipso facto* excommunication and suspension until he separated from the woman. In 1585, the Third Provincial Council of Goa, legislating for the St Thomas Christians, declared that marriage was an impediment to Holy Orders. (session III, decree 3). However, ordination of married men and marriage of ordained men continued to take place exceptionally under Mar Abraham.

The Synod of Diamper took up the issue in Session VII, Section I. Decree No. 16 forbade clerics in Holy Orders to marry, in virtue of obedience and under pain of excommunication *latae sententiae*. The clerics who had already married were suspended from sacerdotal acts until they separated from their wives. Clerics who had married twice or married widows were declared bigamists, and were ordered to put off their wives under pain of excommunication. Decree No.17 permitted married priests, after putting away their wives, to exercise Holy Orders. By these decrees clerical celibacy was made obligatory for the St Thomas Christian Church.

(b) The Archdeacon as the *Jathikku Karthavyan* for the central administration of the Church: In the special situation of the St Thomas Christian Church governed by the East Syrian foreign bishops, the indigenous organs assisting the foreign bishops in the governance of the Church had loomed large in competence and authority. The first assistant to the Metropolitan of All-India was the Archdeacon of All-India from the family of Pakalomattam, which claimed to have provided ecclesiastical ministers from the time of the Apostle Thomas. The Archdeacon, who was recognized by the kings of Malabar, functioned also as the national head (*Jathikku Karthavyan*) of the St Thomas Christians. The central administration of the St Thomas Christian Church had been practically in the hands of the Archdeacon, especially in the temporal and judicial matters.[48]

(c) The *Desathu Pattakkar* and *Palliyogam* for the local church administration: The clergy was ascribed to the local churches, not to the eparchy. The local clergy (*Desathu Pattakkar*) ministered to the community jointly under the leadership of the seniormost priest, no single priest functioning as the parish priest or curate. The local communities were economically self supporting, contributing a share also for the central administration of the Church. The *Palliyogam* ie. the assembly of the heads of the families and the priests, managed the whole ecclesial administration of the local church.

The Portuguese missionaries of the sixteenth century tried to change this system of church administration by the *desathu Pattakkar* and *Palliyogam,* especially during the periods when the East Syrian bishops were not present in Malabar. But such efforts were not successful in the early period, except in the Portuguese enclaves, such as Cranganore, Cochin and Quilon. For example, after the death of Mar Jacob (1552) and Mar Denha, the missionaries wanted to take over all the fifty churches of the St Thomas Christians. The Franciscans and the Malabar priests trained by them at Cranganore, Cochin and in Portugal in the Latin rite were not numerically strong enough to do it by themselves. So the Franciscans' Custodian requested the Dominicans and the Jesuits to collaborate. After working for three years, the missionaries thought that they were about to succeed, but their san-

---

[48] See J. Kollaparambil, *The Archdeacon of All-India,* Rome 1972.

guine hopes cooled on seeing a Nestorian bishop called Abraham reach Malabar and minister to the St Thomas Christians.[49]

The Portuguese, therefore, used the good offices of the two East Syrian Catholic bishops, Mar Elias and Mar Joseph, whom they had detained at Goa and Baçain, to go to Malabar and persuade Mar Abraham to profess the Catholic faith. But later they deported Mar Abraham from Malabar in 1558. Mar Elias returned to his country. The first bishop of Cochin George Temudo, OP, saw to it that Mar Joseph embarked for Europe in 1563. Thus the scene was cleared for Bishop Temudo and the missionaries to get very active visiting the churches of the St Thomas Christians and stationing in them as vicars some priests whom they had trained in the Latin rite.[50]

Now that the three East Syrian bishops (Mar Abraham, Mar Elias and Mar Joseph) were sent away from Malabar in quick succession, even Archdeacon George of Christ, who was the *Jathikku Karthavyan,* seems to have despaired of getting another East Syrian bishop in the near future. It was in this context that during the celebration of a feast at Parur on 21 November 1563, the Archdeacon, the priests and the faithful gave a solemn reception to Bishop Temudo of Cochin and agreed to receive vicars in all the churches of Malabar whom the Bishop of Cochin might appoint.[51] But this time also the missionaries' plan was foiled, as Mar Joseph returned to Malabar by the end of 1564, all the more fortified with royal endorsement from Portugal.

Again in 1568, Mar Joseph was on his way to Rome, denounced for heresy and simony by Bishop Temudo of Cochin and indicted by Pope Pius V.[52] Meanwhile, Mar Abraham, who was appointed Metropolitan of Angamaly by Patriarch Mar Abdiso as directed by Pope Pius IV was detained at the Dominican monastery of Goa. Then for about two years till Mar Abraham escaped from Goa and reached Malabar, the missionaries were fraternizing with the St Thomas

[49] Fr Fernando da Paz in 1557: A. da Silva Rego, *Documentaçâ ... India,* 6, 247-250.

[50] Cf. the letters of Amador Correia, Francis Lopes, and Melchior Nunes Barreto in 1554 and 1556: J. Wicki, *Documenta Indica,* 6 (1960) 178-180; 413, 427-428.

[51] Cf. letter of Fr Amador Correia, SJ, on 20-1-1564: J. WIcki, *Documenta Indica,* 6 (1960) 180.

[52] Cf. the Apostolic Brief dated 15-1-1567 in G. Beltrami, *La Chiesa Caldea nel secolo dell'unione,* Orientalia Christiana 29 (Roma 1933) 91; Fr Melchior Nunes Barreto in 1568 and 1569: J. Wicki, *Documenta Indica,* 7 (1972) 476; 8 (1964) 135-136.

Christians.[53] But after Mar Abraham returned in 1570, the missionaries met with real apathy among the St Thomas Christians, as they were scandalized by the way the Portuguese missionaries treated their East Syrian bishops. Thereafter, as long as Mar Abraham was alive, the missionaries could not make any serious inroads into the system of church administration among the St Thomas Christians.

After the death of Mar Abraham in 1597, however, the St Thomas Christian community under the leadership of their ecclesiastical Governor and *Jathikku Karthavyan* Archdeacon George of the Cross, could not withstand for long the overwhelming power exercised by the Archbishop Menezes of Goa, which was boosted also by the political power of the Portuguese colonial government and the support exacted of the King of Cochin. Threatened with the loss of his office,[54] Archdeacon George finally gave in under heavy pressure and agreed to collaborate with Dom Menezes on all ten of his demands, one of which was to convoke a Diocesan Synod.

Subsequently, at the Synod convoked at Diamper, triumphed the missionaries' long scuttled project of changing the St Thomas Christians' system of church administration. In an avalanche came the synodal decrees modelled after the Latin canon law. Session VIII, decrees 1-3 ordered the division of the Church into parishes, and to appoint vicars, curates and coadjutors. As per session VII, section I, decrees 21 and 22 the clergy of the St Thomas Christians was to be supported with funds raised by alms, collections, assessments, tithes on the dowry, etc. from the faithful. For the support of the vicars and curates the King of Portugal was requested to grant an yearly subsidy of at least 15,000 Crusados. Until such a subsidy would be granted, Dom Menezes himself volunteered to supply that amount from his own revenues. Thus the self-supporting Church of the St Thomas Christians was made economically dependent on Portuguese subsidies. As per session VIII, decree 26, four lay overseers (*kaikars*) were to be elected yearly to help the vicar in the financial management of the parish funds.

---

[53] See letters of Fr Jerome Rodrigues (1570), Fr Salvador Cortès (1571) and Fr George Crasto (1574): J. Wicki, *Documenta Indica,* 8 (1964) 223, 359, 751-753.

[54] Archbishop Menezes threatened to excommunicate Archdeacon George of the Cross and promote Caçanar Thomas Curia of Angamaly as the Archdeacon. The warning was given by public announcements at Kaduthuruthy and Diamper (A. Gouvea, *op. cit,* f. 46r, 51r) as well as by letters from Thripunithara (Narame) and Cranganore (*ibid.,* ff. 52v, 54r). The Archdeacon gave in to the demands of Menezes at Vaipicotta (*ibid.,* f. 55v).

By subverting the hierarchical structure of the St Thomas Christian Church from the East Syrian pattern into the Latin, the organs assisting the bishop in the governance of the eparchy, such as the Archdeacon, the local clergy and the *Palliyogam* also were gradually deprived of their special competence and authority. The Latin hierarchs who were appointed over the St Thomas Christians after the Synod of Diamper wanted to exercise fully their power of governance by themselves. The Archdeacon was gradually side-tracked and finally ousted totally from the central administration. In half a century matters deteriorated to such an extent that a reaction occurred in the form of the *Koonan Cross* Revolution of 1653,[55] a harbinger of the unfortunate ecclesial divisions that now exist among the St Thomas Christians into Catholic, Jacobite, Orthodox, Mar Thomite Churches, and other ecclesial communities.

VI. Changes in the Spirituality and Ecclesial Life Style of the Clergy and the Laity

Since the first contact with the St Thomas Christians the Portuguese missionaries had great admiration for them for having preserved the Christian faith for so many centuries despite the adverse conditions of living among the Hindus, Muslims and Jews with no special protection from the State as in Europe. The missionaries were favourably impressed by their good Christian practices, such as regular church-going, chanting of the Liturgy of the Hours by the laity and the clergy together, strict observance of fasts and abstinence, and in general a good moral conduct.

However, quite a number of practices and customs of the St Thomas Christians were different from those of the Portuguese, and the missionaries wished perfect uniformity in everything. In their enclaves like Cranganore, Cochin, Quilon, etc. the missionaries insisted that the St Thomas Christians should keep fast and abstinence according to the Latin discipline, that is, the law of abstinence allowing the use of fish, egg, milk, milk products, wine, etc. But the Christians refused to give up their traditions. When too much pressure was brought to bear on them in places under the effective control of the

[55] See J. Kollaparambil, *The St Thomas Christians' Revolution in 1653*, Kottayam 1981.

Portuguese, the Christians preferred to leave those places than to abandon their traditions.[56]

The St Thomas Christians' devotions were mostly liturgy-centered, mainly in the celebration of the Holy Eucharist and in the chanting of the liturgy of the hours. The Synod of Diamper recommended also adoration of the Holy Eucharist outside the celebration of the Holy Liturgy and introduced the feast of the Corpus Christi (Session V, I, dec. 1). After the Synod of Diamper the liturgy of the hours was gradually reduced to a two weeks cycle of the ferial prayers. The *Hudra* and *Gazza* were practically discarded. Those who had no books could satisfy the obligation by reciting a number of *Our Fathers, Hail Marys* and *Glorys* in the morning and evening (Session VII, I, dec. 5). Besides, the devotions of the litany and the rosary of Our Lady and meditation on the Passion of Christ also were recommended (Session III, dec. 5).

In connection with the liturgical feasts and seasons, the St Thomas Christians had many fast days. They observed these fasts very piously, abstaining from meat, fish, egg, milk, milk products, alcoholic drinks and marital sex. The Synod of Diamper approved this as laudable custom (Session VIII, dec. 11). The Synod approved also the custom of beginning the Lent on the Monday after Quinquagesima Sunday, and enjoined the rites of the Ash Wednesday translated from the *Rituale Romanum* (Session VIII, dec, 15).

Further, instead of the St Thomas Christians' practice of abstinence on all Wednesdays and Fridays, the Synod commanded abstinence from meat on all Fridays and Saturdays, leaving the St Thomas Christians free to continue their custom of Wednesday abstinence. In addition to the Lent and Advent they were left free to observe the Three-days-fast of Jonas, the Eight-days-fast preceding the Nativity of Our Lady, the Fifteen-days-fast before the Assumption of Our Lady, and the Fifty-days-fast of the Apostles. To these were added as obligatory many more Latin fasts such as of the *Quatuor tempora*, vigils of the feasts of the Apostles etc.(Session VIII, dec. 10).

The St Thomas Christians used to venerate the cross in the churches and at home, but they had no statues and images. The missionaries slowly introduced the use of statues in the Malabar Church. The Synod of Diamper decreed that the statues and images of Our

---

[56] See Reports by Fr Fernando da Paz in 1557: A. da Silva Rego, *Documentaçâo ... India*, 6, 247-250; by Fr Pero Luis, S.J. in 1580: ARSI, *Goa 13*, ff. 42-43; and by Bishop Ros in 1604 and 1607: BML, *loc. cit.*, f. 90; and ARSI, *Goa 65*, f. 43v.

Lord, Our Lady and Saints must be set up in houses and churches for adoring or venerating the person represented. The contrary custom of the St Thomas Christians was censured as Nestorian (Session III, dec. 1, chc. 11; Session III, dec. 5; Session VIII, dec. 29).

Thus, as a consequence of the Synod of Diamper, the liturgy-centered devotions of the St Thomas Christians had to give way to paraliturgical devotions like the rosary, Eucharistic adoration, veneration of the saints through statues and images, litanies, novenas, etc. They were burdened with fasts and abstinences also of the Latin tradition in addition to their own.

VII. The Synod of Diamper's Censure of Some Inculturated Practices

Some of the customs and practices of the St Thomas Christians were integrated from the local culture. The Synod of Diamper found fault with them as superstitious and idolatrous and imposed severe censures on those who continued with such practices.

Some such practices had nothing to do with superstition or idolatry; they were simple national or cultural habits of the people. Such were, for example, the newly-wed couple not going to the church until the fourth day after marriage (Session VII, Section II, dec. 16); people bathing in the morning of fast days (Session VIII, dec. 13); bathing after a funeral, after which serving a meal for the bereaved relatives; taking back a thread after cutting a peace of cloth; taking back two grains after measuring out the paddy (Session IX, dec. 1); taking part in the games of *Onam* festivities along with the non-Christians (Session IX, dec. 4); men piercing their earlobes to wear an ornament like the Nairs (Session IX, dec. 17), etc.

Likewise the custom of the St Thomas Christian women not going to church for forty days after giving birth to a baby boy, or for eighty days after giving birth to a baby girl, was proscribed as a Jewish custom (Session IX, dec. 5).

Thus the St Thomas Christian Church was forced to shed many elements of inculturation which had been integrated into its life during the course of sixteen centuries.

CONCLUSION

From what I have exposed in this paper it becomes clear that the real function of the Synod of Diamper was to put a legal seal and stamp over the policy of the Portuguese missionaries to latinise the ecclesial life of the St Thomas Christians. This process, started right from their first encounter, continued all through the full span of the sixteenth century. Archbishop Menezes exceeded all the other missionaries before him in his zeal to reduce the St Thomas Christians to the Latin Church and passed very stringent decrees at the Synod of Diamper. Thus Dom Menezes became the symbol of the demise of the Oriental ecclesial identity of the St Thomas Christians.

Before the Synod of Diamper the latinising policy and process were, so to say, unofficial, unilaterally started and maintained by the Portuguese Padroado missionaries. The Synod of Diamper made that process official and legal, obliging the St Thomas Christians to accept and to conform to the synodal legislation. From then on the Latin hierarchs appointed over the St Thomas Christian Church could legally oblige the faithful to willy nilly go along with the plans and programmes of the missionaries to latinise their ecclesial life. The result was that in the course of the following three centuries the St Thomas Christians lost their genuine, Oriental ecclesial identity.

The ecclesial life which they were forced to lead after the Synod of Diamper was essentially Latin, although wrapped in the East Syrian linguistic garb. The East Syrian ecclesial traditions and life-style, however, lingered longer among the simple practising faithful, but the clergy educated and formed in the Latin pattern served only to destroy such Oriental traditions among the ordinary faithful.

The most disastrous consequence was that the St Thomas Christians remained Orientals only in name. In reality, their liturgy was very much latinised except for the celebration of the Holy Qurbana, though several interpolations from the Latin liturgy were introduced into the Qurbana, and many other corrections were made following the Western theology. As for the liturgy of the hours the *Hudra* and *Gazza* disappeared from the practice due to the destruction of the MSS. What remained was only a two-weeks cycle of the Ordinary Sunday and ferial prayers (*Kaskol*). For all the other Sacraments and sacramentals mere Syriac translations of the *Rituale Romanum* came into use.

After the Synod of Diamper the missionaries taught the St Thomas Christian clergy the Western theology, but purposely keeping it to the elementary level. The Eastern theological tradition disappeared gradually from this Church. So also the mostly liturgy-centred spirituality of the St Thomas Christians was replaced with non-liturgical or paraliturgical devotions. Many of their national-cultural practices were to be abandoned. The Latin hierarchy that was imposed over the St Thomas Christians changed also the Oriental system of governance and administration at the central level as well as in the local communities.

The Synod of Diamper sealed with its authority the latinising process initiated and pursued by the Portuguese missionaries from the early sixteenth century, and this was interpreted as the authorization granted by the St Thomas Christians to the missionaries to continue the same latinising process. In spite of the sporadic resistance and even rebellion by the St Thomas Christians, the missionaries succeeded to a great extent in destroying the Oriental identity of this Church. The community suffered tragic divisions, some even changing their ecclesial affiliation from Catholic to non-Catholic, from East Syrian to West Syrian or to Anglican.

Those who remained in the Catholic fold lost their former ecclesial identity and became a kind of hybrid breed made up of a curious mixture of the Law of Thomas and the Law of Peter. In official classification, they are Oriental, but in reality according to their liturgical, theological, spiritual and disciplinary life, they are to a great extent Western. They are the product of a latinising process that had endured for three and a half centuries both under the Latin and the indigenous hierarchs.

In the second half of the twentieth century, the Holy See adopted an official policy to restore the Oriental identity of this Church, but it met with resistance from a considerable section of this Church who, albeit for no fault of theirs, have lost their proper Oriental identity and glory in their so-called "universal Catholic identity". Let us hope that patient and sustained efforts to conscientize this section of their proper Oriental ecclesial identity may succeed to undo the damage done by a latinising process which was unleashed by the Portuguese missionaries in the sixteenth century, a policy that was legally confirmed and accelerated by the Synod of Diamper, and afterwards pursued unabated under the Latin and indigenous hierarchs.

Catholic Bishop's House
Kottayam – 686 001
Kerala, India

Jacob Kollaparambil

Jacob Vellian

The Synod of Diamper and the Liturgy of the Syro-Malabar Church

In the Church of India the East Syrian liturgy was in use from ancient times. Its use in Malabar from the early centuries is attested by the Synod of the Diamper. In session V, section II, decree 1, it is stated: "Whereas the Church has been 1200 years separated from the obedience of the Holy Roman Church ... all the bishops that came from Babylon ... both added to and have taken from the Mass at their pleasure without any order."

Again, when Menezes insisted that the Patriach of Babylon should not be commemorated any longer but must be regarded as a Nestorian heretic and got a document signed to that effect by the archdeacon at Vaipicotta before the Synod, the local people protested saying: "For more than 1200 years we have been governed by the patriarch."[1] This contains an implicit affirmation of the use of the East Syrian liturgy in Malabar from the fourth century onwards.

The Background

Certain events preceded the Synod that shaped its peculiar slant, determined its contents and by and large set the tone of its decrees.

The Jesuit seminary founded at Vaipicotta in 1587 was gradually opened to the training of the Malabar clergy. Unlike the Franciscan seminary of Cranganore, Syriac was taught at Vaipicotta. Fr. Francis Ros, S.J., was professor of Syriac and would later be commissioned to implement the synodal decrees regarding the seminary training, to see to the translation of the Latin Pontifical and Ritual into Syriac, and expunge the Syriac manuscripts of all Nestorian errors. For this last commission he had special credentials. In a report written already in 1586 entitled *De Erroribus Nestorianorum qui in hac India Orientali versantur*,[2] he had ascertained that though the Malaber

---

[1] James Hough, *History of Christianity in India,* vol. 1, pp. 231, 347.

[2] Irenée Hausher, ed., *De Erroribus Nestorianorum...*, (Orientalia Christiana IX/1, Nº 40), Rome, 1928.

Christians professed the true christological faith, and acknowledged Mary as the Mother of God, their books contained Nestorian errors.[3]

The Synod dealt both with doctrine and discipline. By affirming the supremacy of the Roman Pontiff, and the divine motherhood of Mary, it rejected the errors of Nestorianism (§§ 15, 16).[4] It prescribed that the disciplinary regulations promulgated by the Council of Trent should be accepted by the Malabar Church (e.g., §§ 92, 96). Regarding the sacraments, with which we are more directly concerned in this paper, the synodal decrees included a doctrinal part and a disciplinary part concerning each sacrament and its administration.

SOLEMN LITURGICAL INAUGURATION

In the first session, a synodal decree prescribed that all, whether priests or laymen, should make a sincere confession during the Synod and should participate in two Eucharistic liturgical celebrations: first, the Mass of the Holy Spirit in the Latin rite, and the second a Qurbana in honour of the Blessed Virgin Mary in Syriac. The litanies were to be sung also both in Syriac and Latin.

INTERPOLATED DECREES ON THE LITURGY

At the end of the Synod, the participants of the Synod of Diamper put their signatures to the acts in their Malayalam version.[5] But in Goa, Menezes made modifications and additions to the original Portuguese text. The folios with the signatures appended to the Malayalam version of the decrees, were then appended to the enlarged Portuguese text. Some of the additions made in the Portuguese text deal with liturgy.[6]

In session III decrees 8 and 9 it was decreed that the Patriarch of Babylon should no more be commemorated in the Qurbana.

---

[3] Ibid., p. 31.

[4] For the paragraph (§) numbers given here see the Latin translation in Raulin, reprinted in Mansi, Paiva Manso, etc.

[5] K. N Daniel, *Undayamperur Sunahadosinte Kanonakal,* (Malayalam), Thiruvalla, 1952.

[6] Scaria Zacharia, *Randu Pracheena Gadyakrithikal,* (Malayalam), Changanachery, 1976, pp. 181-198. This work contains the decrees of the Synod of Diamper and the *Statutes* of Bishop Francis Ros, S. J. Appendix I, pp. 181–198 gives the decrees that were added to the original Malayalam text.

Session IV decree 22 prescribed that children should be called only by the name received at Baptism.

Session V decree 7 ordered that "seals are to be made to stamp wafers or hosts used at Mass." It added that Vicars are to take care always to provide the flour of wheat to make them; they are to make sure that no other substance is mixed with flour, as is usually done in making common bread, in order not to endanger the validity of the consecration. And the same care shall be taken for wine, that it be no other than that of Portugal, and that it be not mixed with juice of raisins, or with any other wines of the country for the same reason."

Next, decree 8 asks priests to take care that Mass wine does not turn into vinegar.

Decree 9 states that the King of Portugal will be asked to send sufficient Mass wine into Malabar.

Decree 10 prescribes that altar stones be consecrated for the use of the Malabar churches. And the Archbishop decides to give metal chalices to all churches.

Decree 11 provides ecclesiastical vestments for the priests.

In decree 14, the Synod forbade heathen musicians and other pagans to remain in the church when the sacraments are administered.

In session VI, decree 7, it recommends frequent confession, not just the yearly one prescribed in the Malayalam decree (session 4, decree 4).

Session VII decree 6, insists that the Athanasian Creed (*Quicumque vult*) be translated into Syriac and be put into all the breviaries and books of prayer of this diocese and that it is to be read every Sunday in the church immediately after the morning service.

Session VII, decree 7 directed priests to be punctual in their attendance at time of the divine office, morning and evening.

Session VIII, decree 23 speaks of blessing candles on certain days (e.g. 2 February, the feast of the Purification of Mary) using a prayer translated from the Latin into Syriac, and of a procession in or around the church with candles; So also three days before Ascension Thursday, candles may be blessed in the morning, as was the Roman custom at that time and a procession may be organized with the singing of litanies.

Session IX, decree 4, forbade attendance in heathen festivals like Onam.

Leaving aside the sacraments of initiation, on which much study has already been done, I shall here deal with the rest of the sacraments.

PART I
DIAMPER AND LITURGY

A. THE TEXT OF THE QURBANA

It is generally accepted that the East Syrian Qurbana was in use in the Malabar Church at the time of the Synod of Diamper, though not much is known regarding its exact text. The decrees of the Synod in its explanations of the corrections it prescribed, at times gave the full texts on which it worked, but at other times only a partial text.

In his study "The Work of Menezes on the Malabar Liturgy" Connolly suggests that the liturgy prior to Diamper could be traced from the decrees of the Synod, and that it was the East Syrian Liturgy, though it was different, in certain cases, from the standard Nestorian Liturgy.[7]

By a comparison of the Diamper text with a few manuscript texts of the East Syrian Liturgy of the Apostles, Douglas Webb has shown that the text on which the synod worked, and hence was in use in the Malabar Church in the period immediately preceding the synod, was a composite East Syrian text "containing many features which do not usually appear in the ordinary manuscripts," and that its parts were composed mostly after the Alqosh type manuscript.[8]

---

[7] R. H Connolly, "The Work of Menezes on the Malabar Liturgy," JTS 15 (1914) 396-425, 569-589. Until recent times scholars considered the Urmia text, *Litgurgia Sanctorum Apostolorum Addai et Mari* (Urmia 1890), as the standard one. An English translation of this text may be found in *The Liturgy of the Holy Apostles Addai and Mari* (London: S.P.C.K., 1893).

[8] Douglas Webb, "The Versions of the Malabar Liturgy and the Manuscripts," *The Malabar Church*, ed. J. Vellian, pp. 41-54. See also, Douglas Webb, "Antonio de Gouvea's Version of the Nestorian Liturgy of the Apostels." *Studia Patristica*, V, part 3, (*Texte and Untersuchungen*, 80), ed. F. L. Cross, Berlin (1962), 213-240. According to Douglas Webb, the manuscripts of the East Syrian Qurbana could be grouped in two: 1) the complete texts with full rubrics and prayers and 2) the incomplete ones, which do not give the full rubrics and texts. The first is the standard type and is called the Alqosh type ("The Versions of the Malabar Liturgy", p.45).

Changes in the Qurbana

The changes prescribed by the synod in the text of the Qurbana are about forty. They can be thus distinguished: six in litanies, seven in hymns or anthems, four in formulae pertaining to the deacon, one in a response of the people, one in the text of the gospel lesson, one affecting the whole creed. In the prayer of the priest, there are five in the pre-anaphoral part, four within the anaphora and eleven in the four variable *huthame* (final blessings).

Many of the changes made were in view of doctrinal integrity. Thus fifteen of the changes concern the names referring to Christ. This was obviously intended as a safeguard against Nestorianism. For example, the simple titles like Christ, Jesus, and the Son were amplified into expressions like "Jesus Christ His Son our Lord." In the same way the title "Mother of Christ" referring to Mary was changed into "Mother of God." Four changes substituted the name of the Chaldean Patriarch with the name of the Pope.

The liturgical convention of anticipation, by which bread and wine are called the body and blood of Christ, was to be abolished. So also the names of Nestorius, Theodore and Diodore[9] were to be removed from the commemoration. In the Creed, § 116 directed the addition of the phrase, *Deum de Deo, lumen de lumine, Deum verum de Deo vero,* and the substitution *of filius essentiae patris* (Barkyana davui) with *consubstantialem patris* (*Heuvmasios dava*).[10] Actually the Syriac word *bar kyana* means the same as the *homousios* which term was transliterated as *heumasios*. The net result of the changes was to make it conformable to the Creed in the Roman Missal. Following the Roman liturgical laws of the time, the synod prohibited the clerics below subdeacons to touch the sacred vessels (§ 124), and those below deacons to use the stole (§ 126). The bread for the Eucharist was to be of pure wheat flour, and the wine pure Portuguese (§ 126). The Synod also ordered the use of consecrated altar stones, and chalices of precious metal (§ 129).

In the response of the people, "May Christ hear your prayers," the Synod made some modification with the addition from the Roman Te

---

[9] Unknown is the text of the anaphora of Diodore. William Wright suggests that it might be "the sixth century fragment of a Persian anaphora" published by G. Bickell. See W. Wright, *Syriac Literature*, p. 28; Connolly, "The Work of Menezes," p. 425.

[10] Cf. Session V, Sacrifice of the Mass, Decree I.

Igitur: *"et omnibus orthodoxis atque catholicae et apostolicae fidei cultoribus"* (§ 117).

In the rite of the Fraction, the Synod "detected" a sacrilegious and impious action. After breaking the bread into two halves, the priest dips the one held in the right hand in the chalice, and with that signs the other half in the left hand. Then he holds both parts together in his hands, and in order that the moistened and the bent part of the host in the right hand may not fall apart, he presses that moistened part against the portion held in the left hand. The Synod considered it a reflection of the Nestorian faith, according to which, as Menezes seems to have understood it, the Body of Christ did not contain the Blood. (Evidently this is without any foundation.) The Synod misunderstood that the priest, by pressing the moistened loaf against the other at the Fraction, was trying to infuse the Blood into the Body. The Synod prohibited such a ceremony (§ 122).

Institution-Narrative

It is well-known that the Institution-Narrative does not appear in the early manuscripts of the anaphora of Addai and Mari. Though the Synod of Diamper speaks about the Institution-Narrative used in the anaphora of Addai and Mari at the time of the Synod (§§ 109-110) it does not give any specific indication concerning the source of this Institution-Narrative.

In a study on "The Malabar Liturgy," Burkitt pointed out that the Chaldean bishops who came from Mesopotamia were responsible for this addition, since they changed the liturgical texts "at will." The addition, says Burkitt, was made by a bishop "after the Nestorian revival of 1490."[11] This opinion is based on the suggestion of Gouvea, (1606).

In 1944 Alphonse Raes brought to light folio 101 of manuscript Vat. Syr. 66 of Mar Joseph (1566), on which an Institution-Narrative is written. It is written right at the beginning of the Anaphora of the Apostles, with a note where to recite it.

In its observations on the Institution-Narrative, the Synod laid down that the *verba consecrationis* should be the same as in the Roman missal. A comparative study of the Diamper text with those of Mar Joseph and the Roman Missal might shed light on their relation and resemblance to one another (see infra).

---

[11] F. C. Burkitt, "The Old Malabar Liturgy," JTS 29 (1928) 155-157.

Both the texts of Mar Joseph and of Diamper have certain characteristics of the Roman canon, which can be resumed as follows:

Diamper

1. "On the day previous to his suffering."
2. Omission of "which is broken for you."
3. "and raises the chalice a little above the altar";
4. "the chalice of my blood."

At the same time, Joseph and Diamper have their peculiarities:

Mar Joseph

1. "In truth" seen in the consecration of bread and wine;
2. the position of "and whenever you eat this bread and drink this chalice ...";
3. "and this will be for you a pledge for ever."

The text of Mar Joseph contains the characteristic expression of Eastern Rites at the beginning of the Institution-Narrative: "In the night in which he was to be betrayed." This is not preserved in the Diamper text. The clause, "and this will be for you a pledge for ever," was changed by Diamper into "and this will be for us a pledge until the end of the world," since the "pledge for us" is for so long as we are away from the Lord.

In the Diamper text the Institution-Narrative is given after the Epiclesis and before the Fraction. It is placed outside the anaphora. In Mar Joseph, the rubrics indicate that it is recited at the end of the Fraction. This, too, is outside the anaphora.

We may suppose that already before Diamper, possibly in the Synod of Angamaly held by Mar Abraham in 1583, which dealt with the Qurbaba, the Institution-Narrative was shifted to an earlier place, i.e., before the Fraction.

Mar Joseph	**Diamper**	**Roman Missal**
On the Body		
- Our Lord Jesus Christ	- Dominus noster Jesus Christus	- Qui
- on the night in which he was to be betrayed	- in illa nocte, qua tradebatur	- pridie quam pateretur,
- and on the day previous to his suffering		

- took this holy bread in his pure and sacred hands	- accepit panem hunc sanctum in sanctas ac puras manus suas	- accepit panem in sanctas ac venerabiles manus suas,
- and he raised his eyes towards heaven	- et elevavit oculos suos in caelum,	- et elevatis oculis in caelum ad te Deum Patrem suum omnipotentem
- and gave thanks to God the Father, the creator of everything	- et gratias egit Deo Patri, omnium rerum creatori	- tibi gratias agens,
- and blessed + and broke and gave (it) to his disciples, and said:	- et benedixit ac fregit, deditque discipulis suis, et dixit:	- benedixit, fregit deditque discipulis suis, dicens:
- "Take, eat from this bread all of you.	- Accipite et comedite ex hoc pane omnes vos.	- Accipite et manducate ex hoc omnes.
- This in truth is my body"	- Hoc est in veritate corpus meum.	- Hoc est enim corpus meum.
(And raising the chalice a little above the altar, he says over the chalice):		
- And in the same way, after they had supped he took this chalice in his pure hands	- Similiter postquam coenavit, accepti hunc calicem manibus suis puris,	- Simili modo postqaum coenatum est, accipiens et hunc praeclarum calicem in sanctas ac venerabiles manus suas.
- and gave thanks	- et gratias egit	- item tibi gratias agens,
- and blessed + and gave (it) to his disciples and said:	- et benedixit, et dedit discipulis suis, dicens:	- benedixit, deditque discipulis suis, dicens:
- "Take, drink from this chalice, all of you; And whenever you eat this bread and drink this chalice, you will remember me.	- Accipite et bibite omnes vos, ex hoc calice - quotiescumque enim comederitis panem Hunc, et biberitis calicem, mei memoriam recoletis	- Accipite, et bibite ex eo omens.
- This is in truth the chalice of my blood of the New Testament	- Hic est in veritate calix sanguinis mei, novi testamenti	- Hic est enim calix sanguinis mei, novi et aeterni testamenti mysterium fidei,
- which is shed for you and for many	- qui pro vobis et pro multis effundetur	- qui pro vobis et pro multis effundetur
- unto the remission of debts and forgiveness of sins.	- in debitorum propitiationem et in peccatorum remissionem:	- in remissionem peccatorum.
- This will be for you a pledge forever"	- et hoc erit vobis pignus in saecula saeculorum	- Hoc quotiescumque feceritis, in mei memoriam facietis.

Epiclesis

Diamper was very sensitive about the Epiclesis. In the anaphora of Addai and Mari there is no explicit allusion to the changing of the bread and wine by the Holy Sprit. Actually Diamper did not modify it. But it dealt with the hymn, "when the priest enters the sanctuary," which appeared at the Fraction, in which there is a reference to the invocation by the priest to the Spirit to consecrate the bread and wine. The Synod decreed to leave out the expression: "The priest invokes the Spirit who comes down from heaven." Evidently the Synod understood this hymn as epicletic.[12] The position of the hymn, namely among the hymns of Fraction which immediately followed the Institution Narrative, tended to support such a conclusion.

B. SACRAMENTS

Penance

The Dismissal of the unworthy in the Liturgical Homilies of Narsai clearly witness to the practice of public penance in the East Syrian Church of the fifth century.[13]

The complete rite of the East Syrian penance is found only in the later manuscripts such as Diarbekir 48 of the fifteenth century. As Wilhem De Vries points out, the rite consisted of four stages: approaching a priest for penance, the assigning of a penance, fulfilling the penance, and receiving absolution before Communion at a Sunday Eucharist.[14]

Bishop Francis Ros, S.J., says in his report of 1604 that Mar Jacob († 1552) translated the Latin formula of absolution into Syriac, and that Mar Joseph († 1569) modified this formula.[15]

According to Mar Joseph confession takes place in front of the sanctuary or any other solitary place set apart for confession; the penitent kneels down, bowing his head and placing the hands on his breast.

---

[12] Jacob Vellian, "Les Prosternements dans le *Raza* Syro-Malabar," *Or Syr* 11 (1966) 367-73; J. Vellian, "The Raza of the Syro-Malabar Church," *Dukrana* 6/7 (1986) 5ff.

[13] R. Connolly, *The Liturgical Homilies of Narsai*, Cambridge 1909.

[14] Wilhelm De Vries, "Beicht und Busspraxis bei Ost-und West Syrern," *Ostkirchliche Studien* 20 (1971) 273-274.

[15] G. Schurhammer, *The Malabar Church and Rome*, p. 22.

The sacrament of penance was taken up in earnest by the Synod of Diamper and decrees were formulated to conform the Malabar discipline to that of the Roman Church. The Synod found fault with those who received the Euchrist without previously going to confession (§ 100).

In the session on confession, the precept of yearly confession was promulgated (§ 137) and § 139 made annual confession obligatory for all from eight years upwards, while § 146 encouraged frequent confession.

Anointing of the Sick

In the early East Syrian Church there are only very few allusions to the anointing of the sick. Canon 19 of the Synod of Catholicos Joseph (554 A.D.) makes a passing mention of the anointing of the body of the sick person, with oil blessed by a priest.[16] Mar Abed (420 AD), the martyr, is said to have anointed a person with "the oil of grace."[17]

Joseph the Indian (1500 A.D.) is reported to have said that there was no anointing of the sick in Malabar; instead of anointing, the sick person was blessed and was sprinkled with holy water.[18] Besides, biblical passages written on plates were tied to the body of the sick, and dust from the tomb of the Apostle Thomas, mixed with water, was often used as a medication. This latter was called *hanana* (= mercy).[19]

Vat. Syr. 45 and 46, manuscripts written by Mar Joseph, contain a prayer for blessing the sick. It is a prayer for the health of the body and soul. Vat. Syr. 46 includes the rite of the making of the *hanana*, in which the *Thaibutha* (grace = dust from the tomb) of Apostle Thomas is an ingredient.[20]

---

[16] *Synodicon Orientale*, p. 364.

[17] Patrologia Orientalis, XIII, 588.

[18] Montalboddo, *Paesi novamente ritorvati*, ch. 134.

[19] It is important to note that the prayer at the imposition of hands at the ordination of priests and bishops implores the grace "to heal the sick imposing hands on them" (*Syriac Pontifical*: Rome, 1958, p. 158).

[20] Translation of Vat. Syr. 45, fol. 173^{v}: "May God, the giver of all healing and dispenser of all good, whose care of the human race does not end and who does not deny His help to us, extend the right hand of His mercy over you; may He expel from you sickness and (all) enemies, and give you a good life and health of body and soul,

Diamper flatly denied the prior existence of the anointing of the sick in Malabar (§ 154). The Synod exhorted the people to make use of this sacrament. The liturgical rules given were purely Roman (§ 156).

Holy Orders

The East Syrian Synod of Seleucia (410 A.D.) set down the hierarchy of orders; patriarch, metropolitan, bishop, chorepiscopa (bishop of the village), archdeacon, presbyter, deacon, subdeacon and lector.[21]

There are four manuscripts of Mar Joseph of Malabar, which contain altogether five ordination services. Vat. Syr. 45 (fol. 34-133) and 46 (fol. 1-8) have the Chaldean Pontifical. Vat. Syr. 66 contains the Chaldean ordination service (fol. 45-61) and a Syriac translation of the Roman ordination service (fol. 1-10) for the seven holy orders: lector to priest. Vat.Syr. 89 also contains the latter.

In this situation a complete transition to the Roman Pontifical was not difficult to achieve. Nothing was said about the text of the Ordination Service. The Synod simply enumerated the seven Holy Orders as given in the Roman Pontifical (§ 163). Menezes insisted that the seminarians who are preparing to receive Holy Orders should acquire as much knowledge of Syriac as the Council of Trent demanded Latin (of seminarians of the Latin Church).

The practice of the Malabar Church was to celebrate the Divine Office in the church with the faithful participating on Sundays and other feast days, or that the clergy alone celebrate it in choir.[22] The Synod imposed as a grave obligation the private recitation of the Divine Office (§ 163).

C. Liturgical Calendar

Feasts

The existence of Vat. Sir. 22 of 1301 A.D. is definite proof of the use of the East Syrian calendar in Malabar. Joseph the Indian (1500)

---

so that you may render Him glory and make confession of the Father and of the Son and of the Holy Spirit now and at all times."

[21] *Synodicon Orientale*, pp. 263-271.

[22] For testimonies of this in the pre-Diamper period, see T. Puthiakunnel, *Syro-Malabar Clergy and Their General Obligations*, pp. 133-139

recounts, among others, the following feasts as observed in Malabar: St. Thomas, the Trinity, the Assumption of Mary. The feast of the Holy Trinity is not East Syrian, but Roman.

In § 208, the Synod of Diamper pointed out that there was confusion in Malabar regarding the holy days of obligation. It gave a list of the feasts to be observed.

Further, the Synod prescribed that the Malabar Church should observe the *Quatuor Tempora* in order that it might be "conformed to the practice of the universal Church". The curious thing to note here is that the Malabar Christians were thus obliged to observe the combined fasts of both the Roman Church and the East Syrian Church.

D. Other Prescriptions

In addition to the above, the Synod dealt with several areas of the Malabar Church which had some bearing on the liturgy. Thus, for instance, it decreed that marriage should take place only inside the church (188), which indicates that it used to take place elsewhere, most probably at home, as was the early Christian as well as Hindu custom. The Synod prescribed the manner of blessing holy water according to the *Rituale Romanum* (§ 217). According to § 220 when pronouncing or hearing the name of Jesus, all should bow their heads.

In making the sign of the cross, the Malabar Christians followed the general practice of the Orientals, signing from right to left. The Synod, however, wanted the Roman way, that is, from left to right (§ 237). The Malabar Church was criticized for not having statues in its churches and was ordered to furnish them. Following the Roman practice of the time, the Synod directed that priests should wear a surplice and stole when they administer the sacraments (§ 221). The Malabar priests were given the privilege of the Roman priests to celebrate three Masses on the feast of Christmas (§ 221). For the celebration of 2 February the Synod asked the priests to follow the prayers of the Roman Ritual, translated into Syriac (§ 223). The Synod ordered priests to use a stamp-press to make the altar bread (§ 126) to ensure that only wafers were used.

As we have seen, the only four borrowings from the Roman Mass for the Qurbana were the Institution-Narrative, part of the Creed, and a phrase from the *Te Igitur* in one of the responses of the faithful, and the Agnus Dei. The texts of the sacraments were taken care of by the simple direction to use the Syriac translation of the *Rituale Romanum*. Thus, most of the directives were meant to replace the East Syrian rite with the Roman liturgical rite. To ensure that the transition was successful, parish priests were supplied with several things at the end of the Synod: consecrated altar stones, a chest containing three holy oils, a Syriac translation of the *Rituale Romanum*, a Malayalam catechism, surplice, corporal, vestments, frontalia for the altar, chalices, and other things necessary for the service of the altar.

PART II

BISHOP ROS AND THE MALABAR LITURGY

Francis Ros was a Jesuit priest from Catalonia. He was well known to the Malabar Christians as a professor, especially of Syriac, and well versed in Malayalam. In the spirit of obedience to ecclesiastical hierarchy, he worked closely with Menezes for the success of the Synod of Diamper. Barely six months after the conclusion of this Synod, on 20 December 1599, Ros was appointed bishop of the diocese of Angamaly and was consecrated on 25 January 1601.

Once he assumed the pastoral charge of his diocese, he openly criticized the dishonest procedure of Menezes who forced the participants to sign the decrees and added some new canons after the conclusion of the Synod.

SOURCES

There are two main documents that help us to understand the work of Ros on the liturgy of Malabar: his diocesan Statutes(1606): and the Raza text which he promulgated (1603). The Statutes is in Malayalam and is preserved in the Vatican Library MS Borgiano Indiano 18.[23] A copy of the manuscript of the Raza of Ros is kept in the Mannanam monastery.

The Statutes refers to the Qurbana text, which he prepared to avoid the confusion in the celebration of the Qurbana. "Hence the Qurbana should be celebrated as it is written in the Taksa according as we have commanded in the second Synod of Angamaly" (fol. 45).

---

[23] It has been published by Scaria Zacharia, ed., *Raṇṭu prācīna gadyakṛtikal*, Changacherry, 1976, pp. 111-177.

The Taksa is entitled *The Rites of Raza in the Church of India. Arranged by Francis in the fourth year, fourth month of his episcopacy in the Synod of Angamaly.*

QURBANA OF ROS

> Fol. 44^{V}. On the celebration of Qurbana and on the priests who celebrate it.
> 45^{V}. There is much confusion in the diocese because the priests celebrate the Qurbana in serval ways. The Qurbana, therefore, shall be celebrated as we ordered in the second Synod of Angamaly. If the priests will not do so every day, they shall not celebrate the Qurbana at all.

A comparative study of the Diamper text and the Rosian text shows that Ros made further latinization. For instance, he begins the Qurbana with the Sign of the Cross, "In the name of the Father." He corrected the position of the reading, placing it before the Offertory" (fol. 37^{r}).

The rubrics of the Raza contain other specifically Roman practices. The celebrant is directed to read the Gospel privately even though it is sung aloud by the deacon. The servers are asked to sit on the steps of the altar during the first and second reading.

Dealing with Holy Communion among other things, Ros says: "So let only those who confessed their sins (properly) dare to receive the Eucharist. The blessing that is given before the distribution of the communion was exactly that of the Roman rite. The prayers, *the Lamb of God, Lord I am not worthy,* are mentioned therein (fol. 38^{v}).

The rubric "A cloth should be spread over a bench placed in front of the kneeling communicants" refers to a Roman practice of the time (fol. 40^{r}).

In the case of the sacrament of penance it is prescribed that the confessor should put on the surplice and the *biretta*. As for the confessional, there should be a wooden plank about 5 feet in height with holes at their centre, kept on either side of the priest in between the penitent and the confessor (fol. 52^{r}). And an image of Christ crucified should be fitted on the plank for the penitents to see (fol. 52^{v}).

The penitents should make the sign of the cross and should recite half of the *confiteor*. The absolution formula is simply Roman (fol. 64^{v}, 67^{v}).

Ros speaks of the sacrament of *"Extreme Unction"* after the pattern of the Roman Liturgy.

He also directs that the candidates to priesthood should be given the tonsure before the Minor Orders are conferred (fol. 78^{v}).

Following the Roman legislation of the time, Ros specified that the blessing (*Intra missam*) should not be given to those who married in the prohibited times. So also it is specified that feast days and fast days are to be observed from midnight to midnight.

On fol. 18 it is said, "all priests of all churches should recite the Divine Office which we, with great labour codified from scattered sources." Possibly this could be the Kaskol (ferial office with a Sunday office), which was in use in Malabar until recently. It left out the year-around prayers and offices of the Syro-Malabar Liturgy of the Hours.

Ros gives the impression that he was engaged in the steady Romanization of the Malabar liturgy, not because he wanted to annihilate the Eastern liturgy, but because he thought that it was the only way to remedy the laxity he saw in the liturgical discipline of the Church he presided over. However, for all his latinization, he was more considerate than Diamper in preserving some of the Malabar customs.

Part III

THE IMPACT OF THE LITURGICAL CHANGES OF DIAMPER AND OF BISHOP ROS ON THE MALABAR LITURGY IN THE SUBSEQUENT FOUR CENTURIES

The policy of latinization was adopted and legalised in the Synod of Diamper, but it was Bishop Ros who applied it officially and extended it further to change the whole physiognomy of the liturgy of the Malabar Church. Three reasons can be suggested why the Synod adopted the policy of latinization: the fear of heresy in the East Syrian liturgical texts; the idea that the Eastern liturgy is imperfect because of the lack of medieval western devotions; and the supposition that the "Latin" (Roman) liturgy was superior (*praestantia ritus romani*), if not faultless and ideal. All these reasons can be found, in one form or another, as underpinning the sixteenth century liturgical reform of the Malabar Church, and even later down to modern times. Such has been the impact of Diamper. To evidence this we have to discuss in chronological sequence the major events in the history of Malabar liturgy since the Diamper-Rosian period, and to examine the activities of the important persons who have exercised great influence on the later Malabar liturgy.

THE PRINTING OF THE LITURGICAL BOOKS: TAKSA

The Syro-Malabar Taksa (missal) was first printed in Rome in 1774 with the Latin title, *Ordo Chaldaicus Missae juxta morem Ecclesiae Malabaricae, superiorum permissu editus.* An Instruction of the Sacred Congregation for the Propagation of the Faith to the Latin Vicar Apostolic of Malabar, dated 3 September 1757, indicated that the text of the Qurbana corrected by Menezes in the Synod of Diamper should be sent to Rome with a Latin translation so that a Syriac missal for the Malabar Church could be printed.[24]

It is not known how this Instruction was followed up. MS Borgiano Latino 280, fol. 241^{v}-282^{v}, of the eighteenth century, gives a report on the procedure that was followed in selecting the text for the printing. It can be summarized as follows.

Father Charles of Conrad, a Carmelite, brought two copies of the Malabar missal to Rome, and another Carmelite brought a third copy of the same. Because of the difference in their contents, Rome had to find out which of those manuscripts was in use in Malabar. To get further light on the issue the Syriac scholar J. S. Assemani was consulted. He suggested either to print the Menezian Missal, which was partially Roman, or to get another copy subscribed to by all the Malabar priests. With this he was actually discouraging the use of the manuscripts brought by the missionaries. These suggestions were sent to the *Congregatio super correctionem librorum Ecclesiae Orientalis*, for a decision. Cardinal Antonelli, one of the consultors of this Congregation, suggested that the Chaldean missal should not be given to the Malabar Church without knowing the will of the people of Malabar. This suggestion was adopted by the Congregation. However, as a compromise two copies of the Chaldean printed missal were sent to the Malabar Vicar Apostolic asking him to convoke an assembly of all the Malabar priests. In the assembly of the priests the Chaldean missal was rejected — a telling proof of the impact of the Diamper-Ros latinization after a century and half. In accordance with this development, one of the two manuscripts brought by Fr. Charles

24 See the text of the Instruction given in *Subsidium ad Bullarium Patronatus Portugalliae* (Alleppey, 1903), pp. 55-56.

was printed.[25] In the edition of 1774 several prayers which were not in the East Syrian Qurbana were added:

1. "The Father of Truth":
2. A final blessing in honour of the Virgin Mary:
3. A prayer of bidding adieu to the altar:
4. Four other *hutamas*
5. *Agnus Dei* before the minor Elevation
6. Two prayers before the celebrant receives the chalice
7. Three Post-communion prayers.

Of these the first three prayers were taken from the Maronite missal due to the influence of J. S. Assemani, who served as a consultant in the committee which edited the Malabar missal.

It prescribed that the celebrant should enter the sanctuary with *biretta* on, and that the server should carry the Taksa (missal). The Qurbana was to begin with the Sign of the Cross and the prayer "In the name of the Father..."

The printed text followed the Roman manner of blessing the deacon before the Gospel. The communion rite was a translation taken from the Roman missal. The Taksa prescribed a genuflection every time the sacred species are handled after the Instituion-Narrative. It contained only the Anaphora of Addai and Mari, leaving out the Anaphoras of Theodore and Nestorius, in accordance with the decrees of Diamper (§ 121). There was no provision for the *propria* (that is, the variable prayers) of the Qurbana.

The Congregatio super correctionem Librorun Ecclesiae Orientlis directed on 1 June 1766 to retain the Elevation of the sacred species immediately after the words of Institution.

In the printed missal, the East Syrian calendar was replaced with the Roman calendar, adding only the feast of 3 July (St. Thomas), and 18 December (St. Thomas), and the feast of the Ninivites, eighteen days before the beginning of Lent. The readings were given as in the Roman missal, generally only two each for every day, and making the text of the Pshitta conformable to the Vulgate whenever the for-

[25] Placid J.Podipara, "The Present Syro-Malabar Liturgy Menesian or Rosian?" OCP 22 (1957) 313-333. This study has shown beyond doubt that the Malabar printed missal was more Rosian than Menesian. It may be noted that the Mannanam missal of Ros, on which Podipara based most of his study, is identical with another Vatican manuscript, Borgiano Syriaco 36, which was probably the manuscript brought to Rome by Father Charles.

mer varied notably. Prayers for the vesting were translated and were printed in the Taksa.

Further, the missal contained the Syriac translation from the Roman missal of the services for Ash Wednesday, Palm Sunday, Maundy Thursday, Passion Friday and of the Candlemas of the second of February. The Mass of the Presanctified was translated from the Roman missal.[26]

A Syriac translation of certain ceremonies of the *Rituale Romanum* was printed in 1775 in Rome. It contained the rites of baptism, confession, anointing of the sick and marriage. A second edition of the same was printed in Rome in 1845 with translations of other ceremonies from the *Rituale Romanum*, such as formulas for blessing holy water, a place, candles, food, statues and holy pictures.

The painting of Archbishop Joseph Kariattil on the wall of the Ramapuram parish church (Malabar) depicts him as a Roman prelate in choir dress, with an archiepiscopal pectoral cross. In a work he composed in 1768, entitled *Apologetics* he cherished the ideas of the contemporary Roman Church regarding the marriage of the clergy, leavened Eucharistic bread, and kneeling.

The travelogue of Kariattil, composed in Malayalam, reports that in Portugal he ordained seminarians to the Lectorate, making use of a Syriac translation of the Roman Pontifical, which his travel-mate, Father Thomman Paremakkal, had prepared.[27]

---

[26] Later editions followed the same line. For example, *Ordo Chaldaicus Rituum et Lectionum juxta morem Ecclesiae Malabaricae, superiorum permissu editus a Matheo Vadakel* (Alwaye, 1946). The prayers and rubrics that were given in different places in the Roman edition are put together in the text of the Qurbana of this edition. The feasts which were only mentioned in the calendar of the early Roman edition are inserted in the *Proprium Sanctorum*. The server's prayers, which were only indicated in the Roman edition, are given fully in this. Readings for the feast of the Ninivites are given in the appendix, which were not included in the Roman edition, and which for the first time were added to the missal in the 1879 Koonammavu edition. The contents and the order of the missal are as follows: Reading for Sundays: 1-205 pages; Preparation for Mass: 206-210; Ordinary of the Mass: 211-257; Thanksgiving after Mass: 257-258; The Raza: 258-264; Server's Part of the Mass: 264-266; The Common of the Saints: 266-296; Votive Masses: 296-317; Proper of the Saints: 330-436

[27] Placid J. Podipara, *Varthamanappusthakam*: "The Archbishop ordained him (the nephew of Padre Mesquita) in the Syriac rite, which was a translation of the Latin" (p. 238).

ARCHBISHOP BERNARDINE BACCINELLI (1853-1868)

Archbishop Bernardine Bacinelli, an Italian who was appointed Vicar Apostolic by the Congregation of Propaganda Fide, issued *decreta* in Malayalam containing "remedies against disorders" which he saw in Malabar parishes during his pastoral visits.

Before the Qurbana the celebrating priest should himself prepare the chalice in the sacristy, carry it to the altar, and take it back after the Qurbana. Five liturgical colours are to be used : white, red, black, green and violet. The colours proper to the feasts and seasons to be used are those in use in the Roman Church.

The use of holy water should be encouraged. There should be a sufficient number of confessionals in all the churches. The service of fire conducted on Christmas night is Jewish and pagan, and hence anyone who dares to conduct it will fall under interdict. This service survived the prohibition of Bernardine and is conducted even today.

Following Diamper, Ros had tried to introduce statues in the churches. It seems that the zeal was too great, or the people responded in a very excessive way. Hence Bernardine had to discourage "abuse" in this matter.

Bernardine prescribed the recitation of the acts of faith, hope and charity at the end of the Qurbana. He also encouraged the recitation of the Rosary at home.

FATHER ELIAS KURIAKOSE CHAVARA († 1871)

Father Chavara Kurikose, Vicar General of Bacinelli for the Syro-Malabarians and founder of the Congregation of the Carmelites of Mary Immaculate, published in 1868 the first *Thúkása*, the rubrics for the celebration of the Qurbaba. He adopted whatever was possible from the Roman Rite, closely following the *Ritus Servandus in Celebratione Missae* of 1570, given at the beginning of the Roman missal of Pius V.

The diary (Nalagamam) of the Mannanam monastery reports that it was Chavara who introduced the "High Mass" with a deacon and a subdeacon assisting. In this he inserted the *Gloria in Excelsis* in full, as it is done in the Roman Mass. The *Gloria in Excelsis* is originally a Syriac composition, which was then received into the Roman rite. In fact the East Syrian Divine Office has a variation of the complete *Gloria in Excelsis*, the introduction of which might have been more justifiable than its Roman version.

In a letter he wrote in Syriac on 31 May 1861 and sent to the Prefect of the Congregation for the Propagation of the Faith, Chavara asked permission for certain liturgical reforms, most of which were intended to conform the Malabar Church to the Roman.

One of them was a Syriac translation of the Holy Saturday Service of the Roman Church. "Since the Malabar Church makes use of the Roman service from Ash Wednesday to the Passion Friday, and since the long service of ancient East Syrian service for the day is no more in use" the present translation was prepared.

> As it is prescribed and practiced in the Mass of the Holy Church, our Qurbana also could end with the reading of the prologue of Saint John's Gospel. We use incense in our daily Qurbana. This is at variance with the practice of the Roman Church here, which uses it only on Sundays and feast days. Let us follow the Roman custom in this matter.[28]

Chavara dedicated each day of the week to some saint. In this scheme, Saturday was dedicated to the Blessed Virgin Mary, though the East Syrian divine office assigns Wednesday to Mary's special commemoration. Chavara also encouraged monthly devotions, for instance, May for Mary and November for the departed souls, and translated western books for such devotions from European languages. (*Vanakkamásam*).

For the first time in Malabar, a forty hour adoration was conducted at the C.M.I. monastery at Koonammavu in the first week of Lent of 1886. And later it spread into other monasteries and parish churches. A Syriac translation from Latin of the services for this devotion and a Malayalam translation about the manner in which the church is to be adorned for the Adoration were prepared by Chavara. It is believed that it was Father Chavara who translated into Syriac the Roman service of the Benediction of the Blessed Sacrament with *Pange Lingua*.[29]

ARCHBISHOP LEONARD LOUIS MELLANO (1868-1887)

When Archbishop Leonard of St. Aloysius, O.C.D. (Joseph Anthony Mellano) returned from Rome after the First Vatican Council, he brought along copies of a printed sheet in Syriac, which was to replace a sheet in the 1844 edition of the Malabar missal printed in

---

[28] Valerian, *Chavara Kuriakose Elias*, Mannanam, 1939, pp. 225-226.

[29] *Nalagamam*, pp. 89-90.

Rome. The sheet in question had the commemoration of the Patriarch: "For all the Patriarchs". The newly printed sheet did not contain the commemoration of the Patriarch. Another sheet printed was the nuptial blessing to be imparted *intra missam* translated from the *Rituale Romanum*.

The pastoral letters of Leonard Mellano contained certain regulations regarding liturgy. The choir should wear choral cope or surplice. All churches should have tabernacles for preserving the Eucharist. Monthly devotions to Holy Mary and to Saint Joseph are to be fostered. The Rosary of the Blessed Virgin should be prayed in churches and in homes.

In 1881 an *Enchiridion* for priests was printed at Verapoly. Father Geevarghese Valiaveettil, a professor of the Puthenpally seminary, had prepared it from the Roman liturgical prayers and Western popular devotions.

Native Bishops

In 1896 the former two Vicariates Apostolic (Trichur and Kottayam) were replaced by three — Trichur, Ernakulam and Changanacherry, all three being entrusted to native bishops of the Syro-Malabar rite. And in 1911 a fourth one was given to the Southist community of Kottayam. Hereafter all the hierarchs presiding over these eparchies would be of the same rite.

A report of the activities of Bishop Mar Louis Pazheparampil (1896-1919) and Archbishop Mar Augustine Kandathil of Ernakulam (1919-1956) has been published in Malayalam. The parts pertaining to liturgy can be summarised as follows:

In 1905 permission was obtained from Rome to add an appendix to the Taksa in order to include new feasts (Roman feasts).

A new service was translated from the Roman Rite for the bishop officiating the ceremony of confirmation.

Services for the pastoral visit of the bishop, and for the vestition of women religious were translated from Latin and were printed in Syriac with the approbation of Pazheparampil.

Permissions were obtained to celebrate the feasts of Christ the King, and of St. Therese of Lisieux, and to use the Syriac translations of the scriptural readings for them.

The Syriac version of the Holy Saturday service was printed in 1943. The printed text had been modified using the Roman missal.

The rubrics for the Pontifical High Mass were fixed. The ceremonies, vestments and other accessories are the same as that of a Latin rite bishop pontificating. The only difference is that the Malabar bishop wears his pectoral cross outside the vestments, while the Latin bishop wears it inside.

In the period of the indigenous bishops, with the permission of Rome, the fasts, abstinence, holy days of obligation and the prohibited time of marriage were fixed, making them conform to those of the Roman Church. All the liturgical books had several editions in this indigenous period, with minor variations, which were mostly intended to conform ever closer to the Roman rite and Latin practices.

Several devotions were spelled out in detail in the *Book of Decrees* (Malayalam) of Bishop Makil of Kottayam († 1914). It gives rubrics for the Exposition of the Blessed Sacrament, *Missa coram Sanctissimo*, Solemn Qurbana, the Benediction of the Blessed Sacrament, the Litany of the Blessed Virgin, the pastoral visit of a bishop to a church, etc.

In general, the first half of the twentieth century saw the latinization of the Malabar liturgy by indigenous bishops in their attempt to foster popular devotions.

The Malabar prelates had a choice between the Chaldean Pontifical, the West Syrian Pontifical, and the Roman Pontifical. The first and the second were practically unknown to them, and hence the choice fell on the third. Ladislaus Zaleski, a Pole who was the Apostolic Delegate to India, pleaded that since the hybrid liturgy had existed in Malabar for the past three centuries it was to be considered to have become the authentic liturgy of this Church. In 1896 he asked for permission to make a translation into Syriac of the Roman Pontifical, and for the use of the Roman Pontifical for the interim period. The Congregation for the Propagation of the Faith, poorly informed and ill-equipped to tackle such an issue, asked the Malabar bishops to proceed with the translation. In an address presented to Pope Pius X in 1908 the Malabar bishops requested him to approve the Syriac translation of the Pontifical in preparation. In 1918 the then Apostolic Delegate, Fumasoni-Biondi, pointed out to the Congregation the inconvenience and inappropriateness of using the Pontifical in Latin with an Ordination Qurbana in Syriac.[30] The same problem was pointed out by the Malabar bishops in a common petition in 1920.

The Syro-Malabar hierarchy was established in 1923 with Ernakulam as metropolitan see with three suffragan sees: Trichur, Kottayam and Changanacherry. Immediately afterwards the bishops sent to Rome a Syriac translation of the Roman Pontifical asking for approbation. Monsignor René Graffin, the editor of *Patrologia Orientalis*, was approached for the printing of the Syriac Pontifical. He replied in a tone of decisiveness that he would not do it, even under orders, since it would be to cooperate in a mischief. Thereupon Father Cyril Korolevsky, Dom Placid de Meester and Monsignor Eugene Tisserant, who were all eminent scholars, were consulted on the issue, and they all with one voice stoutly opposed such a Pontifical. However, in the Plenary Session of the Oriental Congregation the Cardinals were divided in their opinion. In December 1934, in an audience, Pope Pius XI decided the matter authoritatively siding with the scholars, stating that latinization was no more to be encouraged, and he appointed a Commission to restore the ancient East Syrian Pontifical. This commission was headed by James Vosté O.P. and when it completed its work the Syriac Pontifical was finally published from Rome in 1957.[31] Along with it was published also the *Ordo persolvendi ritus pontificalis juxta usum Ecclesiae Syro-Malabarensis* (Rome, 1958). The restored Syriac Pontifical came into use in Malayalam for the priestly ordinations in 1960 and for the episcopal ordination in 1968.[32]

The Malabar bishops had stood for the Roman Pontifical, with which alone they were familiar. They thought that its translation into Syriac would be suitable for the Malabar rite, already latinized for so long and for so much. Rome was ill-informed also by the Apostolic Delegates, who were not leading Orientalists. Finally, it was the energetic decision of Pope Pius XI, himself a scholar who chose to second scholars against his curial cardinals, that helped the Malabar Church

---

[30] Joseph Valiaveettil, *Biography of Father Geevarghese Valiaveettil,* Alwaye, 1948, p. 63.

[31] For the manuscript tradition of the Pontifical, see Isaac Allencherry, "The Ordination Ritual of the Chaldean and Malabar Churches," *The Malabar Church*, ed. Jacob Vellian, pp. 74-78.

[32] The new Pontifical was used for the first time on 24 February 1968 for the episcopal ordination of Kuriakose Kunnacherry, Bishop of Kottayam.

to find its way to its own ancestral tradition and recover its ancient East Syrian Pontifical.

RESTORATION CONTINUED

The Oriental Congregation entrusted a special committee (appointed on 5 December 1931) with the restoration of other items of the Malabar liturgy. In 1957 the recommendation of this committee regarding the Qurbana and its accessories were examined by the plenary session of the Congregation. The suggestions of the Malabar hierarchy also were taken into account. On June 26, 1957, Pope Pius XII approved the conclusions of the plenary session. In accordance with the papal approbations, the following books were published by the Oriental Congregation.[33]

Taksa d'Quddasa including the Syriac text of the restored Qurbana with the *Anphora of Addai amd Mari* (Alwaye, 1959).

Ordo celebrationis Quddasa juxta usum Ecclesiae Syro-Malabarensis containing rubrics in Latin for the different forms of celebrating Qurbana (Rome, 1959).

Supplementum Mysteriorum sive Proprium de Tempore et de Sanctis juxta ritum Ecclesiae Syro-Malabarensis, which is a collection of the variable parts of the Qurbana, the restored Calendar and the scriptural passages to be read in the Qurbana.

The missal (*Taksa d'quddasa*) was edited in 1962 (Alwaye) with a partial Malayalam translation. In 1968 it appeared entirely in Malayalam (Alwaye), with minor modifications.

The *Supplementum Mysteriorum* contained variable parts for every Sunday and feast day of the liturgical year. A unit of the variable prayers for each season (and not for every Sunday or feast day) was inserted into the 1968 edition of the missal.

In 1968 the restored Malayalam Sacramentary came into use. Restored services for Hosanna Sunday, Passion Thursday and Passion Friday were introduced in 1969.

The whole process of restoration was mainly intended to deromanize all items of the Malabar liturgy. But the 1968 Malayalam edition of the missal prepared by the Syro-Malabar Liturgical Committee in India re-introduced certain Roman elements which the Alwaye

[33] For a detailed description of the process of the restoration of these books see Jacob Vellian, *The Restored Syro-Malabar Qurbana,* (Malayayalam), Aloor, 1962.

edition of 1962 had left out; for example, the genuflection after the words of Institution.[34]

The first draft of the restored Sacramentary, prepared by me was in accordance with the ancient East Syrian sacramentaries. But the final text which was published on 18 December 1968 contained some Roman elements like the formulas of baptism, penance, and anointing of the sick in indicative mood.[35]

CONCLUSION

In the course of centuries the Malabar Christians lost for the most part the sense of an Eastern Church. They are no more familiar with the East Syrian Liturgy except for the Qurbana. But even this was enveloped with Roman accessories and presented in a language unknown to them. The structure of the church edifice, the shape and colour of the vestments and the liturgical gestures were nothing but Roman, with the effect that it would have been difficult to distinguish a Malabar priest celebrating Qurbana "privately" from a priest celebrating the Roman Mass. The Holy Week service, the liturgical calendar, the sacraments and sacramentals were replicas of those of the Roman Church. The funeral service and the Divine Office remained essentially East Syrian, but with a lot of Roman modifications, such as gcsturcs and prayers.

The Malabar clergy were trained in seminaries run by the Western missionaries. They (and the future bishops from among them being no exception) were impressed by the western devotions and liturgy, and developed an attitude of toleration of their own liturgy. The effect of this western training of the clergy was so strong that in the absence of any formal information about their liturgy, they opted for the Roman liturgy whenever they had an occasion to do so. Thus it was that the native bishops, unfamiliar with their own East Syrian Pontifical, opted for the Latin one.

The 1968 text of the Qurbana was *ad experimentum.* Hence there was a need to finalize its text. But in this process the Romanization

---

[34] For a critical analysis of the 1968 Malayalam edition, see George Vavanikunnel and Johannes Madey, "A 'Reform' of the Restored Syro-Malabar Qurbana," *The Malabar Church*, pp. 86-97.

[35] For a critical observation on this see George Vavanikunnel and Johannes Madey, "Baptism and Confirmation in the Syro-Malabar Church," *Ostkirchliche Studien* 20 (1971) 43-54.

tendency was still there. Moreover, there is an unresolved question: How far are we to go back in de-latinizaion?

Four hundred years of Romanization was, in effect, a brain-washing, so that the very thinking pattern became thoroughly westernized. Today, with sensible instruction and with the lapse of time, the Malabar Christians are getting more and more used to the restored liturgy and the Eastern Liturgical tradition.

St. Thomas Apostolic Seminary Jacob Vellian
Vadavathoor, Kottayam
Kerala, India

Paul Pallath

The Synod of Diamper: Valid or Invalid?

Introduction

Three doctoral dissertations about the Synod of Diamper were defended in Rome in the twentieth century. Gregorio Magno Antão, a priest from the Archdiocese (patriarchate) of Goa defended his doctoral dissertation *Synodus Diamperitana* in 1938 at the Faculty of Canon Law of the Pontifical Gregorian University in Rome, which was published in 1952 from Goa, under the title *De Synodi Diamperitanae natura atque decretis*.[1] In this dissertation he endeavours to demonstrate that the Synod of Diamper is valid. In 1958 Jonas Thaliath defended his doctoral dissertation at the Section of Oriental Canon Law of the same Faculty at the Pontifical Oriental Institute in Rome, entitled *The Synod of Diamper,* refuting the arguments of Antão and trying to establish the invalidity of this Synod.[2] The third Dissertation, *The Disciplinary Legislation of the Synod of Diamper*, was submitted to the Canon Law Faculty of the Oriental Institute in 1975 by Joseph Kuzhinjalil. Though the scope of this thesis is to demonstrate that most of the disciplinary norms of the Synod were the fruit of ignorance concerning the Eastern liturgico-sacramental discipline and the indigenous customs and traditions of the St Thomas Christians, in the introductory chapter the author considers the invalidity of the Synod as an established fact.[3] The Protestant and Eastern authors generally consider the Synod of Diamper invalid, while some Western authors without probing accurately into the facts, take its validity for granted, considering the greater good derived from this synod, which in their opinion consists in the "reduction of the St Thomas Christians to the Catholic faith and to the obedience of the

[1] G. M. Antão, *De Synodi Diamperitanae natura atque decretis*, Goa, 1952.

[2] J. Thaliath, *The Synod of Diamper*, (Orientalia Christiana Analecta, 152), Rome 1958. I am specially indebted to Thaliath for the articulation of my arguments. It is remarkable that even J. Wicki has not put forward any valid argument to refute the conclusions of Thaliath. See his article, "Die Synoden der Thomaschristen (auch Syromalabaren genannt)," *Annuarium Historiae Conciliorum* 18/2 (1986) 433-438.

[3] J. Kuzhinjalil, *The Disciplinary Legislation of the Synod of Diamper*, (Unpublished doctoral dissertation: Pontifical Oriental Institute), Rome, 1975, 21-23.

Roman Pontiff."[4] In this article, we shall try to evaluate as objectively as possible the various circumstances and historical facts which will permit us to arrive at a correct judgement about the validity or invalidity of this synod.[5]

1. The Juridical Nature of the Synod of Diamper

In order to consider the validity or invalidity of the Synod of Diamper, it is necessary to determine the juridical nature of this Synod. From the time of the apostolic council of Jerusalem itself different kinds of synods, councils and assemblies began to emerge both in the East and the West. In the East there developed provincial synods, patriarchal synods and the Permanent Synod of the Church of Constantinople. In the West, although there were a few synods of a patriarchal character in which some bishops from the whole Latin Church participated, gradually they gave way to national councils or plenary councils. Naturally provincial councils or metropolitan synods existed also in the West.[6]

The diocesan synod of the Latin Church originated only in the ninth century. No reference can be found in the "sacred canons" of the first millennium regarding the celebration of such synods. Though some diocesan synods took place from the IX century onwards,[7] it is the Fourth Lateran Council (1215) which for the first time ruled that bishops have to see to the observance of the things that they decree in the provincial synods, publishing them "in episcopal synods which are to be held annually in each diocese."[8] The norms for the convocation and celebration of diocesan synods were confirmed by the Council of Basel – Ferrara – Florence – Rome

---

[4] For an overview of the positions of various authors until 1975, see J. Wicki, "Die Synode von Diamper in Malabar (1599) und ihre Beurteilung (1600-1975)," *Annuarium Historiae Conciliorum* 1-2 (1977) 190-205.

[5] Since the scope of the present study is only to evaluate the validity or invalidity of the Synod of Diamper at the time of its celebration, we consider neither the impact of the synodal decisions on the Christian community during the four succeeding centuries nor the canonical status of the customs and particular laws stemming from the decrees and canons of this synod.

[6] See P. Pallath, *Local Episcopal Bodies in East and West*, OIRSI, Kottayam 1997, 24-90.

[7] W. Plöchl, *Storia del diritto canonico*, vol. 1, 366.

[8] Fourth Lateran Council (1215), Constitution 6, Norman. P. Tanner, ed., *Decrees of the Ecumenical Councils*, vol. 1, 236-237.

(1431-1445) and the Council of Trent (1545-1563).[9] After the council of Trent, Pope Benedict XIV (1740-1758) published his comprehensive work entitled *De Synodo Dioecesana* which treats the nature, structure, membership and all other aspects of the diocesan synod. The diocesan synod (at the time of Diamper) may be described as an assembly of the representatives of the priests, religious and sometimes of the lay faithful, convoked and presided over by the diocesan bishop.[10] Since the only legislator or law giver in a diocesan synod (at that time and even today) is the diocesan bishop, the role of other participants is merely to discuss the matters on the agenda and to express their opinion even through a vote, which has only a consultative value.[11]

In the patriarchal synods, metropolitan synods and permanent synods of the East, as well as in the regional, national or plenary councils and provincial synods of the West more than one diocesan bishop participate (bishops of a province, patriarchate or nation), but in the diocesan synod only the diocesan bishop, the head of the diocese (at present together with the auxiliaries, if any) will be present.

The Synod of Diamper convoked and presided over by Alexis de Menezes, the Archbishop of Goa, is to be considered a diocesan synod presumably in accordance with the canonical norms of the Latin Church at that time. The only bishop present in the Synod was Menezes and he was the sole legislator in the Synod, although the archdeacon, and representatives of the clergy and laity attended it. Even though the see of St Thomas Christians was considered a metropolitan Church, any synod celebrated for this Church in 1599 could not but be a diocesan synod, because it was not canonically divided into suffragan sees.

It is evident that Menezes himself understood this synod only as a diocesan synod. In the convocation letter itself Menezes designates the Synod of Diamper as a diocesan synod three times: "to assemble a diocesan synod in some convenient place," "We do call and assemble a diocesan synod in the said town of Diamper," "to celebrate a dioce-

---

[9] The Council of Basel – Ferrara – Florence – Rome, Session 15 (26-November 1433): see Tanner, ibid., p. 473; Council of Trent, Session 24, canon 2: see Norman P. Tanner, *Decrees of the Ecumenical Councils*, vol. 2, 761.

[10] Benedict XIV, *De Synodo Dioecesana*, lib. I, cap. 1, n. 4 & lib. III, cap. 1-9; D. Bouix, *Tractatus de Episcopo*, ubi et de *Synodo Dioecesana*, vol. 2, Parisiis 1859, 348.

[11] Benedict XIV, *De Synodo Dioecesana*, lib. XIII, cap. 1-2.

san synod conformable to the holy canons."[12] The minutes of the opening session of the Synod held on 20 June 1599 states: "in the bishopric of Angamaly of the Christians of St Thomas in the Serra of Malabar ... there assembled in a diocesan synod according to the holy canons ...."[13] Similarly in the decrees wherever the nature of the assembly is to be specified it is referred to as a "diocesan synod."[14] In 1606, when Gouvea, the historian of Menezes, published the acts and decrees of the synod in Protuguese, he entitled the book: *Synodo Diocesano, de Igreja e bispado de Angamale dos antigos christãos de Sam Thome*.... Raulin repeated the same in his Latin translation published in 1745: "Synodus Dioecesana Ecclesiae et Episcopatus Angamalensis Antiquorum Christianorum Sancti Thomae..." From all this we can conclude that it is beyond doubt that the Synod of Diamper was a diocesan synod.

2. The Titles Claimed by Menezes for Convoking the Synod of Diamper

In order to know the titles claimed by Menezes we have to examine the official convocation letter of the Synod and the opening address of Menezes in which he explains his faculty to convoke the Synod and set forth its objectives. In the convocation letter addressed to "the Reverend in Christ, Father George, Archdeacon of the Christians of St Thomas in the Serra of the Kingdom of Malabar, and to all other priests, curates, deacons and subdeacons, and to all towns, villages, and hamlets, and to all Christian people of the said bishopric," Menezes refers to his authority to convoke the Synod in the following words:

> We give you all, and every one of you in particular to understand, that the most Holy Father Pope Clement VIII, our Lord Bishop of Rome, and Vicar of Our Lord Jesus Christ upon earth, at this time presiding in the Church of God; having sent two briefs directed to Us, one of the 27th of January in the year 1595, and the other of the 21st of the same month, in the Year 1597; in which, by virtue of his pastoral Office, and the universal

[12] The convocation letter may be found in A. De Gouvea, *Synodo Diocesano da Igreja e bispado de Angamale dos antigos christãos de Sam Thome das Serras do Malavar das partes da India Oriental*, Coimbra, 1606, ff. 1-3, Eng. tr. M. Geddes, *The History of the Church of Malabar, Together with the Synod of Diamper*, London 1694, 89-96.

[13] A. De Gouvea, *Synodo Diocesano da Igreja e bispado de Angamale ...*, f. 3.

[14] Synod of Diamper, session 1, decree 1; session II, decree 1, session IX, decree 25.

> power bequeathed to the Supreme, Holy and Apostolic Chair of St. Peter over all the Churches in the world by Jesus Christ the Son of God our Lord and Redeemer, he commanded us upon the death of the Archbishop Mar Abraham to take possession of this Church and Bishopric, so as not to suffer any bishop or Prelate coming from Babylon, to enter therein, as has been hitherto the custom, all that come from thence being schismatics, heretics, and Nestorians, out of the obedience of the Holy Roman Church and subject to the patriarch of Babylon, the head of the said heresy; ...which being read by Us, we were desirous to execute the apostolic mandates with due reverence and obedience; besides, that the same was incumbent on us of right (the said Church having no Chapter to take care of it during the vacancy of the See) as Metropolitan and Primate of this and all the other Churches of the Indies, and the Oriental Parts.[15]

The Synod of Diamper began on Sunday, 20 June 1599 after the Holy Mass. Gouvea, the Portuguese historian, gives the minutes of the opening session of the Synod before the first decree. Gouvea affirms:

> ... the Mass being ended, he (Menezes) re-invested himself in his pontifical robes, and read the Office for the beginning of a Synod, as it is in the Roman Pontifical; which being over, and the Metropolitan seated in his chair, with all the ecclesiastics and secular procurators about him in their order, he told them that he celebrated this holy synod by virtue of two Briefs of the Holy Father our Lord, Pope Clement VIII, in which His Holiness had recommended to him the government of that Church, after the death of the Archbishop, Mar Abraham, until such time as it should be provided of a pastor and prelate; besides that the same belonged to him as the Metropolitan thereof, and Primate of the Indies, and all the oriental parts, by the canons, the see thereof being vacant, and it having no Chapter to take care of it during the vacancy.[16]

Since the validity or invalidity of the Synod of Diamper depends primarily on the question whether the one who convoked and conducted the Synod had the authority or legitimate canonical title to do so, we consider briefly the objectivity of the three titles claimed in the convocation letter and mentioned in the minutes of the opening session.

---

[15] A. De Gouvea, *Synodo Diocesano da Igreja e bispado de Angamale* ..., f. 1; Eng. tr. M. Geddes, *The History of the Church of Malabar*..., 89-90.

[16] Gouvea, *Synodo Diocesano*, f. 2; Eng. tr. M. Geddes, *The History of the Church of Malabar* ..., 98-99.

2.1. *The Authority of Menezes as the Metropolitan of the St Thomas Christians*

1. Menezes claims that he is the metropolitan of the St Thomas Christians (the Archdiocese of Angamaly) and therefore he has the right to convoke the Synod of Diamper according to the canons of the Church. In the convocation letter we read "... besides, that the same was incumbent on us of right (the said Church having no Chapter to take care of it during the vacancy of the See) *as Metropolitan* (and Primate) *of this* and all the other Churches of the Indies...." Similarly in the minutes of the opening session it is stated: ...besides that the same belonged to him as the Metropolitan thereof...." In brief, Menezes and Gouvea consider the Diocese of Angamaly as a suffragan of the Archdiocese of Goa and therefore Menezes as the legitimate metropolitan of the St Thomas Christians.

We shall now examine whether the Archdiocese of Angamaly was a suffragan of the Archdiocese of Goa at the time of the Synod of Diamper. Since there was no Latin diocese in India when the Portuguese came in the beginning of the sixteenth century, the whole of India was placed under the jurisdiction of the Diocese of Funchal in Portugal (and also all other places which Portugal would explore in the future), erected in 1514.[17] On 3 November 1534 Pope Paul III through the Bull *Aequum reputamus* separated Goa from Funchal, and erected the first Latin diocese in India, as a suffragan of Funchal. The territory of Goa stretched from the Cape of Good Hope in South Africa to China in East Asia.[18] The first bishop of Goa was the Franciscan Juan de Albuquerque who was nominated in 1538 and installed in Goa in 1539.[19] Until 1557 Goa was the only Latin diocese in India and all the Latin Christians were under its jurisdiction. On 4 February 1557 by the apostolic constitution *Etsi sancta et immaculata* Pope Paul IV (1555-1559) elevated Goa to an archdiocese and erected the Diocese of Cochin in Kerala and the Diocese of Malacca in Singapore as its suffragan sees. However, the Archdiocese of Angamaly,

---

[17] *Bullarium Patronatus Portugalliae,* 1, 100. Before the erection of Funchal India was under the jurisdiction of the Prior of the Military Order of Christ who used to send Vicars General to India. See, A. Meersman, "Origin of the Latin Hierarchy in India," *Clergy Monthly* 5 (1960) 72-73.

[18] *Bullarium Patronatus Portugalliae,* vol. 1, 148.

[19] Don Francisco de Melo, who was appointed bishop of Goa and was consecrated at Lisbon in 1536, could be considered as the first bishop of Goa, though he died before setting sail for India.

which was under the jurisdiction of the Chaldean patriarch, was not included among the suffragans of Goa.[20] Hence at the time of the Synod of Diamper (1599) there were only two Latin dioceses in India: the Archdiocese of Goa and its suffragan, the Diocese of Cochin.[21]

The see of St Thomas in India existed from the very first century. At the time of the Synod of Diamper the residence of the "Metropolitan of All India" was in Angamaly and therefore the see of the St Thomas Christians was designated the Archdiocese of Angamaly. From time immemorial the Chaldean patriarch used to nominate bishops for India. The last bishop sent by the Chaldean patriarch was Mar Abraham.

After the Synod of Diamper, on 5 November 1599 Pope Clement VIII appointed Francis Ros S.J. (the first Latin Bishop of the St Thomas Christians), a friend of Dom Menezes, as successor to Metropolitan Mar Abraham. On 20 December 1599 Pope Clement VIII reduced the Archdiocese of Angamaly to the status of a simple diocese and made it a suffragan of the Archdiocese of Goa.[22] On 4 August 1600 the same Pope extended also the patronage of the king of Portugal over the Diocese of Angamaly with the brief *In supremo militantis*.[23]

The Synod of Diamper took place from 20 to 25 June 1599. The Archdiocese of Angamaly was made a suffragan of the Archdiocese of Goa only on 20 December 1599, that is, six months after the Synod of Diamper. Evidently at the time of the Synod of Diamper the Diocese of Angamaly was not a suffragan of the Archdiocese of Goa. Consequently Archbishop Menezes was not the metropolitan of the St Thomas Christians and he did not enjoy any metropolitan right over the Archdiocese of Angamaly. Regarding this point there is no dispute. Even those who defended the validity of the Synod of Diamper admit that Menezes was not the metropolitan of the St Thomas

---

[20] *Bullarium Patronatus Portugalliae*, vol. 1, 191, 193, 196. In the course of time Macau in China (1576), Funay in Japan (1588), Mylapore (1606), the prelacy of Mozambique in East Africa (1612) Peking and Nanking in China (1690) were erected as suffragans of Goa.

[21] It was only on 9 January 1606 the Diocese of Cochin was bifurcated and the Diocese of Mylapore (the third latin diocese in India) consisting of Coromandel Coast, Orissa, Bengal and Pegu was erected. No other diocese was erected in India until the nineteenth century.

[22] Paulinus A S. Bartholomaeo, *India Orientalis Christiana*, Romae 1794, 61; cf. *Bullarium Patronatus Portugalliae*, vol. 1, 260.

[23] *Bullarium Patronatus Portugalliae*, vol. 1, 260.

Christians at the time of the Synod. For example, Antão Gregorio Magno states:

> Attamen jam supra vidimus Ecclesiam Angamalensem, tempore celebrationis Synodi Diamperensis, non fuisse suffraganeam Goae. Concludendum ergo est: facultas qua celebrata Synodus Dimapertana non est quaerenda in potestate Archiepiscopi Metropolitani, qua praeditus erat Alexius de Menezes; sed eruenda ex alio fonte... [24]

Even if the Diocese of Angamaly were a suffragan of Goa and Menezes were its legitimate metropolitan he could not have convoked the Synod of Diamper, because the canon law of that time did not permit a metropolitan to convene a diocesan synod in a suffragan see when that see was vacant. So is the law even today. The competence of the metropolitan is limited to nominating an administrator if the Cathedral Chapter has failed to do so, or if a Chapter does not exist in a particular diocese, nor is there any other legitimate custom or tradition for the nomination of the administrator. It is to be noted that cathedral chapter is something unknown in the whole Christian Orient.[25]

2.2. *The Faculty of Menezes to Convoke the Synod as the Primate of the East Indies*

Both in the convocation letter and in the minutes of the first session it is claimed that the right to convoke the Synod of Diamper was incumbent on Menezes also as the "Primate of this and all the other Churches of the Indies, and the Oriental Parts." It is true that on 15 March 1572 Pope Gregory XIII by the bull *Pastoralis Officii Cura* recognized Menezes as the primate of the East Indies.[26] However, such primacy at that time did not carry with it any power of governance in the Latin Church, apart from the prerogative of honour. So is the law even today.[27] With regard to jurisdiction the power of pri-

---

[24] G. M. Antão, *De Synodi Diamperitanae natura atque decretis*, 40.

[25] For a detailed analysis of this question, see Thaliath, *The Synod of Diamper*, 62-68.

[26] *Bullarium Patronatus Portugalliae,* vol. 1, 232.

[27] F. Wernz, *Ius Decretalium*, tom. III/2, Rome 1906, 484-489; Wernz – Vidal, *Ius Canonicum*, tom. II, De Personis, Rome 1928, n. 527; F. Cleys Bouuaaert, "Primat", *DDC* VII, 214; E. F. Regatillo, *Institutiones Iuris Canonici*, I, ed. 5, Salterrae 1956, 317-320; A. Vermeersch – J. Creusen, *Epitome Iuris Canonici*, tom I, ed. 8, Romae 1963, 352; Antão, *De Synodi Diamperitanae natura atque decretis*, 35. The law has remained unchanged till today: see CIC 1917 c. 271 and CIC 1983 c. 438.

mates was equal to that of other metropolitans. In brief, the prerogatives of Menezes as the primate of the East Indies did not grant him any jurisdictional power to intervene in the affairs of another diocese, nor to convoke a synod there. Hence I readily agree with the conclusion of Antão, who as I pointed out, defended the validity of the synod but on other grounds: "Ideo concludendum rationem auctoritatis non esse in Primatialitate Ecclesiae Goanensis ad convocandum et celebrandum Synodum Diamperensem collocandam."[28] Since there is no dispute regarding this point, we pass on to the next one.

2.3. *The Competence of Menezes to Convoke the Synod on the Basis of the Faculty Granted to Him by Pope Clement VIII in the Two Letters*

2. Menezes claims the faculty to convoke the Synod of Diamper on the basis of two briefs sent to him by Pope Clement the VIII on 27 January 1595 and on 21 January 1597, respectively. In the convocation letter he states: "the most Holy Father Pope Clement VIII ... having sent two briefs directed to Us, he commanded us upon the death of the Archbishop Mar Abraham to take possession of this Church ... which being read by Us, we were desirous to execute the apostolic mandates with due reverence and obedience ...." Similarly in the minutes of the opening session of the Synod it is affirmed that "He (Menezes) celebrated this holy synod by virtue of two Briefs of the Holy Father our Lord, Pope Clement VIII, in which His Holiness had recommended to him the government of that Church, after the death of the Archbishop, Mar Abraham ...." It is important to note that Gouvea indicated the faculty of Menezes to convoke the Synod even in the subtitle of his book, which in English reads: "A Diocesan Synod ... celebrated by the most Reverend Lord Dom Frey Aleixo de Menezes, Archbishop, Metropolitan of Goa, Primate of the East Indies *by virtue of the two Briefs* of the most Holy Father Pope Clement VIII...." We analyse these two letters in order to ascertain whether the mandate for the convocation of the Synod of Diamper is contained in them as stated above.

2.3.1. The Contents of the Two Letters

The contents of these letters cannot be understood without reference to their context. Mar Abraham was a Catholic bishop, canoni-

---

[28] G. M. Antão, *De Synodi Diamperitanae natura atque decretis*, 35.

cally nominated by the Chaldean Catholic Patriarch Mar Abdiso (1555-1571), who received ecclesiastical communion and Pallium from Pope Pius IV.[29] Mar Abraham first reached Kerala in 1557. He was arrested by the Portuguese military in 1558 and was brought in custody to Goa to be deported to Lisbon in Portugal. But on the way to Portugal, when the ship anchored in Mozambique he eluded his guards and escaped to Ormuz, from where he made his way to Mozul. Patriarch Abdiso, who had received assurances from the Pope about his jurisdiction over the St Thomas Christians, sent Mar Abraham to Rome with testimonial letters. In Rome the Chaldean bishop made the profession of faith and obtained two recommendation letters signed by the Pope himself dated 28 February 1565, addressed to the Archbishop of Goa and to the Bishop of Cochin, respectively.[30] In these letters the Pope categorically and explicitly confirmed the jurisdiction of the Chaldean patriarch over the St Thomas Christians and asked the Archbishop of Goa and the Bishop of Cochin not to hinder Mar Abraham in any way in the administration of the diocese assigned to him by his patriarch.[31] The Pope also sent a letter to patriarch Mar Abdiso on 23 February 1565 reconfirming his jurisdiction in Malabar.[32]

When Mar Abraham reached Goa in 1568 with the letters of the Pope he was detained in the Dominican monastery of Goa on suspicion that either he might have deceived the Roman Curia or falsified the letters. A few months later he escaped from Goa and reached Kerala. After a few years of peaceful co-existence, the relationship between Mar Abraham and the Portuguese missionaries worsened mainly due to the attempts of westernization of the St Thomas Christians. Many letters reached Rome in which Mar Abraham was accused of immorality, heresy and simony. Authorization was also requested from the Pope to deport Mar Abraham to Goa for conducting

---

[29] For the history of Mar Abraham see: P. J. Podipara, *The Hierarchy of the Syro-Malabar Church,* Alleppey 1976, 64-82; E. Tisserant, *Eastern Christianity in India*, Bombay 1957, 40-47; Bernard Thoma, *Marthoma Christianikal* (Malayalam), Kottayam 1992, 313-349; G. Beltrami, *La Chiesa caldea nel secolo dell'Unione, Orientalia Christiana* XXIX, Roma 1933, 94-119.

[30] These letters can be found in S. Giamil, *Genuinae Relationes inter Sedem Apostolicam et Assyriorum Orientalium seu Chaldaeorum Ecclesiam*, Romae 1902, 69-73.

[31] Cf. S. Giamil, *Genuinae Relationes*, 69-73.

[32] S. Giamil, *Genuinae Relationes*, 69.

a trial against him regarding the accusations indicated above. Finally on 27 January 1595, Pope Clement VIII issued the following letter.[33]

Venerabili fratri archiepiscopo Goano. Clemens Papa VIII.

Venerabilis frater, salutem et apostolicam benedictionem.

Nuper non sine animi nostri dolore ad nos perlatum est Mar Abraham archiepiscopum Angamalensem in regno Concini et in Malabari seu Indiis sancti Thomae apostoli — qui alias catholicam doctrinam amplexus Apostolicae Sedi obedientiam praestitit ac in synodo provinciali Goana de reductione ad catholicam fidem eiusdemque Sedis obedientiam universae ipsius dioecesis tractavit — novissime in recidivos Nestorianae haeresis errores misere prolapsum fuisse, nec monitum respiscere voluisse, minusque permisisse libros caldaicos eisdem erroribus refertos qui in eius dioecesis et provinciae ecclesiis leguntur emendari et corrigi, ac praeterea plures simonias commisisse. Nos qui ob iniuncti nobis apostolici muneris debitum in eam potissimum curam et solicitudinem incumbere tenemur, ut ecclesiarum pastores, praesertim in tam remotis ab Apostolica Sede regionibus, sanam doctrinam teneant et commissas sibi oves catholicae doctrinae salutari pabulo reficiant et pascant, in praemissis ea qua decet ratione consulere volentes ac de tua fide, integritate ac catholicae religionis zelo plurimum in Domino confisi, fraternitati tuae per praesentes committimus et mandamus ut in ip-

Pope Clement VIII, To our Venerable Brother Archbishop of Goa.

Venerable Brother, greetings and Apostolic blessing.

Recently and not without the fact causing us great sorrow, it was referred to us that Mar Abraham, the Archbishop of Angamaly in the Kingdom of Cochin and Malabar or in the Indies of St Thomas the Apostle, — who on another occasion accepted the Catholic doctrine and offered obedience to the Apostolic See and in the provincial synod of Goa agreed to a reduction to the Catholic faith and obedience of his whole diocese to the same See — has in recent times miserably relapsed into the errors of the Nestorian heresy, has not wished to heed any warning, has not even allowed the Chaldean books filled with the same errors which are read in the churches of his diocese and province to be emended and corrected, and moreover he has committed various acts of simony. On account of the responsibility of our Apostolic office we are particularly bound to regard this Church with care and solicitude, so that the pastors of the Church, specially in those regions which are so far away from the Holy See, may preserve the correct doctrine and may restore and nurture (revive) with the health-giving food of the Catholic doctrine the flock which has been entrusted to them, and wishing first of all to advise what is becoming to rea-

[33] This letter can be found in Archivio Brevi Apostolici, vol. 223, f. 89[sq]; printed versions, *Subsidium ad Bullarium Patronatus Portugalliae* ..., Allappe [Alleppey] 1903, 9-10; Gouvea, *Jornada do Arcebispo de Goa*, 10; Beltrami, *La Chiesa caldea*, 248-249.

sius Mar Abrahae vitam, mores, et doctrinam diligenter inquiras et, si per inquisitionem huiusmodi illum in praemissis culpabilem esse repereris, illum ad te Goam venire iubeas et facias, ibique sub tuta et honesta custodia retineas, et processus per te faciendi exemplum in authentica forma ad nos et Apostolicam Sedem transmittas ut, ipso processu diligenter inspecto et examinato, ipsius Mar Abrahae archiepiscopi causam prout iustum fuerit terminare valeamus. Interim vero ne ecclesia, dioecesis et provincia praedictae Angamalensis, ipso archiepiscopo absente et erroribus implicato, in spiritualibus vel temporalibus aliqua patiantur detrimenta, in eadem ecclesia et dioccesi personam aliquam ecclestasticam ex ritu latino qui si fieri possit linguam caldeam seu syriacam calleat, in vicarium apostolicum cum facultate ea omnia quae iurisdictionis sunt non autem ordinis faciendi deputes et constituas, ac illum toties quoties expedire iudicaveris removeas et alium semel et pluries in eius locum surroges et denuo deputes et constituas; nec absente aut decedente ipso Mar Abraha archiepiscopo, alium archiepiscopum eligi vel quomodo deputari aut ibidem admitti permittas, nisi quem Apostolica Sedes iuxta decretum praefatae synodi provincialis Goanae, ab ipso Mar Abraha eiusque ecclesia et dioecesi acceptatum, elegerit. Si quos vero alios quoscumque in dioecesi et provincia praedictis similis erroris labe irretitos reperiri contingat, in eos per te aut Vicarium Apostolicum, a te ut praescribitur deputandum, inquiras et procedas seu inquiri et procedi facias iuxta canonicas sanctiones. Super quibus omnibus et singulis plenam et amplam tibi facultatem et auctoritatem

son, confident in the Lord of your faith, integrity and zeal for the Catholic religion, with this missive we entrust to you our brother and give order that you inquire diligently into the life, morals and doctrine of Mar Abraham and from this inquiry if you find him guilty regarding the above, you shall order him and make him come to Goa and thither you shall keep him in safe and distinguished custody and transmit to us and the Apostolic See an authentic copy of the trial to be conducted by you, so that after the process itself has been diligently inspected and examined, we may be able to settle the case of the Archbishop Mar Abraham as justice requires. In the meantime, lest the Church, diocese and province of the aforesaid Angamaly, since its archbishop is absent and implicated in errors, may suffer any damage in spiritual or temporal matters, you shall appoint and constitute in that same Church an ecclesiastical person of the Latin rite who, if possible, is well versed in the Chaldean or Syriac tongues, to be Vicar Apostolic with the faculty of attending to all those matters concerning jurisdiction but not of conducting Ordinations. You shall remove him as often as you judge it is expedient and you shall duly substitute, nominate and constitute another one in his place once or many times. When the same Archbishop Mar Abraham is absent or after his death you shall not allow another archbishop to be elected, somehow deputed or be admitted except for the man whom the Apostolic See, according to the decree of the aforesaid provincial synod of Goa which was accepted by Mar Abraham himself and his church and diocese, will have elected. Moreover, if it were to occur that any others in the aforesaid diocese and

apostolica auctoritate tenore praesentium concedimus et impartimur. Non obstantibus quibusvis apostolicis ac in provincialibus et in synodalibus conciliis editis generalibus vel specialibus constitutionibus et ordinationibus ac nominatim concilii Tridentini decreto, quo disponitur quod processus etiam informativi contra episcopos formari non possint nisi vigore commissionis manu propria Romani Pontificis signatae; necnon praedictae ecclesiae Angamalensis etiam iuramento, confirmatione apostolica vel quavis firmitate alia roboratis statutis et consuetudinibus ac privilegiis, indultis et litteris apostolicis in contrarium praemissorum quomodolibet concessis, confirmatis et approbatis. Quibus omnibus, illorum tenores praesentibus pro expressis habentes, hac vice dumtaxat specialiter et expresse derogamus, ceterisque contrariis quibuscumque. Volumus autem ut praesentium transumptis, manu alicuius notarii publici subscriptis et sigillo alicuius personae in dignitate ecclesiastica constitutae munitis, eadem quae praesentibus ipsis fides adhibeatur. Datum Romae, apud Sanctum Petrum etc., die 27 ianuarii 1595. Anno tertio.

diocese and province were to be found to have been ensnared by the stain of similar errors, you or the Vicar Apostolic, who must be appointed as prescribed above, shall hold an inquiry about them and proceed (or you shall arrange that others do the same) according to canonical sanctions. For all these and each of the matters, by our Apostolic authority and the contents of this letter, we concede and bestow upon you full and ample faculty and authority. Notwithstanding.... Given in Rome, at St. Peter's, on the twenty seventh of January 1595, the third year (of our Pontificate).

The faculties granted to Menezes in this letter in accordance with the request of the Portuguese authorities can be grouped into four:

1. To inquire into the life, doctrine and morals of Mar Abraham. If from such inquiry he is found suspect of heresy he could be deported to Goa for a formal trial. The acts of the process should be sent to Rome for final decision.

2. To appoint a Vicar Apostolic from the Latin rite (if possible one knowing Syriac), in case Mar Abraham, being found guilty, is to be taken to Goa for a formal trial.

3. To inquire into the life of anyone else in the Archdiocese of Angamaly, suspected of heresy. He can be judged either by the Archbishop himself or by a Vicar Apostolic to be appointed by him.

4. To keep out anyone (bishops) coming to govern the Archdiocese of Angamaly during the absence or after the death of Abraham.

The second apostolic letter[34], dated 21 January 1597 reads as follows:

Venerabili fratri archiepiscopo Goano in Indiis Orientalibus. Clemens Papa VIII.	Pope Clement VIII, To Our Venerable Brother the Archbishop of Goa in the East Indies.
Venerabilis frater, salutem et apostolicam benedictionem.	Venerable Brother, greetings and Apostolic blessing.
Cupientes statui ecclesiae Angamalensis opportune providere, fraternitati tuae ut — si contingat modernum archiepiscopum Angamalensem ab humanis decedere, ne dum eidem ecclesiae de alio pastore canonice providetur, illa propter temporis et locorum distantiam in spiritualibus vel temporalibus aliqua detrimenta sustineat — quamcumque personam ecclesiasticam prudentia, pietate, et doctrina insignitam, quae tibi idonea videbitur, in ipsius ecclesiae in eisdem spiritualibus et temporalibus vicarium apostolicum apostolica auctoritate constituere et deputare valeat, donec nos eidem ecclesiae de pastore providerimus, auctoritate praedicta, tenore praesentium facultatem concedimus. Non obstantibus constitutionibus ... quibuscumque. Datum Romae, apud Sanctum Petrum sub annulo Piscatoris, die 21 ianuarii 1597, pontificatus nostri anno quinto.	If the present Archbishop of Angamaly departs from this life, lest the Church of Angamaly may suffer any damage in spiritual and temporal matters on account of the distance in time and space while canonical provision is being taken for another pastor, in our desire to give opportune provision to the status of the same Church, by our apostolic authority and by the contents of this missive we concede to you our Brother, the faculty of appointing and constituting any ecclesiastical person of outstanding prudence, piety and doctrine who will seem suitable to you as Vicar Apostolic for the spiritual and temporal matters of this Church until we provide it with a pastor. Notwithstanding ... Given in Rome, in St. Peter's, the twenty first of January 1597, the fifth year of our Pontificate.

[34] This letter can be found in Archivio Brevi Apostolici, vol. 248, f. 245; printed versions, *Subsidium ad Bullarium Patronatus Portugalliae* ..., cited in n. 33, 11; Beltrami, *La Chiesa caldea*, 252-253.

This letter was written when news about the illness and probable death of Mar Abraham reached Rome. The content of this letter is crystal clear. Pope Clement VIII commissioned the Archbishop of Goa to appoint any ecclesiastical person of outstanding prudence, piety and doctrine as Vicar Apostolic to govern the Archdiocese of Angamaly, in case of Abraham's death. The Vicar Apostolic, contrary to the first brief, need not be of the Latin rite ("any ecclesiastical person"). The Vicar Apostolic will govern the vacant Church until Rome provides a pastor.

2.3.2. The Two Letters of the Pope and the Synod of Diamper

The principal mandate granted to the Archbishop in the first letter was to inquire into the life and doctrine of Archbishop Mar Abraham. Although information was gathered about Mar Abraham, he was not deported to Goa and no formal trial was conducted by the Goan inquisition. Since he was not deported to Goa for trial, no Vicar Apostolic was nominated in accordance with the first letter. Mar Abraham, the Archbishop of Angamaly died on 3 January 1597. So the mandate given in the first letter to investigate into his life and to nominate a Vicar Apostolic in case of his eventual deportation to Goa for a formal trial became irrelevant. Since the pope issued another letter after the death of Mar Abraham, logically it would seem that the first letter had to be considered as superseded. Even if we consider both letters together the faculties granted to Menezes are:

1. To appoint a Vicar Apostolic as per the second letter;
2. In virtue of the first letter to inquire into the case of any one suspected of heresy or error in the Church of Malabar;
3. To prevent the entry of any bishop into Malabar except the one appointed by the Holy See, as prescribed in the first letter.

In short the two letters which Menezes believed to have granted him the faculty to conduct the Synod of Diamper, state nothing about the convocation of a synod or any kind of assembly, convention or meeting.

Even Gregorio Magno Antão, who strove to defend the validity of the Synod of Diamper, could not find anything in these letters about the convocation of a synod; so he only could assert that such a mandate is implicitly conceded according to the mind of the Roman Pontiff. He states:

> Clarum est in illis duobus Brevibus non fieri explicitam mentionem de potestate celebrandi Synodum Diamperitanam et in ea ferendi praecepta et statuta quaedam. Nobis tamen *videtur* illam potestatem iuxta mentem Pontificis, Brevia concedentis, deputatam fuisse.[35]

It is difficult to believe that since the Pope enumerated explicitly and point by point (even minor things, especially in the first letter) what should be done in the Malabar Church, such a drastic and far reaching act like the convocation of a diocesan synod during the vacancy of a See, when nothing should be innovated (*Sede vacante, nihil innovetur*), is implicitly contained in the letters "iuxta mentem Pontificis." Antão also points out that the mandate to conduct the Synod of Diamper is implicitly contained in the faculty to nominate a Vicar Apostolic, since such a synod was necessary for the efficacy of the nomination.[36]

One can only admit that the faculty to convoke the Synod of Diamper is implicitly contained in the letters of the Pope if the synod was a necessary means for the execution of any of the mandates granted to Menezes (the two letters taken together) by the Pope.

1. Nomination of the Vicar Apostolic

The principal mandate granted to Menezes is to nominate a Vicar Apostolic (both in the first and the second letter under different circumstances). According to the ancient tradition and custom of the St Thomas Christians, after the death of the bishop, the Archdeacon automatically becomes the canonical administrator of the diocese. In accordance with this tradition, in order to avoid all kinds of equivocation, a few days before his death, Mar Abraham canonically nominated Archdeacon George as the administrator of the Archdiocese of Angamaly after he had obtained permission from his patriarch.[37] Although Menezes attempted to nominate Francis Ros S.J. as the administrator, he confirmed the Archdeacon George as the Apostolic Administrator according to the recommendations of Ros himself and the other missionaries in Malabar.[38] He did not nominate any Vicar Apostolic before or after the Synod of Diamper. Hence the Synod of Diamper was not conducted in order to nominate a Vicar Apostolic. In the convocation letter or in the preliminary decree where the

---

[35] G. M. Antão, *De Synodi Diamperitanae natura atque decretis*, 46.

[36] G. M. Antão, *De Synodi Diamperitanae natura atque decretis*, 49.

[37] J. Kollaparampil, *The Archdeacon of All India: A Historico-Juridical Study*, Rome 1972, 207-212.

[38] For details, see J. Thaliath, *The Synod of Diamper*, 89-92.

scope of the synod is explained, nothing can be found about the nomination of a Vicar Apostolic. Similarly if we go through the acts of the synod, it is not possible to find even a single sentence about the appointment of a Vicar Apostolic or anything connected with it.

2. Inquiry and trial of any one suspected of heresy or error in the Church of Malabar. The first letter (if not superseded by the second) grants Menezes the faculty to conduct an inquiry personally or through the Vicar Apostolic to be appointed by him, about anyone suspect of error in faith. In the Synod of Diamper no such inquiry was made about anyone, no trial was conducted and nobody was adjudicated.

3. As Jonas Thaliath points out "There is no need to consider the third faculty invested in Menezes, namely to bar entrance into Malabar of any bishop other than the one sent by the Holy See. ... The Portuguese police were not only effectively screening all the passengers who reached Ormuz, the port through which the prospective Chaldean bishops had to come; they had even taken stringent measures to censor the correspondence between Malabar and Chaldea."[39] Even many years before the papal brief the Portuguese authorities did everything possible to hinder the entrance of Chaldean bishops in India.

So it is evident that these two letters, even if taken together, do not contain anything at all about the conduct of a synod or assembly; nor can such a faculty be deduced in any way from them.

3. Irregularities and Non-Canonical Procedures Which Affect the Validity of the Synod

1. The St Thomas Christians were constrained to participate in the Synod of Diamper. This is evident from the fact that the archdeacon and the priests of the Archdiocese of Angamaly were convoked to the synod *sub poena excommunicatione latae sententiae*. The convocation letter reads: "... by virtue of holy obedience, and upon pain of excommunication *latae sententiae*, We command the Reverend archdeacon of this diocese and all other priests of the same, that will not be hindered by age or some other just impediment, to be present in the said town of Diamper, therewith Us to celebrate a Diocesan

---

[39] J. Thaliath, *The Synod of Diamper*, 110.

Synod conformable to the Holy Canons."[40] Similarly, the second decree of the synod commanded all participants "by virtue of holy obedience and under pain of excommunication *latae sententiae*" not to depart from Diamper before the synod ended and they had signed the decrees thereof with their own hand (that is, if somebody left the synod without putting his signature, he would incur automatic excommunication).[41] Menezes also forbade the participants by virtue of obedience and under pain of excommunication *latae sententiae* to meet together in groups with any persons, ecclesiastic or secular, as long as the synod was in session, to avoid what was called "unnecessary and hurtful debates."[42] Thus it is clear that during the whole synod, from the convocation until the signing of the decrees, the members were under the threat of excommunication, which the St Thomas Christians feared most because they were practising Catholics and did not want to break communion with the Catholic Church.

2. There were no consultations nor discussions nor deliberations in the Synod. Even though in a diocesan synod the only legislative authority is the diocesan bishop, the participants should be permitted to express freely their opinions and considerations in order that the decisions may be synodal and not simply episcopal. But in the Synod of Diamper nothing of this sort happened. Since the members of the synod were not consulted and they did not understand many of the things prescribed by it, there was no form of a synod.

3. After the conclusion of the synod many canons and decrees were added by Menezes at will. Thaliath, after comparing the three Malayalam originals kept in the Vatican archives and the Portuguese version published by Gouvea in 1606, arrived at the conclusion that the Malayalam text is considerably shorter and the wording less offensive; it hardly at any time ascribes heresy proper to St Thomas Christians while the Portuguese text with the many additions and amplifications is nearly twice as long as the Malayalam one.[43] Prof.

---

[40] "... Mandamos em virtude da santa obediencia, e sob pena de excomunhäo *latae sententiae*, ao reverendo arcediago desde bispado, e a todos os mais sacerdotes delle que não tiverem legitimo impedimento de enfermidade, idade, ou outra inevitável ocupação, se achem presentes aos ditos vinte dias do mês de Junho na igreja de Todos os Santos do dito lugar de Diamper para com nosco celebrarem o dito Synodo dioecesano ...." Gouvea, *Synodo Diocesano*, f. 1; Eng. tr. M. Geddes, *The History of the Church of Malabar...*, 93.

[41] See the Synod of Diamper, session I, decree II.

[42] See the Synod of Diamper, session I, decree V.

[43] J. Thaliath, *The Synod of Diamper*, 180.

Scaria Zacharia identified thirty-five new decrees that are found only in the Western versions, in addition to the elaborations and descriptions introduced here and there into the original decrees.[44]

In order to corroborate the irregularities and non-canonical procedures mentioned above we draw on the letters of responsible and competent Portuguese missionaries who had first-hand information about what happened in the Synod. The context which enabled the missionaries to report the true story of the Synod of Diamper is also important and highly helpful to understand the letters. Perhaps convinced of the invalidity of the Synod of Diamper, Bishop Francis Ros, the first Latin Bishop of the St Thomas Christians, convoked another synod in Angamaly in 1603, in which many decrees of Diamper were altered or modified while others were left out. At this time Menezes was trying his best to get the Synod of Diamper approved by the Pope. In the context of the preparations of the new synod he was going to conduct, Francis Ros S.J., who had participated in the Synod of Diamper as an assistant to Menezes, wrote to the Jesuit General Claudio Aquaviva on 20 November 1603 about Diamper in the following manner:

> When I was now going to make amendments in the Synod which His Excellency the Archbishop of Goa conducted here, as our experience has shown that there are many things in it that have to be changed, His Excellency wrote to me asking for signatures of the above-said synod to be sent to the Holy Father for confirmation. I have sent them to His Excellency with the views of our Fathers on the matter, pointing out to His Excellency that if His Holiness confirmed the above-said synod he would be placing all these Christians in a state of mortal sin, as they would not keep it; if His Holiness approved, I say, what has to do with practices in such a way as to make a law. As great evils would follow from such procedure, I request Your Paternity for the love of Our Lord, on receiving this information, to use your influence in the court of Rome so that this step, ruinous to souls, may be averted; and let the Holy Father be informed of it; let not these Christians say that we have duped them; for to tell you the entire truth, some of the canons of the above said synod the Archbishop himself added after the synod was over; not a single canon was discussed or altered, so much so that there was no form of a synod, and it cannot be said to contain anything more than directive principles; they heard them without understanding what was being said, as I can myself bear ample witness as also the other Fathers who understood the language. His Excellency many a time had said that the synod was intended merely to show them the way of their salvation without obstacles.

[44] Scaria Zacharia, *The Acts and Decrees of the Synod of Diamper 1599*, Edamattam 1994, 9.

> This is what transpired within the Synod, and I have pointed out all this to His Excellency the Archbishop of Goa.[45]

After holding a new synod at Angamaly in 1603 Bishop Ros wrote another letter to the same Jesuit General on 26 December 1603, in which he informed the General of the new synod and requested him to impede the presentation of the acts of the Synod of Diamper to the Holy Father (something which Menezes so highly desired) because the synod was not in form. We cite below the pertinent parts of this letter:

> I conducted a diocesan synod at Angamaly this Advent to the satisfaction of all. The Christians renewed their oath of obedience to the Holy Father and abjured their former heretical beliefs. The present synod was conducted in due form and while many things were ordained for the good of these souls, former decisions were altered (which the Archbishop of Goa had taken when he came here); this was done at the insistence of the entire Christian community, who said that at that time they were not consulted on any point and that they did not understand many of the things prescribed by the first synod. This is so very true that the above-said Archbishop made by himself, even after the Synod was over, some canons which he added to the body of the synod. ... I understand that the Archbishop is sending his synod to the Holy Father in the current year; he had written to me to that effect. Your Paternity must ask the Father Procurator General to negotiate with the eminent cardinals to impede the presentation of the above-said synod. It is not in form; besides it contains many

---

[45] Archivium Romanum Societatis Iesu (hereafter ARSI), Goa-Mal. 15, f. 155-156^{v}; Thaliath, *The Synod of Diamper*, 130-131: "Estando agora para recopilar la synodo que el Sr. Arcebispo de Goa celebró aqui por haver muchas cosas que la experiencia nuestra haverense de mudar, el dicho Señor me mandó pedir las firmas de la dicha synodo por la mandar a Su Sd., que la confirme. Yo las mandé a su Sa. con parecer de los padres nuestros advertindo al dicho Señor que si su Sd. confirmava la dicha sinodo, ponia en estado de pecado mortal a todos estos christianos, porque no la guardarian, confirmar digo lo que pertenece a las costumbres, de modo que se haga ley, de lo que se siguen grandes males por lo que pido por amor de N. Sr. a V. Pd. esté advertido tambien desto, porque se obvie a este danno de las almas, nessa corte, y esté su Sd.informado, e no digan estos christianos o que los enganamos porque si se ha de dezir la verdad por entero, algunos de los canones de la dicha synodo, hizo el mismo señor Arcebispo despues de la synodo acabada, e ninguno de los canones fue preguntado ni alterado, de modo que forma de synodo no la uvo, mas que hazer reglas directivas y escrevirlas, y ellos oyren sin hazer concepto de lo que se dezia, como io soy muy bien testimonio, como los mas padres que entendiamos la lengoa, y su Sa. dezia muchas vezes, que no hazia aquello, si no por mostrarles el camino de su salvacion sin impedimento. Esto es lo que passa en el negocio de la synodo, de lo que todo advertí al Señor Arcebispo de Goa."

things we have abandoned in the present synod as they were unbearable to these Christians...[46]

In addition to the letters quoted above, another letter of Francis Ros S.J., written to the Portuguese Jesuit Assistant, John Alvarez on 27 December 1603 is very much revealing:

> The Archbishop of Goa, I think, intends to send to Rome the synod he conducted at Diamper when he came here, because he has written to me asking for signatures which I was keeping. It was no synod since no consultation was made and the Christians were unaware of what was being enacted. If they put their signatures, it was due to my importunity. Hence the Synod should on no account be presented to the Holy Father. Moreover, in the present Synod some unbearable provisions of the former, about which the Christians had no knowledge, were dropped; and the Archbishop himself made some canons even after the synod and the Christians were unaware of them. Hence the promoters of the present synod asked for a copy of the former and some of the provisions were changed as it seemed necessary to all the Fathers.[47]

John Campori, who was present at the Synod of Diamper and was an eye-witness of all the happenings, wrote to John Alvarez, the Portuguese Assistant to the Jesuit General in Rome on 1 January 1604 in the following manner:

---

[46] ARSI, Goa-Mal. 15, f. 176-177v; Thaliath, *The Synod of Diamper*, 131-132: "En este adviento hize synodo diocesana en este Angamalle con mucho contentamiento de todos, donde se juró de nuevo obediencia a S. Sanctidad y se abjuraron las heregias antiguas, ye se hizo synodo en forma, donde se ordenaron muchas cosas de grande bien para estas almas, ye se mudaron otras (que ordenó el Arcebispo de Goa quando aqui vino) por lo pedir assi toda la cristianidad diciendo que no se consultó entonces con ellos cosa alguna, ni entendieron muchas que en la primera synodo se mandaron. Lo qual es tanta verdad que aun despues el dicho Arcebispo hizo por si mismo algunos canones despues de acabada la synodo, y los ayuntó al cuerpo de la dicha synodo. ... El Arcebispo entendo que manda este año su synodo a S. Sanctidad porque assi me lo escrevio. V. Pd. deve mandar al Padre Procurador general que haga con los illmos. Cardenales que se impida mostrarse la dicha synodo, pues no está en forma, y tiene muchas cosas se quitaron en esta, incompartales a estos christianos..."

[47] ARSI, Goa-Mal. 15, f. 179; Thaliath, *The Synod of Diamper*, 133: "O Arcebispo de Goa cuido que quer mandar a Roma a synodo que elle fez no Diamper cuando câ veio. Porque me mandou pedir as firmas della que eu tinha & como auquella synodo não o foi, porque se não consultou nada, nem os christãos fizerão conceito della e se firmarão nella foi por minha importunação, não convem per nenhum cazo que se apresente à sua Sanctidade, pois nesta d'agora se tirarão algumas cousas della que erão insufriveis, e os christãos não souberão dellas e ainda o mesmo Arcebispo fez algunos canones, dêpois da synodo acabada, que os christãos não souberão. Pello que os promotores desta Synodo d'agora pedirão mostra da outra, e mudarãosse algumas cousas, que a todos os padres preccìò ser assi necessario."

> Now I should not like to leave out here a thing of great importance, namely that when the Archbishop of Goa came to visit this Malabar, he conducted a council, to tell the truth, with little form and order of a council; and of his own accord, even afterwards, added some things which were never read in public. And much of what was read, was done in such hurry and confusion that the Christians did not understand, nor consequently accept it... But now that we can proceed with more leisure, it seemed necessary to all the Fathers that the bishop should convoke again a synod in which things could be settled with good order and deliberation... This diocesan synod conducted with all prescribed formalities, the Bishop will be sending to His Holiness next year, it is necessary, and I think His Excellency will also be writing to Your Reverence, that Rome be warned that the Archbishop is sending this year the synod he conducted, to be presented to the Pope; but it should on no account, be approved, as it contains some provisions which are detested by the entire Christian community, since they are impossible to observe and the Christians never understood them.[48]

Albert Laerzio, the Vice Provincial of the Vice Province of Malabar in his letter of 15 January 1604 addressed to Claudio Acquaviva, the Jesuit General in Rome, confirms the irregularities:

> Although he [Bishop Francis Ros] has no great natural talent for administration, his great virtues and compliance compensate for this defect, and Our Lord is favouring him in everything. This year he convoked and concluded a synod to the great contentment and satisfaction of all. In it, all the clerics who numbered over 300 and the heads of the people vowed obedience to the Roman Church with great concord. Since the Synod which the Archbishop of Goa convoked was not read to the convoked and since the assembled did not understand what had been settled in it, as the Archbishop added many things of his choice, in the present one some provisions were revoked and others were confirmed; so much so, it was

---

[48] ARSI, Goa-Mal, 15, f. 182; Thaliath, *The Synod of Diamper*, 134: "Porem não queiro deixar de apontar huma cousa de muita emportança e hè que quando o Arcebispo de Goa veo a visitar esta Serra fez hum concilio, e, per fallar verdade, com pouco modo e ordem de concilio, acrecentando ainda depois a sua vontade algumas cousas que nunca se lerão em publico, e muitas que se lerão foy com tanta pressa e confusão que nem os Christãos as perceberão nem pollo conseguinte as receberão... Mas agora que se procede con mais liberdade pareceo a todos os padres necessario que o Senhor Bispo outra vez ajuntasse o Concilio, no qual se essentassem as cousas com boa ordem e madureça... Este concilio diocesano, feito com todas as circumstancias o anno que vem o Sr. Bispo o manderá s S. Sde., porque agoura não he possivel, e como S. Sra tãobem cuido que escreve a V. R. he necessario que advertião lá que o Arcebispo este anno manda o que elle fez, para se apresentar ao Papa, o que não convem de nenhuma maneyra que se aprove, por ter algumas cousas que toda a christandade repugna aceitar, por ser impossiveis e que nunca entenderão".

determined when I was in Rome that it should not be presented to the Pope; and it is good that it is not presented....[49]

These official letters written by highly competent persons to their superiors in Rome are more than enough to establish the fact that the Synod of Diamper was not conducted according to the norms of the "sacred canons."

4. Papal Approbation of the Synod

In the first millennium, particular councils were convoked and laws were promulgated in harmony with the decrees of the ecumenical councils without any approval or confirmation by the Holy See. From the eleventh century onwards restrictions were introduced for the celebration of provincial and plenary councils. After the Council of Trent, Pope Sixtus V, with the publication of the bull *Immensa aeterni* on 11 February 1587 prescribed the transmission of all decrees and laws of provincial and regional (plenary, national) councils to the Sacred Congregation of the Council for revision and confirmation.[50] However, no such revision nor confirmation by Rome was required for diocesan synods; and even when the acts of diocesan synods were sent to Rome, usually the Sacred Congregation of the Council refused to examine them.[51] Such is the norm and practice also today. Since the Synod of Diamper was only a diocesan Synod no approval nor confirmation of the Pope or the Apostolic See was needed for its validity, if it were convoked by a legitimate diocesan

[49] ARSI, Goa-Mal. 15, f. 209; Thaliath, *The Synod of Diamper*, 136-137: "Posto que não tenha [Francisco Ros] tanto talento natural pera o governo, mas a muita virtude, que tem, e facilidade supre esta falta e Nosso Senhor o vay em tudo favorecendo. Ajuntou este anno sinodo e o acabou com grande contentamento e satisfação de todos no qual assy os ecclesiasticos todos que passão de trezentos como as cabeças dos pouvos, juravão obediencia a Igreja Romana com grande conformidade. E porque o sinodo que o Arcebispo de Goa, Dom Aleixo de Menezes, fez, não se tornou ler aos congregados, nem souberão o que tinhão nelle determinado pollo Arcebispo ajuntar muitas cousas suas, agora neste retratarão algumas cousas e concetarão outras, de modo que foy cousa acertada, não se presentar ao Papa, quando eu la estive, e he bem que não se lhe presente...."

[50] Pope Sixtus V, the bull *Immensa aeterni*, 11 February 1587, in *Bullarium Romanum*, tom. VIII, 1863, 991; cf. also P. Hinschius, *System des Katholischen Kirchenrechts mit Besonderer Rücksicht auf Deutschland*, vol. 3, Berlin 1883, 653-654.

[51] Benedict XIV, *De Synodo Dioecesana*, lib. XIII, cap. III, 6-7.

bishop and conducted according to the norms of canon law.[52] We treat this matter here only because some strove to demonstrate that Pope Clement VIII in the letter *Divinam Dei* of 19 May 1601 ratified or confirmed the Synod of Diamper.[53]

After the conclusion of the synod Menezes made strenuous attempts to obtain at least an apostolic blessing or praise from the pope for his great works in the Malabar Church. Many letters and reports about the happy and successful conclusion of the synod in accordance with the sacred canons were also forwarded to Rome. The Pope was informed that the St Thomas Christians were brought back to the Catholic faith and to the obedience of Rome. Albert Laerzio, the Procurator of the Jesuits, commissioned by Menezes, submitted a report about the Synod of Diamper to the Holy Father through Cardinal Santori on 29 March 1601, in which an apostolic blessing or praise from the Pope was earnestly requested for the whole Christian community which accepted the Roman Pontiff as the head of the Church.[54] It is in response to this request that the Pope issued the letter *Divinam Dei* of 19 May 1601, in order to congratulate and encourage the St Thomas Christians who "promised obedience to him."[55] In this letter, addressed to the "venerable brother, the Archbishop of Angamaly (at that time Francis Ros S.J.) and to the clergy and Christian people converted by St Thomas, the Apostle," the Pope makes a simple passing reference to the Synod of Diamper, in which (he was made to believe) that the St Thomas Christians "abandoned the schism and accepted the jurisdiction of the pope." We quote the relevant part of this letter:

> Wherefore we are filled with great joy and pleasure in the Lord on hearing from many such letters that have been copiously sent to us (*de litteris hoc de genere copiose scriptis*) and on coming to know therefrom that our Venerable Brother the Archbishop of Goa, prompted by his devotion and zeal for the salvation of souls, has conducted a well-attended Synod of

[52] Cf. Fonti, fasc. VIII: *Studi Storici sulle fonti del diritto canonico orientale*, Rome 1932, 705; G. Beltrami, *La chiesa Caldea nel secolo dell'Unione*, 83; C. De Clercq, *Histoire des Conciles*, t. XI, 67.

[53] J. F. Raulin, *Historia Ecclesiae Malabaricae cum Diamperitana Synodo*, Rome 1745, 58; L. V. Pastor, *Storia dei Papi*, vol. XI, 498; G. M. Antão, *De Synodi Diamperitanae...*, 76-82.

[54] For details see Thaliath, *The Synod of Diamper*, 118-122; Beltrami, *La Chiesa caldea ...*, 242.

[55] Archivum Vaticanum Armarium 44, n. 45, ff. 131-135; *Corpo Diplomático Português*, vol. XII, 99-102.

> your priests with the presence of most respectful laymen of your nation. In the Synod, under the inspiration of the Holy Ghost and with overwhelming consensus of opinion, the nefarious errors of Nestorius have been rejected, anathematized and condemned by you, even as they had been already rejected, anathematized and condemned by the Holy See and the Ecumenical councils; books containing the contagion and venom of heretics were thrown into the fire or purged of errors lest they should ruin souls; but what is of utmost importance is that you have accepted and professed the Roman Pontiff as the common Father of the faithful and the Head of the whole Church and have given him due obedience, as the kings, princes and all the Catholics render, for they cannot be Christ's sheep if they do not obey (Peter), to whom Christ himself the eternal Pastor entrusted his sheep to be fed, to whom he gave the keys of the kingdom, the supreme power of binding and loosing and whom he established as the strong and unmoveable rock of God, the edifice of the Church.[56]

It is evident that this letter contains nothing but a simple praise or blessing directed to the whole Christian community (not to Menezes) for the things accomplished in the Synod, as requested in "many such letters that have been copiously sent to us," and no formula of a canonical approval of the Synod.[57] Antão, who set out to defend the validity of the Synod of Diamper, resorted to the theory of implicit approval since he could not find anything explicit about the approval of the synod in the pope's letter. He states:

> Non fuit illa quidem explicite approbata, cum Pontifex totidem verbis non dixerit: *approbamus synodum Diamperitanam*; sed sine dubio fuit approbata *implicite*, licet generice, quia Pontifex Archiepiscopum goanensem

[56] *Corpo Diplomático Português*, vol. XII, 101: "... Quare magno gaudio magna in Domino voluptate repleti sumus, cum ex litteris hoc de genere copiose scriptis audivimus et cognovimus venerabilem fratrem archiepiscopum Goae, pro sua pietate et zelo divini honoris et salutis animarum vestrarum, synodum apud vos frequentem celebrasse sacerdotum vestrorum, praesentibus etiam viris primariis ex natione vestra, qua in Synodo Spiritus Sancti instinctu magno animarum consensu impii errores Nestorii a vobis rejecti et anathemate condemnati sunt, quemadmodum jampridem ab hac Sancta Apostolica Sede ab oecumenicis conciliis hujus quoque Sanctae Sedis congregatis reiecti, damnati et anathematizati sunt, tum libri haereticorum peste ac veneno infecti ne animas interficerent, igne sunt exusti aliique ab erroribus expurgati, sed illud maximi momenti quod Romanum Pontificem communem fidelium Patrem totius Ecclesiae caput agnovistis et professi estis, eique debitam obedientiam detulistis quam ei Reges et Principes et omnes Christiani unanimes praestant et deferunt, non enim esse possunt ex ovibus Christi, qui tebro (*sic*) non obediunt, cui Christus ipse aeternus Pastor agnos, et oves suas pascendas tradidit, cui claves Regni coelorum, et summam ligandi, et solvendi potestatem dedit, quem denique firmam, et immobilem Dei petram, et Ecclesiae aedificationem constituit...."

[57] Beltrami, *La Chiesa caldea...*, 124-125; C. De Clerc, *Histoire des Conciles*, t. XI, 67.

> Synodum illam celebratam laudibus culmavit.... Igitur synodus celeberrima Diamperensis, de cuius approbatione iam diversimode auctores loquuntur, fuit a Clemente VIII approbata. Approbata quidem implicite; sed approbatio implicita est vera et propria approbatio. Quae vero, cum in forma communi et generica data sit, non continet approbationem singulorum decretorum Synodi; quae eundem valorem habent, ac haberent sine illa laude et generica approbationem pontificia.[58]

However, in our opinion, this letter contains only a simple apostolic blessing, which has nothing to do with a formal juridical approval or confirmation of the Synod in the canonical sense, because of the following reasons:

1. In the report submitted to the pope no approval or confirmation of the synod was requested but only an apostolic blessing for the whole Christian community. Therefore, what was granted was a general praise for the things accomplished in Malabar, which has no juridical relevance. Even Gouvea, the Portuguese historian states only that "His Holiness sent his apostolic blessing to the Archbishop in token of his great appreciation of the labour he had undertaken for the good of these souls."[59] It is to be particularly noted that this letter was not sent to Archbishop Menezes as Gouvea states, but to the community of St Thomas Christians.

2. No approval nor confirmation of the Holy See was required for diocesan synods. Therefore, it would be difficult to believe that the Pope formally approved this particular diocesan synod, for which no such approval was required. Hence, authors like A. Coussa, Giamil, Karoloveskij, Beltrami, De Clercq are of the opinion that Synod of Diamper was never approved by the Pope.[60]

3. Approbation was never granted to any synod before the competent authority (at that time the Sacred Congregation of the Council) had examined and corrected the acts and decrees in order to ensure their conformity with the common law and with the norms of sound reason, justice and canonical equity.[61] But before the date of the papal letter *Divinam Dei* (19 May 1601) the acts of the synod were not presented to the Pope nor to Apostolic See because they were not yet

---

[58] G. M. Antão, *De Synodi Diamperitanae natura atque decretis*, 82.

[59] Gouvea, *Jornada do Arcebispo de Goa*, f. 130.

[60] For the opinions of various authors, see Thaliath, *The Synod of Diamper* 114-117.

[61] Wernz, *Ius Decretalium*, t. II, pars ii, 835; Wernz – Vidal, *Ius Canonicum*, II, *De personis*, 577-578.

translated into Latin. Albert Laerzio who was commissioned by Menezes to obtain an apostolic praise from the Pope states in his report to the Pontiff: "The Archbishop of Goa has written a letter to his Holiness on this subject and gives information about the state of the Church. He has also forwarded the acts of the said council which are being translated into Latin and will be presented to His Holiness on completion of the translation."[62] Albert Laerzio, who later became the Vice Provincial of the Vice Province of Malabar, states clearly in his letter of 15 January 1604 addressed to the Claudio Acquaviva, the Jesuit General in Rome, what happened to the acts which were being translated into Latin:

> ... Since the Synod which the Archbishop of Goa convoked was not read to the convoked and since the assembled did not understand what had been settled in it, as the Archbishop added many things of his choice, in the present one some provisions were revoked and others were confirmed; so much so, it was determined when I was in Rome that it should not be presented to the Pope; and it is good that it is not presented....[63]

Since Rome never approves a synod before the examination and correction of its acts and decrees, it is unthinkable that the Pope approved the Synod of Diamper even implicitly, the acts of which were not presented to him.

4. Neither Menezes himself nor the Portuguese missionaries considered the letter *Divinam Dei* of Pope Clement VIII as a formal approval of the Synod of Diamper. In the three letters of Bishop Francis Ros cited above concerning the irregularities in the synod written more than two years after the letter *Divinam Dei* (letters of Francis Ros on 20 November 1603 and 26 December 1603 addressed to the Jesuit General and the letter to John Alvarez on 27 December 1603) and in the letter of John Campori, dated 1 January 1604, (that is, two years and seven months after the papal letter) earnest request was made to the authorities in Rome to impede the presentation of the Acts of the Synod of Diamper to the Pope, since at that time Menezes was trying to send them to the Holy See for approval. Therefore, it is evident that even Archbishop Menezes, Bishop Francis Ros and other Portuguese missionaries did not regard the papal letter *Divinam Dei* as a formal canonical approval of the Synod.

---

[62] Archivio de Propaganda Fide, Miscel vol. 17, f. 23-27^{v}; Thaliath, *The Synod of Diamper*, 122.

[63] See note 49.

CONCLUSION

The Synod of Diamper was a diocesan synod convoked and presided over by a Latin Ordinary without any special mandate from the supreme authority of the Church, in the Archdiocese of Angamaly, that is in an Eastern Church. Furthermore, it was conducted during the vacancy of the said See, when nothing should be innovated (*Sede vacante nihil innovetur*), under pain of excommunication *latae sententiae*, contrary to the norms of the canon law of that time.

Congregation for Divine Worship
and the Discipline of the Sacraments
Piazza Pio XII, 10
00193 Rome, Italy

Paul Pallath

George Nedungatt, S.J.

Return to Pre-Diamper Traditions

The Second Vatican Council has given a solemn directive to the Eastern Catholic Churches to *delatinize*, to use a term which the Council did not use. In fact the conciliar directive is primarily concerned with the recovery and preservation of Tradition and hence it is much wider in application than delatinization. But unfortunately this conciliar directive has commonly been misunderstood owing to defective English translations. In this final study we shall address the issue and deal with the question of return to ancestral traditions according to the Council. In the light of this conciliar teaching we shall examine the particular question of return to pre-Diamper traditions in liturgy and canonical discipline, which constitutes the foremost of the Diamperian "lessons of history". What are the principles, directives and norms regulating such a return?

Since the Council was concerned primarily with the recovery and preservation of the genuine traditions of the Eastern Catholic Churches, we need to start with the conciliar understanding of traditions in the framework of Tradition. Hence we shall devote the first section to this subject. As we shall see in the second section, the Eastern and Western traditions are complementary and are open to healthy reception and mutual enrichment. In the third section we shall distinguish between two different phenomena, namely latinization and catholicization. We shall then attempt an exegetical study of the conciliar directive of return to ancestral traditions (fourth section). After this, in the fifth section, we shall address the particular issue of return to the pre-Diamper traditions in general, which concerns the Syro-Malabar Church in particular. Two concerns of such return are in the matter of liturgy (sixth section) and canonical discipline (seventh section). In the concluding eighth section we shall hear Pope John Paul II formulating a guiding principle that sheds exegetical light on the conciliar directive to return to ancestral traditions, maintaining a double fidelity: "fidelity to traditions" and "fidelity to the men and women of today."

Briefly, then, the following will be the contents of our study:

1. Tradition and Traditions
2. Orientalization and Occidentalization
3. Latinization and Catholicization
4. Return to Ancestral Traditions
   a) Textual History of the Conciliar Directive
   b) English Translations of the Conciliar Text (OE 6)
   c) Meaning of the Conciliar Text
   d) The Rule of Return and the Centennial and Immemorial Customs
   e) The 1996 Instruction of the Congregation for the Eastern Churches
5. The Rule of Return to the Pre-Diamper Traditions in General
6. Return to the Pre-Diamper Liturgical Tradition
7. Return to the Pre-Diamper Canonical Tradition
8. Summary and Conclusion: Double Fidelity

1. Tradition and Traditions

It is in the light of Tradition as the carrier of revelation that the Second Vatican Council spoke of the traditions of the East and of the West as constituting the one precious patrimony of the Catholic Church. The conciliar directive to return to ancestral traditions must also be set in this wider framework. Hence we have first to take stock of what this council has to tell us about Tradition and traditions. The Council has dealt with Tradition in its dogmatic constitution on revelation (DV 7-10), in which Tradition has a rich, positive meaning.

> What was been handed on by the Apostles comprises everything that serves to make the People of God live their lives in holiness and increase their faith. In this way the Church in her doctrine, life and worship, perpetuates and transmits to every generation all that she herself is, all that she believes. The Tradition that comes from the Apostles makes progress in the Church with the help of the Holy Spirit.... The sayings of the Holy Fathers are a witness to the life-giving presence of this Tradition and show how its riches are poured out in the practice and life of the Church as she believes and prays (DV 8).
>
> Sacred Scripture is the word of God as it is put down in writing under the inspiration of the Holy Spirit. And Tradition transmits the word of God, entrusted by Christ the Lord and the Holy Spirit to the Apostles, in its entirety to their successors.... Hence both are to be accepted and respected with equal religious reverence (DV 9).
>
> Sacred Tradition and sacred Scripture make up a single deposit of the word of God (DV 10).

The tradition that transmits the word of God and together with sacred Scripture makes up a "single deposit of the word of God" is sacred Tradition. It is integral to "the deposit of faith entrusted to the Church"[1] and is to be "respected with equal religious reverence" as sacred Scripture. Obviously, not all traditions in the Church go into the making of the "sacred Tradition," written conventionally with a capital T or as tradition in the singular.[2] This is not simply a matter of orthography: if sacred Scripture and sacred Tradition are to be "respected with equal religious reverence" then it is proper that "Tradition" is also capitalised just like "Scripture." A leading Orthodox theologian explains the difference between Tradition and traditions clearly and succinctly as follows.

> 'Tradition' is used in a variety of senses, some wide-ranging and others more restricted. (1) In an inclusive sense it designates the whole Christian faith and practice — not only doctrinal teaching but worship, norms of behaviour, living experience, sanctity — as handed down within the Church from Christ and the apostles down to the present day. Understood in this comprehensive way, Tradition is not to be contrasted with holy scripture but seen as including it; scripture exists within Tradition. (2) In a narrower sense Tradition may be distinguished from scripture, and taken to mean the teaching and practice of the Church, not explicitly recorded in the words of the Bible, but handed down from the beginning within the Christian community. (3) More narrowly still — especially when used in the plural 'traditions' — the term may refer, often in a pejorative sense, to a belief or custom which cannot claim any divine or apostolic origin.[3]

Apostolic tradition, transmitted through the Fathers, "is part of the divinely revealed, undivided heritage of the universal Church." And the Church wants that "the traditions of the Particular Churches remain whole and entire" even while updating their lifestyle (OE 1, 2). The Eastern Code recognizes five major traditions: Alexandrian, Antiochene, Armenian, Chaldean and Constantinopolitan. Besides these

---

[1] See CIC canon 747 § 1 and the corresponding CCEO canon 595 § 1 (with minor variations).

[2] Yves M.-J. Congar, *La Tradition et les Traditions*, 2 vols., Paris, Fayard, 1960-1963; see vol. 2, p. 55 (trans. *Tradition and Traditions: An Historical and Theological Essay*, London, Burns and Oates, 1966). Since the document of Faith and Order (Montreal, 1963) entitled "Scripture, Tradition, traditions," the distinction of meaning of Tradition in the singular and traditions in the plural as going beyond mere grammar, is widely accepted and is ecumenically significant.

[3] Kallistos Ware, "Tradition and traditions," *Dictionary of the Ecumenical Movement*, ed. Nicholas Lossky et al., Geneva, WCC Publications, 1991, pp. 1013-1017.

five Eastern traditions, there is the Western or Latin tradition disciplined by the Latin Code. From these traditions have originated rites, "which are the complex of liturgical, theological, spiritual and disciplinary heritage, which is diversified by culture and the circumstance of history" (CCEO c. 28). Though this word "Rite/rite" has been used by the Second Vatican Council not only in this sense but also to refer to the Eastern Catholic Churches as well as liturgical rites (symbolic and other gestures usually accompanied by words in worship), we follow here the univocal usage established by the Eastern Code to avoid all ambiguity. Some writers still keep to the former usage of "Rite/rite" for "Church," following the "example" of the conciliar decree on the Eastern Churches. It is true that in this decree the Council adopted the existing usage, if only to be understood by its readers, but in no other conciliar document has it done so. In fact it would be to betray the ecclesiology of *Lumen Gentium* to continue with such a usage, which was a latinization of the time of uniatism. In an ecclesiology that conceives only of one Church, the (Roman) Catholic Church, and not of a plurality of Churches in any sense, the other "Churches" could at best be conceived as ritual variations in the one Church, or simply as *ritus*, since according to such an ecclesiology they cannot be designated as Churches in the plural.

The conciliar decree on ecumenism affirms: "It is of supreme importance to understand, respect, preserve and foster the rich liturgical and spiritual heritage of the Eastern Churches in order faithfully to preserve the fullness of the Christian tradition, and to bring about the reconciliation between Eastern and Western Christians" (UR 15). For the Council the ritual patrimony of the Churches of the East merit equal regard as that of the West so that no Church is superior to another by reason of its rite (OE 2, 3, 5). The Council has further proclaimed the right and the duty of the Eastern and Western Churches each to follow its own rite (OE 3, 5). This right is not something that the Council has created and conferred. It is a right that pre-existed the Council, a right that the Council has only articulated and proclaimed — just like the rights all the Christian faithful have to a Christian education or to freedom in the choice of a state of life (GE 2 and 26; CCEO cc. 20 and 22). These and other such rights are prior to councils and codes, and they cannot be abrogated by any ecclesiastical authority. Such is also the right and duty of Churches and persons to follow their own rite (CCEO cc 17 and 40).

Like life itself, tradition is kept alive through growth and change. Hence rites too are subject to growth and change. But such growth and change is not to be erratic or noxious. The Church is not only a society but the Body of Christ in the first place. Hence there is a profound ecclesiological reason, beyond any canonical prescription, why growth and change of its traditions, rites and institutions should follow the laws of organic progress (OE 6).[4] We shall consider this concept more in detail farther below.

2. Orientalization and Occidentalization

"From their very origins, the Churches of the East have had a treasury from which the Church of the West has drawn largely for its liturgy, spiritual tradition and law" (UR 14). Thus the Second Vatican Council refers to the process of the *orientalization* of the Western Church in the first millennium in a tone of appreciation: The Eastern treasury had been formed through creative innovation till about the eighth century mostly in the East.[5] Part of it was received in the West, which was on the whole less creative and innovative than the East during the first millennium. If such *orientalization* has been beneficial to the Western Church for its development, it cannot be excluded *a priori* that a similar *occidentalization* (westernization) of the Eastern Churches can be beneficial to them in areas where they are underdeveloped in comparison with the genuine progress made in the West.

Here are a few examples. In the post-Vatican liturgical reform the Latin Church has received from the East several elements like the Anaphora of St Basil (thoroughly adapted), and rediscovered elements like the Prayers of the Faithful, and restored institutions like the permanent diaconate, which had ceased in the Latin Church but not in the East. The Eastern icons and the Prayer of Jesus have be-

[4] The term rite has been used in several senses in the past, but the new Eastern Code has assigned to it a uniform meaning in law (CCEO 28 § 1). See George Nedungatt, *The Spirit of the Eastern Code*, Rome, CIIS (Bangalore, Dharmaram Publications), 1993: chapter 6, "Churches, Traditions and Rites," pp. 60-84.

[5] Robert Taft says incisively: "Every single innovation in Christian liturgical practice, except the December 25 date of Christmas, originated in the East before migrating westward." See his study, "The Missionary Effort of the Eastern Churches as an Example of Inculturation," in: La Congregazione per le Chiese Orientali, *Le chiese orientali e la missione in Asia: Riflessioni in preparazione all'Assemblea Speciale del Sinodo dei Vescovi*, Vatican City, 1998, pp. 28-45, at p. 35.

come favourites in the West. So much for orientalization. As for occidentalization, here are two recent examples from the Russian Orthodox Church that are absolutely free of all suspicion of undue western influence. The *Ratio fundamentalis institutionis sacerdotalis,*[6] containing guidelines for clerical formation issued by the Roman Congregation for Catholic Education, was received gratefully by Metropolitan Nikodim, the official delegate of the Patriarchate of Moscow for relations with the West, and translated into Russian as well suited for seminary formation in the Russian Orthodox Church. Again, the same Metropolitan Nikodim had the Constitutions of the Society of Jesus translated into Russian to serve as the constitutions of a religious group of the Russian Orthodox Church. Further, in the areas of biblical and liturgical studies, in patristics, catechetics and homiletics, free reception from the West has been taking place in the Catholic Eastern Churches and to some extent also in the Eastern Orthodox Churches. For the latter may be named the foremost Orthodox theologian of liturgy, Alexander Schmemann, who avowedly was indebted to Western scholars like Jean Danielou and Louis Bouyer and the Western liturgical movement in general, which in its turn drew on the East ever since it was launched by Lambert Beauduin in 1909.[7] The text of the Stations of the Cross conducted by Pope John Paul II at the Colosseum in Rome on Good Friday 1994 was written by His Holiness Bartholomew, the Ecumenical Patriarch of Constantinople. Western saints like St Francis of Assisi and Therese of Lisieux have been received into several Eastern liturgical calendars. Such a process, whether orientalization or occidentalization, is basically the ecclesial act of "reception" in accordance with the nature of the Church as *koinonia* or communion of Churches.[8] Such reception of course presupposes that it is a free act from within and not an imposition from outside, which would be ecclesiologically an aberration, morally reprehensible, and canonically illegitimate. Evidently, free reception does not mean adopting elements indiscriminately without regard to

[6] AAS 62 (1970) 321-384.

[7] Alexander Schmemann, *Liturgy and Tradition: Theological Reflections of Alexander Schmemann*, ed. Thomas Fisch, Crestwood, St. Vladimir's Seminary Press, 1990, pp. 4, 5, 101. See also his *Introduction to Liturgical Theology,* Portland, The American Orthodox Press, 1966.

[8] Yves Congar, "La réception comme réalité ecclésiologique," *Revue des sciences philosophiques et théologiques,* n° 56, 1972, pp. 369-403: reprint in Idem, *Église et Papauté*, Paris, Cerf, 1994, 229-266.

organic progress: it does not imply licence to mutilate and disfigure, or to graft and produce a monster, or to remove or adopt elements that destroy the proper ritual identity.[9] Reception by taking in elements that are lethal is like the "freedom" for the ingestion of poison. Changes in the rite may only be admitted for organic progress (CCEO c. 40 § 1).

3. Latinization and Catholicization

The latinization of the Thomaschristian Church was the unnatural child born to the ideology of the superiority of the Latin rite. This ideology had been generated as a reaction to and a reversal of the earlier ideology of the superiority of the Greek rite (*"superbia Graecorum"*). The Western reaction in the second millennium was shored up by and confused with the Roman doctrine of the primacy of the See/Church of Rome. It was fuelled by the colonial drive for Western dominance, which was not seldom rationalized as the triumph of "culture" over "nature" in the age of the Enlightenment. The ideology of the superiority of the Latin rite had been fostered even by certain popes and the Roman Curia, in practice if not in theory, before Pope Benedict XIV articulated the doctrine of the superiority of the Latin rite (*praestantia ritus latini*) as the authentic doctrine of the Church.[10]

---

[9] The metaphor of "organic progress" indicates that whereas to have one's hands or nose cut off is mutilation, it is not mutilation to have one's nails paired. To graft fresh skin on a burn is not like grafting a "third eye." An injection of penicillin may be all right but not the ingestion of a lethal dose of poison. A heart transplant is not done so routinely as a tooth replacement. Models of healthy and successful reception may be found also outside Churches and rites: for example, Rabindranath Tagore's religious music is rooted in Indian ragas and kirtans but was inspired also by Christian church music, Western operas, classical music and folksongs (Irish, Scottish, and German).

[10] In his apostolic constitution *Etsi pastoralis* (26 May 1742) Benedict XIV asserted the superiority (*praestantia*) of the Latin rite over the *Greek* rite since the former is the rite of the Roman Church : "Ritus enim latinus propter suam *praestantiam* eo quod sit ritus Sanctae Romanae Ecclesiae omnium Ecclesiarum Matris et Magistrae, sic supra Graecum ritum *praevalet*, maxime in Italicis regionibus, ubi latinis Episcopis subiecti sunt, ut non modo ab ipso ad Graecum transitus nullatenus permittatur, verum etiam a Graecis semel assumptus absque Apostolica dispensatione deseri nequeat" (P. Gasparri, ed., *Codicis Iuris Canonici Fontes* I, Rome, 1926, p. 730).

In his encyclical letter *Allatae sunt* (26 June 1755) Benedict XIV went a step further and asserted the superiority of the Latin rite over *all* the other rites: "Cum Latinus Ritus is sit, quo utitur Sancta Romana Ecclesia, quae Mater est et Magistra aliarum Ecclesiarum, reliquis omnibus Ritibus *praeferri* debet. Ex quo porro sequitur, haud licere a Latino Ritu ad Graecum transire; nec illis, qui semel a Ritu graeco vel

Consequently, in the subsequent centuries the reform of the Eastern Catholic Churches was guided by this doctrine of the superiority of the Latin rite. We are not surprised, therefore, if as a practical corollary, the latinization of these Churches was pursued not only by the Latins but also by the Easterners themselves, if only moved by religious *obsequium* to the Roman magisterium, which was not uniform or constant in this matter.

The most elaborate example of such latinization is the Synod of Mount Lebanon of the Maronite Church (1736). The Maronite Church had already received the Tridentine norms in four synods held between 1580-1590, operating widespread latinization, so much so Pope Paul V had to call for moderation. But the process was resumed later and completed in the Synod of Mount Lebanon in 1736, which was steered by the Maronite scholar Joseph Assemani giving rise to the most telling example of massive auto-latinization of an Eastern Catholic Church. What is more, Pope Benedict XIV approved this synod *"in forma specifica"* with the bull *Singulari Romanorum* on 1 September 1741, the only instance of an Eastern Catholic synod ever approved specifically by a Roman Pontiff. Clearly, the Synod met the pope's idea of the application of the Tridentine norms in the Catholic Church, without distinction of rites.[11] And the message was clear to the other Eastern Catholic Churches till the Second Vatican Council would declare the equal dignity of the various rites and determine that they were all to be preserved and protected as the precious patrimony of the one Catholic Church.

Against this wider canvas it becomes understandable why and how in Malabar latinization was carried out by the Synod of Diamper on a massive scale (see for details the studies of Kollaparambil and Vellian in this volume), and after it the process was carried on not only by the foreign Latin bishops who governed the Thomaschristians till 1896 but also by native Syro-Malabar bishops after them.

---

orientali ad latinum transierunt, integrum esse ad pristinum Graecum reverti." (P. Gasparri, ed., *Codicis Iuris Canonici Fontes* II, Rome, 1924, p. 459).

On the policy and many instances of latinization under Pope Benedict XIV, see H. L. Hoffmann, *De Benedicti XIV latinisationibus*, Vatican, 1955.

[11] As a rule, Pope Benedict XIV's doctrine of the superiority of the Latin rite prevailed over the occasional contrary signals like the warnings of the Roman Propaganda Congregation against undue changes of local rites and disciplines and the partial correctives under Pope Leo XIII (Apostolic letter *Orientalium Dignitas*, 1894) and Pope Benedict XV's creation of the Congregation for the Eastern Church and of the Pontifical Oriental Institute in 1917. See the sources cited under CCEO c. 40 § 1.

The repeated attempts to make the Syro-Malabar rite conform more closely to the Roman rite have been detailed by Jacob Vellian in his study. Our post-Vatican hindsight was not the view of the latinizers whether foreign like Menezes or native like Blessed Chavara Kuriakose (1805-1871, beatified 1986). Their good intention need not be called into question, whatever be the havoc done to the identity and purity of the Syro-Malabar rite and in particular to its liturgy and discipline.

Moreover, for those times it would be anachronistic to think in terms of Churches *sui iuris*, as we understand this concept today, not to speak of the equal dignity and equal rights of the Churches. The prevailing ecclesiological view was monarchic, with the pope at the summit of the one Church of Christ, with patriarchs and primates and bishops governing under him and in communion with him with whatever powers he had granted or recognized. The ritual differences did not amount to a plurality of Churches *sui iuris*. In Leo XIII's *Ecclesiarum dignitas orientalium* the plural denoted rather dioceses/eparchies. And indeed, Benedict XIV spoke of the "praestantia *ritus latini*" and not of "praestantia *Ecclesiae latinae* ratione ritus" (cf. OE 3). In short, the dominant ecclesiological idea was that there was only one Church with a number of dioceses/eparchies united together in one body, in which the "Patriarchal Churches" are but administrative collectivities with their heads having a jurisdiction that is but a participation in the supreme power vested in the Roman Pontiff and the ecumenical councils.[12]

The Second Vatican Council spoke of latinization only in veiled terms, without ever using this term itself, much less making a frank confession born of repentance (as Pope John Paul II would do on 12 March of the Great Jubilee Year 2000 for the sins of the Church or churchmen). However, the Council's declaration that "no Church is superior (*praestat*) to the others by reason of its rite" (OE 3) is clear and resonant and it quietly disclaims the magisterium of Benedict XIV.[13] The Council then directs the Eastern Catholic Churches "to

---

[12] Ivan Žužek, *Understanding the Eastern Code*, (Kanonika 8), Rome, Pontifical Oriental Institute, 1997, see "Incidenza del CCEO nella storia modern della Chiesa universale" (p. 266,-327; see pp. 291-293).

[13] Each one of the thirty paragraphs (except the final peroration) of the conciliar decree on the Eastern Catholic Churches is fortified with footnotes, except one paragraph, OE 3, which declares the equality of all rites in the Church and thus disclaims the doctrine of Pope Benedict XIV on the *praestantia ritus latini*. This omission is not casual but seems to be due to a piety that recoiled from presenting a pope as a loser

return to their ancestral traditions" (OE 6), a directive that has been widely misunderstood and misapplied (see below). Here we have a very vital and complex issue. In the Syro-Malabar Church in particular it continues to agitate minds and spirits as the lingering billows and backflows of Diamper.

The Synod of Diamper has been cited fifty-three times in the Code of Canons of the Eastern Churches (CCEO).[14] A casual reader might wonder if this means approval of the source cited. Ivan Žužek, S.J., former Secretary of the Pontifical Eastern Code Commission (PCCICOR), intervening in a discussion during the 1999 Symposium on the Synod of Diamper held at the Pontifical Oriental Institute, explained that a mere citation is not necessarily an indication that the canon in question is based on the source cited. Sometimes the canon departs from the source and may even be opposed to it, thus pointing to canonical development. In fact this methodology had been adopted already by the decree on the Eastern Churches of the Second Vatican Council; for example the 1963 Schema contained citations of source texts that were "contrary to the canonical discipline in force."[15]

The Code of Canons of the Eastern Churches (CCEO) has incorporated quite a number of canons based on the teachings of the Council of Florence and the Council of Trent. Does this mean latinization of the Eastern Catholic Churches? To legislate on the authority of the Council of Trent may appear to be at first sight latinization. Some see all Tridentization[16] as latinization. However, this is erroneous since Trent often draws on the earlier ecumenical councils. And in such cases what appears at first sight as Tridentization (and latinization)

---

to the Council. However, the reference to the pope can be read in the text itself ... *praestet ratione ritus*. Of old the councils did not show such pious regard for bishops, patriarchs or popes.

[14] I am grateful to Sunny Kokkaravalayil, S.J., who ascertained this number fifty-three. For example, among the sources cited for c. 373, which canonizes both clerical celibacy and the state of the married clergy, we find the Synod of Diamper cited. After the Quinisext canons 3, 6, 13, and 30 have been cited among the sources for the institution of the married clergy, the Synod of Diamper is cited with its prohibition of ordaining married men (Action VII, section 1, decree 16/12).

[15] It was noted at the end of the first part of the Schema that among the footnotes there were also "quae nova omnino sunt vel vigenti disciplinae canonicae contraria videntur." — *Acta Synodalia Sacrosancti Concilii Oecumenici Vaticani Secundi*, vol. III, pars V, Vatican, Polyglot, 1975, p. 751.

[16] "Tridentization" is derived from *Tridentum*, meaning Trent in English and Trento in Italian. Note that the Council of Trent is *concilium tridentinum*, in Latin.

may turn out to be catholicization. This distinction is often neglected but is important, since conformity to Trent is not always mere latinization but at times is catholicization. Trent itself did not make this distinction and imposed its doctrine and most of its discipline on all Catholics. It follows that it will be superficial and deviant to dub as latinization all instances of Tridentization by the Synod of Diamper. For example, what is sometimes called the post-Diamper latinization of the role of the bishop in the Thomaschristian tradition, especially with regard to the administration of Church temporalities, is really catholicization in the above sense.[17] Obviously, the concept of latinization is not so simple as some people make out with a proof-text methodology.

The Synod of Diamper promulgated not only the doctrine of the Council of Trent but also its decrees "regarding the reformation of the Church, and all Christian people, promising and swearing to govern itself according to the rules thereof, and to observe the same forms that are observed in the Catholic Church, and as are observed in this province of the Indies, and in all the other provinces and suffragans to the metropolis of Goa" (Session III, decree 21). The pre-comprehension was that only "the forms that are observed in the Catholic Church" [read: the Latin Church] are "Catholic," and standard, and any differentiation was unwarranted deviation. In other words, for unity it is necessary to have uniformity. The Council of Trent itself had not made that mistake as it had "mainly been concerned to condemn and anathematize the chief errors of the heretics of our age, and to hand on and teach the true catholic doctrine."[18] The Tridentine decree regarding the reform of the Roman missal and breviary, which was perhaps open to misinterpretation in its extreme brevity,[19] did not prescribe the substitution of the liturgical books of the Eastern rites with the Western counterparts, as was widely done by the Synod of Diamper. In other words, whereas the distinction

[17] George Nedungatt, *Laity and Church Temporalities: Appraisal of a Tradition,* Dharmaram Canonical Studies, 1), Bangalore, Dharmaram Publications, 2000, pp. 163-179.

[18] Session XXV, closing decrees: *Decrees of the Ecumenical Councils*, II, ed. Norman E. Tanner, Georgetown, Sheed and Ward, 1990, p. 798.

[19] The council orders the correction of books "by the judgement and authority" of the Roman Pontiff. "It gives similar orders in the matter of the catechism prepared by the Fathers who have been commissioned for this, and of the missal and the breviary" (ibid., p. 797).

between catholicization and latinization was maintained at Trent, it vanished almost entirely with the massive latinization of Diamper.

However, Diamper was not simply a drive at wholesale latinization. Though the liturgy as a whole was much latinized, the Qurbana and the Liturgy of the Hours were left in the original Syriac, albeit with several mutilations, corrections and interpolations. And knowledge of Syriac needed to understand the texts was henceforth to be required of candidates for sacred orders.[20]

The pre-Diamper Thomaschristian Church is not to be harked back to as an ideal best made in Eden. Some seem to see everything pre-Diamper as hallowed by the Law of Thomas, with no "falling short." It is thus, for example, that the *malpan* system is viewed by some, with no critical questions being asked. Some Syro-Malabar writers regard the *malpan* system ("malpan"is Syriac for "teacher") as proper and peculiar to the Law of Thomas. Some also hold that it was unduly replaced by the Seminary system through Tridentization and latinization. As a matter of fact, clerical formation in the West prior to the Council of Trent (1545-1563), too, was essentially identical to the *malpan* system (clerical students being entrusted to a single teacher attached to the cathedral) and was disciplined by canon 18 of the Third Lateran Council (1178) and canon 11 of the Fourth Lateran Council (1215). Though this system favoured personal attention, it was not free of serious defects: 1) a single teacher taught all the different subjects, not several 'specialists' who today ensure better quality instruction; 2) the neglect of the clerical vocation of the poor, who used to be left out. The Seminary system, experimented already before the Council of Trent, was geared to remedy these and other such defects of the "*malpan* system" and was prescribed by this Council (Session 23, canon 18). Now, though it is not perfect (no system on the earth is), to cry latinization and to call for a return to the *malpan* system would be obscurantist chauvinism, not organic progress envisaged by the Second Vatican Council. From the fruits you judge the tree. Why is it that the *malpan* system did not produce any notable theologian in the Malabar Church? It lent itself easily to bribery, in the absence of a "controller of examinations," resulting in

[20] "Whereas it has been hitherto the custom of this diocese to ordain boys even priests, and that without examining their lives and manners, having for money and not for any extraordinary sufficiency, all the inferior orders as well as holy orders conferred upon them in one day, contrary to the holy canons and the laws of the Church" (Session VII, decree 1).

the promotion of the richer boys and the neglect of vocations from poor families. A parallel would be English education under the British Raj, which for all its merits, was tailored to producing subordinate clerks to aid the colonial masters. The malpan system could at best produce local pastors, not specialists in the sacred sciences.

In the matter of the administration of the Church property during the Chaldean period under foreign bishops there was an anomalous deviation from the discipline established by the ecumenical councils. Although this deviation may not have been morally imputable, it was objectively a failure to conform to the decrees of the ecumenical councils. Though the canonical discipline in the Chaldean Church conformed to the norm of the ecumenical councils in this matter, the chaldean bishops failed to enforce it in the Malabar Church. Their option to exercise almost exclusively the power of orders and practically eschew the exercise of the power of jurisdiction was objectively or formally "undue." Here conformity to the sacred canons of the ecumenical councils would be not latinization but catholicization, even though this conformity was de facto brought about by Latin bishops: This may be explained as follows.

> Though the Latin bishops followed an overall policy of latinization, in this matter of the administration of Church property what they did was basically to enforce the discipline established by the sacred canons of the ecumenical councils. According to this discipline, the bishop is to have authority over the temporal goods of the diocese. Hence the enforcement of this discipline was effectively catholicization, not latinization, though superficially it appeared to be latinization. For, just as when the Latin missionaries taught dogmas of the Christian faith defined by the ecumenical councils this cannot be called latinization, even so the enforcement of the discipline sanctioned by the same ecumenical councils for the universal Church cannot be called latinization. Latinization is not simply something done by the Latins as *persons*; it has to do with the *thing* called the Latin rite that is not an integral part of the Christian Tradition. And such latinization can and has been done by non-Latins or Orientals themselves out of ignorance or due to the notion of the superiority of the Latin rite, which was the official Roman magisterium at least from Pope Benedict XIV onwards till the Second Vatican Council. ...
>
> As for the latinizing Synod of Diamper and the post-Diamper latinization of the Church of the Thomaschristians there is much that deserves to be disapproved for the deviations and mutilations, especially in the area of liturgy; they are infamous as "unbearable provisions." But in the matter of the administration of temporal goods, as also in a few other areas, the Thomaschristian discipline was brought into conformity with the Catholic discipline, which it had "fallen short of owing to circumstances of times and persons." The Latin period, therefore, is a

> move away from an exception to the rule, from illegality to legality in the matter of temporalities. ...
>
> Traditionally, the "Latins" have claimed: "We have catholicized you;" and the "Syrians" have rebutted: "No, you have latinized us." Both absolutize, both are extremist positions. The truth is in between, in the distinction. Illegitimate latinization is to be condemned, but not catholicization. Catholicization simply because it is done by the Latins does not become latinization but remains what it is, catholicization.[21]

When a person or group or community opts for the Catholic communion, it is necessary to profess the Catholic faith, share in its sacramental life, and be governed by its essential regimen or government, without prejudice to ritual variety. This is catholicization. For example, if a Presbyterian community wants to enter into the Catholic communion, it has to accept the episcopal structure of Church government besides making the profession of the faith of the Catholic Church. Thus, when the Thomaschristians came into the Catholic communion with the profession of faith made by John Sulaqa in 1553, they virtually renounced their presbyteral-lay church organization, in which the bishop had hardly any power of jurisdiction and accepted an episcopal church order established by the sacred canons of the ecumenical councils. This catholicization, however, was not carried into effect fully and consistently till the Latin bishops took the matter up seriously. Although many of their reforms were latinizations and not catholicization, some of those reforms commonly and loosely called "latinization" were legitimate and beneficial catholicization.

The Synod of Diamper has been denounced on the one hand for its "aggressive, polemic and westernising ideology" but on the other hand lauded for "the many positive aspects which the Portuguese fostered in India, for which India should be thankful to them."[22] For the Thomaschristians, "had several errors against the positive laws which had not yet been received by them because these had not been promulgated among them."[23] The lack of promulgation of laws or canons is some excuse for those errors and deficiencies. But if the

---

[21] George Nedungatt, *Laity and Church Temporalities: Appraisal of a Tradition,* Dharmaram Canonical Studies, 1), Bangalore, Dharmaram Publications, 2000, pp. 460-463.

[22] Mathias A. Mundadan, *History of Christianity in India.* From the Beginning up to the Middle of the Sixteenth Century (CHAI History of Christianity in India, I), Bangalore, Theological Publications, 1984, pp. 521.

[23] Mathias A. Mundadan, op. cit., pp. 503, 507.

promulgation was due and was possible and yet was neglected, the excuse is less. When those errors and deficiencies are finally addressed and corrected through legislation or reform, it would be unfair and illogical to speak of illegitimate latinization solely because this was done by the Latins.

4. Return to Ancestral Traditions According to the Second Vatican Council

The Second Vatican Council has enjoined on "all members of the Eastern Churches" that "they should acquire an ever increasing knowledge of their legitimate liturgical rites and discipline, and if they have unduly fallen short of them owing to circumstances of times or persons, they are to strive to *return* to their ancestral traditions" (OE 6).[24] This is the key Vatican text about "delatinization," though the Council did not use this term. This conciliar text is of wider intent and application. It may be noted that corresponding somewhat to the Western phenomenon of latinization there is the Eastern phenomenon of byzantinization to the detriment of the Alexandrian and Antiochene rites. It is regrettable that the key conciliar text cited above has mostly been misunderstood, especially in the English-speaking world, chiefly because of defective translations, as we shall proceed to show now. Let us start by setting the text in its historical context and examine its formation.

a) *Textual History of the Conciliar Directive (OE 6)*

The textual history can shed light on the meaning of the text itself. The present text is the abridgement and condensing of the 1963 Schema of the Decree on the Eastern Churches prepared by the conciliar commission on the Eastern Churches. That 1963 Schema had 54 paragraphs. Paragraph 49 ran as follows:

> Sciant ac pro certo habeant omnes Orientales se numquam coactum iri legitimos suos ritus suamque disciplinam relinquere aut mutare. Nam Ecclesiarum Orientalium dignitas, pervetustis rerum monumentis eisque insignibus commendata, magna gaudet in toto christiano orbe veneratione et honore. Maxima igitur fidelitate prae ceteris ipsi Orientales suos ritus liturgicos et disciplinam ecclesiasticam observent, eorumdem cognitio-

---

[24] This is my translation, since, as will be seen, the current English translations are all defective. In the phrase "fallen short ...owing to persons..." the reference is to persons like Menezes.

> nem in dies maiorem usumque perfectiorem usque acquirant, et, si ab iis ob temporum vel personarum adiuncta *aliquomodo fortasse* defecerint, ad avitas *memorias* redire satagant, *quantum fieri potest, bono fidelium et adiunctis locorum et temporum prae oculis habitis.*[25]

This paragraph starts with a veiled reference to the historical phenomenon of forced latinization, but avoiding this term with a periphrasis. There is a veiled confession of guilt in the promise not to repeat the offence in the future: *Sciant ac pro certo habeant omnes Orientales se numquam coactum iri legitimos suos ritus suamque disciplinam relinquere aut mutare*. But during the revision of the Schema this confession was omitted, as the time for ecclesial repentance had not yet matured. The Schema was also condensed and reduced to 30 paragraphs mostly by combining and reordering some of them and by omitting some others. This revision was effected in the light of the "Animadversiones" or observations of the Fathers of the Council on the Schema. Archbishop Mauritius Baudoux of St. Boniface, for example, made a long and detailed criticism. He sniffed that the Schema was the work of Latins and/or latinised Orientals. Commenting on paragraph 49 he asked that the whole sentence "*Nam Ecclesiarum ... et honore*" be omitted as it was inappropriate and betrayed arrogance.[26]

Till now the Schema had only spoken of maintaining intact the rites and discipline of the Oriental Churches. In 1964 there was a new development. During its third session, the Council approved the Constitution on the Liturgy, which set out the conciliar teaching on liturgy and spoke of the need to make necessary and opportune changes in the liturgy. For liturgy consists of invariable and variable elements. "These latter not only may be changed but should be changed in course of time if they have suffered from the intrusion of anything out of harmony with the inner nature of the liturgy or have become less suitable" (SC 21). Now this conciliar law of change had to be integrated into the Schema on the Oriental Churches. Hence the

---

[25] *Acta Synodalia Sacrosancti Concilii Oecumenici Vaticani Secundi*, vol. III, pars V, Vatican, Polyglot, 1975, p. 756; also vol. V, pars I, Vatican Polyglot, 1989, p. 434.

[26] Ibid., pp. 769-774, at p. 774: "*inoppurtuna videtur et prae se fert quamdam superbiam in verbis*." This is rather an understatement. To promise the Orientals that their rites and discipline would no more be forcibly changed was to remind them that they had once been forcibly latinized. And then to offer as the ground for the promise the explanation ("*Nam*") that "the dignity of the Orientals enjoys great veneration and honour all over the globe" was a crumb of consolation that only added insult to injury with a complimentary lie.

following clause was added to the Schema, allowing changes and envisioning progress: *"ac nonnisi ratione proprii et convenientis progressus mutationes inducendas esse."* This new stance, however, was cautioned against as dangerous and anti-ecumenical by Bishop Garabed Amadouni of Cyprus, who proposed instead *"respectu habito semper spiritu et stylo proprio ritus."*[27] Another suggestion was to replace *"convenientis"* with *"harmonici."*[28] What was finally accepted was the proposal of Archbishop Maurice Baudoux of St. Boniface that the changes should be of the nature of *organic progress: "ac nonnisi ratione proprii et organici progressus mutationes inducendas esse."*[29] Thus the idea of "organic progress" as the criterion of liturgical and canonical changes was introduced into the decree on the Oriental Churches. This idea if not the term as such was in fact borrowed from the conciliar Constitution on the Liturgy: "there must be no innovations unless the good of the Church genuinely and certainly requires them and care is taken that the new forms in some way *grow organically* from the already existing forms' (SC 23). This "organic growth" of SC 23 and "organic progress" of OE 6 are obviously one and the same thing.

In the final redaction paragraph 49 of the 1963 Schema became, in its revised form, the first half of the 1964 Schema and finally emerged as the first half of OE 6. Here is the text:

> Sciant ac pro certo habeant omnes Orientales se suos legitimos ritus liturgicos suamque disciplinam semper servare posse et debere, ac nonnisi ratione proprii et organici progressus mutationes inducendas esse. Haec omnia igitur maxima fidelitate ab ipsis Orientalibus observanda sunt; qui quidem harum rerum cognitionem in dies maiorem usumque perfectiorem acquirere debent, et, si ab iis ob temporum vel personarum adiuncta indebite defecerint, ad avitas traditiones redire satagant.

This text may be rendered as follows in a literal translation:

> All members of the Eastern Churches are to know and be assured for certain that they have the right and the duty always to preserve their legitimate liturgical rites and their discipline and that changes are not to be introduced into them except for their organic progress. They themselves are to observe these norms with the greatest fidelity. And of these things they should acquire a progressively greater knowledge and more perfect practice, and if they have *unduly* fallen short of them owing to circumstances

[27] Ibid., pp. 850-851.

[28] Ibid., p. 858.

[29] Ibid. p. 854.

of times or persons, they are to strive to return to their ancestral traditions.

In the above version, which is by the present writer, *unduly* is italicised in order to draw attention to the fact that it is *omitted* in some current English translations (see below). It may be noted that "unduly fallen short" renders *indebite defecerint,* which replaces *aliquomodo fortasse defecerint* of the 1963 Schema. The phrase "they are to strive to return" renders the Latin *redire satagant*, literally, "do the needful to return." The return according to the Schema was to *avitas memorias,* that is, "ancestral memorials or monuments," meaning "traditions." And the return prescribed was not in absolute terms but *quantum fieri potest, bono fidelium et adiunctis locorum et temporum prae oculis habitis:* "in so far as possible, taking into consideration the good of the faithful and the circumstances of the places and times." These conditions and reservations obviously hold good always and therefore were omitted in the revised text as all too obvious.[30]

b) *English Translations of the Conciliar Text (OE 6)*

Unfortunately, this crucial conciliar text has been translated incorrectly or defectively into English. Three different translations are available today. In the commonly used edition by Austin Flannery, O. P., the key word "unduly" is missing. What we read is the following. "They are to aim always at a more perfect knowledge and practice of their rites, and if they have fallen away due to circumstances of times and persons, they are to strive to return to their ancestral traditions."[31] Even in the newly revised edition of 1996 this omission has not been noted and made good, and the text still runs without translating *indebite* ("unduly").[32] Most people who rely on this English version do not realise the absence of the key word "unduly," and so

[30] Neophytos Edelby and Ignace Dick, *Les Églises orientales catholiques: Décret "Orientalium Ecclesiarum,"* (Unam Sanctam, 76), Paris, Cerf, 1970, p. 254. "Au besoin, restaurer les rites et la discipline de l'Orient ... pour les ramener à leur pureté authentique" (p. 259). The restoration the Council envisages needs "patience, tact and prudence," say the authors. "Brusque restorations have often bad results and provoke a contrary reaction which delays the goal pursued. ... Under the pretext of liturgical or disciplinary purism disorders are unleashed, which are ultimately more serious than the ones meant to be corrected" (pp. 259-260).

[31] Austin Flannery, ed. *Vatican Council II. The Conciliar and Post Conciliar Documents,* Collegeville, The Liturgical Press, 1975, p. 443.

[32] *Vatican Council II: Constitutions, Decrees, Declarations*, ed. Austin Flannery, O.P., Northport, N.Y., Castello, 1996, p. 528.

naturally they are misled into understanding and applying the conciliar directive wrongly. This has given rise not only to unjustified popular demands and expectations but even to unsatisfactory official Roman directives about the return to ancestral traditions (see below).

In the Abbot edition of the Vatican II documents, the word *indebite* was translated as "improperly, which is not an accurate translation: "... if they have improperly fallen away from them because of circumstances of time or personage, let them take pains to return to their ancestral ways."[33] However, "ancestral ways" used to render "ancestral traditions" is unsatisfactory: surely "ways" cannot substitute "traditions."

In the Tanner edition *indebite* is translated correctly as "unduly" : "... if they have fallen unduly short of this they should have recourse to their age-old traditions."[34] In this version, though the first part or protasis ("if they have fallen unduly short of this") is well rendered, the second part or apodosis ("they should have recourse to their age-old traditions.") is a defective or deviant rendering. In Latin "redire" means usually to "return, to go back." It *can* mean "to have recourse to" in a *judicial* context, which is not the case here. Moreover, "age-old" means "having existed for a very long time," which is not the same as "ancestral."[35] It is not a question of searching for what is more ancient, but of regaining one's own lost family heritage. On the whole the meaning of this conciliar text is not faithfully conveyed in this translation. Contrast the standard German version: "Wenn sie aber wegen besonderer Zeitumstände oder persönlicher Verhältnisse ungebürlich von ihren östlichen Gebräuchen abgekommen sind, sollen sie sich befleißigen, zu den Überlieferungen ihrer Väter zurückzukehren."[36]

---

[33] *The Documents of Vatican II*, ed. Walter M. Abbot, S.J., New York, Guild Press, 1966, p. 376.

[34] *Decrees of the Ecumenical Councils*, II, ed. Norman E. Tanner, Georgetown, Sheed and Ward, 1990, p. 902.

[35] *The Concise Oxford Dictionary*, 9th ed., Oxford, Clarendon, 1995, s.v. "Age-old" does not render the Latin adjective "avítus, -a, -um," which means instead "of or belonging to a grandfather, inherited from a grandfather, of one's forefathers, ancestral, family."(*Oxford Latin Dictionary*, ed. P. G. W. Glare, Oxford, Clarendon, 1990 (1982), s.v.

[36] LThK, *Das Zweite Vatikanische Konzil,* I, p. 373.

c) *Meaning of the Conciliar Text (OE 6)*

Now, in order to understand this key conciliar text let us look at it again in a correct rendering as was given earlier:

> All members of the Eastern Churches are to know and be assured for certain that they have the right and the duty always to preserve their legitimate liturgical rites and their discipline and that changes are not to be introduced into them except for their organic progress. They themselves are to observe these norms with the greatest fidelity. And of these things they should acquire a progressively greater knowledge and more perfect practice, and if they have unduly fallen short of them owing to circumstances of times or persons, they are to strive to return to their ancestral traditions.

The Second Vatican Council was concerned about the loss of the precious Eastern traditions in several Churches, chiefly owing to latinization; and therefore the Council wanted to urge their proper recovery. However, it was not the mind of the Council to state (because it is not true) that *all* ancient Eastern traditions without exception were precious and were *by all means* to be preserved or recovered. Accordingly, the conciliar decree both delimits the area or subject matter, namely *legitimate* (or *lawful*) *liturgical rites and discipline*, and specifies the reason or condition, namely *undue falling short* (or departure or deviation or indent). The Council is, therefore, not enjoining simply a switch-button return to *all the ancestral traditions.* If it is the right and duty of the Eastern Churches "to preserve their lawful liturgical rites and their discipline," the injunction to return is also restricted to the lawful liturgical rites and discipline," which are referred to later with the word "traditions."

The return (*redire*) in question is not at all a matter of regression or setting the clock back but of true progress. For the Council is asking for a return in view of the recovery of those legitimate liturgical rites and discipline which have suffered from undue loss or indent. And such a recovery far from being a regression should make for *organic progress* since, as is clearly stated before, "*no change* is to be admitted unless it makes for *organic progress*" (OE 6). This norm of organic progress applies equally to the recovery or restoration of ancestral traditions as to innovations.

The conciliar directive is "redire *satagant,*" and not simply *redeant.* This latter would mean "let them return," an apodictic or absolute command. The former (*satagant*: from *sat+agere*, *sat* being the abbreviated form of *satis*, hence "to do enough" literally, or "busy oneself with") implies a qualified return, "try to return, or strive to return" (in German: *sollen sie sich befleißigen*). And this recaptures synthetically the qualifications that had been articulated in three phrases in the 1963 Schema: "in so far as possible, taking into consideration the good of the faithful and the circumstances of the places and times." But as we saw, these qualifications were omitted as obvious and replaced in the final shortened redaction with this succinct directive.

The return in question is to "*ancestral* traditions," that is "traditions of the forefathers," meaning those traditions that obtained *before* they were changed through *undue* falling off or deviation. This is not primarily a chronological concept with focus on antiquity. Hence there is no point in asking about the century or epoch before which those traditions qualify as *ancestral*. Ancestry is not just antiquity. The undue deviation may have occurred indeed in the early Christian centuries, in the Middle Ages, or in more modern times, or even in the twentieth century. Ancestral traditions are not determined simply by consulting tomes of ancient history nor by calculating their age.

In the phrase "ancestral *traditions*" the latter term "traditions" refers back to "the lawful liturgical rites and discipline" through the intervening pronouns "*harum rerum*" (of these things) and "*ab iis*" (of them, from them). Hence there is no question here of all and sundry traditions but *only of lawful traditions in the matter of liturgical rites and canonical discipline*. In other words, in this text the Council is not concerned about the recovery of *all* ancient Eastern traditions, not even of all *lawful* ones, but only the lawful traditions regarding liturgy and canonical discipline.

In prescribing the return to those liturgical and canonical traditions the Council is not presupposing a golden age of Eastern Eden. In liturgical matters some seem to work with the presupposition that the more ancient the liturgical forms, the purer and more genuine they are. The analogy is: the nearer you get to the source of a stream, the purer the water. The Council has no such precomprehension regarding liturgy or antiquity. Nor does its directive to return to ancestral traditions guarantee that the Eastern forms are per se superior to the Western forms. By rejecting the *praestantia latini ritus* the Council did not teach the opposite, the *praestantia ritus orientalis*. For the Council East and West, like their theological formulations, are "complementary rather than conflicting" (SC 16). Or, as the poet Pope John Paul II likes to repeat, they are like two lungs with which one and the same Church had long breathed and must relearn to breathe again to mutual benefit and common good.

Finally, though the Council did not refer in this text explicitly to the identity of the Eastern Churches, this concept is implicit in the principle and norm of organic progress. The insistence on organic progress is related to the concern to preserve the identity of the Church as a living organism. What then is the identity of a Particular Church?[37] And when does a Church reach and realise its identity? When did, for example, a twenty-centuries old Church reach and realise its identity? When it was two centuries old? four centuries old? Ten centuries old? Fifteen centuries old? Or later? These are not idle questions as they bear on the issues of undue deviation and return to ancestral traditions. They may be better understood in relation to the analogous questions about the identity of a human being: when did he/she reach his/her identity? At birth? At seven years with the age of reason? At puberty with clearer and definite masculine or feminine biological differentiation? With maturity, physical, intellectual, affective, etc.? Ontological identity (present from the first moment of existence of a human being) is different from psychological identity. Evidently, there is no rule of thumb in determining identity whether of a human being or of a Church, nor consequently undue deviation or the return to ancestral traditions.[38]

In the matter of return to ancestral traditions it may be helpful to answer the following questions. 1) Was the ancestral tradition in question good, better, legitimate or lawful — or the opposite? 2) Was it changed through an *undue* deviation or "falling short" — or was the change a lawful one, say by way of enlightened free reception? 3)

---

[37] Congregazione per le Chiese Orientali, ed., *L'identità delle Chiese orientali cattoliche*, Vatican, Libreria Editrice Vaticana, 1999. "The Eastern Catholic Churches should be careful not to fall into the temptation to define their own identity in contrast or opposition to the Latin Church" (Michel Van Parys, O.S.B., p. 28). The identity of the Eastern Catholic Churches is not to be defined exclusively in terms of liturgy, however important a factor this be, but the whole proper rite in the sense of CCEO c. 28 § 1 (Robert Taft, p. 134). Rite in this sense includes also historical circumstances (Enrico Morini, pp. 35-70).

[38] An immature adolescent may join a cloistered religious institute and take vows but later quit the institute to find his or her true vocation in the world. That is not defection or deviant behaviour but genuine progress, though through zigzag ways. Not so when a finally professed religious is infatuated with a chance encounter and elopes with his or her sweetheart: the person has the moral obligation to return to his or her institute. The case of undue falling short or deviation and return to ancestral tradition in the Church is analogous.

Was the change in mere minutiae or in a matter of some importance so that a return or restoration is worth while and not simply a question of form? 4) Is this change going to make the end result better or worse? 5) Is it needed or is it at least useful for the Church? 6) Can it be enforced without disrupting the peace of the Church and provoking disproportionate unrest, or revolt, or schism? 7) Does the change make for organic progress? 8) Does it meet with the genuine sensibilities of contemporary culture and the higher values of our age? 9) Does the change conform to the rules of the practice of ecumenism, so that there is no unnecessary or undue departure from the respective Orthodox counterpart, if any?

The *Code of Canons of the Eastern Churches* is an authoritative example of return to the ancient common canonical traditions of the Eastern Churches formed by the sacred canons, but hardly any of them was literally lifted from their ancient *situs* and placed in the Code textually. Most of the sacred canons have undergone some transformation, some have been abolished; others have only been partly received; in some cases the norm contained in the Code is just the opposite of the ancient norm. For example, CCEO (cc. 608 and 610 § 4) allows the laity to preach in certain circumstances, whereas laypeople were forbidden to "teach in public" by the Council in Trullo (c. 64). However, the new norm is not simply the contradiction of the old one but meets the exigency of inculturation in keeping with the changed conditions of our times.

d) *The Conciliar Directive and Centennial and Immemorial Customs*

Some may wonder if there is some conflict between the conciliar directive to return to ancestral traditions and the canonical provision that centennial and immemorial customs are not abrogated or affected by common law. Since most latinizations in the Eastern Catholic Churches are centennial or more than a hundred years old, or their origins are immemorial, it would seem that they fall under this canonical prescription and so could continue unaffected by the present conciliar directive.[39] Let us therefore first look at the canonical norm in question.

[39] A. Van Hove, "Coutume," *Dictionnaire de Droit Canonique*, IV, cols. 731-755, writes: "Coutume centenaire, celle dont l'origine remonte a cent ans; immémoriale, celle que les contemporains ont toujours vue appliqué et dont ils ont appris de leur aînés qu'elle a toujours été appliquée. It ne s'agit donc pas ici d'une coutume immé-

> A custom, whether it is contrary to or apart from the law, is revoked by a contrary custom or law; but a law does not revoke centennial or immemorial customs, unless it makes express mention of them; as regards other customs, canon 1502 § 2 applies (CCEO c. 1509).

The provision of canon 1502 § 2 regarding those customs that are not revoked by CCEO c. 1509 cannot be rendered into English with precision without recourse to the two terms used in Latin *lex* and *ius*, for which in English there is only one corresponding word, "law." In the following canon a literal translation of the first phrase would be the awkward "a law of common law."

> A *lex* of common *ius*, unless it is expressly provided otherwise in the *lex* itself, does not deorogate from the *lex* of a particular *ius*, nor does the *lex* of a particular *ius* enacted for a Church *sui iuris* derogate from a more particular *ius* in force in the same Church (CCEO c. 1502 § 2).[40]

What corresponds to CCEO cc. 1502 § 2 and 1509 may be found in CIC cc. 5 and 28. These canons on customs in both the codes, their force, and relationship to law (*lex*) cannot and need not be fully discussed here since we are concerned for the moment only with a very limited question: the force of these canons in the application of the conciliar directive OE 6 to return to *ancestral traditions*. These ancestral traditions may consist not only of customs but also of laws. If these traditions were legitimate or lawful but a contrary custom or law was introduced to their detriment, then the conciliar directive demands that measures be taken to return to the former. Historically, the latinization of the Eastern Catholic Churches (introduction of contrary custom or law) is not a recent phenomenon but on the whole it took place more than a centenary ago at the least. In so far as the prescription of the two codes about centennial and immemorial customs apply to these measures, which will normally be enactment of particular law, express mention should be made of these customs and laws. The conciliar directive itself is not a *lex iuris communis* (CCEO cc. 1502 § 2) abolishing all latinizations but a directive

---

moriale au sens historique du mot: on peut en connaître parfaitement l'origine historique. Une coutume immémoriale peut être plus ancienne ou moins ancienne qu'une coutume centenaire." (col. 733).

[40] On the need for and justification of such an inelegant English rendering in the interests of juridical precision, see George Nedungatt, *A Companion to the Eastern Code: For a New Translation of Codex Canonum Ecclesiarum Orientalium*, (Kanonika 5), Rome, Pontifical Oriental Institute, pp. 342, 346.

of common law requiring proper legislation by the competent legislative authority.

That centennial and immemorial customs that are contrary to law are not revoked unless they are expressly suppressed by it, is rather new in the history of canon law. This norm or rule is not found in ancient Roman law (*Corpus Iuris Civilis*), nor in the classical canon law (*Corpus Iuris Canonici*). Gratian does not know of it. In the sources of the relative canons 5 and 30 of *Codex Iuris Canonici* (1917) indicated in the *Fontes Iuris Canonici* there are but two entries. The first cites a Roman jurist Julian, who recognizes the juridical value of custom, but not mention the force of centennial or immemorial customs to prevail over a contrary legislation.[41] And as for the second entry, it is another Roman law citation by Gratian, which leaves to the discretion of the Prefect of the Province to let a long standing custom prevail over a contrary law or not.[42] It is significant that in this matter no papal decretals are cited in the sources, which shows how recent this provision for saving centennial and immemorial customs is. According to canonist Bishop Yves de Chartres (1090-1098) no custom can prevail against law.[43] Pope Gregory VII played up truth against custom, however old.[44] Indeed it may not be wrong to see the twentieth century canonical high regard for centennial and immemorial customs as a bow to the nineteenth century German

---

[41] "Inveterata consuetudo pro lege non immerito custoditur, et hoc est ius quod dicitur moribus constitutum. Nam cum ipsae leges nulla alia ex causa non teneant quam quod iudicio populi receptae sunt, merito et ea, quae sine ullo scripto populus probavit, tenebunt omnes: nam quid interest suffragio populus voluntatem suam declaret an rebus ipsis et factis? Quare rectissime etiam illud receptum est, ut leges non solum suffragio legis latoris, sed etiam tacito consensu omnium perdesuetudinem abrogentur" (D 1. 3. 32).

[42] "Quidquid contra longam consuetudinem fiet, ad sollicitudinem suam revocabit praeses provinciae" (D I dist. 12, c. 7). See A. Van Hove, "Coutume," *Dictionnaire de Droit Canonique*, IV, cols. 731-755, "coutume immémoriale," (col. 733); Idem, *De consuetudine, de temporum supputatione*, Mechliniae-Romae, Dessain, 1933; Gommarus Michiels, *Normae generales juris canonici*, II, 2 ed., Paris, Desclee, 1949, "De consuetudine," pp. 1-220; Paolo Picozza, "Consuetudine: diritto canonico," *Enciclopedia Giuridica*, VIII, Roma, Enciclopedia Italiana, 1988, pp. 1-10.

[43] "Consuetudinis ususque longaevi non vilis auctoritas est, verum non usque adeo sui valitura momento, ut aut rationem vincat aut legem" (PL 161, col 309C; Gratian, Decretum, pars IV, c. 202).

[44] "Dominus dicit: Ego sum veritas et vita. Non dixit: Ego sum consuetudo, sed veritas. Et certe, ut beati Cypriani utamur sententia, quaeliber consuetudo, quantumvis vetusta, quantumvis vulgata, veritati omnino est postponenda et usus qui veritati est contraria abolendus" (cit. Gratian, Dist. VIII, c. 5).

school of the history of law headed by Frederick Carl Savigny (1779-1861), who opposed all codification of law starting with the Napoleonic Code as stifling custom, which is the spontaneous expression of the will of the people. But Savigny had his day. Today, unlike canon law civil law does not bow to custom in like manner. Modern legislation tends to leave ever dwindling space to the operation of customs.[45]

The sacred canons of the ecumenical councils of the first millennium did not allow customs, whether particular or universal, to prevail over canonical legislation. The presupposition was that uniformity was needed for unity. Hence East and West clashed over issues big and small, from the discipline of clerical celibacy or married clergy to the use of leavened or unleavened bread at the Eucharist. Particular customs, like the Armenians not mingling water with wine at the Eucharist, were to yield to the common law, as the Council in Trullo (691/692) demanded.

> This council tried to enforce uniformity of discipline at the expense of legitimate diversity. This mistake was recognised and corrected in 880 at the Council of Constantinople, a council of reconciliation between the sees of Rome and Constantinople, which put an end to the so-called Photian Schism. This council acknowledged the diversity of the customs of the two Churches, as well as those of the Eastern sees, as legitimate and proper and not as a matter of contention or polemics. Today it has become a commonplace to say that uniformity of discipline is not integral to the unity of the Church; rather, if pressed too far, uniformity can even be harmful to unity. But this is a lesson that the Church has learnt all too slowly and not without repeated failures of memory.[46]

In the light of history, therefore, it would be anachronistic to invoke the very recent canonical norm saving centennial and immemo-

---

[45] In modern legal systems when there is "una norma consuetudinaria che risulti contraria ad una norma di legge, ... deve ritenersi che ... la norma legislativa prevalga sulla norma consuetudinaria con conseguente obbligo di disappliczione di quest'ultima, non solo da prate di qualunque autorità pubblica, ma anche da parte dei privati..." (Alessandro Pizzorusso, "Consuetudine 1) Profili generali," *Enciclopedia Giuridica*, VIII, Roma, Enciclopedia Italiana, 1988, pp. 1-12, at pp. 5-6).

[46] George Nedungatt and Michael Featherstone, eds., *The Council in Trullo Revisited* (Kanonika 6), Rome, Pontifical Oriental Institute, 1995, p. 13. For the text of the accord see p. 37-38: "The Holy Council said: each See had by tradition some ancient customs. On their count there should not be mutual contention and polemics. The Church of the Romans for its part preserves some customs which are proper to it, and it is fine that this is so. So, too the Church of the Constantinopolitans keeps some proper customs, which it has received from the beginning; so do also the Thrones of the East" (Mansi, 17, 489B).

rial customs from the operation of contrary legislation by the first seven ecumenical councils. Thus, for example, the peculiar customs of the Thomaschristians in the matter of Church temporalities ceased to be lawful when confronted by the contrary canonical legislation of the ecumenical councils. It is true that as long as this legislation was not promulgated in Malabar it did not morally and legally oblige formally. But that is not the end of the matter. The lawfulness of the non-promulgation itself is in question since a non-Ephesian Church in canonical separation from the one and catholic Church lacked legal justification in the light of the sacred canons, irrespective of the question about the orthodoxy of its christological faith.[47] Consequently, it can be said that where the ancient Thomaschristian particular law including customs deviated from the common law, it was not legitimate or it "fell short unduly (*indebite defecit*)," and so there would not be any warrant to return to it after a period of catholicization.

e) *The 1996 Instruction of the Congregation for the Eastern Churches*

Before concluding this section mention must be made of a recent *Instruction* of the Congregation for the Eastern Churches *for Applying the Liturgical Prescriptions of the Code of Canons of the Eastern Churches*.[48] Without wishing to present here a summary we shall only highlight some points. After rightly stressing the paramount importance of liturgy in the life of the Church and of the riches of the Eastern liturgies in particular, this Instruction insists on the recovery of the Eastern traditions. And it states: "The insistence on the full recovery of tradition does not mean a move at the expense of the necessary adaptation to the contemporary cultural sensibility."[49] Further, there is "the rightful exigency to express the gospel, as much as possible, in a plain and clear way for the contemporary man and woman" (n. 18).

---

[47] George Nedungatt, *Laity and Church Temporalities: Appraisal of a Tradition,* Dharmaram Canonical Studies, 1), Bangalore, Dharmaram Publications, 2000, pp. 178-179, 462.

[48] Congregation for the Eastern Churches, *Instruction for Applying the Liturgical Prescriptions of the Code of Canons of the Eastern Churches* (Vatican City, Editrice Vaticana, 1996).

[49] The original Italian runs as follows: "L'insistenza sul pieno recupero della Tradizione non vuole andare a scapito del pur necessario adattamento alla sensibilità contemporanea" (n. 112, p. 89). "To restore or to reform" is a false dilemma, since what is recovered from tradition is not meant to be kept intact in a museum but is to be adapted for life today according to the exigencies of inculturation.

In this the *sensus fidelium* has a decisive role, although pressure groups should be guarded against (n. 23). Not every change once introduced in the ancient patrimony is necessarily to be remade but "that which has altered the authenticity of the liturgical traditions" (n. 18). In trimming out extraneous forms and developments sometimes popular habits may have to be corrected but the restoration of the genuine forms must be done "with prudence without perturbing the sensibilities of the people" (n. 18 *"con prudenza per non turbare gli animi,"* in the original Italian). With these and other such very sensible and practical directives the Instruction has rightly interpreted the mind of the Second Vatican Council and offered a valid help in applying the norms of CCEO.

However, regrettably the Instruction is flawed in that in its English edition the conciliar text OE 6 about return to the ancestral traditions is cited wrongly. In this text the keyword "unduly" (*indebite*) is left out, following the Flannery translation (see above), though the original Italian text of the Instruction contains *indebite*. Here is the relevant passage of the English version (n. 12):

> The Council specifies that changes in the rites and disciplines of these Churches are not admitted except by reason of their own organic progress and adds that whenever they have fallen short, due to circumstances of time or persons, they are to strive to return to their ancestral traditions (OE 6).[50]

In this version, following the faulty translation of the Flannery edition of the conciliar documents, the key word *"unduly"* (*indebite:* Italian *"indebitamente"*) is omitted. Hence, unfortunately, the agenda of "return to ancestral traditions" risks being misguided officially in the English language area, as if what is required by the conciliar directive were an undiscerning pan-return to all ancestral traditions whether lawful or not. This is surely not what the Council has enjoined, though according to the conciliar text cited in the instruction of the Oriental Congregation in English it is. But evidently such is not the mind of this Congregation, as is evident from the original Italian text of the instruction as well as the caution that efforts at return

---

[50] The original Italian text, which reproduces the conciliar text correctly, is as follows: "Il Concilio precisa che non si possano introdurre mutazioni nei riti e nelle discipline di queste Chiese, se non per ragione del proprio organico progresso e aggiunge che qualora, per circostanze di tempo e di persone, queste fossero *indebitamente* venute meno, si procuri di tornare alle avite tradizioni (OE 6)."

should not be at the expense of perturbing the sensibilities of the faithful.

This caution points to the fact that in the program of returning to ancestral traditions there is not only place for reason (*ratio*) but also for the heart (*cor*): "the heart has reasons which reason has not" (Pascal). Consequently, the ecclesial discernment of return cannot be a matter of mere brain storming or syllogistic reasoning. The following ancient fable of the rape of the Sabines offers a good illustration of the reasons of the heart not to perturb long settled sensibilities.

> Romulus, the legendary and eponymous founder of Rome, had peopled the new city with adventurous immigrants. In order to obtain wives for them and increase the population, he organized a lavish feast and invited the nearby tribes. The Sabines came in large numbers. At a signal the young Romans ravished and carried off the Sabine belles. The Sabines needed time to organize an armed attack in order to recover their lost women folk. But then it was too late. As the battle raged, the Sabine women ran into the middle holding their babies in their arms and crying: "You are our fathers and brothers, but here are our husbands and these are our babies. We are the cause of the massacre of our husbands and fathers. Rather kill us. It is better for us to die than live as widows and orphans." Touched to the heart, all stood still. Peace was signed, and the Romans and the Sabines were reconciled and fused into a single, powerful and peaceful nation under the united reign of the Roman Romulus and the Sabine Titus Tatius.

The moral of the fable: once valuable elements of different traditions have forged happily into an organic unity, instead of a forced separation and a troubled return to patrimonial purity (*reason*) a better choice would be peace and unity (*heart*).

5. Return to the Pre-Diamper Traditions in General

Following the Second Vatican Council, the Syro-Malabar Church has been making serious and concerted efforts to return to the "ancestral traditions" (OE 6) through studies, seminars, and debates. The debates have at times even crossed the boundaries of moderation through excessive zeal. Much of the zeal is unenlightened as it is based on a wrong understanding of the conciliar directive occasioned by defective English translations, as we have shown above. The "ancestral traditions" in question are generally identified as the pre-Diamper traditions and are globally included in the expression "the Law of Thomas," though of course these traditions cannot all be linked with St Thomas the Apostle historically. The modern equivalent of "the Law of Thomas" would be the Thomaschristian rite, if rite is understood as it is defined in the new Eastern Code (CCEO 28 § 1).[51] With the Synod of Diamper and during the following Latin period the Thomaschristian liturgy[52] and discipline[53] were latinized and changed drastically. Most of these changes did not make for organic progress. So, following the conciliar directive (OE 6), the Syro-Malabar Church is now engaged in the reform of its liturgy and canonical discipline or particular law. In this context, the question of the return to ancestral traditions (practically, the pre-Diamper traditions) is crucial both in liturgy and in discipline.

As we have seen in the previous section, to return to the ancestral traditions is not a categorical imperative according to the Council. If it were, and the Syro-Malankara Church were to heed it, it would be suicidal for it! Even for the Syro-Malabar Church undiscerning return to certain pre-Diamper traditions will be a fatal regression where they were mixed up with superstition and magic. Some other traditions were unjust or unfair (like daughters having no right of inheritance) or retrograde (like child marriage). The practice of caste and untouchability was common and almost unquestioned. The Synod of Diamper rightly pointed its accusing moral finger at the practice of usury (interest over 12%), the use of unequal measures in buying and selling, the killing or abandoning of babies born on inauspicious days. Certain other traditions or practices were pastorally and spiritually negative or deficient. For example, for Holy Scripture there was as yet no translation into Malayalam, not even of the Four Gospels. There was no catechism in the language of the faithful, who recited prayers like the Our Father and formulas of catechetical doctrine in the Syriac language without understanding them. Clerical formation, as we saw, was based on the *malpan* system, which had its merits and defects, but a return to it today would be obscurantist chauvinism, not organic progress as envisaged by the Second Vatican Council in the area of clerical formation prescribed in its decree *Optatam totius,* which is normative for the entire Catholic Church.

---

[51] George Nedungatt, *The Spirit of the Eastern Code*, Rome, CIIS (Bangalore, Dharmaram Publications), 1993: chapter 6, "Churches, Traditions and Rites," pp. 60-84.

[52] For the more significant changes in the liturgy, which had been thoroughly latinized, see the study of Jacob Vellian in this volume.

[53] For the changes in discipline, see Joseph Kuzhinjalil, *The Disciplinary Legislation of the Synod of Diamper* (Unpublished doctoral Dissertation), Rome, Pontifical Oriental Institute, 1975.

Certainly, reforms formerly effected by the Latin missionaries and by the Synod of Diamper in the above areas were not perfect but they were a very positive and appreciable service to the Thomaschristian Church and community, and any return to the pre-Diamper traditions in these areas would be unwarranted.

It is not such an indiscriminate pan-return that the Council has ordered and the Holy See has instructed but a discerning return.[54] But this discernment is not always easy, as may be illustrated by the controversy over the so-called St. Thomas Cross. What was in common use in the Thomaschristian churches before Diamper was not the crucifix but the plain cross without the figure of the crucified. Should there be a return to that plain, figureless cross? And if so (this is only a supposition, not an admission) should the return be to the so-called St. Thomas Cross? The use of this latter, however, was rather marginal compared to the kind of crosses erected in front of churches or installed or painted elsewhere, even apart from the debate about whether the so-called "Mar Thoma Cross" is a Manichaean cross or not. The thesis that the crucifix is incongruous to the Thomaschristian tradition is an unproven theorem. The following questions have been raised. 1) Is this tradition so perfect as not to need to benefit by the process of ecclesial reception? 2) Have the lives of its two saintly daughters, who were great devotees of the crucifix, Blessed Alphonsa and Blessed Mariam Thresia (the latter gifted in addition with the stigmata), have no message for the Syro-Malabar Church in this regard, even though by beatifying them the supreme pontifical magisterium has proposed them as models for imitation to the members of this Church? 3) Does the fact that according to the history of iconography the first ever icon of the crucifix originated in the Syriac tradition[55] invite a return to a more ancient tradition beyond the pre-Diamper tradition. Here we have an emblematic case that shows that not all return to the pre-Diamper traditions is a simple matter. Indeed, in the final analysis, all return must be an act of ecclesial discernment, not individual interpretation or imposition.

---

[54] The above examples illustrate the relevance of the keywords "legitimate" and "unduly" in OE 6. Unfortunately, as we pointed out earlier, owing to defective English translations an indiscriminate return to all pre-Diamper traditions is mistakenly read by some as the authentic directive of the Council and as the mind of the Congregation for the Oriental Churches (See above sections 5 d and e).

[55] The first known religious picture of Christ nailed on the cross is in the sixth century manuscript of the Syriac Rabbula Gospels preserved in the Medici Library in Florence, Italy.

It is generally agreed that in order to realise the proper identity of the Syro-Malabar Church there is need to recover its pre-Diamper ritual patrimony, although there can be difference of opinion as to what in particular is to be recovered and whether the recovery should be a simple restoration or a creative restoration with inculturation and updating. In liturgy no written texts of the first Indian period have survived. Nor does the Council prescribe return to the more ancient tradition if different traditions have succeeded one another. Indeed such a rule would create troublesome problems. For example, in the search for an alternative name for the current Syro-Malabar Church if the more ancient tradition were the norm, the choice would fall on *Tarijanes* since the Thomaschristians bore this noble name before being called *Nasrani* by "the Moors and Turks," which was a later foreign designation that gradually came into common native use as well.[56] Was this changeover to *Nasrani* already an "undue deviation owing to persons and circumstances," which points to the possibility or need of returning farther to the former name *Tarijanes*? Surely, such straining after the more ancient is not the mind of the Council. It can smack of an archaeologism and obscurantism that does not make sense to the men and women of today.

6. Return to the Pre-Diamper Liturgical Tradition

The current liturgical reform of the Syro-Malabar Church is a slow and even painful process for various reasons. One difficulty is the lack of critically edited source texts. This generates either unreserved praise on the one hand or undeserved condemnation on the other of the Chaldean liturgy, both extremes being in addition innocent of comparative liturgy. Paradoxically, the extremes call forth and reinforce each other. What is needed is not a compromise but a realistic and critical appreciation. A well-known scholar of comparative lit-

[56] "The king who granted the Quilon Plates calls the Christians of St Thomas *Tarijanes,* that is to say kings or first kings. It seems that these Christians used to be called thus from ancient times for having descended from the ancient kings whom St Thomas made Christians. Later [they were called and even] now they are popularly called *Nasarani,* i.e. *Nasareus,* for they are so called by the Moors and Turks. Still, in the southern parts beyond Quilon they retain the ancient name" (Francis Ros, "Report on the Serra,' see Appendix IV, 13). In short, "Nasrani" loses out to "Tarijanes" on seniority. But there are more substantial objections than seniority against the name "Nasrani"in its global setting and for its heretical connotations: See George Nedungatt, *"Nasrāni* or *Kristiāni," Tanima* 7 (1998) 112-126.

urgy has written: "The East-Syrian tradition, which took root in the cradles of Syriac Christianity, Edessa and later Nisibis, remains the most purely Semitic form of Catholic worship still in use today."[57] The Anaphora of Addai and Mari heads the most ancient, developed anaphoras and is indeed very beautiful and rich in contents, though it has been disfigured by certain later accretions, not to mention profuse latinizations. The same praise is not due to the other two anaphoras of the East Syrian or Chaldean Church, the Anaphora of Nestorius and the Anaphora of Theodore, both of which are found in the pre-Diamper Taksa of the Thomaschristian Church. The former is a lengthy theological tract, and not liturgical prayer, according to independent scholarly judgement.[58] The latter is less wordy and is better suited as liturgical prayer and can be *adapted*, but is hardly suitable as it stands.[59] It is true that before the Second Vatican Council, in 1957, Pius XII had approved the *restoration* of all these three anaphoras, and the Oriental Congregation has dutifully and repeatedly prescribed their *translation* and introduction in the Syro-Malabar Church.[60] The bishops, however, rightly *received* the first anaphora and put it into general use, in Malayalam translation, but not the other two, since these do not meet the criteria of reformed liturgical prayer as envisioned by the Second Vatican Council. In doing so,

[57] Robert Taft, "The Missionary Effort of the Eastern Churches as an Example of Inculturation," in La Congregazione per le Chiese Orientali, *Le chiese orientali e la missione in Asia,* (op. cit. n. 75), p. 38.

[58] We only need to quote an Anglican scholar, Bryan D. Spinks, "The Anaphora of Nestorius: Antiochene Lex Credendi through Constantinopolitan Lex Orandi?" *Orientalia Christiana Periodica* 62 (1996) 273-294. The most likely compiler of the Anaphora of Nestorius is Patriarch-Catholicos Mar Aba (540-552), who conflated some writings of Nestorius, whose works he had brought from Constantinople and translated into Syriac. "In the past it may be that the association with the name Nestorius, condemned at Ephesus for his christological views, has cast a shadow over this prayer. More importantly, though, the anaphora is clearly a conflation, lacking originality and is rather tedious in length and language" (p. 273). "The compiler has cleverly combined the anaphoras in use at Constantinople to form a composite. In what Bouyer described as 'exhausting dissertations which have more the feeling of coming from a professorial chair than an altar,' the compiler has expressed the concerns of a particular strand of Antiochene theology..." (293).

[59] For a critical edition of the Anaphora of Theodore, see Jacob Vadakel, *The East Syrian Anaphora of Mar Theodore of Mopsuestia*, Kottayam, OIRSI Publications No. 129, 1989. For a critical study, Bryan D. Spinks, *Prayers From the East*, Washington, D. C., Pastoral Press, 1993: "The East Syrian Anaphora of Theodore: Its Sources and Theology," (pp. 47-64).

[60] Cf. the decrees and directives of the Oriental Congregation dated 20 January 1962, 9 May 1969, 1 March 1983, etc.

though their explicit motives may have been different, the bishops seem to have acted as if they instinctively anticipated the recent directive of the Congregation for the Oriental Churches about "the rightful exigency to express the gospel, as much as possible, in a plain and clear way for the contemporary man and woman."[61] Indeed, the anaphoras II and III (euphemistic substitute names for the anaphoras of Theodore and Nestorius) do create "the feeling of coming from a professorial chair rather than an altar," though for some bishops what was offensive was their presumed authorship by two heretics, Theodore and Nestorius. In the words of Bryan D. Spinks, "Use of ancient anaphoras simply by way of modern translation is rarely successful. It is doubtful whether any modern Western Church would want to use or benefit from use of either of these two anaphoras."[62] Nor would any Eastern Church unless they are first adapted and updated, as the Eastern Anaphora of Basil was adapted before being approved for use in the Latin Church.[63]

Even before the Second Vatican Council the Mass (Qurbana) and the Pontifical had been delatinised and restored.[64] This restoration proved to be a kind of mixed blessing. On the one hand, with such prior liturgical restoration to go by, the Council was able to speak from experience and not in the abstract when it directed the Eastern

[61] Congregation for the Eastern Churches, *Instruction for Applying the Liturgical Prescriptions... (*op. cit. n. 46), §18, p. 19.

[62] Bryan D. Spinks, *Prayers From the East,* op. cit.: "The East Syrian Anaphoras and Current Liturgical Revision,"(pp 125-132) at p. 130.

[63] Jacob Vadakel writes instead: "In accordance with the teaching of the Second Vatican Council (OE 6) the Syro-Malabar Church has an imperative duty to *restore* [my emphasis] the anaphora of Theodore to her liturgical tradition, since it belongs to the lost tradition of our Church" (*The East Syrian Anaphora of Mar Theodore*, op. cit. [n. 104], p. 252). The Council's teaching to "return" (not to *restore*) is much more nuanced, as has been shown in our study (see section 5). Likewise in his study of the Anaphora of Nestorius, Robert Mateus, uncritically regrets that "in spite of approbation by Rome in 1957, still today, in 2000, it has not been introduced by the local authorities" (*The Order of the Third Sanctification* [OIRSI 240], Kottayam, Paurastya Vidyapitham, 2000, p. 1). As a matter of fact the bishops' stand is an instance of responsible "non reception," vindicated by studies of outstanding scholars like Bouyer and Spinks, who state equivalently that the pre-conciliar approbation by Rome of these two anaphoras did not stand the test of the cunciliar norms for liturgical reform.

[64] The Anaphora of Addai and Mari was restored by a liturgical committee set up in Rome and approved by Pius XII on 26 June 1957 and it was published in *Taksa d'Quddasa* (Alwaye, 1959). Likewise, the East Syrian Pontifical, restored by a Roman liturgical committee, was published from Rome in 1957.

Catholic Churches to return to their ancestral traditions. On the other hand a preconciliar liturgical reform invites the question if indeed it anticipated and applied the principles of liturgical reform which the Council would later enunciate. The presumption is that it did not. And this presumption has in fact been verified in the differentiated reception of the *undifferentiaed* restoration of the three anaphoras, which seems to have taken for granted that what was pre-Diamper was good for restoration.

But, according to the Council, all liturgical reform should "retain sound tradition and yet leave the way open to legitimate progress." To ensure this "careful research should first be made — theological, historical, and pastoral — about each section of the liturgy to be revised" (SC 23). There is question here of a threefold research: theological, historical, and pastoral. Now, the Roman liturgical committees appointed to reform the Qurbana and the Pontifical were surely competent in the areas of theological and historical research. But what about the *pastoral research* as a prerequisite of liturgical reform? In the analogous case of the reform of the canon law of the Eastern Catholic Churches, the pastoral sense of Pope John XXIII suggested the deferring of the promulgation of the Eastern Code (which had been presented to him in 1959 in its finished form for his signature), till after the Council. As a result the postconciliar CCEO and its preconciliarly finalised Schema differ enormously. As regards liturgy, it is pertinent to ask if the preconciliarly restored Syro-Malabar Qurbana is like the aforesaid Schema. The painful process and consequences of the liturgical reform in the Syro-Malabar Church raises the question about pastoral research as required by the Council.

Pastoral research (by no means a strong point of traditional Eastern Christianity) does not consist only in consulting the faithful — the laity, the clergy, and the religious — though this is one of the important elements of pastoral research. In fact, long before the Second Vatican Council, before the 1774 Roman edition of the Syro-Malabar missal, the Holy See itself had *consulted* the priests of the Syro-Malabar Church.[65] Cardinal Antonelli, a member of the Congregation for the Correction of the Liturgical Books of the Eastern Church, moved in session that no Chaldean missal should be ap-

[65] Vatican Archives, Borgiano Latino, MS 280, fol. 241v-282v, summarised by J. Vellian in his study, in which he also refers to the "unresolved question" as to "How far are we to go back in de-latinization?"

proved for use in the Syro-Malabar Church without ascertaining whether the people of Malabar wanted it. This proposal was accepted by the Congregation, which therefore sent to the Vicar Apostolic Florence of Jesus of Nazareth O.C.D. a printed copy each of two Chaldean missals, which differed among themselves in contents, to ascertain if and which of the two the people of Malabar wanted. This the Vicar Apostolic was directed to do by convoking an assembly of all the priests (priests only, so it was not a *Mahāyōgam* of the pre-Diamper tradition) of the Vicariate Apostolic. In this assembly the priests rejected both the Chaldean missals, seemingly because they were used to a third version, which was more Rosian than Menezian. And respecting their preference the 1774 Roman edition of the Syro-Malabar missal was made, with the addition of some prayers and rites borrowed from the Roman missal and the Maronite missal (e.g. the prayer of bidding adieu to the altar at the end of the Qurbana).

If in 1774 the priests rejected a *less* latinized version of the missal, it was because they had become familiar with a *more* latinized version believed to be superior on the principle of the *praestantia ritus latini*, instilled into them by the magisterium and doctrine. Moreover, those priests had no more at hand the pre-Diamper or Chaldean *taksa* to make a comparative study. A real choice implies two *known* alternatives. The 1774 consultation of the priests could not have yielded any enlightening results in terms of pastoral research. As the saying has it, *ignoti nulla cupido,* no one desires something unknown. The same danger lurks also in the consultation of the faithful without information based on prior research, scholarly and popular publications, catechesis, liturgical experimentation, use of mass media, group media, etc. There is indeed more to pastoral research than simply "consulting the faithful."

In the restoration of the Pontifical, the Syro-Malabar bishops were consulted, but not the priests. But what finally prevailed was not the vote of the bishops (who opted for the Roman Pontifical they were used to) but the vote of the leading Western Orientalists. Seconding them Pope Pius XI, himself a scholar, took the enlightened and energetic decision not to approve the Roman Pontifical for use in the Syro-Malabar Church, contrary to the vote of some of his own curial cardinals. It was thus that the Malabar Church found its way to the recovery of its ancient East Syrian Pontifical.

If in former times only bishops and priests were consulted, today the consultation should be widened to embrace the whole portion of the People of God whose interests are involved. This is not to yield to the modern democratic principle or bow to the majesty of the majority. Liturgical reform following upon pastoral research can better ensure that the reform enacted is received freely and joyfully by the portion of the People of God entrusted to the pastoral care of the bishops. Here the ancient but recently recovered theology of *reception* is pertinent.[66] In this connection it may be recalled that Thomman Paremmakkal referred approvingly to the non-reception of the Synod of Diamper by several northern parish communities.[67] Besides, a doctrine or reform that is not freely received but has to be enforced with sanctions serves rather to undermine the efficacy of the *reception* of the doctrine and the application of the reform, as was evidenced long ago by the hard lesson of the Council of Chalcedon.[68] A liturgical law like any other law that is imposed on an unwilling people will normally be evaded, thus compromising its efficacy; and this can gradually generate a contrary custom in an eparchy that can obtain force of law in thirty years (CIC c. 26; CCEO c. 1507 § 3), and then even prevail over the law itself by making it fall into desuetude.

7. Return to the Pre-Diamper Canonical Tradition

The promulgation of the Code of Canons of the Eastern Churches in 1990 has also made it necessary for these Churches to reform their particular law according to the norms of this Code. Accordingly, the reform of the particular law of the Syro-Malabar Church has been undertaken. In this process, too, as in the reform of the liturgy, there is question about return to "ancestral traditions." Here are a few examples.

---

[66] Gilles Routhier, *La reception d'un concile* (Cogitatio Fidei 174), Paris, Cerf, 1993: "If the Spirit is the principal actor during the celebration of a council, this is no less so during the spiritual process of its reception" (p. 8). Hence non-compliance by the faithful is not simply disobedience. It can be a word from the same Spirit to the hierarchy to reconsider. Reconsideration does not deny the action of the Spirit at the earlier consideration: for the Spirit does not teach the whole truth all at once since we cannot receive it all at once. Hence the spiritual dialectics of reception includes the antithesis of rejection, which is obedience to God while it may *appear* to be disobedience to man. But non-reception is not necessarily disobedience.

[67] Paremmakkal Thommakkathanar, *Varthamanappusthakam*, Athirampuzha, 1933, pp. 508-509; English transl., Placid Podipara, OCA 190, Rome, 1971, p. 267.

[68] Alois Grillmeier, *Mit ihm und in ihm: christologische Forschungen und Perspektiven*, Freiburg, Herder, 1975: "Konzil und Rezeption," (pp. 303-334).

The Synod of Diamper introduced the canonical obligation of annual confession under pain of excommunication (Session VI, decree 1), enforcing the discipline initiated by the Fourth Lateran Council in 1215 (DzSch 812) and reinforced by the Council of Trent in 1551 (Session 24, *de paenitentia,* can. 8: DzSch 1708). Again, the Synod of Diamper (Session VII, On Marriage, decree 1) enforced the Tridentine norm of 1563, whereby Catholic couples are to be married publicly after three banns in the church by the parish priest or his delegate, before two or three witnesses (Session 24, *de matrimonio*, decree *Tametsi*, DzSch, 1813-1816). The Synod of Diamper forbade the Christians to file suits before the tribunals of kings rather than before the bishop (Session IX, decree 15), a norm that recalls a directive given by St Paul to the Corinthians (1 Cor 6:4-6). These are but a few of the many disciplinary reforms of the Synod of Diamper, which do not permit to be undone by a mere return to the pre-Diamper traditions.

There are several canonical norms concerning priests (priestly dress, formation, ordination, etc.), or bishops (appointment, powers, etc.), or laypeople (role, competence in Church affairs, especially temporalities), etc., in which there can be question of return to the pre-Diamper ancestral traditions. As an example of interpretation in the matter of such a return, let us examine the pre-Diamper Thomaschristian institution of the married clergy in some detail. The question may be framed as follows: is the Syro-Malabar Church to return to the pre-Diamper discipline of optional celibacy?

Undoubtedly, married clergy was a *legitimate* canonical discipline of the Thomaschristian Church forming part of the Law of Thomas. In fact it continues to be so in the sister Church, namely the Syro-Orthodox Church. Indeed the institution of the married clergy goes back to the apostolic tradition (1 Tim 3:2, 12), and is preserved uninterruptedly in the Eastern Churches (of the Byzantine or Constantinopolitan tradition like the Ukrainian Catholic Church, of the Antiochene tradition like the Maronite Church, of the Chaldean tradition like the Chaldean Church, etc.), though not in the Armenian Catholic Church or in the Syro-Malabar Church as a consequence of latinization. The Western Church in fact increasingly forbade the institution of the married clergy from the fourth century onwards (DzSch 119, 185). The Council of Trent hurled anathema on those in sacred orders who married; it also declared their marriage invalid.[69] The traditional Church teaching that virginity is superior to marriage was canonized by the Council of Trent: "If anyone were to say that the conjugal state is superior to the state of virginity or of celibacy, and that it is not better and more blessed to remain in virginity and celibacy than be united in marriage, let him be anathema."[70] This Tridentine teaching is to be understood in the context of the established discipline of clerical celibacy in the Latin Church, which was defied by the Protestant Reformers. Trent did not pronounce on the discipline of the married clergy followed by the Eastern Churches from apostolic times but tolerated it. The Synod of Diamper recognized the discipline of clerical marriage "in the Greek Church, and in some that are subject to the Apostolic See, by which it is tolerated for just reasons." (Session VII, decree 16).

But what the Council of Trent and the Apostolic See of Rome "tolerated" was not tolerated by the Latinizers in the Malabar Church, which like the other suffragan dioceses of Goa had to conform to the metropolis "observing the same forms." Already the First Synod of Angamaly (1583), which was a Vorschau or rehearsal of the Synod of Diamper, not only forbade priests to marry after ordination under pain of excommunication and suspension *ipso facto* till separation from the partner[71] but also introduced, among other latinizations, the

---

[69] Council of Trent, Session 24, Canons on the Sacrament of Marriage, can. 9 (DzSch 1809).

[70] Ibid., can. 10 (DzSch 1810).

[71] The general canonical tradition forbidding marriage after ordination is constant and common to the East and to the West. However, theology does not seem to offer a convincing justification, beyond the symbolism of the bishop as spouse of the local Church, of the prohibition of marriage *after* ordination; while the canonical justification is the constancy and the universality of this *tradition* itself. Those who are in "*sacri ordines*" (episcopate, presbyterate, diaconate) are forbidden to marry by the *sacri canones*. The Council of Trent (Sessio XXIV, *canones de matrimonio*, can. 9) confirmed this prohibition of the ecumenical councils. Hence, in the Eastern discipline which admits married clergy, the remarriage of widowed clerics is forbidden: marriage must always precede ordination. But why cannot ordination precede marriage? The usual canonical answer from tradition did not convince the Protestant Reformers. Perhaps it had not convinced the pre-Diamper Thomaschristian priests either. While some of them practised voluntary celibacy, some others were married twice or more times even after the sacred ordination. After the Synod of Diamper, which received the Tridentine norm and confirmed the relative decree of the First Synod of Angamaly, Archbishop Menezes went round the Malabar parishes, according to the account of Gouvea, cursing priests guilty of this "abominable crime" and terrorising them with anathemas and hell fire. The Statutes of Ros (IV, 3) kept the excommunication of priests who married.

law of the Latin Church on clerical celibacy.[72] This was indeed an "undue" deviation from or "falling short" of the authentic Thomaschristian tradition "because of circumstances of persons and times," in the language of Vatican II (OE 6). The mere fact that this "reform" had the support of Mar Abraham does not make it a legitimate reform for the following three reasons.

1) It was not catholicization, since the institution of married clergy and clerical celibacy are both two legitimate expressions of the catholic tradition.
2) It was not Tridentization since the Council of Trent did not abrogate the institution of married clergy, a recognized discipline in the Eastern Churches. In fact the Apostolic See of Rome did not require of Patriarch John Zulaqa on his union with the Catholic Church in 1553 to enforce clerical celibacy in the Chaldean Church.
3) It was *ultra vires* for Mar Abraham in as much as a metropolitan cannot validly change a law of his Patriarchal Church. Or, in the language of CCEO, a particular law cannot be abolished by a more-particular law.

The Chaldean tradition was optional clerical celibacy. Indeed, a Patriarchal Synod of the Chaldean Church held in 486 had gone to the extent of approving a legislation authorizing all clerics, including bishops and patriarchs to marry or remarry. But this canon, made under pressure of Barsauma (ca 415 – ca 495), Bishop of Nisibis, who was himself married and had allowed even his monks and nuns to marry, was later revoked synodically in 543-544 since the new liberal practice had led to much disorder, decline of monastic discipline and scandal. Hence the former discipline of celibacy was re-established for bishops, monks and nuns, whereas clerics below bishops could be optionally married or celibate. This was the law in force also in the Thomaschristian Church, though we cannot ascertain whether it was received from the Chaldean Church or originated in the first Indian period. At any rate the Latin bishops enforced the institution of clerical celibacy in the Thomaschristian Church, and the Syro-Malabar

[72] Joseph Wicki, *Documenta Indica* XII, 826. This one-day synod held on 26 October 1583 was a *Mahāyōgam* in form, though not in substance, and was geared to the latinization of the Thomaschristian Church according to a Jesuit design devised by the Jesuit Visitator Alessandro Valignano: see Andrews Thazhath, *The Juridical Sources of the Syro-Malabar Church*, (OIRSI, 106), Kottayam, Paurastya Vidyapitham, 1987, p. 131.

bishops who followed them in time followed also their example, so that the discipline of clerical celibacy, even if at first it was an undue deviation has become, according to common doctrine, a centennial customary law with legal force.

CCEO holds both voluntary clerical celibacy in great esteem and the state of the married clergy in honour according to the practice of the primitive Church and the age-old tradition of the Eastern Churches (c. 373 § 1). It leaves to particular law the admission of married men to priestly orders unless this is prohibited in particular cases by the Roman Apostolic See (c. 758 § 3), a veiled reference to the prohibition of ministry by married priests to the Ukrainian emigrants in America around the turn of the twentieth century, later extended also to Australia. The episcopate is barred to those bound by a marriage bond (c. 180, 3°), which is a canonical norm that is common to the Orthodox Churches as well since the Council in Trullo (692).[73] The Second Vatican Council sees the ancient discipline of the Oriental Churches as "better suited to the mores of their faithful and better fitted to the good of their souls" (OE 5).[74]

In the reform of the particular law of the Syro-Malabar Church on clerical celibacy the question of the application of the conciliar directive to return to ancestral traditions cannot obviously be evaded. On the one hand no law prevents the Syro-Malabar Synod of Bishops from legislating the restoration of the institution of the married clergy whereby married men are admitted to the diaconate and presbyterate, thus restoring the discipline of the Chaldean period as it has been preserved in the Syrian Orthodox Church. Such a restoration would distinguish the Syro-Malabar Church as an Oriental Church from the Latin Church even more than certain differences in liturgy do. Some would even argue that differentiation from the Latin

---

[73] Canons 12, 13, 48. For an English translation see George Nedungatt and Michael Featherstone, eds., *The Council in Trullo Revisited* (Kanonika 6), Rome, Pontifical Oriental Institute, 1995. In the Latin Church the sacrament of orders, except the diaconate, is barred to married men (CIC c. 1042 1°). Among the Protestants, even the episcopate is normally open to married men, and in some cases even to women.

[74] There is no contradiction between Trent and Vatican II on this point: Trent spoke of the superiority of virginity and widowhood over marriage in the abstract. Vatican II speaks of what is more suitable and fitting in the concrete. What is per se superior or higher may be less suitable in concrete cases and circumstances. Thus, for example, St Paul recognized that virginity, though more fitted for the eschatological phase of waiting, was not for all, indeed marriage was more suitable for "each" Christian in the Corinthian context (1 Cor 7: 2).

Church is a practical principle of liturgical reform and that it should apply in canonical reform as well. If so, the restoration of the discipline of the married clergy would be a most notable distinction — if indeed there is any such principle.[75]

The proper methodology of the Syro-Malabar canonical reform is not first to computerise the pre-Diamper traditions and then to retrieve them. According to the Council, "no change is to be made" if it does not make for *organic progress* (OE 6). And this general principle applies also to the restoration of ancestral traditions. Canonical reform is not simply a matter of ascertaining the ancient canonical institutions and restoring them without ecclesial discernment as to whether they are good also for today. And such discernment has to gauge the pastoral situation of the Church in the world today, having regard for the *sensus fidei* of the People of God (LG 12). Nor is discernment simply a question of identifying the ideal best, which can at times be the enemy of the real good. Where the return to ancestral traditions does not make for organic progress, there should be no return at all. What was good once in certain definite circumstances need not necessarily be so in changed circumstances.[76]

The concept of organic progress evokes the mystery of the Church as the Mystical Body of Christ. The Church is not simply a society nor can the *mechanical theory* of society be applied to it, according to which theory the component parts of a society are autonomous, independent and dispensable. On the contrary, in the *organic theory* of society, the components are members of a living organism, and their functions and rights have to be composed harmoniously in their exercise in view of the common good of the whole. This will need a value judgement, an ecclesial discernment, which is essentially the perception and articulation of what "has been seen good to the Holy Spirit and to us" (Acts 15:28).

---

[75] "Be different from the Latins" is not a principle or practical guideline given to the Eastern Catholic Churches, but it is sometimes recited as a slogan. If it were a guideline, all these Churches would have to distinguish themselves with the institution of married clergy so as to be different from the Latin Church with its celibate clergy. This "difference principle" has indeed no conciliar or canonical support. Some wonder if it has a biblical basis in the parable of Jesus about the two men who went to the temple to pray — and one of them invoked the difference principle (Lk 18: 11).

[76] A boy or girl cannot wear today the dress he or she wore with comfort and elegance five or ten or years ago for the first communion. So, too, what was suitable for a Church five or ten centuries ago is not necessarily so today.

The directive Pope Paul VI gave to the Pontifical Commission for the Revision of the Eastern Code seems to be applicable in the revision of particular law as well. "Since the norms of the Church have to contribute to the perennial growth of the People of God and the ever new needs, they cannot absolutely be inert, immovable, as if dead."[77] In other words, disciplinary norms are for life: they are not mummified museum pieces or archaeological findings.

8. Summary and Conclusion: Double Fidelity

Anyone who revisits the Synod of Diamper today needs first of all to be aware of a new holistic appraisal of Nestorianism. The Synod of Diamper promulgated and applied the norms and reforms of the Council of Trent, without distinguishing between catholicization and latinization but applying the ideology of the superiority of the Latin rite and serving the interests of the Portuguese hegemony.

The current efforts to return to the pre-Diamper traditions in accordance with the directive of the Second Vatican Council (OE 6) are bedevilled by complex problems. The first and foremost of them is, strangely enough, the wrong understanding of the conciliar directive itself following an incorrect English translation of the original Latin text. The omission to translate a keyword of the original Latin text, namely *indebite* ("unduly"), has misled unwary readers into intransigent positions. Incredibly enough, even the 1996 Instruction of the Congregation for the Eastern Churches has used the same incorrect and deviant English translation, which has only served to reinforce the confusion (though the Italian original is free of this defect). According to the conciliar directive, the recovery of pre-Diamper traditions, like any change in the proper rite of the Churches *sui iuris,* must make for organic progress. This applies in the matter of liturgy as well as discipline, like the celibate or married clergy. The conciliar directive of return does not mean setting the clock back mechanically. A mere "repristination" can be noxious in certain cases. All return is ultimately a matter of ecclesial discernment and should make for organic progress.

This ecclesial discernment starts with the initial question whether the original change was an *undue* falling off or deviation, a mere

---

[77] Pope Paul VI, Address (18 March 1974), "AAS 66 (1974) 243-249; *Nuntia* 1 (1975) 4-8, at p. 6.

latinization, or was it a needed catholicization. It is the irony of Diamper that where Menezes claimed catholicization most (christological faith replacing Nestorianism) he has been shown to have erred most, in the light of the ecumenical reappraisal of historical Nestorianism, as evidenced by the 1994 Common Declaration of Pope John Paul II and the Assyrian Patriarch Mar Dinkha IV. This profoundly significant event can serve to purify the historical memory of the "Latins" and the "Syrians" in the Church of Kerala.

The concept of latinization is more complex than many people make out. There is latinization, born of the ignorance of the Eastern heritage held to be erroneous or inferior for no better reason than the principle of *praestantia ritus latini.* This principle, which formerly carried a papal blessing, was exorcised by the Second Vatican Council. That having been said, one can only hope not to be misunderstood when one notes that sometimes behind the facade of latinization may be lurking genuine catholicization. Such crypto-catholicization needs to be distinguished from crass latinization. And to do so, it is not enough to look just at the Thomaschristian tradition and regard it as something unique, as if it were not subject to the test of catholicity in the light of the universal Catholic tradition articulated especially by the ecumenical councils.

It is only honest to recognize that there is much that the East can receive (by free *reception*, not imposition from outside!). Indeed, in the first millennium it was the West that was at the receiving end and it borrowed freely from the rich Eastern heritage of liturgy, spirituality and discipline. Then the East declined owing to various historical vicissitudes, while the West advanced in several sectors like biblical studies, critical edition of patristic literature, catechetical and liturgical renewal, missiology and evangelization, media education, etc. Here the East has been left behind. But not a few Easterners borrow from the West, with or without acknowledgement. There is nothing to be ashamed of in learning or receiving from the West — or for that matter from the north or the south. Besides the cross fertilisation of cultures, there is in the Christian vision the mystery of the communion of saints, with the corollary of *reception*. In the process of reception, however, the East should not let latinization barter away its heritage, as the Congregation for the Eastern Churches warns: "...the Eastern uniqueness, which risks being compromised or even eliminated in the contact with the Latin Church, her institutions, her doctrinal elaboration, her liturgical practices, and her internal organization which is often more developed also because of more favourable historical vicissitudes."[78]

This is what happened to the Church of the Thomaschristians with the Synod of Diamper. The Eastern and Indian heritage was replaced by the "institutions of the Latin Church, her doctrinal elaboration, her liturgical practices, and her more developed internal organization." This process was not free *reception* contributing to organic progress but hybridism, loss of identity, rejection and disgregation. That was the unmaking of tradition. However, the resistance by the Thomaschristans has prevented their Church from going the way of Goa, a fully latinised local Church, which, according to some well-informed modern Goan historians, was at first a portion of a far-flung Thomaschristian Church. The resistance of the Malabar Thomaschristians preserved Eastern Christianity in India, when for nearly three centuries Rome (except for an occasional act like the 1774 edition of the Taksa) remained by and large a mute onlooker till Pope Leo XIII took some decisive steps to stem the current. The ongoing return to the pre-Diamper traditions in the Syro-Malabar Church is caught up between the dilemma of restoration and reform. It is a painful process, complicated by the misunderstanding of the conciliar directive, unenlightened zeal, factionalism and infighting, sometimes verging on disgregation. Such are the simmering waves of the Synod of Diamper still breaking on the distant shores of history.

In the Church's pilgrim journey of adventure with the Holy Spirit, there is more than mere fidelity to or recovery of tradition. So we are told by Pope John Paul II, who has recently spoken of a twofold fidelity. After citing the conciliar directive about return to ancestral traditions, the pope gives us what can perhaps be called an authentic interpretation of the conciliar concept of return to the ancestral traditions.

> The Eastern Catholic Churches are thus called to maintain a twofold fidelity. First is fidelity to the traditions which have been handed down to them, so that they may in turn hand them on faithfully; useful in this regard are the bonds which unite them to their own Mother Churches. Second is fidelity to the men and women of today with their joys and hopes, their sorrows and pain, their desires and expectations, as they thirst for the truth and the fullness of life that finds its source only in God; this is faithfulness to the continuing search, especially in consumer-oriented so-

---

[78] Congregation for the Eastern Churches, *Instruction for Applying the Liturgical Prescriptions ...*, (op. cit., n. 46), p. 8.

cieties, for the deeper meaning of life. This twofold fidelity is fidelity to God and to his revelation — shining brightly in the many different traditions which come from the Apostles through the Fathers (OE 1) and fidelity to man and to his need of God, in the various ways in which this is expressed.[79]

This is a rather new voice of the magisterium.[80] Addressing the Eastern Catholic Churches the magisterium had so far insisted almost exclusively on tradition and "the mission they have of bearing witness to an ancient doctrinal, liturgical and monastic tradition." And there was good reason for such insistence. However, with such an exclusive focus on tradition, hardly ever had the magisterium pointed to the Vatican II pastoral constitution *Gaudium et Spes* as applicable also to the Eastern Catholic Churches. Pope John Paul II says it does. He speaks of a double fidelity: first, fidelity to their respective traditions, which, however should not make them fix their gaze on the past and lose sight of the present (not an unreal hypothesis); and secondly, "fidelity to the men and women of today in their joys and hopes, their sorrows and expectations." For this double fidelity, according to the Holy Father, the genuine Eastern tradition itself contains "elements [that] are capable of giving a more complete Christian response to the expectations of the men and women of today."[81]

The return to the pre-Diamper traditions, as intended by the Second Vatican Council, is not like retrieving history files in a computer. It is for the Church to determine with a pastorally enlightened discernment whether a return makes for organic progress or not in a double fidelity to God and to the men and women of today.

Pontifical Oriental Institute George Nedungatt, S.J.
Rome

---

[79] John Paul II, Letter dated 1 November 1999 to Cardinal Achille Silvestrini at the meeting of Bishops and Religious Superiors of the Eastern Catholic Churches in America and Oceania in Boston, 7-12 November 1999, *L'Osservatore Romano*, 8-9 November 1999, p. 5.

[80] Actually the phrase "double fidelity to God and man" in the sense of "inculturation of the gospel" was already used by Cardinal Silvestrini, Prefect of the Congregation for the Oriental Churches, in his address to a preparatory session for the Special Assembly of the Synod of Bishops for Asia. "Santi e Crillo e Metodio ... nella duplice fedeltà a Dio e all'uomo, si sono prodigati nell'annuncio del Vangelo di Cristo nel rispetto delle diverse culture alle quali si rivolgevano" See Congregazione per le Chiese Orientali, *Le chiese orientali e la missione in Asia,* (op. cit., n. 5), p. 5.

[81] John Paul II, Apostolic Letter (2 May 1995) "Orientale Lumen," AAS 87/5 (1995) 749.

Appendix I

PAPAL BULL ON THE RECEPTION OF PATRIARCH JOHN SULAQA IN THE CATHOLIC CHURCH (1553)

We reproduce below the text of the pontifical bull of Pope Julius III issued after receiving the profession of faith of John Simon Sulaqa and confirming him as patriarch of the Chaldean Church on 20 February 1553. This papal document was edited nearly a century ago by Samuel Giamil in his *Genuinæ Relationes inter Sedem Apostolicam et Assyrorum Orientalium seu Chaldæorum Ecclesiam*, Roma, Loescher, 1902, pp. 15-23. However, this book is now long out of print and is not generally available in young libraries. That seems to be the reason why this papal bull is not mentioned in certain publications on the Synod of Diamper like a recent book which proposes to deal "with the complete suppression of Nestorianism by the Catholic missions with the arrival of Portuguese missionaries," a book which is otherwise enriched with several papal bulls dealing with Christianity in India.

We reedit the text of this pontifical document with a few minor corrections in the text as edited by Giamil. These are chiefly typographical errors and are indicated in the footnotes. As for orthography, we let stand spellings like *litera* and *quicquid*, since they are recognized as alternate forms, though less than standard. Sulaqa's name is written as Sulaka in the bull. As a rule, we do not point out the few changes in punctuation like the omission of commas: Giamil's text abounds in commas. Instead of his *de quinque panibus, quinque millia hominum satiavit* we give *de quinque panibus quinque millia hominum satiavit*. Occasionally, where commas would preferably be in place, but are not found in the text of Giamil, we supply them, as for example, *circumcisionis, Sabbati, Ciborum eadem lege prohibitorum, reliquarumque legalium observatores*. Since the use of capital letters is very variable in Latin, we leave them mostly as found in Giamil's text (exception, e.g. footnotes 7 and 9), although today it would be more common to write *sabbati* and *ciborum* in the text above.

We give below a summary description of the contents of this papal bull. We have divided it into several sections or paragraphs and numbered them.

SUMMARY OF CONTENTS

1. Introduction: It is the right and the duty of the Roman Pontiff to provide for the pastoral government of the Churches which are without proper pastors.

2. Responding to a faction of the Chaldean Church, divided over the election of a new patriarch, Pope Julius III receives into Catholic communion its elected candidate John Sulaqa, a monk of the monastery of Hormisd, in order to provide a valid successor to the late Simon Bar-Mama, Patriarch of

the Assyrian Church (Chaldean Church). Among the territories subject to the patriarch Pope Julius III mentions "China, Calicut, and the whole of India."

3. The pope absolves John Sulaqa of excommunication and all other ecclesiastical censures and appoints him patriarch and pastor entrusting to him "the care and the administration of the same Church in spiritual and temporal matters."

4. The bishops and the clergy are to render him obedience and reverence.

5. The people are to receive him as their "Father and Pastor."

6. Profession of Faith required of John Sulaqa and subscribed to by him

a. Confession of the Most Holy Trinity

b. Confession of the Incarnation of the Son of God. "I accept and embrace and approve the first Synod of Ephesus of two hundred Fathers. And I believe whatever it decreed, and I reprobate whatever it reprobated, but especially the Nestorian heresy together with its author Nestorius" (Giamil, p. 22).

c. Mary, the mother of Jesus, is truly the Mother of God

d. No one is saved except through the blood and death of Jesus Christ

e. The legal prescriptions of the Old Testament ceased with the Christ event

f. I believe and profess the seven sacraments.

g. I believe in the purification after death with the sufferings of Purgatory

h. I hold and abide by the Nicene Creed according to the hereby subscribed text

i. I accept the canonical books of the Old and the New Testaments.

j. I embrace and receive the first four ecumenical councils: Nicea, Constantinople, Ephesus and Chalcedon. I abjure the heresies and heretics condemned by these councils.

k. I approve and embrace whatever the Holy Catholic and Roman Church teaches.

l. I hold and confess (*teneo et confiteor*) that the Holy Apostolic See and the Roman Pontiff have authority in the entire world, and that the pope is "truly the Vicar of Christ and the head of the entire Church and the father and teacher of all Christians (*verum Christi Vicarium, totiusque Ecclesiæ esse caput, omnium Christianorum patrem ac doctorem existere*)" with full powers. "I confess that none can be saved outside the Catholic Church or have a share in the eternal life" (p. 23).

m. "Besides, I promise obedience ... to Pope Julius III, the present pope, and to his successors" (p. 23).

7. Conclusion. The date of the Profession of Faith, 15 February 1553. Papal bull of Julius III issued on 20 February 1553.

George Nedungatt, S.J.

JULIUS EPISCOPUS
SERVUS SERVORUM DEI
DILECTO FILIO
SIMONI SULAKAE DANIELIS DE DOMO BELLU
ELECTO DE MUZAL IN ASSYRIA ORIENTALI
SALUTEM ET APOSTOLICAM BENEDICTIONEM

(*Regest. Vat.* Bull. secr. Julii III, anno III, t. 70, N. 1793, pag. 235)

1. Divina disponente clementia, cuius inscrutabili providentia ordinationem suscipiunt universa, in Apostolica Sedis culmine, meritis licet insufficientibus, constituti, ad universas orbis ecclesias aciem nostræ considerationis extendimus, et pro earum statu salubriter dirigendo Apostolici favoris auxilium adhibemus. Sed de illis propensius Nos cogitare convenit quas propriis carere Pastoribus intuemur, ut eis iuxta cor nostrum Pastores præficiantur idonei, qui commissos sibi populos per suam circumspectionem providam salubriter dirigant et informent, ac bona ecclesiarum ipsarum non solum gubernent utiliter, sed etiam multis modis efferant incrementis. Dudum siquidem provisiones ecclesiarum omnium tunc vacantium et in antea [vacatarum necnon][1] vacaturarum ordinationi et dispositioni nostræ reservavimus, decernentes ex tunc irritum et inane, si secus super his per quoscumque quavis auctoritate scienter vel ignoranter contingeret attentari.

2. Postmodum vero Ecclesia Patriarchali de Muzal in Syria (Assyria) Orientali, cui bo[næ] me[moriæ] Simon Maria (Bar-Mama) Patriarcha de Muzal, et insulæ Tygris, ac ceterarum civitatum et terrarum Orientalium eidem Patriarchæ subiectarum, necnon monasteriorum eiusdem nationis in Sin, Massin et Calicuth, ac tota India existentium eidem etiam Patriarchæ subditorum dum viveret præsidebat per obitum eiusdem Symonis patriarchæ qui extra Romanam Curiam debitum naturæ persolvit, Pastoris solatio destituta, Nos, vacatione huiusmodi fide dignis relatibus intellecta, ad provisionem eiusdem Ecclesiæ celerem, et felicem, de qua nullus præter Nos hac vice se intromittere potuit, sive potest, reservatione et decreto obsistentibus supradictis, ne Ecclesia ipsa longæ vacationis exponatur incommodis, paternis et sollicitis studiis intendentes, post deliberationem, quam de præficendo eidem Ecclesiæ personam utilem et etiam fructuosam cum Fratribus Nostris habuimus diligentem, demum

[1] Some words are obviously missing here which we supply in [ ]. Cf. Giamil: "antea vacaturarum (*sic*)".

ad te Monachum Monasterii Hormisd ordinis sancti Basilii,[2] Muzal diœcesis ordinem ipsum expresse professum, in quadragesimo, vel circa, tuæ ætatis anno et Presbyteratus ordine constitutum, ac de legitimo matrimonio procreatum, de cuius integritate, doctrina, puritate, sinceritate, fidei constantia, religionis zelo, vitæ ac morum honestate et denique in omni virtute summa conspicuitate dilecti filii universi clerus et populus illius regionis per eorum literas Nobis testimonium perhibuere, direximus oculos nostræ mentis.

3. Quibus omnibus debita meditatione pensatis, ac confessione tua, quam præsentibus de verbo ad verbum inseri et annotari voluimus et mandamus, prius audita et in scriptis redacta ac diligenter examinata et in Consistorio nostro perlecta, et ea catholica, teque per eam fidei capace et vero fideli ac idoneo reperto,[3] horum intuitu te a quibusvis excommunicationis, suspensionis et interdictis aliisque ecclesiasticis sententiis, censuris et pœnis a iure vel ab homine quavis occasione, vel causa latis, si quibus quomodolibet innodatus existis, ad effectum præsentium dumtaxat consequendum harum serie absolventes et absolutum fore censentes, de persona tua Nobis et fratribus ipsis ob tuorum exigentiam meritorum accepta, eidem Ecclesiæ de eorundem fratrum consilio Apostolica auctoritate providemus, teque illi in Patriarcham præficimus et Pastorem curam et administrationem ipsius Ecclesiæ tibi in spiritualibus et temporalibus plenarie committendo, in illo, qui dat gratias et largitur præmia confidentes, quod dirigente Domino actus tuos præfata Ecclesia sub tuo felici regimine regetur utiliter, et prospere dirigetur, ac grata in eisdem temporalibus et spiritualibus suscipiet incrementa.

4. Quocirca discretioni tuæ per Apostolica scripta mandamus, quatenus eiusdem Ecclesiæ curam et administrationem prædictas sic exercere studeas sollicite fideliter et prudenter, quod Ecclesia ipsa Gubernatori provido et fructuoso administratori gaudeat se commissam, tuque præter æternæ retributionis præmium nostram et Apostolicæ Sedis benedictionem et gratiam exinde uberius consequi merearis: nec non Venerabilibus fratribus nostris universis suffraganeis, ac dilectis filiis Capitulo et Vassallis dictæ Ecclesiæ nec non Clero, et populus[4] civitatis et diœcesis de Muzal quatenus suffraganei tibi tamquam membra capiti obsequentes, et Capitulum tamquam Patri et Pastori animarum suarum similiter inten-

---

[2] Instead of "Basilii" perhaps Antonii Abbatis (?). So Giamil, who explains that the Chaldean monks followed then and still follow the Rule of St Anthony, not of Basil, though they do venerate the latter, too.

[3] repertis (Giamil)

[4] Cf. nec non Clero, et populs (Giamil)

dentes exhibeant tibi obedientiam et reverentiam debitas et devotas, ita quod mutua inter te et ipsos suffraganeos gratia gratos sortiatur effectus, et Nos devotionem ipsorum possimus propterea in Domino merito commendare; nec non Clerus te pro nostra et dictæ Sedis reverentia benigne recipientes et honorifice pertractantes tua salubria monita et mandata suscipiant humiliter et efficaciter adimplere procurent.

5. Populus vero te tamquam Patrem et Pastorem animarum suarum devote suscipientes, et debita honorificentia prosequentes tuis monitis et mandatis salubribus humiliter intendant ita, quod tu in eis devotionis filios, et ipsi in te per consequens Patrem benevolum invenisse gaudeatis. Vassalli autem prædicti te debito honore prosequentes tibi fidelitatem solitam ac consueta servitia et iura tibi ab eis debita integre exhibere studeant; alioquin sententiam, sive pœnam, quam rite tuleris seu statueris in rebelles, ratam habebimus, et faciemus auctore Domino usque ad satisfactionem condignam inviolabiliter observari.

6. Tenor vero dictæ confessionis sequitur et est talis: Ego, Simon Sulaka de Danielis de Domo Bellu, ex civitate Muzal et Assyria Orientali oriundus, monachus Monasterii Hormisd ordinis sancti Basilii,[5] Muzal diœcesis ordinem ipsum expresse professus,

6a. credo ex corde et confiteor ore quod unus solus est verus Deus omnipotens incommutabilis, qui est incomprehensibilis, ineffabilis et æternus Pater et Filius et Spiritus Sanctus, Unus in essentia, Trinus in personis, Pater ingenitus, Filius a solo Patre genitus, Spiritus Sanctus a Patre Filioque procedens non sicut a duobus principiis, sed ab utroque tanquam ab uno principio. Pater non est Filius aut Spiritus Sanctus, Filius non est Pater aut Spiritus Sanctus, Spiritus Sanctus non est Pater aut Filius, sed Pater tantum Pater est, Filius tantum Filius est et Spiritus Sanctus tantum Spiritus Sanctus est, nullus alium aut præcedit æternitate, aut excedit magnitudine, aut superat æternitate, absque initio semper est et sine fine. Pater est generans, Filius nascens, Spiritus Sanctus procedens, consubstantiales, coæquales, coomnipotentes et coæterni: hæ tres personæ sunt Unus Deus non tres dii, una essentia, una substantia, una immensitas, unum Principium, unus creator visibilium omnium et invisibilium, corporalium et spiritualium, qui quando voluit, universas condidit creaturas sua bonitate, quas et valde bonas voluit, et ideo reprobo et anathematizo omnes hæreses ac hæreticos sentientes et docentes contraria.[6]

---

[5] See note 2.

[6] Cf. Giamil: docentes contraria, firmiter etiam credo et profiteor,

6b. Firmiter etiam credo et profiteor, quod Unigenitus Dei Filius Patri consubstantialis, semper cum Patre et Spiritu Sancto existens, in plenitudine temporis, quam divinæ misericordiæ consilium inscrutabile disposuit, ut nos a peccato Adæ ac ceterarum culparum nostrarum sordibus mundaret, et a morte et inferno liberaret, incarnatus est de Spiritu Sancto in immaculato utero Mariæ semper Virginis, veram et integram hominis naturam assumpsit, corpus videlicet et animam rationalem in unitate personæ divinæ tanta unitate, ut unus et idem Christus sit Deus et homo, Dei Filius et hominis Filius ita, quod una natura non confunditur ab altera, nec una transit in alteram, nec una miscetur alteri, nec altera evanescit,[7] sed in persona omnino una sint duæ naturæ perfectæ scilicet divina et humana, salvis earundem naturarum proprietatibus, duæ voluntates, duæ operationes ita ut Christus sit tantum unus, et sicut formam servi Dei forma non adimit, ita formam Dei servi forma non minuit. Qui enim verus Deus est, idem verus est homo, Deus per id quod in principio erat Verbum et Verbum erat apud Deum et Deus erat Verbum, homo per id quod Verbum caro factum est et habitavit in nobis,[8] Deus per id quod de quinque panibus quinque millia hominum satiavit, quod Samaritanæ aquam salientem in vitam æternam promisit, quod Lazarum quatriduanum a mortuis resuscitavit, homo per id quod esurivit, sitivit, fatigatus est, et in ligno clavis transfixus est, unus et idem secundum divinitatem, æqualis æterno Patri, immortalis, impassibilis; secundum vero humanitatem minor Patre, mortalis et passibilis.

6c. Insuper firmiter credo et prædico eundem Dei Filium incarnatum vere natum esse ex Maria semper Virgine et ideo ipsam Virginem fateor Dei Matrem atque Genitricem, item vere passum, vere mortuum et sepultum, vere cum anima descendisse ad Inferos ad liberandum Patres et ad ligandum insatiabilem homicidam, et subinde vere ex mortuis resurrexisse, et per quadraginta dies Apostolos docuisse de Regno Dei, moxque ad Cælos ascendisse, sedereque ad dextram Patris et venturum in fine sæculorum ad iudicandum vivos et mortuos.

6d. Credo et profiteor nullum unquam hominem ex semine Adæ conceptum et natum fuisse salvatum, aut fore salvandum nisi per fidem Mediatoris Dei et hominum Domini Nostri Jesu Chrisi in sanguine et morte ipsius, qua nos reconciliavit æterno Patri, et delevit chirographum iniquitatum nostrarum, æterna redemptione inventa.

6e. Item firmiter credo legalia omnia Veteris Testamenti seu Mosaicæ legis, quia Christum figurabant, licet divino cultui illa ætate congruerent,

---

[7] Cf. avanescit (Giamil)

[8] Cf. Nobis (Giamil)

ipso adveniente cessasse et iam promulgato Evangelio servari non posse sine interitu salutis æternæ.[9] Omnes igitur post illud tempus circumcisionis, Sabbati, Ciborum eadem lege prohibitorum, reliquarumque legalium observatores alienos a fide denuntio, et salutis æternæ non posse esse participes, nisi aliquando ab his erroribus resipiscant, ab his enim omnibus liberavit nos[10] Christus, et septem novæ legis sacramenta instituit, quæ veneror.

6f. Credo et profiteor unum Baptismum, Confirmationem, Eucharistiam, Pænitentiam, Ordinem, Matrimonium et Extremam Unctionem, quæ omnia nobis gratiam Dei conferunt, et virtute passionis Domini nostri Jesu Christi ea sumentibus applicant.[11] Ista septem sacramenta perficiuntur tribus, verbo videlicet et rebus ac Ministro: rebus in Materia, verbis in forma, Ministro qui facere intendat quod facit Ecclesia. Recipio insuper quicquid de eisdem Sacramentis Sancta et Catholica Ecclesia Romana docet et prædicat.

6g. Credo quod si vere dicti pænitentes[12] in Dei charitate decesserint, anteqnam dignis pænitentiæ fructibus de commissorum et commissorum pœnis satisfecerint coram iustitia divina, eorum animas pœnis Purgatorii post mortem purgari,[13] utque a pœnis huiusmodi releventur prodesse eis fidelium vivorum suffragia Missarum scilicet sacrificia, orationes et eleemosinæ ac alia pietatis officia, quæ a fidelibus pro aliis fidelibus fieri consueverunt secundum Ecclesiæ instituta, illorumque animas, quæ post baptisma susceptum nullam omnino peccati maculam incurrerunt, illas etiam, quæ post contractam peccati maculam, ut dictum est, purgatæ sunt, in cælum mox recipi et intueri clare ipsum Deum Trinum et Unum, sicuti est, pro meritorum tamen diversitate alium alio perfectius; illorum vero animas qui in actuali mortali peccato, vel solo originali decedunt,

---

[9] The sentence "Item firmiter credo … salutis æternæ" is a summary restatement of a passage from the *Decretum pro Iacobitis* of the Council of Florence (DzSch 1348). Unfortunately, the precision of the original (which only reproduces the teaching of St. Thomas Aquinas that the *ceremonialia,* one of the three components of the Mosaic *legalia,* have come to an end with the Christ event) is lost in the summary, which as it stands is not fully faithful to the teaching of the original decree. Giamil inserts *sic* after the phrase "ipso adveniente cessasse (*sic*)," but it is not clear what he is drawing attention to.

[10] Cf. Nos (Giamil)

[11] Cf. Giamil: … ea sumentibus applicant, ista septem sacramenta perficiuntur …

[12] Cf. Giamil: … Ecclesia Romana docet et prædicat, credo quod si vere dicti (*sic*) pœnitentes

[13] Cf. Giamil: … eorum animas pœnis Purgatorii post mortem purgari. utque a pœnis…

mox in Infernum descendere pœnis tamen disparibus perpetuo puniendas.

6h. Firmiter etiam teneo et credo Simbolum Fidei a Trecentum et octo Patribus Concilii Niceni acceptatum, et usque in hæc tempora servatum in Ecclesia in hac forma, videlicet: Credo in unum Deum Patrem Omnipotentem factorem cæli et terræ, visibilium omnium et invisibilium, et in unum Dominum Jesum Christum filium Dei unigenitum, et ex Patre natum ante omnia sæcula, Deum de Deo, lumen de lumine, Deum verum de Deo vero, genitum non factum, consubstantialem Patri per quem omnia facta sunt. Qui propter nos homines et propter nostram salutem descendit de cælis et incarnatus est de Spiritu Sancto ex Maria Virgine et homo factus est. Qui conceptus et natus, crucifixus etiam pro nobis[14] sub Pontio Pilato, passus et sepultus est, et resurrexit tertia die secundum scripturas et ascendit in cælum.[15] Sedet ad dexteram Patris et iterum venturus est cum gloria iudicare vivos et mortuos, cuius regni non erit finis. Et in unum Spiritum Sanctum, Spiritum veritatis, Dominum vivificantem, qui ex Patre Filioque procedit. Qui cum Patre et Filio simul adoratur et conglorificatur, qui locutus est per Prophetas et Apostolos. Et unam Sanctam Catholicam et Apostolicam Ecclesiam.[16] Confiteor unum baptisma in remissionem peccatorum. Et expecto resurrectionem mortuorum et vitam venturi seculi. Amen.

6i. Confiteor, teneo et prædico unum eundemque Deum Veteris et Novi Testamenti, hoc est, Legis et Prophetarum atque Evangelii auctorem esse, quoniam eodem Spiritu Sancto inspirante utriusque Testamenti sancti loquuti sunt. Itaque suscipio omnes libros canonicos, quos suscepit Sacrosancta Romana et Catholica Ecclesia, quorum tituli sunt hi, videlicet: quinque libri Moysi, idest, liber Genesis, Exodi, Levitici, Numeri, Deuteronomii, Josue, Judicum, Ruth, quatuor libri Regum, duo Paralipomenon, Esdræ primus et secundus qui dicitur Neemias, Tobie, Judith, Job, psalmorum David, liber Proverbiorum, Ecclesiastes et Cantici Canticorum, Sapientiæ, Ecclesiastici, Isai, Hieremiæ, Baruth (sic), Ezechielis, Danielis. Teneo etiam Libros duodecim Prophetarum minorum, idest: Osee, Joelis, Amos, Abdie, Jone, Michee, Naum, Abacuc, Sephoniæ (sic), Aggei, Zachariæ, Malachiæe et duos libros Machabeorum. Etiam teneo quatuor libros Evangeliorum Matthei, Marci, Lucæ et

---

[14] Cf. Giamil: ... pro Nobis

[15] Cf. Giamil: ... et ascendit in Cœlum sedet...

[16] Cf. Giamil: ... qui locutus est per Prophetas et Apostolos et unam Sanctam Catholicam et Apostolicam Ecclesiam.

Joannis. Accepto quatuordecim Epistolas divi Pauli, unam[17] videlicet ad Romanos, ad Corinthios duas, ad Galatas unam, ad Ephesios unam, ad Philippenses unam, ad Colossenses unam, ad Thessalonicenses duas, ad Timotheum duas, ad Titum unam, ad Philemonem unam, ad Hebræos unam. Item suscipio epistolam Jacobi unam, Petri duas, Joannis Apostoli tres, Judæ unam, librum Actuum Apostolorum et Apocalipsim Joannis Apostoli.

6j. Item amplector, suscipio et approbo Sanctam Nicenam Synodum Trecentorum decem et octo Patrum et profiteor ac sequor quicquid illa decrevit, et reprobo ac damno quicquid illa damnavit, et maxime impiam hæresim Arianorum cum suo auctore Ario. Item amplector, suscipio et approbo Sanctam Constantinopolitanam Synodum primam centum et quinquaginta Patrum, et credo quicquid illa decrevit, et reprobo quicquid illa reprobavit, et maxime impiam hæresim Macedonii cum ipso auctore. Item suscipio, amplector et approbo primam Ephesinam Synodum ducentorum Patrum, et credo quicquid illa decrevit, et reprobo quicquid illa reprobavit et maxime hæresim Nestorianam cum suo auctore Nestorio. Item suscipio, amplector et approbo Sanctam Chalcedonensem Synodum, quartam in ordine Generalium Synodorum, et credo ac sequor quicquid illa decrevit, et reprobo ac damno quicquid illa reprobavit et maxime impiam hæresim Euticetis (sic) et Dioscori et reprobo secundam Ephesinam Synodum.

6k. Item suscipio, approbo et amplector quæcumque alia concilia, quæ recipit et approbat Sancta et Catholica Ecclesia Romana, ac damno et reprobo omnes hæreses et auctores earumdem, quas et quos reprobat et damnat dicta Sancta et Catholica Romana Ecclesia, nec non quidquid tenet et docet Sancta Sedes Apostolica et Romana ac Catholica Ecclesia cum omni devotione et reverentia suscipio et accepto. Illos quoque doctores et Sanctos Patres quos Ecclesia Romana approbat, reverenter suscipio.

6l. Teneo et confiteor Sanctam Apostolicam Sedem et Romanum Pontificem in universum orbem tenere Principatum, et ipsum Romanum Pontificem successorem esse Beati Petri Principis Apostolorum, et verum Christi Vicarium, totiusque Ecclesiæ esse caput, omnium Christianorum patrem ac doctorem existere, et ipsi in Beato Petro pascendi, regendi et gubernandi universalem Ecclesiam a Domino Nostro Jesu Christo plenam potestatem traditam esse. Cuius Ecclesiæ unitatem et congregatio-

[17] Cf. Giamil: ... Machabeorum, etiam teneo quatuor libros Evangeliorum Matthei, Marci, Lucæ et Joannis: accepto quatuordecim Epistolas divi Pauli unam

nem tam valde credo, ut nullos extra dictam Ecclesiam Catholicam existentes æternæ vitæ participes fieri posse confiteor.

6 m. Insuper promitto me tamquam obedientiæ filium ordinationibus, præceptis, censuris ac iussionibus Papæ Julii III moderni, et successorum suorum Romanorum Pontificum callonice intrantium, et Sedi Apostolicæ fideliter et semper obtemperaturum. Ita Deus me adiuvet et Sancta Dei Evangelia. Et Deus testis est mihi quod corde credo, confiteor ore hanc confessionem fidei mere sinceram et veram, quam scribi feci, ac manu propria subscripsi, et humiliter Patri Sanctissimo Julio III Pontifici Maximo ad pedes eius prostratus obtuli die quintadecima mensis Februarii anni millesimi quingentesimi quinquagesimi tertii.

Ego indignus Simon Sulaka feci scribere hanc fidem et manu propria subscripsi.

Datum Romæ apud Sanctum Petrum anno Incarnationis Domini millesimo quingentesimo quinquagesimo tertio,[18] decimo Calendas Martii,[19] Pontificatus nostri anno tertio.

JAC. CARD. PUTEUS.

A. DIAZ.

Concordat
L. † S.

PETRUS WENZEI,
Subarchivista.

[18] Giamil edits the text enigmatically as follows: Jo. tertio (*sic*) la. secundo.

[19] *Decimo kalendas martii* is 20 February as is rightly noted by Giamil (p. 17) according to the Latin reckoning, and not 18 February as is given by Andrews Thazhath, *Juridical Sources of the Syro-Malabar Church*, (OIRSI, 106), Kottayam, Paurasthya Vidyapitham, 1987, p. 67.

Appendix II

INFORMATION ABOUT MAR ABRAHAM (1593/1594)

by Francisco Ros, S.J.

Joseph Wicki, *Documenta Indica*, XVI, (Roma, 1984),
Document 159, "Enformação do Prelado do Serra" pp. 1029-1039

Francisco Ros, S.J., the author of this treatise, was the right hand man of Archbishop Alexis Menezes at the Synod of Diamper. On the life and works of this Jesuit priest see the detailed study of Angel Santos, S.J., "Francisco Ros S.J., Arzobispo de Cranganor, primer obispo Jesuita de la India," *Missionalia Hispanica* 5 (1948) 325-393; 6 (1949) 79-142.

Francisco Ros was born in 1557 in Catalonia, north eastern Spain, entered the Society of Jesus in 1575 and arrived in India in 1583. Professor of Syriac at the Jesuit seminary of Vaipicotta since 1587, he accompanied Mar Abraham to the Third Provincial Council of Goa in 1885. Appointed by this Council as Mar Abraham's aide with a mandate to watch over the execution of his reform promises, Ros wrote in 1586-1787 a tract, "De erroribus Nestorianorum...", which has been edited by Irenéé Hausherr in *Orientalia Christiana*, IX/1, 1928, N° 40, pp. 5-36. This tract recommended Mar Abraham's deposition by the pope since he continued to hold on to the Nestorian heresy and neglected all reforms and pastoral care. Again in 1993 or early 1994 Ros wrote another more detailed and harsher denunciation of Mar Abraham singling out the various reforms that were needed in the Church of the Thomaschristians. We are publishing in this Appendix II an English translation of the Portuguese original of this tract published by Joseph Wicki in 1984. After the death of Mar Abraham in 1997 when the Synod of Diamper met in 1999, Ros (who alone among the foreign missionaries knew Syriac well) acted as the chief aide of Alexis Menezes for the formulation of several synodal reforms. Having succeeded Mar Abraham in the See of Angamale in 1601, Ros held a diocesan synod in 1603 revising some decrees of the Synod of Diamper that had most given offence to the Thomaschristians. Though the acts of this synod seem to have got lost, probably their main thrust has been preserved in the Diocesan Statutes of Angamale, which Bishop Ros promulgated in 1606. Through his endeavours the See of Angamale was detached by Pope Paul V in 1608 from its subjection as a suffragan see to the Archdiocese of Goa and transferred to Cranganore. Thus Ros became the Archbishop of Cranganore. With his knowledge of Syriac he did much to latinize the liturgy of the Thomaschristians. After 23 years of pastoral government he died on 16 February 1624 and was buried at Cranganore. When the tomb was opened two years later with a view to its transfer, his body was found incorrupt as certified at the official examination. His epitaph with an inscription in vattezhuth (Malayalam paleography) still exists at Parur.

The DATE of the present document is given in the Portuguese text as 30 December '94, that is 1594, but in the Spanish text (Text 2 or B) it is given as 30 September 1594. Joseph Wicki, in his introductory note, adopted the date 30 December 1594, but there are good reasons to hold that this is erroneous. Probably the original documents bore no dates, as they were not letters, and the dates were added later at Goa. See *Translator's Note* at the end.

The ENGLISH TRANSLATION, which follows the Introductory notes and Summary by Joseph Wicki, has been made by Jacob Kollaparambil. In it are kept the footnotes, but the textual variants between Text 1 (A) and Text 2 (B) noted in the critical apparatus of the edition by Joseph Wicki are omitted. These variants in fact are not very important, except for the last one concerning the date of the document, for which see the *Translator's Note*.

George Nedungatt, S.J.

I. TEXTS:

1. Goa 32 *I*, ff. 529ʳ-32ᵛ, earlier 196-98 and LI: Portuguese copy or quasi original, divided into several paragraphs with corresponding numbers in the margins. Number 12 is omitted by oversight. Folio 532*r* is blank. Some phrases were underlined in Rome.

2. Goa 32 *I*, ff. 525ʳ-28ᵛ, earlier LI: Spanish version of text 1 probably made at Goa. There are some omissions and corrections (see crit. app.). Folio 528*r* is blank. In f. 528ᵛ is the title of the document and this note: "Embíala el P.e Provincial de la India [Francisco Cabral] a nuestro Padre General."

II. AUTHOR and PLACE: are not indicated in the document. The author of this information twice speaks of himself in the first person (see nn. 4 and 10). In n.10 he says: "em Goa li eu este tratado todo em caldeo." No other Jesuit in the province except Fr. Ros, could read Chaldean at that time. Hence we conclude that Fr. Ros is the author of this information. As the habitual residence of Fr. Ros was Vaipikotta, we presume that this information was written there, and sent to the provincial, who resided in Goa.

III. OUR EDITION: We publish text 1 (A) and note the most important variants of text 2 (B) in the critical apparatus.

SUMMARY

1. Mar Abraham has not corrected the errors and heresies contained in the liturgical books in use among the Thomas Christians. – 2. Some of the errors and heresies prevalent among them. – 3. Some heretical books in the possession of Mar Abraham. – 4. Mar Abraham and some of his priests pray to Nestor and celebrate his feast in secret. – 5. In the whole of the Serra, feasts in honour of Theodore, Diodore and Nestor are celebrated every year. – 6. In the Chaldean translation of the profession of faith, made by Mar Abraham in Rome, some words are interpolated. – 7. The Christians of the Serra call their patriarch "universal pastor" and Mar Abraham "father of our

fathers," "pastor of our pastors" and "sun of the Catholics." – 8. Mar Abraham has asked two patriarchs to send a pastor to his flock. – 9. He has taught his people not to meditate on the Passion of Christ. – 10. He wrote to his patriarch that the theologians gathered at the Goan synod read and approved a Nestorian treatise on Incarnation. This is false. – 11. A strange question asked by Mar Abraham. – 12. Mar Abraham and his priests use a book of exorcisms full of superstitions. – 13. They possess a letter against the Church of Rome which, they claim, fell from heaven. – 14. A list of accusations against Mar Abraham and his priests. [15]. Mar Abraham has been promising reform for seventeen years. – [16]. After the Goan synod he has become inimical to the Church of Rome. – [17]. He tries to set his people against the ministers of the Church of Rome. – [18]. The need to send a really Catholic bishop to the Serra and of punishing Mar Abraham before it is too late.

† INFORMATION ABOUT THE PRELATE OF THE SERRA

1°. Though Mar Abraham, the Archbishop of Angamale, was admonished and advised many times that he should correct the errors and heresies found at present in the Chaldean books of the Serra, he never wanted to do it either by himself or through someone else.[1]

2°. The heresies and errors among others are the following:

(1) that the Divine Word did not become incarnate in the manner the Catholics profess, the said Catholics having erred in the understanding of the divine Scriptures and not understanding the power of God;

(2) that in Christ Our Lord there are two persons, divine and human;[2]

(3) that Jesus and the Emmanuel are different *supposita*;[3]

(4) that Jesus Christ is not God by nature but the temple of God;[4]

(5) that Our Lady did not give birth to God, but only to a mere man;[5]

(6) that the body of the Virgin, Our Lady was carried to the air by the Apostles and the ministry of the angels after her death to the terrestrial paradise, and thus the soul and the body of the said Lady have to remain in the terrestrial paradise till the day of judgement;[6]

---

[1] Letters of other Jesuits contradict this assertion. Cf. DI XIV 454, 563, 784.

[2] See also *De erroribus Nestorianorum* pp.16, 27; as also the Synod of Diamper, Session III, decr. 1, c.2.

[3] See also *De erroribus* 16; the Synod of Diamper, Session III, decr. 14.

[4] See also *De erroribus* 16 22; the Synod of Diamper, Session III, decr. 14.

[5] Se also *De erroribus* 17 22; the Synod of Dimaper, Session III, decr. 1, c. 3; decr. 6.

[6] See also the Synod of Diamper, decr. 14.

(7) that the souls of the just will not go to heaven till the day of judgement;[7]
(8) that St. Joseph, the spouse of the Virgin, actually had another wife besides the said Lady;[8]
(9) that the Annunciation by the Angel took place at Jerusalem;[9]
(10) that the Magi Kings did not merit anything by adoring the Infant Jesus, nor did they believe much even after they had adored him;[10]
(11) that St. Ephrem, the Catholic Doctor [of the Church], trod the steps of Nestorius;[11]
(12) that when Emperor Constantine went to war against the barbarians he made a vow to Nestorius to get back victorious from the war;[12]
(13) that St. Joseph used to teach and rebuke the Child Jesus, and to ask him why he did unseemly and naughty tricks;[13]
(14) that the said Joseph, angered by the Child Jesus, caught him by the hand and spanked him;[14]
(15) that he took him many times to school for instruction;[15]
(16) that the Eternal Father also became incarnate.[16]

And other things like these can be seen and read many times in the books of this Serra; and they are in the possession of certain priests and are placed publicly in the churches for use in prayer. And especially in a commentary of the Gospels, used by them, written by a heretic Nestorian bishop, in which are written many heresies and fables and lies and temerities, which have been read and noticed in the said book.[17]

3°. So also the said Archbishop of the Serra has a book in which it is treated and proved that the Holy Spirit does not proceed from the Son.[18] He has also another book of Nestorius, in which it is said that the penal-

---

[7] *Ibid.*

[8] *Ibid.*

[9] *Ibid.*

[10] *Ibid.*

[11] *Ibid.*, decr. 15; *De erroribus* 32.

[12] Cf. *De erroribus* 32.

[13] Cf. the Synod of Diamper, Session III, decr. 14.

[14] *Ibid.*

[15] *Ibid.*

[16] The Synod of Diamper, Session III, decr. 15; *De erroribus* 24.

[17] *Exposição dos evangelhos.* Cf. Synod of Diamper, Session III, decr. 14.

[18] *Da processão do Spirito Santo.* Cf. *ibid.*

ties of human nature were not due to the original sin,[19] which is against the divine Scripture in the epistle to the Romans.[20] So too all the texts in the canonical epistles which can be used against the Church of Nestorius, where the dying and shedding of blood is attributed to God, are adulterated by the Nestorians.[21] All this I have seen and read, and the books still exist as witnesses.

4°. When the said Archbishop was in Goa, one of his caçanars,[22] who had in his ignorance lived in the error of Nestorius, told me[23] that the said Archbishop and three or four persons here in the Serra were wont to recite the Divine Office [Liturgy of the Hours] of Nestorius in secret every year and celebrate his feast.

5°. In the whole of the Serra the feast of Theodor of Mopsuestia, Diodor and Nestorius[24] is celebrated every year. However, after we warned them of this they introduced into a few books the names of Catholic Doctors. Nevertheless, the prayers and readings are proper to the said heretics, and their prayer is full of their praises in as much as they had maintained that God had not died for men. They invoke God's justice on those who believe the contrary of what the said heretics have taught. They call Rome *Ur Caldeorum*[25] and they say that Nestorius was exiled and persecuted out of envy, the envy of St. Cyril who opposed Nestorius and presided over the Council of Ephesus. They say that he was persecuted not only for the envy of St. Cyril, but also for that of his party; and they call St. Cyril devil's worker.[26]

6°. In the profession of faith which the said Archbishop made in Rome at the time of Pius IV,[27] written in his hand and translated from Latin into Chaldean, I[28] found those words of faith adulterated which say "We believe that the Son of God took human nature"; in its place stood in

[19] The book on the Incarnation by Jonas Bar Kaldun. Cf. *De erroribus* 27, 33; the Synod of Diamper, Session III, decr. 1, c. 5.

[20] Cf. Rom. 5. 12 ss; 6, 23.

[21] These passages are cited by Francisco Ros in one of his letters to Fr. Acquaviva (DI XIV 564, 3). See also *De erroribus 19-20;* The Synod of Diamper, Session III, decr. 3.

[22] A priest of the Thomas Christians.

[23] Evidently, it is Fr. Ros who is referred to. See an identical passage in one of his letters to Fr. Acquaviva (DI XIV 564, 4).

[24] *Ibid.;* as also *de erroribus* 34; Synod of Diamper, Session III, decr. 9.

[25] Cf. Gen. 11, 31; 15, 7.

[26] Cf. DI XIV 564; *De erroribus* 32; Synod of Diamper, Session III, decr. 14.

[27] Mar Abraham was in Rome in the beginning of 1565, perhaps even at the end of 1564 (cf. DI XIV 563). See also the third Council of Goa (1585), Session III, decr. 1.

[28] It is Fr. Ros who speaks.

Chaldean in the handwriting of the said Archbishop the contrary of what the faith teaches, namely, the Son of God took the human person. And when I showed it to the said Archbishop he laughed, and then a caçanar cancelled those words. And where in Latin it is said "I abjure" and "I give up all the heresies," in the said profession it is in the future, namely "I will give up" and "I will abjure all the heresies"; and so is written also in the translations of the said profession made in the Serra.

7°. In the Daily Office they call their Patriarch "universal pastor,"[29] though he is a heretic and schismatic. And the same Archbishop of Angamaly, in a letter he wrote to the said Patriarch, calls him "Father of our Fathers" and "pastor of our pastors" and "the sun of the Catholics." And seeing this, we requested him many times to replace it with the name of the Pope, but till now he has never wanted to do so.

8°. In the said letter the Archbishop of Angamaly requested two patriarchs,[30] to whom he wrote asking them to send promptly a prelate to this Christianity of St. Thomas, because he was already old and those adversaries, namely, we of the Roman Church, are like a sledgehammer poised over it and over the heads of these Christians. And when a pastor for this Christianity is sent, he must bear patent letters stating to this effect: "I, N., by the grace of God and of the Holy Church of Rome, Mother of all Churches, Patriarch of such a place, am sending N. as Bishop of the Christians of St. Thomas." And after this he concluded the letter, "to those who understand well, a few words are enough to understand much."[31]

9°. The said Archbishop has taught the people prohibiting them to meditate on the passion of the Saviour, saying that it would despise and insult Christ Our Lord.[32]

10°. In the letters which the said Archbishop wrote to the heretical Patriarch of Babylon, he says that in Goa he translated into Latin from Chaldean a treatise on the Incarnation written by a Nestorian, called

---

[29] A title attributed by the Latins to the pope alone. Cf. the Synod of Diamper, Session III, decr. 8: « sendo o apelido, e titulo devido somente ao Santissimo Padre Pontifice Romano, successor do principe dos apostolos São Pedro, e vigayro de Christo na terra [....] ».

[30] At this time there were two lines of patriarchs in Babylon, one united with the Church of Rome and the other not. At the head of the first was Simon Denha (1581-1600?) and at that of the second Elias VIII (1591-1617). See Podipara 56.

[31] A well known proverb. Cf. XV 231 note 5; as also Wicki, *Das Sprichwort* 246-247.

[32] Cf. the Synod of Diamper, Session III, decr. 5.

Joan Caldeu[33]; and he says that he showed the Latin version to the doctors who had assembled in the Synod of Goa,[34] and that they all read it and liked it much and praised God. That is false, and is to make the Catholics heretics; because in Goa I read the entire treatise in Chaldean. And I saw the heresies that were in it, namely, that the Incarnation is common to the three Persons, that all became incarnate, and that Christ Our Lord is not God by nature but by grace, in the same way as is written about the just, *Ego dixi: dii estis et filii Excelsi omnes,*[35] and also other most wicked things against Christ. Leaving these heresies out, I translated that treatise in the Catholic sense, without saying any thing to the Archbishop, lest he should hide the other books from me. And having translated it thus, I showed it to some persons. Afterwards I showed it to Mar Abraham, how such and such heresies were in that book, and he cancelled them at once out of fear. After all this, he wrote to the Patriarch maligning us that we praise the blasphemies which were contained in that book, without saying that he had been admonished that they were heresies against the Catholic faith. I do keep with me that letter.[36]

11°. The same Archbishop asked me once, whether it could be affirmed that the union of Incarnation was union of love and will. In saying this, before I answered him, he turned pale, because the question was Nestorian.

12°. The said Archbishop and his priests have a book, which they use to cast out devils and to cure diseases, in which there are many superstitions and unknown names, even of demons, and certain words to charm entangled women with sacred words [*mantras*].[37]

13°. They have many other superstitions and pseudo-miracles, and a letter against the Roman Church, which, they say, fell form heaven.[38] In it is written that the members of the Roman Church are apostates who have abandoned the faith. Hearing this the people believe it all to be true. Their caçanars narrate in their sermons fabulous stories, temerities and even heresies, etc. [530v]

---

[33] Cf. *supra* note 19.

[34] The third Provincial Council of Goa (1585), in which Mar Abraham participated. Cf. DI XIV 16, 103, 672.

[35] Ps. 81, 6.

[36] Now lost.

[37] The book is entitled *Paresman* or *Medicina persica.* Cf. *De erroribus* 33; the Synod of Diamper, session III, decr. 14. Following the Synod of Diamper some 21 of these books were burnt. Cf. Wicki, *Synode* 198.

[38] Cf. the Synod of Diamper, Session III, decr. 14: « Item a carta que chamão *De domingo,* fingem deceo de ceo, na qual são acusados […] ».

14°. With regard to this Bishop in particular; first of all the way he lives is a scandal to this Christianity and even to the heathens:-

† Many times he has given Communion to many people without confession, and for that he has been receiving money.

† We saw him absolving a dead person at Maladurte[39] and we told him that it was not possible, nevertheless he gave sacramental absolution.

† He administers all the sacraments simoniacally, receiving money.

† He does not bless the oils, nor has he the form for it; everyone uses oil in the [administration of] baptism, but we do not know if it is blessed by the Bishop.

† He takes the *são tomés*[40] placed over the chalices or altar stones he blesses.

† He uses old chrism, as may be available, but does not administer the sacrament of the Chrism [Confirmation], while that of Extreme Unction only rarely.

† He does not keep the feasts of the Apostles, although he and all others had accepted them.[41]

† He does not implement any provision of the Synod which he had accepted.

† He persecutes the ministers of the Roman Church.

† Up to now he has not handed over the books, as he had promised, for correcting the errors of Nestorius.

† He does not put the priests under obligation to recite the Divine Office, and as a result they recite it rarely. They say Mass when a stipend is given to them.

† He is ill-affected towards the Roman Church. He does not want to ordain those of his own people who learn Latin and the Roman customs, not even the Syrians who study with the Fathers of the Roman Church.

† He helps and favours the non-Christians against the Fathers of the Roman Church and those Christians who follow their doctrine.

† He does not have the form for Holy Orders,[42] and being admonished by our Father who knows the language[43] he re-ordained many priests

---

[39] Mulanthuruthy (Thevarmannil, *Mar Abraham* 194).

[40] A unit of money. Cf. doc. 123, note 13.

[41] See the *Constituciones do arcebispado de Goa,* Tit. XII: *Das festas do anno,* where a list of the feasts to be observed in that diocese is given. The feasts of the apostles figure prominently in this list (cf. Silva Rego, *Documentação* X 572-574).

[42] Cf. DI XIV 104-105, 454.

[43] Francisco Ros.

who had been saying Mass and hearing confessions. He said clearly before the Fathers that he used to pour only water in the chalice when giving the Holy Orders, not observing or wanting to observe what is ordered in the Pontifical translated by Ours into Syriac.[44]

† He confers Holy Orders on many who do not have the learning or qualities for it, contrary to his promise and the injunction the Council of Goa gave him.[45]

† He wrote letters to the Patriarch of Babylon, insistently requesting him to send a prelate, as was said above.

† In the collects he never mentions the name of the Pope, but puts the name of the Patriarch and he names as saints the companions of Nestorius.

† He does not care about the doctrine and the life of the Christians, nor to baptize babies soon after their birth; hence it happens that there are many unbaptized adults and elderly people, and they receive the other sacraments. There are many who want to be married, but are not married. The Christians die without confession, etc.

† In the Lent he does not care who confesses and who does not; and there are many who do not confess and no one is there to encourage them to do it. He does not give Communion unless they put money into his hand; so too do his caçanars like him.

† There are many places that have been abandoned without priests.[46] He threatens the caçanars who study with the Fathers of the Latin Church, who know the language and instruct them.

† There is no excuse in saying that this Christianity exists among the heathens, because he can easily govern his own people according to the ecclesiastical laws without anyone preventing him form doing so.

† He says Mass rarely, nor does he arrange to hear it, nor does he preach to the people.

† Sometimes he has been heard saying a shortened and mutilated Mass beginning with the Credo.

† Some of his caçanars preach the errors of Nestorius in order to please him. And his archdeacon[47] some years ago preached in this church that there is no purgatory, etc., and many ridiculous things about the infancy of the Saviour.[48]

---

[44] Translated by Ros.

[45] The third Provincial Council of Goa, Session III, decr. 3.

[46] Cf. DI XIV 454, 4.

[47] George of the Cross.

[48] Cf. the Synod of Diamper, Session III, decr. 14.

† These Armenians[49] have so entangled these Christians as to suppose that without paying money nothing spiritual will benefit them.

† A few days ago this Prelate was passing across a hill country where he found a rich Christian who was keeping a young pagan girl as his wife. He sent for him and imposed on him the penalty of a sum of money without obliging him to separate from her. This Christian requested him to allow him to continue as before and keep the pagan woman. The Archbishop told him that, if he wanted to do so, he would have to pay an amount of money. He pocketed it and was quite satisfied, to the great scandal of the Christians.

15°. For the last sixteen years we have been carrying on working with this Prelate.[50] All this while we have been reminding him of what is needed for his salvation and for the care of his sheep, often suggesting particular items. He never wanted to put them into practice, nor did he let us come to an understanding with the archdeacon for the reform of this people. Although in the past he got along and collaborated with us, promising to correct himself; it was simply for the purpose of getting certain things form His Highness[51] and His Holiness[52] through us – and also with the hope that the Christians would never take a liking to us and that we would never learn his language[53] and get to know his errors.

16°. However, after his return from the Council, as he saw us build and organize the seminary and learn Malayalam and Chaldean, and teach the caçanars, he changed his mind and turned into an enemy of the Roman Church. He would by no means give up his errors in which he keeps this people ensnared, requiring nothing more of them than that each one live as he pleases, content with the name of St. Thomas Christian, adhere to him and pay him cash. The ground principle with which he deceives them is that he has the law of St. Thomas while we that of St. Peter[54]; and that it would be a great sin and dishonour for the Christians to abandon their ancient law of St. Thomas to accept another new law which the Portuguese want to impose on them. For this he tells fables and lies, for example, that when he attended the Council of Goa, the prelates promised him much money etc. to have him take to the law of St. Peter, etc.

---

[49] Read *Caldeos*.

[50] Since 1577 (DI X 10*-14*).

[51] The King of Portugal (cf. doc. 152, 4).

[52] Pope Gregory XIII. Cf. DI XI 829-831.

[53] Syriac.

[54] Cf. *De erroribus* 34; the Synod of Diamper, Session III, decr. 7.

17°. Now that he sees that his errors are known, and that the greater part of the Christians are following the doctrine of the Roman Church, he is creating divisions among the people against the ministers of the Catholic Church. He is also trying to forge new friendships with the other Religious of the Roman Church,[55] who do not understand his language and his mischiefs. And together with them, who are simple, he wants to justify and revive another schism in the Serra. And they promise him favours, although he is a schismatic and an enemy of the Roman Church. By this he seeks to stick on to his errors and schisms and to justify his cause, fearing to be caught and imprisoned.

18°. This is the state of the Christians of the Serra and Malabar and their Prelate. Hence one clearly sees the necessity it has for a diligent Catholic prelate and for the remedy by which this one is punished before some greater evil creeps in and the wolves enter,[56] etc.

On the 30th of December [15]94.

Title [532v:] Information on the Bishop of Angamale and the Christianity of the Serra called Christians of St. Thomas.[57]

Translator's Note on the Date

This report, which is very critical of Mar Abraham, was written in the context of unfriendly relations between Mar Abraham and the Jesuits of Vaipicotta. As the documents so far published show, these mutual relations were at the lowest ebb by the end of 1593, but they began to improve suddenly in the spring of 1594 and were very good by the end of that year. Therefore, I think Fr Ros must have written this report in Spanish by the end of 1593 or early in 1594 and sent it to the Jesuit Provincial at Goa. The Provincial sent a copy of the original Spanish text and a Portuguese translation to Rome along with the annual letter of 1594. The ARSI has those copies: the Spanish text is dated 30th September 1594, the Portuguese text 30th December 1594. Probably these dates were noted when copies were made at Goa.

Let me explain: After Mar Abraham returned from the Goan Council of 1585, Fr Ros writes that the Metropolitan was not interested in introducing in his Church the reforms decreed by the Goan Council. He was not making the Syriac books available to Father Ros for doctrinal scrutiny and correction. He was refusing to ordain the seminarians formed by the Jesuits

---

[55] The Franciscans and Dominicans. Cf. DI XIV 907 ss.; *supra*, docs. 86, 9; 93, 4; 94, 1.

[56] Cf. Acts 20, 29; Jn. 10, 12.

[57] This report contrasts sharply with the letter of Mar Abraham to Fr. Acquaviva (doc. 152), which shows him to be a man united with the Church of Rome, interested in the good of his flock and appreciative of the work of the Jesuits.

at Vaipicotta. He was trying to promote his own interests through other Religious, especially the Franciscans of Cranganore. Towards the end of 1593 several other Jesuits including Fr Jerome Xavier, Fr Abraham de Georgiis, and Fr Manuel Carvalho, wrote bitterly against Mar Abraham suggesting that the Inquisition should prosecute him (see *Documenta Indica*, XI, pp. 246-247, 560-566, 590-592, 596-597). The main accusations contained in the present document can be seen in summary form also in the letter of Fr Abraham de Georgiis.

However, by the spring of 1594 the relations between the Jesuits and Mar Abraham improved, as we read in the annual report of 1594. Mar Abraham promised to ordain the seminarians, and handed over some Syriac books to Fr Ros for correction. Archdeacon George of the Cross began taking Syriac lessons from Fr Ros; he even prepared a sermon under the guidance of Fr Ros and preached it on the feast of the Assumption (see *ibid.* pp. 740-743). The fourth Provincial Congregation of the Jesuits held at Goa on 22-29 October 1594 requested the Jesuit General to propose Archdeacon George to the Pope as a worthy candidate to be appointed as successor to Mar Abraham (see *ibid.* pp. 650-652). On 19 December 1594 Mar Abraham wrote a letter in Spanish to the Jesuit General requesting him to recommend Archdeacon George to the Holy See and have him appointed as his successor, and expressing appreciation for the good works of the Jesuits among his Christian faithful (*ibid.* pp. 989-991). In such a tempo of improved relations it is unlikely that Fr Ros would criticize Mar Abraham so severely as he does in our document.

In a letter to the Jesuit General dated December 24, 1593 Fr Ros mentions an "Information on the Serra and its Nestorian Archbishop" taken to Rome by Fr Monclaro early in 1589 but not given to Father General (*ibid.* p. 596). The present Information probably was an updated text of that earlier information of 1589. Since it was forwarded by the Provincial only at the end of 1594, it had no influence on the issuance of the Apostolic letter dated 27 January 1595, which authorized the Archbishop of Goa to proceed against Mar Abraham. On the other hand, Fr Abraham de Georgiis, a young Maronite Jesuit who had come to Vaipicotta in 1592 and who must have discussed with Father Ros the Syriac texts of the Serra, wrote a letter in 1593 containing a short list of accusations against Mar Abraham; this letter, along with the aforementioned letters of the other Jesuits suggesting to move the Goan Inquisition against Mar Abrham might have influenced the Jesuit curia to ask the Holy See to issue the said Apostolic letter.

The present Information, probably written in 1593, or at the latest early in 1594, most likely bore no date in the Spanish original, as it was not a letter, and the dates were added only when copies and a Portuguese translation were made at Goa. In any case, along with his previous *De Errorbus Nestorianorum* this tract of Ros did directly influence the acts of the Synod of Diamper, especially its third session, as Fr Wicki, the editor of the Portuguese original, has shown with several cross references in the foot notes.

Jacob Kollaparambil

Appendix III

A REPORT ON THE SYNOD OF DIAMPER (1599)

by Giovanni Maria Campori, S.J.

Five months after the conclusion of the Synod of Diamper, on 28 November 1599, the following letter was written by Giovanni Maria Campori, S.J. (1574-1621), a recent addition to the Jesuit community of Vaipicotta. An eyewitness of the synod, the young Italian Jesuit is in admiration of the accomplishment of Archbishop Menezes, whom he sees as the saviour of the Christians of the Serra (Malabar) from the heresy of Nestorianism. "The Fathers of our Society moved by the love for the salvation of neighbours, and devoured by untiring zeal, worked in collaboration with the Archbishop, or better as protagonists, taking him to places and bringing him back, always ready with advice and the spirit of enterprise." This "letter of edification" addressed to the Jesuits, was probably written originally in Italian. A Latin translation made by Antoin Possevin, S.J., has been edited by Vincenzo Poggi, S.J., for the present volume with the following introduction and summary. In his article Father Poggi has translated the entire text into Italian.

Lettera di Giovanni Maria Campori S.I., da Vaipicotta il 28 novembre 1599. Non è escluso che il Campori abbia scritto originariamente in italiano e che da qualche parte si conservi tale redazione della lettera. Non l'ho trovata. Ne do la redazione, latina probabilmente fatta da Antonio Possevino S.I., buon latinista, pubblicata nel suo *Apparatus Sacer ad Scriptores veteris et novi Testamenti etc.,* Tribus Tomis distinctus, Venetiis MDCVI, Tomus primus, 392-394. La suddivisione del testo in 16 paragrafi numerati è mia. (Vincenzo Poggi S.J.).

SOMMARIO

Premessa del Possevino. – 1. Sabato che precede la Domenica di Passione: ordinazione di numerosi nuovi sacerdoti. – 2. Solenne liturgia della Settimana Santa. 3. Commozione dei fedeli. – 4. L'Arcidiacono è persuaso dall'Arcivescovo di Goa. – 5. L'arcivescovo lo abbraccia e gli dona una croce pettorale preziosa. – 6. Indizione e celebrazione del sinodo di Diamper. – 7. Nomina di parroci per le varie chiese. 8) Visita pastorale. – 9. Processioni alla maniera indiana. – 10. Amministrazione del sacramento della confermazione. – 11. Censura dei libri ereticali. – 12. Catechismo dei bambini. – 13. Le singole chiese sono fornite di sacra suppellettile. – 14. Cambio d'atmosfera e d'abitudini. – 15. Che parte esercitano i gesuiti nel sinodo. – Colofone.

Diamperiense Concilium Provinciale habitum anno 1599 ab Archiepiscopo Goensi in Oppido Diamper, quod est in Asia, prope Civitatem, quae dicitur S. Thomae, non tam statuit, quam ad effectum perduxit, quae ad Catholicam religionem, atque ad disciplinam omnem Ecclesiasticam restituendam pertinent. Quod ut planius intelligatur, expedit, ut Epistolae partem ad nostros missam, ab eo qui toti rei interfuit, huc adtexam. Sic autem scribit.

[1.] Archidiaconus paullatim ab Archiepiscopo recipit, Patriarchae nomen delendum negat, multa alia submurmurat redolentia empietatem. Paucis post diebus archiepiscopus sollemnem Ordinum celebrationem indicit. Archidiaconus autem maximum iurisdictionis argumentum impedire laborat, timorem incutit promovendis eorumque parentibus, sed frustra. Sabbatho ante dominicam Passionis plurimos ad sacros ordines promovet, admirantibus laudantibusque omnibus universis Ecclesiae Romanae sacras ceremonias.

[2.] His absolutis, confert se *Carturtem*, ut ibi Hebdomadae Sanctioris sacramenta peragat. Palmarum ramos solemni apparatu benedicit; quinta feria in Coena Domini S. Chrisma conficit; pedes duodecim Sacerdotum abluit lachrymis et aqua; Sanctissimum Christi Corpus de more sepulturae mandat.

[3.] Virtutem Spiritus Sancti addit sacris ceremoniis, maxima enim hominum frequentia tam divinos intuens ritus Divinitus movetur; emollescunt lapides, petrae scinduntur, fluunt lachrymae, talia siccis oculis contemplari unusquisque sacrilegium ducit; mixtis vocibus lachrymis omnes proclamant: Pastor hic noster est, nos oves eius, hunc omnes recipimus, huius vocem audire volumus. Babyloniae mercenarii, lupi rapaces abeant in malam crucem, discedant a nobis Operarii iniquitatis, quoniam Dominus magnificavit facere nobiscum; Romanae Ecclesiae filii sumus; haec omnium Ecclesiarum caput esse atque magistram confitemur. Talia iam corde credentibus, ore oculisque confessio fiebat a salutem. Quae tunc essent archiepiscopi gaudia, qui animi sensus, lachrymarum impetus laetificantes Civitatem Dei declarabant.

[4.] Maximo igitur fructu redit archiepiscopus eo consilio ut, si nolit obedire Archidiaconus, hunc deponat, alterum constituat; itaque ad illum litteras mittit, admonens, ut resipiscat, et intra sex dies quibusdam conditionibus acceptis Vaipicottam se conferat; sin minus, anathemate, utpote pertinacem haereticum sciat se publice faciendum esse. Ipse metu perculsus respondit conditiones oblatas se accipere eique in omnibus parere paratum esse. Interim Patrem Franciscum Roz rogat per litteras ut eo se conferat, ubi ipse statutam diem expectabat. Pater paterno affectu admonet, hortatur, obsecrat, finem imponat scandalis, misereatur animae suae, in quot pericula se conjiciat, contempletur, Antistitis clementiam, et facilitatem agnoscat, non abutatur patientia Dei ad poenitentiam ipsum vocantis; ne ponat ipse spem suam brachium carnis, sciat Reges omnes infideles, quorum auxilio defectionem aggressus erat, ei futuros parum fideles. Victus ille tandem, sive verbis Patris, sive metu, accedit ad Archiepiscopum;

[5.] pius Pater filium prodigum amplectitur, largitur veniam, Crucem pretiosissimam in amoris signum donat, maiora promittit si persistet in bono.

[6.] Sequenti die in Ecclesia indicit Concilium Provinciale ad haereses extirpandas, mores corrigendos, superstitiones evellendas, omnia demum ad Divinum cultum spectantia componenda. Convocantur per litteras omnes Ecclesiastici, ex omnibus oppidis praecipui viri quattuor statuta die. Maxima omnium laetitia, summoque omnium consensu celebratum est concilium in oppido Diamper, in quo haereses omnes, earumque auctores, sectatoresque praecipue, Babyloniae Patriarcham, anathematizarunt, Romanum autem Pontificem Christi Vicarium, et Ecclesiae caput agnoverunt, eique obedientiam promiserunt: nullumque Episcopum, nisi a Romana Sede destinatum recepturos se Sacramento obstrinxerunt.

[7.] Sub finem singulis Ecclesiis Parochi deputati sunt, quod quidem in hac Dioecesi novum fuit. Ad eorum sustentationem mille aureos e suis redditibus quotannis ipse Archiepiscopus assignavit. Insumpsit in hac visitatione pius Pastor fere sex et decem millia, sed fructu millesimo.

[8.] Peracta Synodo, Archiepiscopus totam Dioecesim visitare aggreditur, ut executioni mandentur, quae legitime decreta fuerant in Concilio. Statim igitur proficiscitur Angamale (Metropolis est Dioeceseos et Episcopi Sedes); excipitur ab omnibus maximo triumpho. Ipsum solum stratum candidis linteaminibus, floribus, frondibus respersum.

[9.] Praeibant triginta fere viri ex nobilioribus laeto tripudii genere, subsequebantur alii ludentes armis maxima celeritate, plaudebat immensa hominum multitudo manibus, vocibus, tympanis, tubarum sono, magnis acclamationibus aerem complebant, nec deerant bellica instrumenta, quae ex tanti viri adventu acceptam laetitiam ceteris testabantur.

[10.] Hic quatuor in ecclesiis sacro chrismate maximum hominum numerum confirmat; Sacerdotes clericique, qui Concilio non interfuerunt, publice haereses, et Patriarcham abiurant, Romano Pontifici obedientiam spondent, sicut in Concilio sancitum fuerat.

[11.] Interim Pater Franciscus Roz, et ego, libris examinandis incumbimus, delemus, scindimus, integra volumina in ignem coniicimus: quanta animi voluptate explicare non possum. Duodecim pene dies in hoc labore consumpsimus; volumina enim omnia tam defuncti Episcopi, quam aliorum sacerdotum, fidei Catholicae puritati aut flammis restituimus. Miraculo tribuebant omnes hoc opus; adeo enim prius libris suis addicti erant, ut nobis nec aperiri paterentur. Iam vero pro libito eos abradere, detruncare, integrosque comburere non moleste ferebant.

[12.] Prosecutus est Archiepiscopus visitationem maxima, ut ipse testatur, animi suavitate. Ubique excipiebatur ut pastor bonus, ipseque boni pastoris officium exsequebatur; Confirmabat, pueros baptizabat, uxoratis sacerdotibus expellebat socias; pueris puellisque indutus Pontificiis vestimentis Docrinam Christianam per alumnos nostri Seminarij maximo fructu tradebat; contionabatur quotidie, perpetuas eleemosinas pauperibus erogabat, accurrebant reges singuli Malabarum, ut viderent talem virum, tam humiliter, benigneque oviculas suas tractantem.

[13.] Ipse res omnes ad Ecclesiae bonum spectantes statuebat, superpellicea, capsulamque Chrismatis, aram consecratam, vestes ad faciendum Sacrum necessarias in singulis ecclesiis collocabat. Baptizandi, inungendi infirmos, nuptias celebrandi modum, a Patre Francisco Roz e latina in syriacam linguam conversum, una cum doctrina Christiana lingua Malabarica conscripta, singulis Parochis tribuebat. Libros ubique examinabamus; expurgatis eis maxima diligentia, iam huius Ecclesiae faciem alteram diceres.

[14.] Ubique enim in Ecclesiis Summi Pontificis nomem resonat; Augustini, Hieronymi, Ambrosii, aliorumque Sanctorum, quos Catholica veneratur Ecclesia, nomina sanctissima exaudiuntur. Obmutuit Nestorij, aliorumque haereticorum impudentissimum os; Sacramentorum usus de more Ecclesiae Romanae frequentior, maximamque denique in omnibus ager Dominicus ubertatem promittit in segete.

[15.] Haec in genere; nam minutissima quaeque scribere esset immensum. Patres Societatis nostrae, proximorum salutis amore, indefessum laborem devorabant ducebant Archiepiscopum, reducebantque, in omnibus consilij, studij, laboris participes effecti (ut melius dicam) Auctores. Agnoscit ipse Archiepiscopus nostrorum operam, praedicat diligentiam, laudat Societatis institutum.

Haec Joan. Maria Camporeus Societatis nostrae ex Collegio eiusdem Societatis, S. Crucis, Vaipicottae in India Orientali 28. Novembris, ann. 1599. qui etiam adiecit quibus quisque Nestorianorum liber scatebat erroribus, quae quidem omnia apud nos extant ab eodem scripta.

Appendix IV

REPORT ON THE SERRA (1603/1604) BY BISHOP FRANCISCO ROS, S.J.

British Library MS Add. 9853, ff. 86-99 (525-538)*

MS Add. 9853 is one of the codices of the manuscripts presented to the British Library in 1835 by William Marsden, who had been an employee of the East India Company in Sumatra. This MS originally belonged to the Professed House of the Society of Jesus at Goa. How it came into the possession of Marsden is a matter of conjecture. Fr. H. Hosten, S.J. thinks that after the suppression of the Society of Jesus it was taken possession of by Pombal and after his death it was auctioned off and Marsden acquired it. (See John Correia-Afonso, S.J., *The Jesuit Letters and Indian History 1542-1773,* Oxford University Press, Bombay, 1969[2], p. 135).

This document originally formed part of a series of manuscript folios numbered in ink as 525-532, 591-596. Folios 591-596 were later renumbered as 533-538, presumably when the intervening 58 folios were set apart for a different document. Now in the British Library volume MS Add. 9853 these folios are numbered in pencil as 86-99. We follow this numbering in the present edition.

About a century ago doing research for his book *India and the Apostle Thomas,* Bishop Adolph Medlycott discovered this document in the British Library among the MSS on the Jesuit missions. He obtained an English translation of it made by, or by order of, Mr. W. Rees Philipps, and included several passages from it in his article on "Saint Thomas Christians" in *The Catholic Encyclopedia, XIV* (1913) 678-688. Fr. H. Hosten, S.J. made his own translation of the whole document (see *Kerala Society Papers* (1930) pp. 189-190, note 22; p. 193, note 39), and published some extracts in his article "Thomas Cana and His Copper Plate Grant," *Indian Antiquary* 56 (1927) 121ss, etc. However, to my knowledge, neither Hosten nor any one else has published this very informative document in its entirety either in the original Portuguese or in English translation. Two partial editions may be found in Gregorio Magno Antão, *De Synodi Diamperitani Natura atque Decretis,* (Doctoral dissertation in the Faculty of Canon Law, Pontifical Gregorian University, Rome), Goa, 1952, Documentum XX, pp. 174-177 (marked #-# in our edition); and in original Portuguese and in English translation in Jacob Kollaparambil, *Historical Sources on the Knanites,* Kottayam, 1986, Document VIII, pp. 13-20 (marked *-* in our edition).

---

* The Portuguese text is edited by Vincenzo Poggi, S.J., and Jacob Kollaparambil; it is introduced and translated into English by Jacob Kollaparambil.

The author is not named in the document, but from internal evidence Bishop Ros can be identified as the author. The major part of the text is written by one amanuensis, seemingly Fr. John M. Campori, S.J., who was Bishop Ros's secretary. Some small portions in the text are written in three other hands. A marginal note on f. 88^{v} and the only paragraph on the last f. 99^{v} are definitely in the typical handwriting of Bishop Ros.

There are only very few paragraph divisions in the original MS. For easy perusal we have divided the text into twenty-six paragraphs and given them numbers topic-wise. For the same purpose a few subheadings have been added [in square brackets] to the Portuguese text by Poggi, while the following summary has been made by Jacob Kollaparambil. The translation has been reviewed and edited by the editor of the volume George Nedungatt, S.J., in dialogue with the translator.

EDITOR'S NOTE

The document is dated 1604. This need not mean that all of it was composed in that year. In fact internal evidence would seem to point to certain portions bearing the marks of an earlier date. This is probably true of the short but laudatory account of the Synod of Diamper, about which in December 1603 Ros himself had written to the Jesuit General with reservation, censuring Menezes and calling it "no synod at all." Are these "contradictions" due to Ros's "eccentric" character, as Poggi asks himself?. A more benign interpretation could be that perhaps the account about the Synod of Diamper in the present document (n. 25) is to be dated earlier than that revised account of December 1603. It is possible that Bishop Ros availed himself of materials from several files of different dates to put together the present document during his busy work schedule as a diocesan bishop, with the help of Giovanni M. Campori, S.J., his secretary. This benign hypothesis of a dossier seems to fit well particularly the very long last section of the document about miracles (n. 26), which begins abruptly at the end of the proportionately brief but all too positive account of the Synod of Diamper (n. 25). In fact the statement "in this year of 1603 the Nairs set fire to the said church of Mattam" (n. 26 c) attests that that section on miracles was written in 1603. The same dating may apply also to the paragraph on the Synod of Diamper (n. 25). In any case, though the long section about miracles (n. 26) does not have the same importance as the earlier ones for the present volume, we have included it for the sake of completeness rather than for its value for illustrating the historical background of the Synod of Diamper.

SUMMARY

1. The Apostle St Thomas preached the gospel in Socotra, India, China and Great China; he died at Maliapur according to the Chaldean Breviary, a lithic inscription in Maliapur and traditions. — 2. Because of wars and famine the Christians left Maliapur; those who went to Bepar and Todamala became heathens. — 3. Those who went to Malavar fared better. — 4. Prelates came from Babylon to Socotra, India and China, but Hendu was the

principal See. — 5. The church architecture in Malavar; the church of Maliapur is the most ancient. — 6. The arrival of Thome Cananeo [= Thomas of Kynai] and the church of Cranganor, but already there was a church at Magoderpatanam. — 7. The text of the Copper Plates Grant by Xeram Perumal to Thome Cananeo. — 8. The Christians of Magoderpatanam later built the church at Parur. — 9. Two groups among the St Thomas Christians: the descendants of those converted by Apostle St Thomas and the descendants of Thome Cananeo. They have separate churches.

10. The progress of Cranganor through the Chaldean connection: Thome Cananeo is commemorated as a saint; three churches at Cranganore. — 11. The Chaldean Bishops in Malavar after the arrival of the Portuguese in India: Mar Johanan, Thomas, Jaballaha, Jacob, Denha, Joseph, Elia and Abraham; their dress and the miracles wrought by them. — 12. Mar Sapor and Mar Aprot miraculously built a church at Quilon. Sapor and Aprot were venerated as saints, but Dom Menezes ordered the feast of SS. Gervasis and Protasis to be celebrated instead. — 13. The St Thomas Christians were first known as *Tarijanes* and then *Nasarani*. — 14. How the king of Biliarte (Villarvattam) became the protector of the St Thomas Christians. Later the King of Cochin had that position. — 15. Cranganore was the principal centre of the St Thomas Christians, but due to vexations by the Portuguese they left it. — 16. Why Xeram Perumal did not give a kingdom to the St Thomas Christians — 17. The Jews in India: Castillians since AD 493; the black Jews from the time of Solomon. — 18. The nature and qualities of the St Thomas Christians. — 19. Their ecclesiastical language is Syriac; their Bible is defective, and books are infected with Nestorian errors. — 20. The priests, ministers and their wives.

21. The Sacraments and Worship: (a) Baptism, (b) Confirmation, (c) Eucharist, (d) Confession, (e) Extreme Unction, (f) Holy Orders, (g) Marriage. — 22. Their liturgy and worship: (a) Syriac translation of the Latin Rituale for all sacraments except the Mass, (b) the Liturgy of the Hours (c) veneration of the Cross and the Bible, (d) feast of Fridays between the Christmas and the Lent, (e) Holy Water, (f) Rituals for the Dead, (g) Procession around the fire at the Christmas night, (h) practices while fasting, (i) feasts of St George, Holy Cross and St Cyriac, (j) sexual abstinence, (k) clerical habit and respect for the churches, (l) Agape, (m) the respect of non-Christians for the churches, (n) sign of the Cross from the right shoulder to the left, and respect for the priests.

23. The Franciscans conducted a seminary at Cranganore since 1541. — 24. The Jesuits started a seminary at the Vaipicotta; Mar Abraham attended the Council of Goa in 1585, but was reluctant to put its decrees into practice.

25. **The Synod of Diamper**. Dom Menezes conducted the Synod of Diamper. The Jesuits collaborated with him.

26. Miracles related to the churches of: (a) Palur, (b) Enamaque, (c) Mattam, (d) Mattancher, (e) Xaregate, (f) Balianate, (g) Mangate, (h) Paru, (i) Corlengate, (j) Molandurte, (k) Caramatete, (l) Colingere, (m) Muttam, (n) Angamale, (o) Molandurte again.

|| [86r]# Relação sobre a Serra feito em 160

[S. THOME]

[1.] O Apóstolo S. Thome segundo o que achamos escripto nos Libros Caldeos se vendeo assy mesmo a hum senhor embaixador do Rey de Bisnaga para assy vir a India como veo a pregar o santo Evangelho como pregou baptizando inumeravel gente em Cambaya e terras do Mogor, Socotera, Malavar e Bisnaga, chegando atee a China e a grande China, segundo o breviário Caldeo lé do dito Apóstolo. Perseverando atee oie o rastro do Apostolo nas mais destas terras, cuia charidade se estendeo atee os Cafres, aos quaes tambem pregou como lé o mesmo breviario. Na pedra escrita de letras antigas que oie está em Maliapur, leem os Christãos de S. Thome, que estão versados na declaração daquellas letras, que o santo Apostolo converteo a fee tres Reis principaes. O de Bisnaga, chamado na sua língoa Xoren Perumal. E o rey do Pandi que chamão Pandi Perumal; e o Rey de todo Malavar chamado Xaram Perumal, com outros dous Reis de menos qualidade, e outros muitos povos, mas disem na dita pedra que morrera o santo aos vinte e hum de dezembro no anno trigessimo depois de promulgação do Evangelho. Do qual tempo em que a gentilidade começou a cair e da dita Era contão os que oie são gentios e tendo sua origem em Maliapur, se sahirão dali e vierão a morrar neste Malavar. De modo que depois da morte do santo perseverando seus discipulos muito tempo, a ley de Deus foi promulgada com gram glória e acrecentamento da Igreia.

[2.] *Mas depois socedendo guerra* e fome, os christãos de S. Tome, moradores em Maliapur se forão para diversas partes segundo a tradição, que têm estes Christãos de seus antepassados e muitos ficarão gentios como são os de Bepar, que se chamão Taridaical naiquemar, como elles mesmos confessão serem de casta Christãos, os que morão nas serras de Todomala, que se chamão Soder que quer dizer gente primeira e antiga; os quaes vivem como bestas sem ley e reverencião huma bufara, como referirão dous clerigos que mandamos a aquellas serras dous annos há, e o anno passado o Padre Jacome Finicio da Companhia de Jesu foy lá mesmo por sua muita charidade e tratou com elles e achando-os mui pouco capazes e em lugares inacessiveis, donde não poderião ser cultivados, os deixou e se tornou, dandolhes boas esperanças. O mesmo aconte-

[86r]

Report on the Serra written in 1604.

[1.] The Apostle St Thomas, as we find written in the Chaldean books, was sold to a Lord Ambassador of the King of Bisnaga [Vijayanagar] to come to India. He came and preached the holy gospel and baptized numberless people in Cambaya and the lands of the Moghuls, Socotera, Malavar and Bisnaga, and reached as far as China and Great China, as we read in the Chaldean Breviary about the said Apostle. To this day in all these lands the remembrance of the Apostle is alive, whose charity extended even to the Cafres[1] to whom also he preached, as may be read in the same Breviary. On a stone with a writing in ancient letters, which now exists in Maliapur, the Christians of St Thomas who are versed in deciphering those letters, read that the Apostle converted to the faith three leading kings: the one of Bisnaga called in their language Xoren [Chola] Perumal, the King of Pandi whom they call Pandi Perumal, and the King of Malabar called Xeram [Cheraman] Perumal, with two other kings of lesser importance and many other people. They also say that it was on the said stone that the Saint died on the twenty-first of December of the thirtieth year after the promulgation of the gospel. From that time paganism began to lose ground, and from that era are to be reckoned those who are pagans today. Even the Christians who had their origin in Maliapur went away from there and came to live in this Malavar. Thus after the death of the Saint, his disciples persevered for a long time in the law of God, and it was promulgated with great glory and growth of the Church.

[2.] But afterwards since there were wars and famine, the Christians of St Thomas who lived in Maliapur were scattered to different places according to the tradition which these Christians hold from their ancestors. And many became heathens. Such are those of Bepar who are called Taridaical Naiquemar, as they themselves confess that they were of the Christian caste. So do also those who live in the forests of Todamala; these are called Soder, which means primitive and ancient people, and they live like beasts without law and venerate a female buffalo. This has been reported by two clerics whom we sent to those forests two years ago. And last year Fr Jacob Fenicio of the Society out of his great charity went there and conversed with them, but seeing that they are backward in intelligence and live in places inaccessible where they cannot be educated, he left them and returned giving them good hopes. The same lot

[1] "Cafres" mean heathens or pagans.

cerá aos de Tyrinancor que vivião como gentios, e sem baptismo. Mas quando veo o senhor Arcebispo de Goa aqui deu princípio ao baptismo delles, e põs ali vigairo; o qual baptizou a todos e recebeo, os que tinhão necessidade disso, e começou a confessálos: E deixando suas superstições vivem agora christammente.

[3.] Todavia os Cristãos, que se estenderão por estas partes de Cochim tiverão milhor ventura sobre todos os outros, espalhandose todos, desde Coulão atee Palur, terra do Samorym. Porque com a vesinhança depois dos Portugueses que vierão os aiudou Nosso Senhor e os acrecentou muito. E porque o Apostolo baptizou a gente de toda casta dos quais estes Christãos descendem; também || [86ᵛ] entre estes Christãos ha alguns da casta del Rey de Cochim, que chamão Covilmar, e outros bramenes, e outros Belalas gente honrada em Bisnaga.

[4.] Antes dos Portugueses virem a India estiverão muito tempo sem clerigos, nem Pontifices, postoque deste tempo que não se sabem quanto durou e depois forão visitados sempre de Arcebispos Armênios segundo lemos nestes livros Caldeos antigos, e não somente vinhão pera qua Prelados com titulo de Arcebispos, mas tambem de Babilõnia, erão mandados outros a Socotera e mais a China, todavia a principal cadeira era esta, que chamão em Caldeo, Hendu, id est Malavar donde se acharão ia tres bispos suffraganeos, ainda depois que os Portugueses vierão a India.

[5.] Os templos que antes da vinda dos Portugueses edificarão estes Christaõs erão na forma dos Gregos. A capella mor mui estreita com hum altarsinho arrimado na parede no meio para o Oriente. A mão esquerda estava um retrete com uma portinha para o Ponente e neste lugar baptisavão. Outro retrete tinhão da banda do Norte e quando não em riba do sobrado da Igreia. Em riba da capelinha mor tinhão hum lugar onde fazião as hostias no modo que fasem os Gregos resando quando as fasião, certo numero dos psalmos, por huma portinha que estava aberta no mesmo sobrado, que vinha a cahir no meio da capela mor, davão aquelle bolo descendo-o com muita solemnidade. Não usavão de casulas, tinhão hum veo, que cobria a porta da capela mor, o qual abrião e fechavão em certas horas quando disião missa (additur: que era tres ou quatro veses no anno). Nenhum leigo por nenhum caso podia entrar na Capela mor, nem leigo nenhum se atrevia a cuspir na Igreia. As antigas edificadas antes dos Portugueses virem a India são poucas, e deixando aparte a santa Igreia que o Apostolo edificou em Maliapur que he a primeira e mais antiga de todas; depois della não se podia tam facil saber qual seia a primeira e mais antiga que houve no Malavar.

happened to those of Tyrivancor, who live like heathens without baptism. But when the Lord Archbishop came here from Goa he started to give them baptism, and he appointed a vicar there who baptized everyone and received what was necessary for it, and began to hear their confession. And having abandoned their superstitions they now live like Christians.

[3.] The Christians who migrated into these parts of Cochin, however, had better fortune than all the others as they sprawled out all the way from Quilon to Palur in the land of the Samorym. For with the presence close by of the Portuguese, who came afterwards, Our Lord helped them and made them grow much. Since the Apostle baptized people of all castes, from whom these Christians are descended, [86v] among these Christians there are some who belong to the caste of the king of Cochin, whom they call Covilmar, and others Brahmins, and yet others Belalas, honourable people in Bisnaga.

[4.] Before the Portuguese came to India, they got on for a long time without clerics or Pontiffs. However, it is not known how long this period lasted. Afterwards they were visited by the Armenian Archbishops, as we read in these same ancient Chaldean books. And not only did Prelates come here with the title of Archbishops, but also others were sent from Babylon to Socotora and China. However, the principal see was this, which they call in Chaldean Hendu, that is, Malavar where there were three suffragan bishops even after the Portuguese came to India.

[5.] The temples which these Christians had built before the arrival of the Portuguese were in the style of the Greeks. The main chapel is rather narrow, with a small altar in the centre built on to the wall at the East end. On the left there is a closet with a small door to the West, and in this place they used to baptize. Besides they have another closet on the North side, or otherwise they have a place on the floor above the main chapel, where they make the hosts in the manner the Greeks make them, reciting a certain number of psalms while making them. Through an opening in the centre of the floor above the main chapel they would let down that bun with great solemnity. They have no chasuble. They have a veil which covers the door of the main chapel, which they open and close at certain times when they say Mass {which was three or four times a year}. No lay person for any reason could enter the main chapel, nor would any lay person dare to spit in the church. The ancient churches built before the Portuguese arrived in India are few. Leaving aside the holy church which the Apostle built in Maliapur, which is the first and most ancient of all, it is not easy to know which was the first and most ancient one here in Malavar.

[THOME CANANEO]

* [6.] E porque estes Christãos não têm Livros de historias antigas mais que tradições dos antigos, das quaes são muy tenases, pello que nos hemos de aiudar nisto das coronicas e conta de tempos que ha entre os gentios Malavares, e coniecturas graves, que achamos em diversos lugares destes Reynos. Consta o primeiro, que o derradeiro Emperador do Malavar chamado Xaram Perumal, foy o que deu em Cranganor chão para Igreia e povoação aos Christãos de S. Thome, e preeminências muy grandes, como consta por suas ollas cuio original de cobre foy levado a Portugal por meio dos religiosos de S. Francisco ficando aqui o treslado dellas. Este Perumal ha mil e duzentos e sincoenta e oito annos que morreo no primeiro de Março. As testemunhas que se acharão presentes no escrever da olla do dito Perumal, em que deu o dito chão de Cranganor, são os que agora são Regulos ou Reis em diversas terras do Malavar, e então quando se escreveo a olla, erão paijens do dito Perumal como consta pellas mesmas ollas. Donde se segue que passa de mil e dozentos annos a dedicação da Igreia de Cranganor || [87r] que foy fundada no mês de Abril do dito anno e se fundarão logo setenta e duas casas no dito chão.

A occasião foy como diz na mesma olla do Perumal que pousando o dito Rey da outra banda em hum Pagode grande, que estava em Parurpatanam, chão de fronte de Paliporto, quis o dito Rey hum dia ir a cassa, e foy da outra banda donde agora está o Cranganor, que tudo era mato e foy por elle chamado hum Armenio muy rico, que era vindo de Babylonia chamado Thome Cananeo: o qual deu boa somma de dinheiro ao dito Rey e lhe comprou aquelle mato todo, e fundou nelle a Igreia de S. Thome e o bazar. O chão que comprou, era de 264 couados de Elifante.* Porem antes da dita Igreia ia muitos annos antes ouve no dito lugar Patanam huma Igreia e povoação grande de Christãos, que se naõ sabem o quando se começou e ainda atee oie o lugar donde esteve a dita Igreia, se chama *Paliparamb* id est campo da Igreia, e logo alli perto há outro lugar que se chama, *Palimoc* id est canto da Igreia, e daqui se chama a Ilha que está de fronte, *Paliporto* id est outra banda de fora de fronte da Igreia. A qual ilha há dozentos e sesenta e sete annos que se descobrio por onde, consta que no dito lugar ouve Igreia, que da povoação de Christãos que alli ouve hé hum grande pagode, não se duvida por onde se chama, Magoder Patanam, id est grande cidade do grande pagode, e alli chegava o mar e surgião as embarcações antes de se descobrir a ilha de

[6.] These Christians have no books of ancient histories but only traditions of the ancients, to which they cling tenaciously. Hence we have to help ourselves with the chronicles and chronology obtaining among the Malavar heathens and with weighty conjectures which we come across in different parts of these kingdoms. Accordingly, it emerges first that the last emperor of Malavar, called Xeram Perumal, was the one who at Cranganor gave land for a church and a settlement to the Christians of St Thomas and very great privileges, as is seen from their ollas. The copper original of these ollas was taken to Portugal by the Religious of St Francis, while a copy of them remains here. That Perumal died on the first of March one thousand two hundred and fifty-eight years ago. The witnesses who were present at the writing of the Perumal's olla, by which he gave the said land of Cranganor, are those who now are kinglets or kings in different parts of Malavar. But when the olla was written they were pages of the Perumal, as is evident from the same ollas. Hence it follows that the dedication of the church of Cranganor took place more than one thousand two hundred years ago. [87r] It was founded in the month of April of the said year, and soon seventy-two houses were built on the said land.

The occasion as related in the olla of the Perumal was as follows. The said king was lodging on the other side in a big pagoda at Parurpatanam, a place over against Paliporto. The said king wished one day to go hunting. And he went to the other side, where Cranganor is now, the whole of which was then a shrubland. It happened that he called for a very rich Armenian named Thomas Cananeo, who had come from Babylon. He gave to the king a good sum of money and bought the whole of that shrubland and founded on it the church of St Thomas and the bazaar. The land which he bought measured 264 elephant cubits. However, already many years before that church was built there was in that place Patanam a church and a large village of the Christians. It is not known when it began. And even today the place where that church stood is called *Paliparamb,* that is, the land of the church. And close to it there is a place which is called *Palimoc,* that is, the corner of the church. And hence the island that lies in front of it is also called *Paliporto,* that is, on the other side in front of the church. This island surfaced 267 years ago[2]. Hence it is certain that there was a church in that place and that the Christian community there had a big pagoda. There is no doubt why it is called Magoderpatanam, that is, great city of great Pagode. The sea then reached there and the embarkations were from there before the island of

[2] 1604 A.D.- 267 = 1337: Vaipim era?

Paliporto. Por onde os Christãos de S. Thome em todas as ollas, que escrevem de contas poem a era de Magoder Patanan sem saber o princípio della, porque tem este lugar por hum dos mais antigos em que morarão Christãos de S. Thome.*

[7.] O treslado da olla, que deu o dito Xaram Perumal a Thome Cananeo, em que lhe concedeu o chão de Cranganor, diz fielmente assy. *Coquarangon seia prosperado* e tenha longa vida e viva cem mil annos, divino servo de Deus, forte, verdadeiro, iusto, cheo de boas obras, racionavel, poderoso sobre toda a terra, ditoso, vençedor, glorioso, prospero no ministerio de Deus direitamente, no Malavar, na cidade grande do grande Idolo. Reynando elle no tempo de Mercurio de fevereiro no dia septimo do mes de Março antes de luna chea o mesmo Rey Coquarangon estando em Carnelur chegou Thome Cananeo homem principal em huma não determinado de ver a derradeira parte de Oriente. E vendo-o alguns homens como chegara forão a diser a El Rey. E veo o mesmo Rey e vio e chamou ao dito Thome homem principal, e desembarcou e veo diante del Rey, o qual falou com elle amigavelmente e lhe poz sobrenome para o honrar, o seu proprio, chamando-o Coquarangon Cananeo. E elle recebeo del Rey esta honra e foy se a pousar no seu || [87v] lugar. E El Rey lhe deu a cidade de Magoderpatanam para todo sempre.

E estando o dito Rey nesta grande prosperidade foy hum dia a caça ao mato, e o mesmo Rey cercou o mato todo. E chamou de pressa a Thome, o qual veo, e esteve diante del Rey em hora ditosa. E perguntou El Rey ao adivinhador. E depois falou El Rey com Thome, que edificaria huma cidade naquelle mato. E respondeo al Rey fazendolhe primeiro reverencia, e disse: Eu quero este mato para mim. E o Rey lhe concedeo, e deu para todo sempre. E logo outro dia alimpou aquelle mato. E poz os olhos nelle no mesmo anno a onze de abril, e deo por herança a Thome em tempo, e dia ditoso, em nome del Rey, o qual póz o primeiro tijolo para a Igreia e para a casa de Thome Cananeo, e fez alli huma cidade a todos, e entrou na Igreia e fez alli oração no mesmo dia, depois destas cousas Thome mesmo foy aos passos del Rey e lhe offereçeo presentes e depois disto dice al Rey que lhe desse a elle e a seus descendentes aquella terra. E mediou dozentos e sesenta e quatro covados de Elefante, e deu a

Paliport surfaced. Hence the Christians of St Thomas mark the date of the era of Magoderpatanam in all the ollas which they write without knowing its origin. For they hold this place to be one of the most ancient ones where the Christians of St Thomas lived.

[7.] The translation of the olla which the said Xeram Perumal gave to Thomas Cananeo, in which he granted him the ground of Cranganor, says textually thus: "May Coquarangon be prosperous, enjoy long life and live one hundred thousand years, divine servant of God, strong, true, just, full of good works, reasonable, powerful over the whole earth, happy, conqueror, glorious, rightly prosperous in the ministry of God, in Malavar in the great city of the great Idol!" During his reign at the time of Mercury[3] in February, on the seventh day of the month of March, before the full moon, as the same king Coquarangon was staying at Carnelur, there arrived in a ship Thomas Cananeo, its Commander, who had resolved to see the uttermost part of the East. And some men who saw him arriving went to inform the king. And the king himself came and saw and called Commander Thomas, who disembarked and came before the king. The king spoke graciously to him and to honour him he gave him as surname his own name, calling him Coquarangon Cananeo. And he received this honour from the king and returned to his palace for rest. [87^{v}] And the king gave him the city of Magoderpatanam for ever.

And being in great prosperity, the said king went one day to hunt in the shrubland and encircled it. And he called in haste for Thomas, who came and stood before the king in an hour of good fortune. And the king consulted the soothsayer. And after that the king spoke to Thomas that he should build a city in that shrubland. After first making an act of reverence he answered the king, "I want to have this shrubland for myself." And the king granted it to him and gave it for ever. And forthwith the next day the king cleared the shrubland. Casting his eyes on it in the same year on the eleventh of April, he gave it as a royal grant to Thomas in inheritance at a propitious time and on a propitious day. The king laid the first brick for the church and for the house of Thomas Cananeo, and made there a city for all. Entering the church he made his prayers there on the same day. After these things Thomas himself went to meet the king in his palatial buildings and offered him presents. Then he requested the king to give that land to him and to his descendants. And he measured two hundred and sixty-four elephant cubits and gave it to

[3] Mercury or Jupiter ?

Thome e a seus descendentes para todo sempre. E iuntamente sesenta e duas casas que alli se fizerão logo e hortas e arvores com seus circuitos e com seus caminhos, e terminos e pateos interiores. E concedeolhe sete modos de instromentos musicos e todas as honras, em falar e andar como Rey, e nas bodas faserem as molheres certo sinal com o dedo na boca, e concedeolhe peso distincto, e ornar o chão con panos e concedeolhe abanos reaes e dobrar o sandal no braço, e tabernaculo e sobreceo real em toda parte de seu Reyno para todo sempre, e afora disto cinco tributos a Thome, e a sua geração e a seus confederados para homens e para molheres e para todos seus parentes e a os filhos de sua ley para todo sempre. O dito Rey em seu nome o deu testemunhas estes principes, Codaxeri Canden. Cherucaraprota Chaten Comeren, porteiro del Rey. Areunden Counden, conselheiro del Rey, Amenate Counden Guerulen, capitão do campo. Chirumalaprata Tirivicramen Comeren, Regedor da banda do Oriente no Malavar. Perubalanata Aditen Chingan cantor do dito Rey. Perubalanata Cottocoulem guarda do porto do reyno. Bichremen Chinguen de Carturte, Camareiro do dito Rey. Araniperumcovil escrivão de todos os negocios *com sua mão escreveo esta escritura se dilate e seia bem-afortunada.*

[8.] Esta he a escritura do chão de Cranganor, que deu o Emperador de todo Malavar a Thome Cananeo Armenio e aos mais Christãos de S. Thome. E porque naquelle tempo contavão de doze em doze annos conforme o curso da planeta Mercurio, por isso dizem na olla || [88^{r}] que se fundara a dita povoação no anno do Mercurio de fevereiro. A qual conta esta de todo esquecida, porque ha setecentos e setenta e nove annos que se conta em todo este Malavar polla era do Coulão.* Todavia porque o dito Perumal como dicemos arriba ha mais de mil e dozentos annos morreo, e assy parece o mesmo que ha em Cranganor Igreia e Christaõs, e muito primeiro os avia em Paru no dito Magoderpatanam.

Thomas and his descendants for ever together with sixty-two houses[4] which by then had been built there, and gardens and trees with their enclosures and with their paths and boundaries and inner yards. And he granted him seven kinds of musical instruments and all the honours to speak and move about like a king. And it was granted to women at weddings to cheer with the finger in the mouth.[5] And the king granted him the use of a distinct weight and to adorn the ground with cloths. And he granted him royal fans, and to wear double sandal marks on the arm, and to put up a tent and royal canopy in every part of his kingdom for ever. Besides five tributes were granted to Thomas and to his lineage and to his confederates, in favour of men and women, and of all his relatives and of the children of his Law for ever. The said king granted it in his name. Witnesses are these princes:[6] "Kōṭaśśēri Kaṭan. Ceṛukaṭapṛattụ Cāttan Komaran, the king's chief doorkeeper. Accutan Kaṇṭan, the king's councillor. Amēnāṭṭụ Kaṇṭan Kēruḷan, Captain of the army. Cerumalappṛ aṭṭụ Trivikṛamen Komaren, governor of the Eastside in Malavar. Peruvaḷanāṭṭụ Ātittan Ciṅṅan, singer of the said king. Peruvalanāttụ Cāttan Komaran, guard of the kingdom's port. Kaṭutturutti Vikṛamen Cingen, Chamberlain of the said king. Airāni Perumkōvil, the scribe of all the affairs, with his own hand wrote this document. Let this be made public and bring good fortune!"

[8.] This is the document of the land of Cranganor, which the Emperor of All Malavar gave to Thomas Cananeo, the Armenian and to all the Christians of St Thomas. And because at that time they counted from twelve to twelve years according to the course of Mercury, it is said in the olla [88r] that the said town was founded in February in the year of Mercury. This manner of reckoning is now quite forgotten, because for the last seven hundred and seventy-nine years they calculate in the whole of Malavar by the Quilon era.[7] Nevertheless, because the said Perumal, as we said, lived and died more than one thousand two hundred years ago, it seems that the Church and the Christians of Cranganor are also of the same age, but those of Paru in the said Magoderpatanam may be much earlier.

---

[4] It should be rather *seventy-two* houses, as is said twice elsewhere in this Report, as also in the tradition among the Southist community.

[5] Cheers of *kurawa* is still in use in the Middle East.

[6] These names given here are in the Malayalam form as rendered by T. K. Joseph, *Kerala Society Papers, I* (Trivandrum, 1930) p.198.

[7] Quilon era began in 825 A.D. So, 825 + 779 = 1604, date of writing. But September 1603 is already Quilon era 779 since the first month of this era (Ciṅṅan) begins in mid-August. However, see below "in 1603, that is last year" [N. 9].

Depois com a prosperidade de Cranganor e a adversidade dos tempos a dita Igreia e povoação de Christaõs se tirou do dito lugar e se poz a Igreia no lugar donde agora esta por revelação particular, que teve hum Christaõ de S. Thome de Paru, como se tém por tradição certa entre estes Christaõs de geração antiga e se conservou atee agora. * De modo que ia muito antes da vinda do dito Thome Cananeo ia havia Christãos de S. Thome neste Malavar, que erão vindos de Maliapur cidade de S. Thome. E as familias principaes saõ quatro: Cotur, Catanal, Onamturte, Narimattan. Oie em dia conhecidas entre todos estes Christaõs os quaes se multiplicarão, e se estenderão por todo este Malavar aiuntando também assy alguns dos gentios que se convertião.

[9.] Todavia os descendentes de Thome Cananeo sempre ficarão sobre sy, sem querer# casar nem misturarse com estes outros Christãos e assy atee oie ha entre elles duas gerações. Huma que descem de Thome Cananeo da parte de pay, porem a may disem que era Malavar gentia e depois se baptisara. Outra geração he do que da parte de pay e may descem originalmente de Christãos de S. Thome, os quaes tiverão mais cuidado que os outros de acrecentar a Igreia, e assy receberão em sy gentios muitos que baptisarão, e ainda bem que em algum tempo servirão aos outros filhos de Thome Cananeo, tamben conservão em baixo de sua proteição, e ficando estes ricos e honrados, os outros os quiserão adoperar dizendo serem seus negros. Do qual resultou entre os Christãos de S. Thome e os outros grande discordia e ouve entre elles grandes brigas antigamente. Pelloque em Carturte e Cotete foy necessario faseremse Igreias differentes afastandose huns dos outros. E os da parcialidade de Thome Cananeo ficaraõ em huma Igreia e os outros em outra. E o anno passado de 1603 esta mesma foy a causa das brigas entre os de Udiamper e Candanada, defendendo cada hum sua parcialidade. E he cousa estranha ver o asco, que tem huns aos outros sem se poderem esquecer de suas antiguidades e fabulas, que tem nesta materia. Os Christãos de S. Thome descendentes de Thome Cananeo são poucos. Estão no Udiamper e na Igreia grande de Carturte e na Igreia grande de Cotete, e em Turigure.

Pello dito se vem haver sido mal informado o autor, que tratando da origem || [88^{v}] dos Christãos de S. Thome no livro que fez da fundação dos mosteiros do ordem do glorioso S. Francisco que escrevendo de

Afterwards with the prosperity of Cranganor and due to adverse times that Church and the community of Christians moved out from that place and were established where they are now, following a particular revelation received by a St Thomas Christian of Paru. This is held as a sure tradition among these Christians handed down from ancient generation till now. Therefore, already long before the coming of the said Thomas Cananeo, there were Christians of St Thomas in this Malavar who had come from Maliapur, the Town of St Thomas. And the chief families are four: Cotur, Catanal, Onamturte and Narimattan, which are well-known today among these Christians, who have multiplied and spread throughout the whole of this Malavar. To be added to them are some heathens who were converted.

[9.] However, the descendants of Thomas Cananeo have always kept to themselves without wishing to intermarry or to mix with these other Christians. And so up to this day there are among them two lines of descent: one descending from Thomas Cananeo on the father's side, while the mother, they say, was a Malavar heathen who got herself baptized later. The other lineage is of those who both on the father's side and mother's side were originally descended from the Christians of St Thomas. The latter took greater care than the former to spread the Church, and so they received into their community many heathens whom they baptized and took under their protection, even though for some time these had been in the service of the former, namely the children of Thomas Cananeo. They became rich and honourable, but these others wanted to employ them saying that they had been their slaves. Because of that there arose between the Christians of St Thomas and these others great discord and there were great disputes among them in olden times. So much so, at Carturte and Cotete it became necessary to make separate churches, each party keeping aloof from the other. Those of the Thomas Cananeo's group went to one church and the others to the other. And in 1603, that is, last year the same was the cause of quarrels between those of Udiamper and Candanad, each one defending his own party. And it is very strange to see the aversion one party has for the other, without being able to forget their ancestries and fables they have in this matter. The Christians of St Thomas who have descended from Thomas Cananeo are few. They are in Udiamper, the great church of Carturte, the great church of Cotete and at Turigure.

From what has been said it is clear how ill-informed that author was who dealing with the origin [88^{v}] of the Christians of St Thomas in the book he wrote on the foundation of the monasteries of the Order of the

Cranganor da por principio a todos os Christãos de S. Thome no Malavar ao dito Thome Cananeo. No que parece não haver tido informação plena desto porque afora da tradição antiquissima e coniecturas certas de haver ia no Malavar Christãos de S. Thome antes do dito Cananeo, a olla de Xeram Perumal dà testemunho claro disto, pois dize que se puserão setenta e duas casas no dito chão de Cranganor, as quaes erão de Christãos, iuntamente com a Igreia e claro està que não tinha o dito Thome tanta gente comsigo, pois vinha a faser mercancia, e como não ouue mais espasso entre sua vinda e a fundação da cidade de Cranganor senão de sete de Março atee onze de Abril do mesmo anno, claramente esta que não podia a dita cidade estar edificada de seus descendentes, polloque esta firme e claro ouve ia no Malavar Christãos de S. Thome o que também confessão os outros Christãos, que descem do dito Thome Cananeo.

[10.] Assy que por via deste Thome aiudou Nosso Senhor muito aos Christãos, que estavão neste Malavar dessemparados, aindaque antes e depois erão algumas veses visitados de alguns Armenios peregrinos, que hião a visitar o sepulchro do Apostolo S. Thome. E alguns se deixavão ficar em Maliapur, outros no Malavar. Nesta Igreia de Cranganor ouve hum Bispo antes da vinda dos Portuguezes, chamado Mar Iohanan, doqual se lé em hum livro antigo scripto da mão em Caldeo que o resuscitara ao samchristão da dita Igreia, que morrera dhuma caida.

Achey mais o nome do dito Thome Cananeo entre os nomens dos santos que na missa nomea o diacono, attribuindolhe que dera huma gran summa de dinheiro al Rey do Malavar para comprar aquelle chão em Cranganor. Polloque cuido ser fabula o que contão estes Christãos disendo que o dito Thome teve huma molher, e huma concubina, das quaes descendem dous generos de christãos, que ha neste Malavar, dos quaes tratamos arriba.

Em o livro antigo da resa scripto da mão dhuma Igreia de Mangate achey no fim delle scripto: como o dito livro fora feito e escripto em Cranganor donde dize que havia tres Igreias: huma de S. Thome, outra da Nossa Senhora e outra de S. Cyriaco, digo são Quirce martyr menino, filho de santa Julita muy celebrado entre estes Caldeos, cuio dia celebrão aos quinze de Julho. Segundo a Era, em que foy escripto o dito livro ha neste anno, de 1604 noventa e sete annos que foy scripto*.

glorious St Francis and writing about Cranganor, attributed the origins of all the Christians of St Thomas in Malavar to the said Thomas Cananeo. It is clear that he did not have full information about them, because besides the most ancient tradition and certain conjectures of the Christians of St Thomas in Malavar dating before the said Cananeo, the olla of Xeram Perumal gives clear witness to it: for it says that on the said ground of Cranganor seventy-two houses were built which were of the Christians along with the church; and it is clear that the said Thomas did not have so many people with him since he came for trade. And since the interval between his arrival and the foundation of the city of Cranganor was only from the seventh of March to the eleventh of April, it is clear that the said city could not have been built for his descendants. Therefore, it is clear and certain that there were Christians of St Thomas in Malavar, and this the other Christians who descend from Thomas Cananeo also admit.

[10.] Likewise, Our Lord helped very much the Christians through this Thomas as they were living forsaken in this Malavar, although at times they had been visited by some Armenian pilgrims on their way to visit the sepulchre of the Apostle St Thomas. And some used to stay in Maliapur, and others in Malavar. In this church of Cranganor before the coming of the Portuguese there was a Bishop called Mar Johanan, of whom one may read in an old book written by hand in Chaldean that he resuscitated the sacristan of the said church who had died of a fall.

Moreover, I found the name of the said Thomas Cananeo among the names of the saints whom the deacon names in the Mass, attributing to him that he gave a large sum of money to the king of Malavar to buy that ground of Cranganor. Hence I consider it to be a fable what these Christans narrate, namely that the said Thomas had a wife and a concubine from whom are descended the two kinds of Christians living in this Malavar of whom we spoke above.

In an old book of prayers written by hand in the Church of Mangate I found written at the end that the said book was made and written at Cranganor where, it says, there were three churches, one of St Thomas, another of Our Lady and another of St Cyriac — I mean St Quirce, a martyr-child, son of St Julita, very famous among these Chaldeans, whose feast they celebrate on the fifteenth of July. According to the era in which the said book was written, it was written ninety-seven years before this year of 1604.

[PRELADOS ARMENIOS]

[11.] *Os Armenios e prelados* que aqui vinhão forão todos Nestorianos e poucos Jacobitas. E foy tempo, que não ouve aqui no Malavar mais que hum so Diacono, ao qual os Christaos vendose sem prelado e ignorantes fizerão diser missa, e ainda ordenar a outros. E vindo logo prelados de Babylonia concertarão a desordem do dito Diacono [additur alia manu: o qual depois morreu com se lhe apodreceo a mão, confessando [...?] culpas que fizera].

Os Bispos de que se tem lembrança e governarão esta Igreia são:

|| [89r] Mar Johanan, Mar Jacob, Mar Thoma, Mar Jabala, Mar Denon, Mar Elia, Mar Johanan, Mar Habraham, que veo primeiro sem ter nenhumas ordens e depois foy em Roma ao tempo de Pio quarto e foy ordenado em Venesa e vendo de outra ves qua outro. Mar Joseph se vinho, segundo dizem, de Mar Abdiso Patriarcha dos Nestorianos, que se achou no fin do concilio tridentino e esta impressa sua profissão em algums concilios Tridentinos. O dito Mar Denon foy ordenado aqui no Malavar Bispo por Mar Jabala como consta por un libro dos Evangelhos, que esta na Igreia de P[...]. Mar Jabala foy Metropolitano e teve por suffraganeos alguns dos ditos bispos. Mar Elia se tornou outra vez para Babylonia. Os ditos prelados todos, que vinhão de Babylonia trazião suas toucas e huma madexa de cabellos compridos no meio da cabeça donde nos fazemos a coroa. E assy tambem andavão os clerigos, que elles qua ordenavão; do que me espanto, porque nos livros seus caldeos mandão os canones que os clerigos tragão tonsura. Por onde não veio como, e de donde tomarão este costume, que foy opprobrio para elles no Malavar, donde os gentios trazem huns poucos de cabellos compridos no meio da cabeça consegrados ao demonio, que chamão Curumbi.

Contão estes Christãos alguns milagres que estes fizerão. Que não creo por ser esta gente muy fabulosa nestas materias, e serem elles hereges, e schismaticos e gente alguns delles que não derão bona conta de sy: postoque sabemos não ser impossivel facer Deus por virtude de seu nome, por meio de tal gente facer algum milagre para o bem comum da Igreia. *Usavão os* ditos [additur: Prelados] com seus clerigos da invocação occulta do demonio por meio de certas palavras, e nomens obscuros, que estavão em hum livro que trouxerão de Babylonia, pello qual fazião algumas cousas miraculosas, e outras ruims, e mais a detrimento das almas.

[12.] *Virão tambem* aqui a esta Serra dous Irmãos naturais Armenios. Os quaes quando vierão ter huma ponta do mar da fronte de Paliporto da

[11.] The Armenians and the prelates who came here were all Nestorians, but a few were Jacobites. And there was a time when in Malavar there was no one else but a single deacon, and the Christians, being ignorant and having no prelate, made him say Mass and even to ordain others. But as soon as the prelates came, they put an end to the disorder of the said deacon [*added in the margin in a different hand:* who afterwards died with a putrid hand, ... confessing the faults he had done].

The bishops about whom there is information and who governed this Church are: [89r] Mar Johanan, Mar Jacob, Mar Thoma, Mar Jabala, Mar Denon, Mar Elia, Mar Johanan (*sic* for Mar Joseph), and Mar Habraham. This last came at first without having received any ordination, and later went to Rome at the time of Pope Pius IV and was ordained in Venice, and came here a second time. Mar Joseph came, as they say, from Patriarch Abdiso of the Nestorians, who was present at the end of the Council of Trent, and his profession of faith is printed in certain acts of the Tridentine Council. The said Mar Denon was ordained bishop here by Mar Jabala as is clear from a book of Gospels which is in the church of P[...]. Mar Jabala was metropolitan, and had some of the said bishops as suffragans. Mar Elia returned to Babylon. The said bishops who came from Babylon wear hoods and a tuft of hairs on the top of the head where we have the tonsure. So do also the clerics whom they have ordained, which surprises me; for the canons in their Chaldean books say that the clerics should wear the tonsure. Hence I do not see from where they took this custom, which is a shame for them in Malavar, as the heathens wear some hair tied together on the top of their head and dedicated to a demon, whom [which ?] they call Curumbi.

These Christians narrate some miracles which these bishops performed. I do not believe them, for these people are rather credulous in such matters, and they are heretics and schismatics, and [... followers ... ?] some of them did not give good account of themselves, although we know it is not impossible that God work some miracle by the power of his name through such people for the common good of the Church. These [prelates] and their clerics used to make use of occult invocation of the devil by means of certain words, and obscure names which are to be found in a book they brought from Babylon, by which they used to perform some miraculous things and other mischiefs, more to the detriment of souls.

[12.] There came also to this Serra two brothers who were natives of Armenia. They first arrived at a promontory in front of Paliport on the

banda do Norte que se chama Maliamquera que quere dizer porto ou terra do Malavar donde disem estes Christãos que tem por tradição, que os ditos ambos irmãos aportarão com hum pao muy grande para edificarem huma Igreia. Em memoria do qual em tempos passados todos os Christãos de S. Thome se aiuntarão [additur: em certos tempos] com seu prelado no dito lugar, e disião missa com grande solemnidade. E em tempo de Mar Joseph, que havera oie trinta e tantos annos, se aiuntarão no dito lugar passante da oitenta mil Christãos de S. Thome. Os ditos dous irmãos se chamavão Sapor e Aprot, dosquaes nesta Serra nos Livros Caldeos não ha mais menção, senão que forão dous irmãos, que vierão a Coulão, e fizerão alli huma Igreia, e obrarão alguns milagres, sem dizer quaes, só tem por tradição os Christãos que naõ tendo os ditos Irmãos dinheiro para pagar aos culles, que trabalhavão na Igreia, que edificavão com a madeira, que elles trouxerão, davãolhe arêa (areia), que se tornava em arros.

Chegarão || [89v] os ditos Irmãos a Coulão e fizerão a dita Igreia iunto do mar no lugar donde esta agora a Sé de Coulão no anno centesimo depois da fundação do dito Coulão que ha agora seiscentos e setenta e nove annos como consta pollas ollas de cobre que estão na mão de Taraga ou o rendeiro de Tevalicare. As quaes no anno de mil seiscentos e hum no mes de Outubro, Etymani caçanar por mandado de Dom Francisco Bispo de Angamale tresladou e authenticou. Nas quaes dizia que Elrey de Coulão dava dos direitos, contagem e copa e peso de cento hum a Igreia dos Apostolos. Tenha para os gastos della e mais setenta e duas honras. A occasião de tresladar esta olla foy por pretender o padre vigairo de Coulão do bispado de Couchim estas rendas todas para a Igreia de Coulão que agora he do Bispado de Cochim, no que se enganava; pois consta polla mesma olla que não se dava aquelle ao chão e paredes da Igreia senão aos christãos de S. Thome que possuião a dita Igreia, aqual mudaram para Coulão de cima donde primeiro tinhão huma cruz.

A causa da mudança, foy como consta do auto que se tirou testimunhas iuradas aos sanctos Evangelhos que quando os Portugueses chegarão a Coulão os Christãos de S. Thome que la moravão, os conhecerão por gente dhuma mesma ley com elles por lhes ver fazer o sinal da cruz e assy os agasalharão. Depois os Portugueses tinhão certas brigas con os

north side, which is called Maliamquera, that is to say port or land of Malavar. Here it was, these Christians say quoting their tradition, that the said brothers arrived at the port with a very big log of timber to build a church. In memory of this the Christians of St Thomas used to assemble in times past at the said place and say Mass with great solemnity. And in the time of Mar Joseph, thirty or more years ago, over eighty thousand Christians of St Thomas assembled at the said place.[8] Those two brothers were called Sapor and Aprot. About them the Chaldean books of the Serra only mention that they were two brothers who arrived at Quilon and built a church there and wrought some miracles, but do not say what. It is held by tradition among these Christians that these brothers, as they had no money to pay the coolies who were building the church with the material they had brought, gave them sand, and it turned into rice.

[89v] Those brothers arrived at Quilon and built the church on the sea shore, at a place where now there is the see of Quilon, in the year 100 after the foundation of Quilon, that is 679 years ago, as is known from the copper plates which are in the possession of the Tarega or the landlord of Tevalicare. In the year 1601 in the month of October, by order of Dom Francis Ros, Bishop of Angamale, Cassanar Etymani copied and authenticated them. In them it is said that the king of Quilon gave to the church of the Apostles the right over one percent of all things counted, measured or weighed. This is collected for the expenses of the church and also for the seventy-two honours. The occasion for copying those plates was that the vicar of Quilon of the Diocese of Cochin claimed the whole of these revenues for the church of Quilon, which now belongs to the Bishop of Cochin. This was cheating, because from the same plates it is clear that the revenues were given not to the plot or to the walls of the church but to the Christians of St Thomas who possessed that church, which they had transferred to Upper Quilon where they had a cross earlier.

The reason of the transfer, as is proved with testimonies sworn on the holy Gospels, was that when the Portuguese arrived at Quilon, the Christians of St Thomas living there recognized them as people of one and the same Law as themselves, as they saw them making the sign of the cross, and so they accepted them. Afterwards the Portuguese had some quarrels

---

[8] On 21 November 1563. See letter of Amador Correia, S.J., dated 20 January 1564: *Documenta Indica* 6 (1960) 178-179. Only eight thousand assembled, not eighty thousand, at that time, and the feast was in commemoration of the landing of St Thomas the apostle at Maliamkara.

Mouros e El Rey quiz dar nelles, os quaes se recolherão por serem seis, ou sete não mais na Igreia dos Christãos de S. Thome. E querendo o dito Rey matar aos Portugueses e dar na Igreia, mandou recado aos Christãos que se sahissem della pois erão seus vassalos e não tinhão nada com elles. Mas elles não quiserão senão morrer com os Portugueses. Polloque El Rey queimou a Igreia e morrerão nella os Portugueses e quarenta Christãos de S. Thome, e hum diacono com elles. E assy se mudarão os Christãos para Coulão de cima e fizerão la a Igreia, que agora tem e forão sempre arrecadando a renda que o dito Rey concedera aos dous Irmaos Armenios para a Igreia que fiserão. Aqual renda por negligencia dos mesmos Christãos não se arrecada oie plenariamente como esta na dita olla.

Os corpos destes dous Irmaos iazem na Igreia que fizerão donde en algumas pedras ha certas letras que eu vi que paressem Abexinas, e não Caldeas, nem Malavares. Esta Igreia, depois da queimada dita, reedificarão os Portugueses e por pura falta de cuidado ficou ao Bispado de Cochim, pelloque o padre vigairo delle, chamado Gregorio dos Reis, pretendeo tirar como de feito tirou hum anno a renda, que os Christãos de S. Thome arrecadavão para sua Igreia de Coulão de cima. Mas o senhor Bispo de Cochim, dou ordem, em que ficassem as cousas no seu primeiro ser como ficarão.

Estes dous Irmãos Armenios vulgarmente se chamão Quadixagal que quer dizer santos e celebravão sua festa aos 19 de Mayo, mas porque não se stribava sua santidade em cousa alguma certa o senhor Arcebispo de Goa quando qua veo mudou isto e mandou que em seu lugar celebrassem a festa de são Gervasio e Protasio a 19 de junho segundo o costume da santa Igreia Romana. E para que estes Christãos não estranhassem outros nomens de outros santos, tomou Sua Senhoria a são Gervaiso e Protasio por serem semelhantes nos nomens, a Sapor, ou Xabor como os Caldeos disem, he [sic] a Prot.

[13.] Há se de notar || [90r] que na sobredita olla de Coulão, o dito Rey o que a passou, chama aos Christãos de S. Thome, Tarijanes: que quer diser Reis, ou Reis primeiros que assy se chamavão antigamente estes Christãos, por descenderem aoque parece, os principais delles dos antigos Reis, que S. Thome fez Christãos. Depois e agora vulgarmente se chamavão Nasarani id est Nazareus, pollos Mouros e Turcos assy os chamavão. Todavia nas partes do Sul alem de Coulão retem o nome antigo não somente elles, mais ainda os que são de sua casta, e estão feito' gentios, sem que herem receber a ley de Deus, como são os de Bepar segundo o dito a cima no principio.

with the Moors, and the king intervened. Six or seven Portuguese took refuge in the church of the Christians of St Thomas. The king wanted to put the Portuguese to death and so he sent a message to the Christians that he had nothing against them, his vassals, and that they should leave the church. But they did not want to leave but opted to die with the Portuguese. Hence the king burned the church down and in it perished the Portuguese and forty Christians of St Thomas together with a deacon. It was in these circumstances that the Christians moved to Upper Quilon and built a church there which they have now. And they used to levy the revenues which the said king had granted to the two Armenian brothers for the church they built. Because of the negligence of the Christians this revenue is not fully levied now, as is stated in the said olla.

The bodies of these two brothers are lying in the church which they built, where on some slabs there is a writing in letters, which seems to me to be Abexinas, and not Chaldean or Malavares. The church, after it was burned down, was rebuilt by the Portuguese, and only due to carelessness did it go to the Diocese of Cochin. Hence its vicar called Fr Gregorio dos Reis put forth claims and levied the revenue for a year, which the Christians of St Thomas used to receive for their church at Upper Quilon. But the Bishop of Cochin gave orders that things should be settled as they were before.

These two brothers are popularly known as *Quadixangal*, that is to say Saints, and they celebrate their feast on the 19th of May. But since their sanctity did not rest upon anything certain, the Lord the Archbishop of Goa when he came changed their feast and ordered that instead they might celebrate the feast of SS. Gervasis and Protasis on the 19th of June according to the custom of the Roman Church. And lest these Christians should feel that the names of these other saints were alien, His Lordship took St Gervasis and St Protasis, as their names are similar to Sapor, or Xabor as the Chaldeans say, and Prot.

[13.] It is to be noted [90r] that in the above mentioned Quilon Plates, the king who granted them calls the Christians of St Thomas *Tarijanes,* that is to say kings or first kings. It seems that these Christians used to be called thus from ancient times for having descended from the ancient kings whom St Thomas made Christians. Later and now they are popularly called *Nasarani,* that is, Nasareus, for they are so called by the Moors and Turks. Still, in the southern parts beyond Quilon they retain the ancient name, not only they but also those who are of their caste who became heathen without wanting to receive the law of God, as are those of Bepar as said above in the beginning.

[14.] *Afora destes* Christãos que estevem e estão nas terras de Rey Biliarte muta covil, que entrou no governo dos Reynos de Curur no primeiro anno da fundação de Coulão, que ha oie setecentos e setenta e nove annos cuio Reyno e terras possuie oie el Rey de Cochim por industria de João de Fonseca capitão que foy de Cochim, e de Proto Christão de S. Thome cabeça que foi na cidade do Udiamper.

Este Biliarte entrou no governo das ditas terras porque, postoque forão dadas por Xaram Perumal a hum Bramene, seus successores não souberão governar arreceando fazer iustiça dos malfeitores. Pelloque se derão elles ao Reyno e ficou Reinando o dito Biliarte. O qual foy particular proteitor destes Christãos por esta causa, que direy. Antes dos Portugueses virem a India pleiarão os Mouros contra os Christãos, aos quaes o dito Biliarte aiudou contra El Rey de Cochim que favoreçia aos Mouros. Mas vencendo os Christãos e querendo remunerar ao dito Biliarte estenderão hum panno no chão, e enriba delle deitarão muito dinheiro para o dar ao dito Rey. O qual elle não quis tomar. Mas disse aos Christãos que não queria senão que lhe dessem cada anno hum fanão cada cabeça delles. E assy ficarão os Christãos muy particularmente seus, e por conseguinte El Rey de Cochim, que herdou o dito Reyno.

E postoque os Reis passados de Cochim fizerão sempre muita conta destes Christãos e os tratarão bem: todavia El Rey Ramormen que foy a morrer ao Ganga, e este, que agora governa chamado Uregueln os tratarão, e tratão muy mal contra todos seus antigos costumes. E a causa principal he por se terem aiuntado com nosco, e serem dhuma mesma ley, e cuidar que por tempo lhe podem façer muito mal servindo elles, a este estado e assy os esbulhão de suas fazendas contra todo direito e iustiça e sofrem mal os Portugueses rogarem por elles.

[15.] Muitos dos que pousão nas terras deste Rey de Cochim, são originalmente de Cranganor donde antigamente estava muita força delles, e alli moravão seus prelados antigamente, e discurrião por todo este Malavar atee chegar a Maliapur. E em todo este tracto do Malavar exercitavão seus actos Pontificaes. E a Cranganor acodiao muitos dos Christãos aos divinos officios. Depois vindo os Portugueses a Cranganor e façendose alli fortalesa Martim Afonso, ainda Mar Jacob, do qual arriba fisemos menção, com outros Bispos Caldeos moravão muito tempo em

[14.] Besides these Christians there were and there are others in the lands of King Byliarte Muta Coil[9], who began his reign of the kingdom of Curur in the first year of the foundation of Quilon, which was 779 years ago. His kingdom and lands are now possessed by the king of Cochin thanks to the diligence of Joao de Fonseca, who was the captain of Cochin, and of Proto a St Thomas Christian, who was the chieftain of the town of Udiamper.[10]

This Biliarte happened to govern the said lands, because although they were given by Xeram Perumal to a Brahmin, his successors did not know how to govern, fearing to mete out justice to the evildoers. Therefore, they gave up the kingdom and the said Biliarte kept on ruling. He was the special protector of these Christians for the reason I shall mention. Before the Portuguese came to India, the Moors waged war against the Christians, whom the said Biliarte helped against the king of Cochin who was favouring the Moors. But the Christians won and, wishing to reward the said Biliarte, spread a sheet on the floor; over it they threw much money to give to that king. However, he did not want to take it but said to the Christians that he only wanted them to give him every year one fanam per head. Thus the Christians became very specially his own; consequently also the king of Cochin who inherited that kingdom.

Although the former kings of Cochin always had much care for these Christians and treated them well, nevertheless King Ramormen, who died at the Ganges, and the one who reigns now and is called Uregueln treated and treats them very badly against all their ancient customs. The principal reason is because they have maintained their union with us and are of one and the same law. And they think that these (Christians) might hurt them very badly serving our state, and so they dispossess them of their properties against all law and justice, and they take it ill if the Portuguese intercede for them.

[15.] Many of those who live in the lands of this king of Cochin are originally of Cranganor, where they had in ancient time great power. And their prelates used to live there and go around the whole of Malavar reaching up to Maliapur. They were exercising their Pontifical acts in the whole length and breadth of Malavar, and many Christians used to go to Cranganor for the divine offices. After the Portuguese landed at Cranganor and even after Martim Afonso built the fortress there, Mar Jacob mentioned above and the other Chaldean bishops lived for a long time in

[9] Biliarte = Villarvattam.

[10] On Fonseca's diligence in 1565, see A. da Silva Rego, *Documentação ...*, vol. 10, p. 151.

Cranganor exercitando o officio de Pontifices no dito lugar como consta por certa relação; porem depois assy os Religiosos de S. Francisco como outros clerigos Christãos de S. Thome do rito Latino, que elles tinhão feito derão contra estes Armenios de feição que nenhum Bispo, nem caçanar podia diser missa senão nos lugares || [90v] fora do Cranganor e isto as escondidas. Prohibindolhes o diser missa in fermentato, segundo do costume dos Gregos. Nem deixavão que os Caçanares casados celebrassem, forçavão aos Christãos que começassem o ieium da Quaresma na quarta feira de cinza, e que comessem peixe, que ellos no comem en tempo de ieium, pelloque se ausentarão muitos Christãos e clerigos de Cranganor e forão amorrar a Paru e Udiamper e Carturte. Acreçentouse tambem o medo da nossa iustiça que elles muito estranhão e o mal tratamento dos capitanis que succederão aos primeiros por onde tambem muitos Christãos de S. Thome que antigamente pousavão em Cochim na rua de Coulão e fazião o que agora fazem os Canarims, se ausentarão de Cochim e forão a pousar a terras de Reis gentios; o que todo consta ser assy por pessoas que ouirão e o mo contarão.

[16.] *Mas he cousa* para se saber a causa porque sendo estes Christãos tam favorecidos dos Reis gentios antigos specialmente do Xaram Perumal oqual repartio todas estas terras do Malavar a seus Regedores que o servião antes de morrer, como sendo estes Christãos privados seus ficarão sem terras e Reynos proprios, antes perderão parte de suas terras que primeiro possuião. A rezão disto he que ouve hum Christão muy principal, chamado Quirian Thome, o qual era Regedor do dito Xaram Perumal, ao qual quiz elle fazer Rey como aos mais Regedores fizera. E pediolhe muito o dito Rey que ninguem o soubesse senão depois de feito. Mas elle descobrio este segredo a sua molher a qual a outro dia tendo humas differenças con huma visinha sua lhe disse: amenhã vos me tratareis de outra manhera, dandolhe a entender que seu marido seria Rey e ella Rainha. A visinha ouvindo diser isto foy o diser a seu marido, e espalhandose a fama, certos enveiosos falarão com el Rey, pelloque o negocio do Reyno que queria dar ao dito Quirian Thome, não veo a effeito. E isto se tem por tradição certa entre estos Christãos. Os quaes não somente tem por vesinhos aos gentios Malavares, senão tambem a Judeos e Mouros, os quaes todos são mercadores. Mas os Christãos de S. Thome são mais venerados que os mais destes gentios.

[17.] *Os Judeos, como* elles dizem vierão a India depois da destroição de Jerusalem feita por Tito, e aportarão a hum lugar alem de Coulão, chamado Caramapaton, ha oie mil e cento e onze annos; Os que vierão,

Cranganor, exercising the office of Pontiffs there, as is clear from certain reports. Afterwards, however, the Religious of St Francis as well as the St Thomas Christian clerics of the Latin rite formed by them decided against these Armenians that no bishop or Cassanar should say mass except in places [90v] outside of Cranganor and that only secretly, prohibiting them to say Mass with the leavened bread according to the custom of the Greeks. Neither did they allow the married priests to celebrate; they forced the Christians to begin the fast of Lent on Ash Wednesday and to eat fish, whereas they do not eat fish in times of the fast. Therefore, many Christians and clerics moved out of Cranganor, and went to live in Paru, Udiamper and Carturte. Likewise, the fear of our justice, which is very much alien to them, waxed also owing to the bad treatment meted out by the Captains who succeeded the first ones. Hence many Christians who lived in Cochin on the street of Quilon and were doing what the Canarims now do, moved out of Cochin and went to live in the lands of the heathen kings. All these things are known from what people who saw them narrated to me.

[16.] It is interesting to learn why these Christians — who had been so favoured by the ancient heathen kings, especially by Xeram Perumal, who distributed all these lands of Malavar to his governors who were serving him before he died — were left without lands and kingdoms of their own, nay lost part of their lands which they formerly possessed. The reason for it was that there was once a prominent Christian called Qurian Thome, who was a governor of Xeram Perumal. This Perumal had proposed to make him a king like all the other governors. The king told him not to tell to anyone else before it was done. But he revealed the secret to his wife. The next day, in a dispute with a neighbour she told her, "Tomorrow you will treat me differently," giving her to understand that her husband would become king and she queen. The neighbour heard this and told her husband. The news spread. Certain envious people spoke about it to the king, with the result the plan to give a kingdom to Quirian Thome was not realized. This is held by tradition among these Christians, who have as neighbours not only the heathens of Malavar but also Jews and Moors, who are all merchants. But the Christians of St Thomas are more esteemed than all these heathens.

[17.] The Jews, as they say, came to India after the destruction of Jerusalem by Titus. And they reached a place called Caramapatan beyond Quilon one thousand one hundred and eleven (1111) years ago. Those

erão Castelhanos, e pareçe ser assy porque ainda oie no construir da Biblia, usão da lingua Castelhana. Antes disto consta tanbem que havia Judeos na India pois se escreve na vida de S. Thome que huma donzela Judea tangia huma frauta louvando a hum só Deus no convite das bodas d'aquelle Rey, que casará seu filho, ao qual tanbem esteve presente o Apostolo. O Padre Gaspar da Trinidade de nasçao Judeo e muy erudito, que foy vigairo de Cranganor, o qual eu conheci, dizia que os Judeos da India, que ha muitos, e pretos, tinhão origem da quelles, que vinhão nas armadas, que mandava Salamão a India: dos quaes alguns ficarão nella, e se multiplicavão, e multiplicarão atee o presente.

[18.] São os Christãos de S. Thome de natural brando, e docil, naturalmente || [91r] sagazes, e inclinados a mercancia, floxos todavia õ que he naturesa de todos estes Malavares. Tem todavia os mais delles bons entendimentos e agudos para todo genero de sciencias e ouve entre elles ia Padres seus naturais muy bons latinos, Artistas e Theologos. São muy pios e tem muita veneraçao a Cruz, a qual fazem ao modo do que deixou S. Thome, rematando os quatro braços della em tres folias de lilio repando.

[ESCRIPTURAS DO VELHO E DO NOVO TESTAMENTO]

[19.] Sua lingua ecclesiastica he e foy sempre Aseyra, lingua vulgar hebrea, no tempo de Christo Nosso Senhor e de seus Apostolos que a falarão e nella pregarão. Tem muitas palavras gregas, outras Arabes, outras Hebreas, e ainda algumas latinas caldaisadas, usarão sempre até oie de escriptura de mão, tem e usão de ambos os testamentos sc. velho e novo na sua lingua. O Velho em alguma parte falando de Christo, e de sua divinidade, Judaisamente. Os Machabeos não os tem, ouvi diser que em Babylonia os tinhão e deve ser assy, porque tampoco tem aqui o livro da Apocalypse de são João, o qual me disse Mar Habraham que o tinhão em Babylonia do que duvido, porque na esposição que tem estes Caldeos de todo o testamento novo falta, nem faz menção do dito Apocalipse, nem das duas epistolas canonicas de S. João, segunda e terceira, nem da epistola segunda de S. Pedro, nem da epistola unica de S. Judas, que nenhuma dellas esta tresladada em syriaco, porque se eu fora fiserão menção dellas os Syros no catalogo da divina scripturas do Testamento novo, oque não fasem, postoque a fação do Apocalypse de S. João. Em cuio Evangelho tambem falta a historia da molher adultera. E os lugares em que claramente em algumas partes dize o Spirito Santo nas escripturas do Testamento novo que Deos morreo por nos, ou deu o sangue por nos, e que em Christo não ha mais que hum so' supposto do Verbo em duas naturesas, estão corruptos pollos Nestorianos. E outros pollo mesmo

who came were Castelhans, and it seems to be so because even now in making a copy of the Bible they use the Castelhan language. Even before that it seems that there were Jews in India. For it is written in the life of St Thomas that a Jewish maiden sounded a flute praising the one only God at the wedding feast of that king who was having his son married, at which the Apostle also was present. Fr Gasper da Trindade of the Jewish nation, who was very learned and was the vicar of Cranganor and whom I knew, said that the Jews of India, who are many and are dark in colour, had their origin from those who came by the fleet sent to India by Solomon. Some of them remained in India and multiplied until the present day.

[18.] The Christians of St Thomas are by nature gentle, docile, naturally [91r] sagacious and inclined to trade, nevertheless flexible, which is the nature of all these Malavares. Most of them have good and sharp understanding for all kinds of sciences, and among them there are indigenous fathers, very good latinists, artists and theologians. They are very pious and have great veneration for the Cross, which they make in the manner of the legacy of St Thomas, the ends of the four arms divided into three leaves of the lily.

[19.] Their ecclesiatical language is and always was Aseyra, the popular Hebrew language at the time of Jesus Our Lord and of the Apostles, who spoke it and preached in it. It has many words from Greek, some others from Arabic, others from Hebrew and even some Chaldeanized Latin. They have always used until today books written by hand; they have and make use of both the Testaments, that is, the Old and the New in their language. The Old Testament is very Jewish in some parts while speaking about Christ and his divinity; they do not have the Machabees. I heard them say that they have them in Babylon, and it must be so. They little use the book of the Apocalypse of St John. Mar Habraham told me that they have it in Babylon, but I doubt it because in the exposition which the Chaldeans make of the New Testament it is wanting. Nor do they make mention of the Apocalypse or of the two canonical letters of St John, the second and the third, or of the second letter of St Peter or the single letter of St Jude. None of them has been translated into Syriac, because the Syrians do not mention them in the catalogue of the divine scriptures of the New Testament, although they do make mention of the Apocalypse of St John. In his Gospel the history of the adulterous woman is wanting. And those texts in which the Holy Spirit says in the books of the New Testament that God died for us, or He gave his blood for us, and that in Christ there is only one suppositum of the Word and two natures,

Nestorio, o qual como se dize no Concilio Ephesino primeiro tirou da primeira epistola de S. João aquellas palavras "qui solvit Iesum non est ex Deo" [1 Gv 4,3] as quaes manifestamente erão contra elles que punhão duas pessoas en Christo Nosso Senhor. Os mesmos erros tinhão tambem, e muitos mais no seus breviarios contra a honra da Madre de Deus celebrando festas a Nestorio e Diodoro e Theodoro Mosuesteno e aos mais hereges seus sequases resando delles e vituperando aos santos que defenderão a santa fee Catholica. Porem todos estes mostruos erros que havia nos ditos livros, assy divinos como ecclesiasticos, todos desaparecerão e os tirarão os padres da Companhia de Jesu do Collegio de Vaypicotta emendando os ditos livros.

[Os Sacramentos]

[20.] Os sacerdotes destes Christãos se chamão Caçanares vocabulo caldeo corrupto de Cahanan id est sacerdos. Os que não são de missa, se chamão chamaxa, palavra Caldea que quer diser ministro, ou illuminador. Sempre conhecerão o sacerdotio e lhe tiverão muito respeito e depois aos Diaconos e subdiaconos || [91v] que sempre tiverão por ordens distinctas. Das menores não acho menção; senão de Lectores. Aos cantores tambem punhão por huma das menores. Assy sacerdotes como os mais clerigos se casavão segundo o costume dos Gregos, depois a ignorancia, a malicia e deseio de dinheiro de seus prelados que lhes consentião tudo, fez que se casassem con viuvas, e a primeira morta segundavão, e ainda terçavão como os mais Leigos. Estas molheres de clerigos ministravão no baptismo das molheres despindoas e vestindoas, a seu modo porque os que se baptisavão assy homens como molheres, nûs' se batisavão immergendo-os dentro dagoa.

[21. a] No qual baptismo usavão tambem de oleo sancto, com que ungião ao baptisado. Nos peitos antes do baptismo, e depois do baptismo na testa. O dito oleo era bento pello mesmo sacerdote, que baptisava. Usavão tambem de padrinhos que tinhão o mesmo officio que tem na Igreia Latina. E tinhão e contrahião parentesco spiritual com o baptisado, e seu pay e sua may e seus filhos. Ouve em tempo passado muita necessidade deste sacramento entre estes Christãos, tanto que me alembro ter eu por minha mão baptisado pessoas de oitenta annos, e de sesenta, e de quarenta. E poucos annos antes se baptisavão de ordinario pessoas adultas, e ia grandes, mas agora ia se baptisão comunmente de oito dias depois do nascimento.

are all corrupted by the Nestorians. Some by Nestorius himself, who as is said in the Council of Ephesus removed from the first letter of St John the words, "Qui solvit Iesum est ex Deo," [1 Jn 4:3] which manifestly were against those who posited two persons in Christ Our Lord. The same errors they also hold, and many more in their Liturgy of the Hours, against the honour of the Mother of God, celebrating feasts for Nestorius, Diodor,Theodor of Mopsuestia and other heretics their followers, praying to them and vituperating the saints who defended the holy catholic faith. However, all these monstrous errors which they had in the said books, both divine and ecclesiastical, have disappeared, as the Fathers of the Society of Jesus at the College of Vaypicotta removed them correcting the said books.

[20.] The priests of those Christians are called *Caçanares*, a Chaldean word corrupted from *Kahanan*, that is, priest. Those who are not of the Mass are called *Chamaxa*, the Chaldean word meaning minister or illuminator. They always had the knowledge of priesthood and they had great respect for it; so too for the deacons and subdeacons [91v] who were always considered as distinct Orders. About the Minor Orders I see mention only of the lectors. They put also the cantors as one of the Minor Orders. The priests as well as the other clerics used to marry according to the custom of the Greeks. Afterwards due to ignorance and malice, and also for the love of money of their prelates, who agree to everything, they started to marry widows. And after the death of the first wife they marry a second or even a third time, like all the laymen. These wives of the clerics used to assist at the baptism of women, stripping them and then dressing them in their manner; for they used to baptise men and women nude by immersion into water.

[21. a] In the baptism they were using also the holy oil, with which they anointed the baptised on the chest before baptism and on the head after baptism. The said oil was blessed by the same priest as was baptising. They have also godparents, who have the same office as in the Latin Church. They hold and contract spiritual relationship with the baptised, his parents and his children. In times past there was so great want of this sacrament among these Christians, that I remember to have baptised with my hand persons who were eighty, seventy, or forty years old. And until a few years ago they ordinarily baptised only adult persons and grown-ups, but now they commonly baptise children on the eighth day after the birth.

[b] *Do sacramento* da confirmação nao ouve uso algum, nem acho em estes Livros Caldeos ser a confirmação sacramento, nem menção disso. Mar Habraham que foy o derradeiro de ritu Caldeo que gouvernou esta Christandade introdusio o uso deste sacramento cuia forma, e oraçoes converteo em Caldeo por meio dos padres da Companhia que morão em Vaypicotta. Mas numqua o deu, senão aos que queria ordenar.

[c] *A Eucharistia* sempre foy conhecida e muy reverenciada desde tempo antequissimo. Porem não cuidavão que era verdadeiramente corpo e sangue do senhor, senão sinal nomais. E como não tinhão nem usavão palavras de consegração, não se enganavão muito na Eucharistia, que na sua Igreia havia. Fazião hum bollo redondo resando quando o fazião certo numero de psalmos, misturavão nelle, sal e oleo. Na missa alevantavão aquelle bollo somente tomando dentro dos indices e dedos pollices, fazendo de todos quatro hum circulo redondo donde ençerravão o dito bollo, e o alevantavão. O calix não acostumavão alevantar. Quando disião missa vestião huma alva, que tinha diante e nas costas algumas cruses e logo emrriba punhão a stola dobrada em forma da cruz diante dos peitos, e logo emriba punhão hum lançol que lhes cubria a cabeça sem lhes tapar os olhos, e o rosto, mas cobria lhes todo o corpo e alevantavão as bordas delle com ambas as mãos que ficavão livres assy como levantão a sobrepelix Portuguesa, e assy disião a missa. Este rito tirou Mar Joseph que governou esta Christandade antes de Mar Habraham e introdusio os amitos, e mais vestiduras sagradas a uso Romano, e assym mais as hostias, e vinho de Portugal porque antes punhão as passas en remolho, e com aquelle liquor que delles sahia, dizião missa. Mais converteo de Latim em Caldeo || 92r as palavras de consagração aindaque mas por falta de interprete que soubesse Caldeo e Latim acrecentando elle algumas outras palavras como lhe pareceo milhor.

[d] *Nao usavão* do sacramento da confissão antes da communhão, mas comungavão grandes e piquenos sem facer distinção alguma. E a mim me alembra ter confessado alguns Christãos destes antigos, que se tinhão comungado muitas veses sem se confessar. E não somente isto, mas nem conheçião a confissao, nem a tinhão por sacramento, nem a nomeão os Livros Caldeos no numero dos sacramentos nomeando a cruz entre elles. Pelloque em nenhum caso usavão estes Christãos de confissão. Mar Jacob que governava esta Igreia no tempo que os Portugueses vierão a India, introdusio a confissão vendo que os Portugueses se con-

[b] About the sacrament of Confirmation they did not have any custom, nor have I found any mention of the sacramnet of Confirmation in these Chaldean books. Mar Habraham, who was the last of the Chaldean prelate to govern this Christianity, introduced the use of this sacrament. He translated the form and prayers of this sacrament into Chaldean with the help of the Fathers of the Society who live at Vaypicotta. However, he never gave it, except to those whom he wanted to ordain.

[c] The Eucharist was always known to them and was much venerated since ancient times. However, they did not consider that it was truly the body and blood of the Lord, but only a nominal sign. And as they did not have nor did they use the words of consecration, they were not much mistaken about the Eucharist which existed in their Church. They used to make a bun reciting a certain number of psalms while making it, mixing in it salt and oil. In the Mass they used to elevate the said bun taking it up with the thumbs and forefingers and encircling the bun within those four fingers. They did not elevate the chalice.

When they say the Mass they put on an alb, which in the front and in the back has some crosses. Over it they put on a stole made in the form of a cross in front of the chest. Over it they put on a mantle which covers their head without blocking their eyes and face, but covers the whole body. Lifting up its brims with both the hands, as in lifting the Portuguese surplice, the hands are made free; and so they say the Mass. Mar Joseph who governed this Christianity before Mar Habraham removed this rite and introduced the amice and the other sacred vestments of the Roman usage. Likewise he introduced the hosts and wine from Portugal. Formerly they used to squeeze raisins and, with the liquid coming out of them, they used to say the Mass. Moreover, he translated from Latin into Chaldean [92r] the words of the consecration, although badly, there not being translators who knew both the Latin and the Chaldean. He also added some other words as seemed better to him.

[d] They were not making use of the sacrament of Confession before Holy Communion. Grown-ups and all children without any distinction used to receive the Communion. I remember to have heard the confession of some of these old Christians, who had received Communion many times without confessing. Besides, they have no idea of Confession, nor do they consider it a sacrament. They do not mention it in the Chaldean books among the sacraments. But they mention the cross among them. Therefore, in no case were these Christians making use of Confession. Mar Jacob, who was governing this Church when the Portuguese came to India, introduced the sacrament of Confession seeing that the

fissavão. Ao qual depois resistio muito Mar Habraham, que não queria admittir por nenhum caso dito sacramento porque a Babylonia não usavão delle, todavia Deus Nosso Senhor aiudou e foy a confissão recibida. Primeiro assy em geral, e depois pouco a pouco aprenderão a confessarse bem, como agora facem commummente todos. As palavras da forma da absolução tresladou o dito Mar Joseph de Latim em Caldeo milhor do que primeiro as tinha tresladadas Mar Jacob. Todavia sem ordem a não muito seguras: digo as palavras essenssiaes da absolvição, por falta como dissem de bom interprete; e tambem porque como monstrão algumas cousas que elle compos, realmente sabia pouco Caldeo:

[e] *O sacramento* da extrema unção numqua foy qua conhecido, nem usado antigamente desta Christandade. Todavia Mar Joseph tresladou a pura forma deste sacramento de Latim em Caldeo, sem mais outra cousa e assy delle usavão algumas veses os sacedotes ungindo algumas pessoas ricas das quaes esperavão boa paga. Agora por industria dos padres da Companhia que tresladarão bem de Latim em caldeo a forma, oraçoes e cerimonias do dito sacramento, ia commummente he usado em toda esta terra graciosamente, nem se tem por venturoso o que não o recebe antes de morrer.

[f] *O sacramento* da ordem foy usado sempre, mas de feição que não usavão dar ordens mais que duas vezes. Huma de diacono na qual tambem davão o subdiacono e lector; foras das quaes no livro ritual caldeo, não se achão outras ordens inferiores distinctas. Da secunda vez davão ordem de presbytero, que entre elles se chama tambem *Caxiça* id est senior. O Diacono com os mais de ordens inferiores se chamão *Camacis*, idest ministro aindaque o Diacono e subdiacono tem particulares nomens de seu officio. Tinhão todos elles antigamente assy Diaconos, como Presbyteros molheres. Porem com hum abuso intoleravel, porque se casavão com ellas depois de tomadas as ordens, o qual fazião com licença de seus prelados, aos quaes peitavão para isto grossamente.

[g] *O Matrimonio* clandestino postoque nos || [92v] Livros Caldeos seia prohibido, e dado por nullo, todavia aqui foy usado, mas sempre que estava algum sacerdote perto o chamavão e a testimunhas diante dos quaes se celebravão as bodas, e os casamentos outros que não erão feitos desta maneira, se tinhão por validos guardando o costume da terra que he amarrar o noivo hum fio no pescoço da noiva a ãqual se le cobre a cabeça com hum panno em sinal de sogeição, com outros sinaes de se

Portuguese were confessing. Mar Habraham afterwards resisted this very much. By no means did he want to accept this sacrament, since they do not have it in Babylon. Nevertheless, God Our Lord helped, and Confession was accepted. In the beginning in general, and afterwards by and by they learned to confess well. Now it is common for all to confess. The said Mar Joseph translated from Latin into Chaldean the words of the formula of the Confession better than they had been translated first by Mar Jacob. Yet it was without order and was not quite correct as regards the essential words of the absolution. The reason for this was the lack of a good translator, as I said, but also because he really did not know Chaldean well, as certain things he composed show.

[e] The sacrament of Extreme Unction was never known here, nor was it used by this Christianity in ancient time. Yet Mar Joseph translated the mere form of this sacrament from Latin into Chaldean without anything else, and thus the priests used to anoint some rich persons from whom they expected good payment. And now by the diligence of the Fathers of the Society who translated well from Latin into Chaldean the form, prayers and the ceremonies of this sacrament, it is already in common use in the whole of the Serra; and people are grateful for that, nor do they consider anyone fortunate who does not receive it before dying.

[f] The sacrament of Order was always used, but with this defect that they were conferring all the orders just in two times: the first time that of the deacon, when the orders of subdeacon and lector also were given; besides these no other distinct minor orders are found in the Chaldean ritual. The second time they were giving the order is that of the presbyter, which among them is called also *Caxiça,* that is, the elder. The deacon with the other minor orders is called *Xamacis* [Śamāśa], that is, minister, although the deacon and the subdeacon have particular names of their office. All these presbyters and deacons in olden times had wives; and what was an intolerable abuse, they used to marry after receiving the orders; and they were doing this with the permission of their prelates, whom they bribed for it grossly.

[g] Although the clandestine marriage [92v] is forbidden according to the Chaldean books and is considered null, nevertheless it was in use here. But when there was a priest close by they called him always and celebrated the wedding before witnesses. But the other weddings not done in this manner were also considered valid, if the custom of the land was observed. That is, the groom ties a thread on the neck of the bride and he covers her head with a drape as a sign of subjection. There are

entregar huma pessoa a outra pondo alguns grãos de arros hum na mão do outro, que he sinal de se entregar perfeitamente e postoque isto do arros, e outras superstições que estes Christãos tinhão nos casamentos se tirarão, todavia ficou o amarrar do fio no pescoço por ser costume da terra, polloque os Malavares na sua lingua chamão a matrimonio Penchetto id est amarrar molher; a qual seus pais desposão logo sendo menina concertandose con os pais do noivo, que tambem de menino dous e tres annos desposão, e a filha dão seus pais o dote conforme sua possibilidade, o qual dote se lhe tornão inteiro por morte do marido morrendo sem filhos. No dia das bodas levão o noivo e a noiva com coroas de ouro na cabeça e a hombros de homens ou em elifantes usando com outras cerimonias das quaes sõ os Reis usão por ser este particular privilegio, que tem os Christãos de S. Thome concedido pollo Rey que arriba dicemos.

[DIVINA LITURGIA]

[22. a] *Da vinte annos* a esta parte por industria dos padres da Companhia moradores de Vaypicotta se tresladou de Latim em Caldeo o livro ritual de todos os sacramentos e tambem da ordem con todas suas formas orações e cerimonias, doqual todos os Parochos desta Christandade usão na administraçao de todos os sacramentos, no qual sò na lingoa se differencião de nos, eseito que o diser da missa he ao modo antigo, mais apurado e aprovado pello Illustrissimo Primas da India, que reconheceo e vio a dita missa que se lhe tresladou em Latim pellos ditos padres da Companhia.

[b] O resar que he em Caldeo he muito mais comprido que o nosso polloque não resem mais que duas vezes cada dia amenhã e a tarde: e tres vezes nos dias de ieium sendo a terceira a meio dia, acabão o psalterio em tres dias.

[c] Sua missa cantada he quasi conforme o costume dos Gregos, fasendo muito caso da adoração da cruz que logo no principio da missa adora o sacerdote que diz a missa e tomandoa nas mãos a dâ â oscular a todo o povo. E o mesmo fazem do livro dos Evangelhos antes de ler o Evangelho o mesmo sacerdote que diz a missa, e dous ministros que lhe aiudão hum lé a epistola e outro huma Lição do Testamento velho.

[d] Nas sestas feiras que são entre Natal e a Quaresma resão na primeira da Madre de Dios e na segunda de S. João Baptista, e na terceira de S. Pedro e são Paulo e mais Apostolos, na quarta dos Evangelistas, e nas outras de S. Estevão e na outra festeiavão antigamente a Nestorio e

also other signs of entrusting a person to another: each places some grains of rice in the other's hand, which is a sign of complete self-commitment. Although this one with the rice and other superstitions which these Christians had at the weddings have been abolished, nevertheless, the tying of the thread on the neck has survived. For it is a custom of the land, for which the Malavarese in their language call the Marriage *Penchetto,* that is, tying a woman. The father betroths his little girl in agreement with the father of the groom, who is likewise a little boy of two or three years. The father gives his daughter a dowry according to his means. The dowry will be returned in its entirety if the husband dies without issue. On the day of the wedding the groom and the bride will wear crowns of gold on the heads and will be carried on the shoulders of men or on elephants. There are other ceremonies also, reserved to royalty, but the Christians of St Thomas enjoy them as a special privilege granted by the king, as we said above.

[22. a] About twenty years back, through the diligence of the Fathers of the Society residing at Vaypicotta, the Book of the Rituals of all the sacraments including Orders, together with all their formulas, prayers and ceremonies was translated from Latin into Chaldean. All the parish priests of this Christianity are now using it in the administration of the sacraments. They differ from us in this matter only as regards the language, except that the saying of Mass is in the ancient manner, but as corrected and approved by the most Illustrious Primate of India, who reviewed and recognized the said Mass which was translated into Latin by the Fathers of the Society.

[b] The recitation of the Liturgy of the Hours is in Chaldean and is much longer than ours, although they do not recite it more than twice a day, in the morning and in the evening; but three times on the days of fast, the third being at noon. They cover the psalter in three days.

[c] In their sung Mass, according to the custom of the Greeks, they make much of the adoration of the cross. Soon after the beginning of the Mass the priest adores the cross, takes it into his hands and lets all the people kiss it. The same they do with the book of the Gospels before the celebrant himself reads the Gospel. Of the two ministers who assist him one reads the Epistle and the other a Lesson from the Old Testament.

[d] Fridays between the Christmas and the Lent: on the first Friday they recite the office of the Mother of God, on the second that of St John the Baptist, on the third that of SS. Peter and Paul and all the Apostles, and on the fourth that of the Evangelists. On one of the remaining Fridays it is of St Stephen and on another Friday they celebrated formerly

seus sequases. E na outra depois resavão de S. Eprehem aiuntando-o com os Doutores Scyriacos hereges, e na derradeira resavão dos fieis || [93r] defuntos sahindo os sacerdotes ao sementerio com huma cruz e agoa benta com que aspergía as sepulturas dos Christãos os quaes por nenhum caso erão enterrados dentro da Igreia senão fora em lugar apartado.

[e] O uso dagoa benta he antequissimo nesta christiandade, fazendoa com incensso, não com sal como nos fazemos, postoque agora usão ia do rito latino no faser dagoa benta.

[f] São observantissimos em celebrar os anniversarios dos seus defuntos dando naquelle dia muitas esmolas e chamando os sacerdotes, os quaes depois de resado na cova do defunto, vão a sua casa, e alli lhe dão de comer, depois do qual resão outros Responsorios. O dó hè deixar crecer a barba e não ir a festas seculares. Jeiunarem quarenta dias e alguns ha que por sua devoção ieiunão hum anno inteiro. Nos quarenta dias logo depois da morte do defunto, vay cada dia o sacerdote a resar na cova do defunto e depois vay a comer a sua casa, donde tambem lhe resa alguns Responsorios. E passados os quarenta dias de trinta em trinta huma vez, atee se acabar o anno, fazem a mesma ceremonia. E nestes Anniversarios e Quarentanarios, e Trentanarios usão de incensso assy na sepultura, como em casa do defunto.

[g] A Vespera do Natal de noite usão queimar os ramos de palma bentos no dia de Ramos, desta maneira fazem huma cova de fronte da porta da Igreia, donde poem os ditos ramos; com outros paos secos, os sacerdotes e povos iuntos se poem ao redor da cova, e resando certas orações e depois cantando tres veses gloria in excelsis Deo, o sacerdote pone fogo aos ramos e incensso no fogo e depois tres veses rodeão ao fogo cantando certos versos em Louvor do nascimento de Christo Nosso Senhor. No dia da Resureição costumão diser missa logo depois da meia anoite.

[h] Jeiunão o Advento, e a Quaresma que começão no domingo da Quinquagessima, postoque agora comecem na segunda feira. Não comem senão depois de meiodia muito tarde nos dias de ieium. E isto depois de idos a Igreia depois das quatro horas da tarde. A resa he mais comprida nestes dias, e os sacerdotes que alevantão muito mais a noite que nos outros dias não são de ieium. Nestes dias não se comem peixe nem laticinio algum, nem se bebe vinho por nenhun caso, nem comem certas folhas que confortão muito o stomago, de modo que està huma pessoa todo hum dia inteiro sem sentir fome. Comem as misturadas com *chunambo* e com outra fruita d'hum arvore que chamão *areca*. Pelloque privaremse das ditas folhas he grande tormento para elles, o qual fazem

the office of Nestorius and his followers. On another Friday they used to recite the office of St Ephrem, adding also their schismatic and heretical Doctors; and on the last Friday they would pray for [93r] the deceased faithful. The priests would go to the cemetery with a cross and the holy water, with which they would sprinkle the graves of the Christians, who in no case were buried in the church but only outside in a place apart.

[e] The use of the holy water is very ancient in this Christianity. Once they made it with incense, not with salt as we do, although now they use the Latin rite in making the holy water.

[f] They are very observant in celebrating the anniversaries of their dead. On that day they give much alms, invite the priests, who after praying at the grave go to the house where they are given meals. After that they recite other responsorials. As a sign of mourning they let the beard grow and do not to go to secular feasts. They fast for forty days following the death of a person. The priest goes every day to the grave to pray and afterwards goes to the house to eat, where also he recites some responsorials. After the fortieth day, they perform the same ceremony once every thirty days till completing one year. On the anniversaries, the Fortieths, and the Thirtieths, they use incense both at the grave and at the house of the deceased.

[g] At the vespers of the Christmas they used to burn in the night the palms blessed on Palm Sunday, in the following manner: they make a pit in front of the church where they place those branches with other dry sticks. The priests and the people stand around the pit, and reciting certain prayers and singing three times "Glory to God in the highest," the priest sets fire to the branches and throws some incense into the fire and then goes around it three times singing certain verses in praise of the birth of Christ Our Lord. On the day of the Resurrection they are accustomed to say the Mass soon after the midnight.

[h] They fast in Advent and in Lent. They used to begin Lent on the Quinquagesima Sunday, although now they begin it on Monday. They do not eat on days of fast until very late in the afternoon, and that too after going to the church at four in the evening. The prayer on these days is longer, and the priests stay awake at night longer than on other days without fast. On fastdays they do not eat fish or milk products; in no case will they drink wine. Neither will they eat certain leaves which soothe the stomach so that a person can remain a whole day without feeling hungry. They chew them mixed with *chunambo* and a fruit of a tree which they call *areca*. To forgo those leaves is a torture for them, and so they do it in times of fasting. On such days their food is rice with blites and vegetables

no tempo de ieium. No qual seu comer he arros com bredos e legumes huma vez ao dia nas horas ditas, postoque muitos porque vivem do seu trabalho comem duas vezes ao dia. Ieiunão tambem tres dias arredo dezoito dias antes da Quaresma. Ieiunão mais quatorze dias antes da Assumpção de Nossa Senhora começando do primeiro de Agosto e no sesto dia sem quebrar ieium fazem grande festa ã Transfiguração de Nosso Senhor. Sesta feira de endoenças antes de solver o ieium comem Absyntio em memoria da paixão e do fel e vinagre de Nosso Senhor Iesus Christo. Esta sesta feira he todo o dia de guarda.

[i] Tem particular devação a S. Jorge, cuia festa celebrão aos 24 de Abril, e a festa da invenção da cruz, aos trese de Septembro, celebrão tambem a são Quirce martyr menino de tres annos, e com sua may santa Julita padecerão martyrio ao quinze || [93v] de Julho, e todo isto dito guardão do tempo immemoravel.

[j] Nos dias de ieium tem por costume estarem os casados afastados, o mesmo fasem nos dias de grandes festividades e nas quartas e sestas de cada semana, nas quaes antigamente tambem ieiunavão.

[k] Os sacerdotes antigamente vestião loubas brancas oque agora tambem muitos usão e criavão a barba oque agora fasem poucos. Seu resar na Igreia he em pê eseito quando resão as horas das matinas. He grandissimo o respeito, que tem a Igreia, donde tem grandissimo medo de diser qualquer mentira. Pelloque quando tratão algum negocio sahem fora da Igreia, temendo que não falem alguma cousa nella que não seia verdade.

[l] Tem por costume immemoravel iuntaremse todos na Igreia e comerem nella certos dias principaes no anno. Porem com toda modestia e sobriedade, sendo de ordinario o comer da dita igreia, pão e certos fruitos todo bento pellos sacerdotes. O que inventarão seus antepassados (disem) para assy ser mais frequentada a Igreia de todo o povo.

[m] São tambem muy reverenciadas as Igreias destes Christãos pollos gentios moradores da terra fasendo Deus algumas veses milagres evidentes, pelloque os ditos gentios não fasem tanto mal, quanto deseião faser a estes Christãos, que por la divina misericordia se conservarão ate agora no coraçao deste infidelidade. Os Reys gentios, em cuias terras estão as ditas Igreias dão certa parte de seus tributos para os gastos dellas.

once a day at the said hour, although many who live by their work eat twice a day. They also keep Three Days Fast eighteen days before the Lent.[11] Likewise they fast fourteen days before the assumption of Our Lady, beginning with the first of August. And on the sixth day, without breaking the fast, they celebrate as a great feast the Transfiguration of Our Lord. On the Friday of the Passion before breaking the fast they eat absinth in memory of the passion and the gall and vinegar given to Our Lord Jesus Christ. The whole of this Friday is a day of observance.

[i] They have a special devotion to St George, whose feast they celebrate on the 24th of April, and the feast of the finding of the Cross on the 13th of September. They celebrate also the feast of St Quirce [12] the martyr, a boy of three years who suffered martyrdom together with his mother St Julita, on the 15th [93^{v}] of July. All these they observe from times immemorial.

[j] On the days of fast it is the custom for the married persons to remain apart. The same they do on the great festivities and on Wednesdays and Fridays of every week. On these days they used to fast in former times.

[k] Formerly the priests used to wear white cassocks, and even now many do wear it. They used to grow beard, but now only a few do so. They recite the office standing on their feet in the Church, except when they recite the morning office. Very great is their respect for the church, where they have great fear to utter a lie. Therefore, when they deal with any business they go out of the church for fear they might say something that is not true.

[l] By an immemorial custom they assemble in the church and eat in it on certain important days of the year, albeit with all modesty and sobriety. The food is given from the church. Ordinarily it is bread and some fruits, everything having been blessed by the priests. This, they say, was invented by their ancestors so that the church might be more frequented by all the people.

[m] The churches of these Christians are venerated also by the heathens, who live in the land. God works sometimes evident miracles, so that those heathens do not do as much harm as they might want to do to these Christians, who by God's mercy have survived until now in the midst of these infidels. The heathen kings, in whose lands exist these churches, grant them a part of their taxes for their expenses.

---

[11] The Three Day Fast, observed in memory of the three days spent by the prophet Jonas in the belly of the fish, ends eighteen days before the start of Lent.

[12] Cyriac, Kuriakose.

[n] Usão estes Christãos benzerense do hombro direito atee o esquerdo o que parece tomarão dos Gregos, que perfidamente creem proceder o spirito santo do Padre somente. Não pode ninguem aiudar a missa sem ter ordens. São os sacerdotes muy respectados destes Christãos, muito mais que entre nos comummente. Não podem, senão quem estiver em ieium, aiudar a missa, aindaque tenha ordens.

[Formação dos sacerdotes]

[23.] O anno de quarenta e hum sobre mil e quinhentos, os Religiosos de s. Francisco fizerão hum seminario em Cranganor, donde ensinavão Latim e bons costumes aos meninos Christãos de S. Thome, que trasião a aquelle seminario, e tiverão nisto muy felices principios, porem depois como estrovavão a estes caçanares a celebrar a seu modo in fermentato, e lhes persuadião que comessem peixes nos dias de ieium e assy outras cousas, que elles tomavão mal, e os sacerdotes latinos que os ditos padres fasião defendião mordicus algumas cousas, que erão de nenhuma importancia para a salvação, como era estrovarlhes os dias de ieium de seu costume, e que não começassem a Quaresma senão a quarta feira de Cinza e que não se iuntassem na Igreia a comer o pão bento, que dissemos. Por amor disto os ditos Christãos de S. Thome e seus sacerdotes tomarão mal isto e se alongarão, porque os sacerdotes que os ditos Religiosos fasião, erão do ritu latino e pretendião mudarlhes os ditos costumes, numqua os tais sacerdotes atee oie tiverão lugar na Serra. De modoque o dito Seminario de Cranganor ficou atee oie Seminario do bispado de Cochim deitando de si muitos e bons clerigos Christãos de S. Thome que sempre administrarão as Igreias do Bispado de Cochim, sem atee oie se achar hum sõ que ficasse na Serra, como he notorio. Proveia bem todavia o dito Seminario a algumas Igreias de cercomvesinhas a Cranganor de hostias e vinho e de outras algumas cousas necessarias ao culto divino segundo a possibilidade do dito Seminario.

[24.] Depois na era de mil e quinhentos e oitenta e quatro se fez em Vaypicotta por ordem do padre Alexandre Valegniano hum Seminario de meninos Christãos de S. Thome, o qual por estar na mesma Serra, e polla grande industria e muito trabalho do padre Jorge de Crasto da Companhia de Jesu foy aceito entre estos Christãos e logo ensinarão os padres da alia manu: Companhia as duas lenguas Latina e Caldea. E fizeram com que Mar Abraham fosse no ano de '85 ao Concilio donde se ordinaram

[n] These Christians used to bless themselves from the right shoulder to the left, which it seems that they received from the Greeks, who perfidiously hold that the Holy Spirit proceeds from the Father only. No one can serve the Mass without being in orders. The priests of these Christians are very much respected, much more than among us commonly. No one, even if he is in orders, can serve the Mass, if he has not been fasting.

[23.] In the year 1541, the Religious of St Francis built a seminary at Cranganor, where they were teaching Latin and good manners to the boys of the Christians of St Thomas, who were brought to that seminary. And in this they had a very happy beginning. However, afterwards they started hindering these caçanares to celebrate in their way with leavened bread. They persuaded them to eat fish on fastdays and thus to do other things which they took ill. And the Latin priests whom the said Fathers trained defended *mordicus* things that were of no importance for salvation. For instance, preventing to hold fastdays according to custom, they insisted that Lent should not begin before Ash Wednesday, and that there should be no assembly in the church to eat the blessed bread, as we said. For their love for it, the Christians of St Thomas and their priests took it ill and distanced themselves. And because the priests formed by the said Religious were of the Latin rite and they tried to change these customs, these priests could not simply be posted anywhere in the Serra till now. Thus the said seminary of Cranganor has been the seminary of the Diocese of Cochin until now, providing many good clerics of the Christians of St Thomas who have always administered the churches of the Diocese of Cochin. But none of them has got settled in the Serra till today. Nevertheless, the said seminary provides some churches around Cranganor with hosts and wine and some other things necessary for the divine worship according to the means of the same seminary.

[24.] Afterwards, in the year 1584, by order of Fr Alexander Valignano, a seminary was founded at Vaypicotta for the children of the St Thomas Christians. Being in the Serra itself and due to the diligence and hard work of Fr George de Crasto of the Society of Jesus it was accepted by these Christians, and soon the Fathers of the Society were teaching there[13] the two languages, Latin and Chaldean. They induced Mar Abraham in the year of '85 to go to the Council [of Goa], in which many

[13] In the original Portuguese text, the last three lines at the end of f. 93^{v} and the first three lines at the head of f. 94^{r} are in a different hand, probably added as a link while removing 58 folios numbered as 533-590 in the original dossier. It is likely that those 58 folios contained a detailed report of the Jesuit seminary at Vaipicotta, its *ratio studiorum*, its students, its impact, etc. and that they were removed in the Jesuit Provincial's curia for some consultation regarding the seminary.

muitas cousas em favor desta Christandade; o que todo Mar Abraham depois desprezou.

[SYNODO NO UDIAMPER]

[25.] Itemque falecendo foy || [94r] o Arcebispo D. Aleixo de Meneses por ordem de sua Santidade visitar os Christãos de S. Thome. Chegando a Cochim a 2 de fevreiro de 1599 D. C. o receberam por su proprio [sic] prelado o dito Arcediago Jorge com os principães christãos de S. Thome da Serra, donde foy recebido com todo aplauso. E expondose a muitos perigos da vida e gastando muito dinheiro em esmolas e edificação das Igreias e outras obras pias, convocou Synodo no Udiamper aos 22 de Junho do dito anno, donde poz em forma todas as cousas eclesiasticas desta Igreia, constituindo Parachos em setenta e sinco Igreias, curadas para os quaes, e para o Arcediago ouve Sua Senhoria del Rey Nosso Senhor dous mil xerafims cada anno com o vinho necessario para as missas desta Serra, e em tanto que Sua Maiestade não o deu, Sua Senhoria de sua fasenda pagou aos ditos e visitou as mais das Igreias desta Serra em pessoa con muito trabalho, mas com tanto fruito; e amor da gente ao dito senhor que foy cousa de pasmo concorrendo Nosso Senhor com cousas miraculosas, com que aprovou o que Sua Senhoria fisera sem ningum resistirlhe.

Postoque no principio ouve alguma desconfiança da parte do Arcediago, e seus seguaces, o que tudo curou a brandura e prudencia do dito Senhor aiudando em tudo e promovendo estas cousas e acompanhando ao dito Senhor os padres da Companhia que lhe mostravão os mais Livros Caldeos hereticos, que ficavão por emendar e manifestandolhe as doenças spirituaes destas almas, que tinhão necessidade de cura: proveendo Sua Senhoria em tudo com grande fervor e liberaldade; e deseiando augumentar esta Igreia, mandou ministros aos gentios remotos aparalhados porem para receberem o Evangelho, como receberão por meio dos padres da Companhia, os Maleas gente, que pousão nos montes muy afastados, donde os ditos padres forão com perigo de suas vidas, e baptisarão as principaes cabeças daquella terra, donde fiserão huma Igreia, que atee oie permanece.

Proveo tambem Sua Senhoria a estas Igreias de Imagens, Retabolos, e vestiduras sagradas, de que estavão muy pobres. Deu o sacramento da confirmação ã maior parte desta Christandade, ordenou algumas pessoas, e supprio a falta das ordens em alguns sacerdotes, que não estavão bem ordenados, polla ignorancia crassa do dito Mar Habrahao.

things were ordered in favour of this Christianity. But later on Mar Abraham disliked them all.

[25.] Therefore, after his death [94ʳ] by order of His Holiness, Archbishop D. Aleixo de Meneses came to visit the Christians of St Thomas. On his arrival at Cochin on the second of February of 1599, they received him as their[14]own prelate. The said [?] Archdeacon George with the chief Christians of St Thomas of the Serra received him with all applause. And exposing himself to many dangers to his life, and spending much money even for building churches and other pious works, he convoked a synod in Udiamper on the 22nd of June of the said year. He thus put into form all ecclesiastical matters of this Church. He appointed parish priests in seventy-five churches. His Lordship cared for them and for the Archdeacon that the King our Lord would give every year two thousand Xerafins and also the wine needed for Masses in this Serra. Till His Majesty started giving them, His Lordship paid them from his own funds. And he himself visited many of the churches of this Serra, a laborious task which, however, bore much fruit. And the people's love for the said Lord was amazing, while Our Lord helped with miracles in approval of what His Lordship was doing without any one to resist him.

Although in the beginning there was some diffidence on the part of the Archdeacon and his followers, the kindness and prudence of the said Lord cured it all. The Fathers of the Society helped him in everything, promoting these things and accompanying the said Lord. They showed him many heretical Chaldean books which were to be corrected, revealing to him the many spiritual maladies of the souls which needed to be cured. His Lordship provided for everything with great fervour and liberality. And desiring to promote the growth of this Church, he sent ministers to the remote and scattered heathens so that they might receive the gospel. Such were the *Maleas* who live on very distant mountains and had received the gospel through the Fathers of the Society, who had been there at the risk of their lives and had baptized the chief heads of that country, built also a church which is there to this day.

His Lordship also provided these churches with pictures, retables and sacred vestments, which they lacked badly. He gave the sacrament of Confirmation to the greater part of this Christianity, ordained some persons and supplied the lack of orders in some priests, who were not well ordained due to the crass ignorance of the said Mar Habraham. And finally he brought this whole Christianity into the form of a Church.

---

[14] What follows is in the usual handwriting.

E finalmente poz em forma da Igreia toda esta Christandade, e a cousa mas admiravel, que aqui fez o dito senhor, a meu parecer, foy fazer em synodo plena anathematizar por boca de tudos em particular ao Patriarcha de Babylonia herege Nestoriano, o qual antigamente igualavão ao sunmo Pontifice e fez nomear o nome do Papa cabeça de toda Igreia nas orações publicas, tirando dellas o nome do dito Patriarcha, como agora se usa nesta Igreia.

Depois de tudo isto ficou esta Igreia com as portas abertas a todo o bem, polloque os padres da Companhia, que morão na Serra ficarão de todo livres para sem impedimento algum promover o bem desta Christandade como fasem com muita gloria de Deus e bem destas almas.

[MILAGRES DE DEUS NA SERRA]

Milagres [in margine] [26.] *E porque o tempo não borre a memoria* dalgumas maravilhas, que Nosso Senhor tem feito nestas Igreias de Serra, determinei de escrever aqui || [94v] algumas dellas mais notorias, e certas, e confirmadas, ou por testemunhas de vista, ou por gente digna de fee, que o ouvio a pessoas verdadeiras ou que o virão.

[a] E começando pollas de mais longe de donde estamos: offerecese logo a Igreia *de Palur*; a qual foy edificada havarà como tresentos annos, e depois reedificada. Deu para ella chão hum christão chamado Mateu Matu. Està esta Igreia deserta digo de Christãos, os quaes pousão longe della, como um quarto de legoa, estando pegados com ella muitos Mouros e Judeos e Gentios, os quaes lhe tem muito respecto. Primeiro havia muitos christãos, que por causa das guerras se forão a outras terras de Reis visinhos, donde fiserão tres povoaçoes. O Rey, que agora governa o Reyno de Palur, foy havido por hum voto, que seus pais fiserão a dita Igreia, porque como tivessem prometido muitas cousas ao demonio, nem isto aproveitasse para terem filhos, fasendo hum voto a Igreia de Palur tiverão logo hum herdeiro, que oie governa o dito Reyno, o qual postoque gentio, he muy amigo dos Christãos. Hum bramene depois de muitos votos feitos ao diabo para ter hum herdeiro, numqua tevem effeito seus deseios, atee faser hum voto a igreia com que ouve o que deseiava.

No tempo en que o Illustrissimo Primas da India estava na Serra, hum homem christão arrepticio do demonio veo a Igreia de Palur, e falando em nome de são Cyriaco martyr cuia invocação tem a dita Igreia, disia muitas cousas, que estavão porvir, e mentindo nas mais dellas como a esperiença mostrava, e fasia tremer a muitas pessoas como se estivessem endemoniados. O qual sabendo o dito senhor mandou huma carta aos Christãos de Palur a qual logo em de acabando de ler cessou tuda aquella illusão do demonio, e o endemoniado numqua mais adivinhou, nen pessoa alguma tremeo.

And the most admirable thing which the said Lord did here, in my opinion, was to make them anathematize in full synod by the mouth of all, in particular the heretic Nestorian Patriarch of Babylon, who had been equalled to the Supreme Pontiff, and to make them name the pope as the head of the whole Church in the public prayers removing from them the name of the said Patriarch, as is done now in this Church.

After all that, this Church remains with doors open for all good. Thus the Fathers of the Society who live in the Serra became altogether free to promote the good of this Christianity without any impediment, as they do it for the great glory of God and the good of these souls.

[26.] [*in the margin* Miracles] And in order that time might not erase the memory of some miracles, which Our Lord wrought in these churches of the Serra I have resolved to write here [94^{v}] some of them more known and certain and confirmed either by eye- witnesses or by people of faith who heard truthful persons or who saw them.

[a] And to begin with those most distant from us, first comes the Church of Palur (Palayur), which was built some 300 years ago and afterwards rebuilt. A Christian by name Maten Matu gave the land for it. This church remains deserted by the Christians, who live a quarter league distant from it, while many Moors, Jews and heathens living close to it have great respect for it. Formerly it had many Christians, who due to wars went to other lands of the neighbouring kings and founded three villages. The king who governs the kingdom of Palur was born after a vow made by his parents to the said church. Though they had promised many things to the devil, nothing of all that helped to have children. After making a vow to the church of Palur, they soon received a heir, the one who is now governing the said kingdom. Though a heathen, he is a great friend of the Christians. A Brahmin who had made many vows to the devil to get an heir never had his desire fulfilled until he made a vow to the said church. Thus he got what he desired.

When the Most Illustrious Primate of India was in the Serra, a Christian man possessed by the devil came to the church of Palur. Speaking in the name of St Cyriac the martyr, who is the patron of this church, he was predicting many things that were to happen. But in most cases he was only lying, as experience showed. He made many people experience tremors as though they were possessed by the devil. Knowing this the said Lord sent a letter to the Christians of Palur. After it was read, all that deception of the devil ceased, and the demoniac never again divined, nor did any one have tremors.

Furtarão os ladrões hum dia o dinheiro do cepo da igreia ha ia muitos annos. E acabando a vida os ditos ladrões em breve tempo muito mal, o dito dinheiro foy offerecido a hum Rey gentio, o qual como soube que era da Igreia não quis tomar por medo que teve. Outro seu parente Rey tambem gentio tomou o dito dinheiro, depois do qual immediatamente lhe socederão muitos desastres, e sobretudo que havendo elle o dito Rey vencido sempre a seus imigos, dalli por diante sempre ficou vencido e abatido delles.

[b] Logo se segue a Igreia de *Enamaqua*, que ha vinte e oito annos, que se fundou em tempo de Mar Habrahão por via de certos christãos ricos, que peitarão ao Samorim e ao senhor da terra, com o que ouverão licença, e comprarão hum chão donde fiserão huma muy pequena Igreia; que atee oie esta da mesma maneira, e gente della num espalhada, e no basar ao presente muy poucos, por causa das guerras presentes. O titulo da Igreia he a Virgem Madre de Deus, a qual defende sua Igreia com muitos castigos que tem dado aos gentios, que a quiserão agravar como diremos a baixo.

O senhor da terra huma noite passando por iunto da dita Igreia com alguns Naires vio muito grande claridade nella e chegando || [95r] mais perto, cuidando que era fogo para o apagar, desapareceo a dita lux e admirando veo ao bazar, e acordou aos christãos, que estavão dormindo e contandolhes o caso elles dicevão que a Igreia era da Madre de Deus, que lhe mostrava aquella visão. Depois doqual o dito senhor da terra foy muy propicio aos ditos christãos, sendolhes primeiro muy aveço, e tomandolhes muitas peitas, depois disto numqua mais usou dista e nos tres dias, que os christãos tem de ieium, cada anno huma vez hia a Igreia, e aiudava aos christãos e lhes pedia que lhe dessem da quelle comer da Igreia, e ellos lho mandavão a casa.

Depois da morte deste hum dos seus herdeiros poz fogo na Igreia em tempo de verão e do muito vento pollo mal que lhes queria. Mas quis Nosso Senor que não accodindo os christãos por espaço de quatro horas apagar o fogo, parecendo a todos os que o uiao que toda Igreia ardia chegando depois acharão, a ola seia toda inteira sem se queimar mais espaço que o redondo, que hum barrete de clerigo e apagado ia do qual pasmarão todos os gentios, que vierão a ver esta maravilha, e da hi a tres dias arderão tres casas do dito que pusera fogo na Igreia, fasendose todas en cinza, sem elle poder morar mais nellas, e dalli a muy pouco tempo por elle ser ruim e mão lhe derão tres cutiladas, e elle ficou manco, e

Many years ago one day some thieves stole money from the coffer of the church. And those thieves died very badly in a short while and that money was offered to a heathen king. Knowing that it was the money of the church, the king did not want to receive it out of fear. Another king, his relative and likewise a heathen, took the said money, but soon many disasters happened to him. Above all, this king, who until then was always victorious over his enemies, from then on was conquered and defeated by them.

[b] Then follows the church of Enamaque [Enammakkel], which was founded 28 years back in the time of Mar Habraham by some rich Christians. They bribed the Samorim and the Lord of the land. Thus they obtained permission and bought a piece of land, where they built a very small church, which exists till today in the same condition. Its people live in a vast area and only a few live in the bazzar at present due to wars. The title of the church is the Virgin Mother of God, who defends her church with many punishments meted out to the heathens who wanted to harm her, as we shall see below.

The lord of the land was passing close to the church with some Nairs one night and saw very much light in it. He approached it [95r], thinking that there was fire in it and he wanted to put it out. The light disappeared. Surprised he came away to the bazaar. He awoke the Christians who were asleep and narrated to them the case. They said that the church was of the Mother of God and she had shown him that vision. After that the said lord of the lands became very propitious to the Christians. Whereas formerly he had been very hostile to them and took much bribe from them, after this event he never did so. During the three days of fast of the Christians every year he would come to the church once. He would help the Christians and ask them to give him that food from the church, and they would send it to his house.

After his death one of his heirs, wishing to harm the Christians, set fire to the church on a summer day which was very windy. But Our Lord helped. As the Christians could not have come to extinguish the fire in four hours time, all who heard about it thought that the whole church would burn down. But when they came they found the entire ola roof intact and unburnt except for the space of the size of a biretta of the clergy. And the fire was already extinguished. All the heathens who came were surprised to see this miracle. Three days later, three houses of the man who had set fire to the church caught fire and were reduced to ashes so that he could no longer live in them. After a short while, this wicked villain became a cripple having received three stabs with a knife.

anda coso con grande ignominia sua sem numqua haver mais bolir con Igreia nem com os christãos.

Hum Christão da pouca fee criava hum galo, o qual tinha offerecido ao pagode, tomando dous christãos disto muita paixão, por ver cada dia andar o galo pollo basar, e passar polla Igreia. Forãose ambos à dita Igreia e pedirão a Nosso Senhor que por sua honra matassem antes da noite aquelle gallo. Em saindo elles de faser oração, o dito gallo no basar cahio morto perante elles.

[c] A Igreia de Mattão tem a invocação de S. Thome apostolo, ha trinta annos que se edificou, em cuio principio tres naires estorvarão muito sua edificação della e hum delles mais atrevido subio no parede e lhe rubou algumas pedras della dizendo o que quis contra os Christãos. Aeste dentro de pouco tempo se lhe podreçeo a lingoa, de feição que lhe caio a metade e elle morreo miseravelmente. Os outros dous tambem se lhes podreçeo o corpo e morrerão o que foi causa de numqua mais estorvarem os naires a obra da dita Igreia.

No basar desta Igreia estavão algumas molheres esteriles, e fazendo voto ã dita Igreia tiverão filhos.

Este anno de 1603 queimarão os naires a dita igreia, depois de quinze dias muitos christãos e gentios virão arder muitas horas huma palmeira que estava iunto da Igreia a cinco horas da tarde no verão com o ceo sereno e depois acharão a palmeira tam verde como primeiro. No que pareçe haverlhes Nosso Senhor declarado, que por mais que queimem Igreias nem por isso perdem seu valor. Tambem neste mesmo tempo depois da Igreia queimada, huma molher velha e devota hum dia depois da meia a noite vio a huma pessoa vestida como clerigo de vestiduras brancas, passear iunto da Igreia, e chamando ella a outras pessoas acudirão e virão a mesma pessoa que loguo desapareçeo: Noque pareçeo haverlhes nosso Senhor dado a entender que elle tinha cuidado de sua Igreia como tem, e se porque o senhor dos naires que a queimarão pagou huma pena boa para a dita igreia. E fiquou mais reverenciada doque primeiro estava.

|| [95v] [d] A Igreia de S. Cruz de Matancher ha poucos annos que se fez postoque a Cruz ha muitos [annos] que alli está, sempre muy acatada de gentios e christãos. Hum menino filho de hum christão, chamado Francisco Dias estando no artigo de morte, prometendo seu pay certa esmola ã dita S. Cruz, logo de improviso o dito menino se achou bem e sarou. Hum Elifante passando hum dia diante da Cruz tomou hum ramo de palma, com que a Cruz estava emramada para a comer. E logo na quelle mesmo dia se lhe incharão os olhos ao dito Elifante, e estando ia

He limped as he walked with great shame and never caused any more disturbance to the church or to the Christians.

A Christian of little faith was raising a cock, which he offered to a temple. Two Christians were very displeased at this as they saw every day the cock go to the bazaar passing in front of the church. Both went into the church and prayed the Lord that they might kill that cock before nightfall. When they went out after making this prayer, that cock fell dead before them in the bazaar.

[c] The Church of Mattâo [Mattam] is in the name of St Thomas the Apostle, and was built thirty years ago. In the beginning three Nairs put many obstacles to its construction. And the most daring of them climbed the wall and stole some stones, uttering all sorts of things against the Christians. Within a short time his tongue became putrid, and losing half of it he died miserably. The other two also had their bodies putrefy, and they died. Because of this never again did the Nairs obstruct the work of the said church.

In the bazaar of this church there were some women who were sterile; and they made vows to the church and had children.

This year 1603, the Nairs set fire to the said church. After fifteen days many Christians and heathens saw a coconut-tree close to the church burning for many hours and afterwards at 5° clock in the evening, with a clear sky, they saw the coconut-tree as green as ever before. By this it seems that Our Lord was declaring to them that, even though they had burned the church, it had not lost its power. Also about the same time, after the church fire, a devout old woman saw a person dressed in white clerical habit walking close to the church after midnight. And she called other persons. They came and saw the same person, who then disappeared all of a sudden. In this it seems that Our Lord made them understand that He cares for His church. So it happened that the lord of the Nairs who burned the church paid a good fine to the said church and it became more respected than before.

[d] [95v] The church of the Holy Cross at Mattancher[i] was built a few years ago, although the Cross existed there for a long time before and was always venerated very much by the heathens and the Christians. A small boy, son of a Christian called Francis Dias, was on the point of death. His father promised certain alms to the said Holy Cross and then all of a sudden the boy got well and was cured. An elephant, passing one day in front of the cross, took a palm branch from the pavilion of the cross and ate it. The same day the eyes of the elephant became suddenly swollen, and the animal was in danger of losing its eyes. The mahout

para os perder, o cornaca prometeo certa esmola a S. Cruz, e logo o dito Elifante sarou.

El Rey de Cochim Ramabrama quiz tirar a Cruz, e mandou para isto hum Elifante, oqual derribou os esteios da igresinha, em que estava a Cruz, e logo dalli a pouco adoeceo El Rey e esteve muito mal, e contava aos seus que hum homem com huma cana na mão estava na cabeceira de sua cama, e lhe não deixava dormir, e sentindo El Rey que isto seria pollo desacato, que fez a S. Cruz, mandou chamar os Christãos, que fizessem hum voto por elle, e logo em o fasendo, e dando certa esmola a Cruz, se achou bem e mandou que se concertassem a dita Igreia, e se fossem por diante na obra de S. Cruz.

O Principe do dito Rey, chamado Codorma, prendeo hum christão, porque fez baptisar sua filha na dita Igreia, e mandou que não se administrasse alli sacramento algum, nem se fizesse obra de pedra na dita Igreia. Pelloque o dito Principe adoeceo logo e esteve a morte e chamou aos christãos e disselhes que fizessem de pedra a Igreia, e administrassem os sacramentos, e logo foi são.

As bexigas são no Malavar, oque entre nos a peste, e adoecendo dellas El Rey de Cochim fez hum voto a S. Cruz da dita Igreia, e não foy a emfermidade pordiante. O que tambem esperimentarão os christãos moradores de Matancher hum anno, no qual dou a dita doença na povoação delles.

Hum gentio furtou hum candieiro da dita Igreia e o dia seguinte logo foy rebatado do demonio o trouxe logo con grandes alvoroços, confessando ser elle o ladrão. Hum Christão uindo hum dia com seu opositor de iurar falso na S. Cruz saltarão certos homens em elle accidentalmente e lhe derão muitas pancadas, e lhe quebrarão as mãos, e os pes.

Huma molher esteril fasendo hum voto a dita Cruz, teve hum filho que oie vive. Outra molher iurando falso na dita cruz, logo de improviso se lhe enchou o braço, e esteve a morte, atee que ella em pessoa, outro dia veo adiante da Cruz e confessou ter iurado falso e restituio huma galinha con seus pintainhos que tinha levado mal pollo dito iuramento, e logo se achou bem. Hum Christão por nome Isac trasia huma cadea douro, no pescoço, a qual fora comprada com dinheiro de S. Cruz por outro Christão defunto, e porfiando elle que a cadea era sua, logo de improviso o dia seguinte se achou com o pescoço enchado, e torcido, e

promised some alms to the Holy Cross, and soon the said elephant was cured.

The king of Cochin, Ramabrama, wished to remove this Cross. For this purpose he sent an elephant, and it destroyed the supports of the small church in which stood the cross. Shortly after that the king got sick very badly. He told his people that a man with a cane in the hand was at the head of his bed and was not letting him sleep. And thinking that it must be because of the disrespect he had done to the Holy Cross, the king sent word to the Christians to make a vow for him. They did so and he gave some alms to the Cross. The king got well and he gave orders that the said church was to be repaired. And thereafter they did the work of the Holy Cross.

The said king's prince Codorma arrested a Christian, because he had his daughter baptized in that church. Cadorma gave orders that no sacrament should be administered there, nor any work in stone should be pursued in that church. The prince soon became sick and was about to die. And so he called the Christians and told them that they could build the church with stone and administer the sacraments there. Soon he got well.

Small pox is in Malavar what plague is among us. When the king of Cochin contracted it, he made a vow to the Holy Cross of the said church. And he did not have the sickness any more. The Christians of Mattancheri also experienced the same during the year when there was that sickness in their town.

A heathen stole a lamp of the said church and soon on the following day he was vexed by the devil. With great repentance he returned the lamp, confessing that he was the thief. A Christian came one day with his opponent to swear a false oath by the Cross. But it happened that some men fell on him and thrashed him thoroughly, breaking his arms and legs.

A sterile woman, making a vow to the said Cross got a son, who is still alive today. Another woman made a false oath by the Cross. Suddenly she had a swelling on her arm and she was on the point of death. The next day she went to the Cross and confessed that she had sworn falsely. She restituted a hen with the chicken which she had wrongly taken with the said oath. And immediately she got well. A Christian by name Isaac was wearing a gold chain on the neck. It had been bought with the money of the Holy Cross by another man who by then was already dead. For contending that the chain was his, his neck became swollen and

confessando seu peccado publicamente tornou a cadea a S. Cruz e logo se achou bem do pescoço.

Hum Regedor del Rey de Cochim quiz com hum Elifante derrubar S. Cruz, e cometendo o dito Elifante a carreira para a derrubar, ia numqua pode ir pordiante, mas arreceiava para tras con grandes bramidos. Muitos gentios e Christãos passando rios, em tempo de tempestades e grandes ventos, forão milagrosamente salvos por votos que fasião a santa Cruz.

|| [96r] [e] A Igreia de Nossa Senhora de Xaragate ha dous annos nomais que se começou por pura devoção e importunação do senhor da terra que postoque gentio he bom homem moralmente e deseia ser christão. A invocação desta Igreia he Nossa Senhora da Conceição. Dous cavoqueiros gentios, que cortavão pedra para Igreia se forão para outra terra levando algum dinheiro, que lhe tenhão dado adiantado os mordomos della. Depois veio outro cavoqueiro tambem gentio, o qual cortando pedras para dita Igreia lhe deu huma mã disposiçao, com que se achou mal. E recolhendosse para casa, foi primeiro ã cruz, e Igreia e dice estas palavras, minha igreia, e minha cruz; eu não posso cortar mais pedra, não me atribuileis mais. E dizendo isto se foi para sua casa; dormindo lhe pareçeo huma menina formosissima que dice estas palavras. Não te enganes tu, nem deixes minha obra assi como deixarão os dous primeiros que se forão. Mas tu por nenhum caso deixes minha obra, e se quiseres, toma outro cavoqueiro contigo, e acordando do sonho sentio são, e foy logo a trabalhar, e publicou isto. O que ouvindo os primeiros dous que se forão tornarão a cortar pedra para a dita Igreia.

Hum Christão chamado Jorge foy a huma festa a outra terra, donde ouvio diser que hum seu filho estava muito mal que lho accodisse e logo pondose no caminho fez hum voto a dita Igreia de lhe dar um real si achasse o seu filho em casa são e salvo. E indo a casa o achou na porta brincado con outros meninos são e salvo. Pello que deu muitas graças a Nosso Senhor.

A may do dito Regedor teve primeiro hum entras [anthrax], do qual sanando disse o medico gentio que se outra ves o tivesse, morreria delle. Estando dalli alguns annos o Regedor ausente da terra, vierão mensageiros que lhe disserão que sua may tinha hum entras, do qual muito sentido, cuidando que morreria, fez hum voto a dita Igreia que se achasse a sua may sem aquelle inchaço daria certa esmola a dita Igreia e compriolhe a Madre de Deus seus deseios, porque chegando a casa achou sua may com o inchaço desfeito e apagado.

curved suddenly on the next day. Then he confessed his sin publicly and returned the chain to the Holy Cross, and he felt well on the neck.

A governor of the king of Cochin wanted to destroy the Cross using an elephant. He brought the elephant along but it could no more advance. It started to walk backwards, trumpeting loudly. Many heathens and Christians crossing the rivers in times of tempests and strong winds were miraculously saved through vows made to the Holy Cross.

[e] [96r] The church of Our Lady at Xaregate [?] was begun two years ago mainly because of the devotion and solicitude of a landlord. Though a heathen, he is a morally good man and wants to become a Christian. The dedication title of the church is Our Lady of the (Immaculate) Conception. Two heathen pikemen who were cutting stone for the church went away to another country, taking some money which was given to them in advance by the trustees of the church. Afterwards there came another heathen pikeman, who while cutting stone for the church suffered from a bad disposition and became ill. He went back home passing by the cross and the church, and said these words: "My church, my cross, I cannot cut stone for the church any more; do not trouble me again." Saying this he went home. While he was asleep a very beautiful young girl appeared to him and told him the following: "Do not let yourself be deceived, and do not abandon my work as the other two have done. In no case shall you abandon my work, but if you wish, take another pikeman with you." After waking up from the dream he felt well. Forthwith he left for work and made the matter public. Hearing of this those two who had gone away returned to cut stone for the church.

A Christian called George went to a feast in another country. There he heard that his son had fallen very ill and that he should return in haste. Immediately he hurried back and made a vow to give a Real to the said church if he should find his son at home safe and sound. And reaching home he found him at the door playing with other boys and in good health. For this he gave many thanks to the Lord.

The mother of the said governor once was suffering from anthrax. The heathen physician, who was treating her said that if she got it again she would die of it. Some years later, when the governor was absent from the country, messengers came to him to say that his mother had caught anthrax. The governor felt very sad and was anxious that she would die. He made a vow to the said church that, if he found his mother without that tumour, he would give some alms to that church. And the Mother of God accomplished his desire, for on reaching home, he found his mother in sound health.

O mesmo Regedor tinha huma bufara que lhe custura muito a qual esteve depois de parida oito dias sem poder botar as parias, pelloque estava para morrer. E o dito Regedor fez hum voto a dita Igreia e logo a bufara botou as parias e sarou.

Hum homem Portugues havia muito tempo que estava mal dhum braço, oqual sentindose sem remedio foy a dita Igreia e fez hum voto a Nossa Senhora de por sua santa imagen nella, o qual feito se tornou para Cochim, e mandando pintar o Retabolo de Nossa Senhra sarou e elle mesmo trouxe a Imagem da Senhora e a poz na Igreia.

[f] A Igreia de Balianate [Velayanadu], he tambem de Nossa Senhora, ha trinta e quatro annos que he feita. Logo no principio deu nos Christãos doença de bexigas que he como peste no Malavar, e desião os gentios que aquillo lhe acontecera, porque edificarão a dita Igreia. Mas quiz Nosso Senhor confundillos, porque nenhum Christão morreo e estando hum todavia muito mal e arrancando ia, lhe appareçeo Nossa Senhora e lhe disse, estas são de tua infirmidade. E assy foy que sarou em breve o que sabendo depois os gentios tiverão muito respeito a dita Igreia.

Ao Rey da quella terra se lhe fez enchaço na nariz e hum seu Principe outro || [96v] nas costas. E vendose muy attribulados fiserão votos a dita Igreia, e sararão tam brevemente e de feição que entenderão claramente ser mercê da Virgem Madre de Deus. Outro gentio deseiava ter huma filha para oqual fez hum voto a dita Igreia, e lhe comprio em breve seus deseios, e elle comprio voto quė tenha feito, que era dar da comer a todos os Christãos, que se aiuntavão na dita Igreia.

Hum carpinteiro gentio disse certas palavras de despreso contra a dita Igreia e perante os christãos, e logo cahio huma trave derriba que lhe quebrou hum pê. Outros gentios estando doentes fasem voto a dita Igreia, assy como os Christãos e sarão de suas infermidades.

[g] A Igreia de Mangate [Alangad] haverà sesenta annos, pouco mas ou menos, que se fundou, seu titulo he, a Madre de Deus. Hauera sete annos que queimarão os inimigos do Rey daquella terra, a povoação dos Christãos de Mangate donde no meio della esta huma cruz de pao muy velha, e nella a parte derriba estavão muitas folhas de palma e muy secas ia do tempo, e pegada com a dita cruz estava huma casinha cuberta de folhas de palmeiras ia muy secas, e tocavão na cruz, nas folhas da palma, que estavão nella bentas do dia de Ramos, ben secas, como palha. Queimouse a pouvação com o todo della, as arvores verdes ao redor della tambem se queimarão, e toda a casinha dita, que estava pegada com a cruz, sem ella, nem as folhas de palma que nella estavão padeçerem det-

The same governor had a buffalo, which had cost him much. Even eight days after the delivery the buffalo did not drop the afterbirth, and was about to die. The governor made a vow to the church, and soon the buffalo dropped the after-birth and was cured.

For a long time a Portuguese man had not been feeling well on his arm. Understanding that there was no remedy, he went to the said church and made a vow to Our Lady to place a picture of hers in the church. Returning to Cochin he gave orders for a retable of Our Lady to be painted, and he was cured. He himself then brought the picture of Our Lady and placed it in the church.

[f] The Church of Balianate [Velayanadu] is also of Our Lady. It was built thirty-four years ago. In the beginning there was the illness of smallpox among the Christians. In Malabar it is like plague. And the heathens were nagging that it happened to them because they built the said church. But Our Lord deigned to confound them, because no Christian died. And to one who was very ill Our Lady appeared and said, These are for your infirmity. And thus he was cured in a short time. Having learnt this the heathens had great respect for the said church thereafter.

The king of that county had a tumour in his nose, and his prince had a tumour [96v] on the ribs. Being very much afflicted, they made vows to the said church and they were cured in so short a time that they recognised it as a favour of the Virgin Mother of God. Another heathen wanted to have a daughter, for which he made a vow to that church. And shortly afterwards God accomplished his desire and he fulfilled his vow, which was to give food to all the Christians who assembled in that church.

A heathen carpenter uttered some words in contempt of the said church in the presence of the Christians. Immediately a beam fell from above and broke his leg. Other heathens when they become sick make vows to the said church, and just like the Christians they get cured of their infirmities.

[g] The Church of Mangate [Alangad] was founded more or less sixty years ago. Its title is the Mother of God. Seven years ago the enemies of the king of that country burned the village of the Christians of Mangate. In the middle of the village stood a very old wooden cross. Over it there were dry palm leaves, and close to it there was a small house thatched with dry palm leaves. And touching the cross they had placed dry palm leaves, blessed on the day of branches [Palm Sunday]. The Christians' village and the green trees around were burned up in the fire, but the cross and the small house with the blessed palm leaves suffered no harm and remained untouched amidst the flames of the fire. Amazed at this

rimento algum ficando illesas com a cruz em meio das chamas de fogo. Doque pasmado o Rey da terra, vio a ver com muita admiração a dita cruz com outros muitos gentios.

O mesmo aconteceo quando se queimou a hermida da S. cruz que esta no dito Mangate, porque queimandose toda a Igreia, estando a cruz, que he muy grande de pao muito seco no meio ficou illesa na metade do fogo. E a esta Igreia accodem muitas pessoas com diversos votos, que fasem a Virgem para particulares beneficios, que della recebem.

A huma molher christaa da dita terra de Mangate alevantarão hum falso, disendo que tinha cometido adulterio, oqual ella sentindo muito, por ser pessoa muy honrada, ieiunou quarenta dias, no cabo dos quaes confessou e comungou, tomou na dita Igreia nas mãos hum ferro quente vermelho, como fogo, e o teve bom espaço de tempo nas palmas das mãos, sem se queimar, disendo estar innocente do que lhe alevantarão. E deitando depois das mãos o dito ferro quente deitarão emrriba delle, humas fullas verdes, as quaes logo com a quentura se desfiserão.

[h] A Igreia grande de Paru, he de grande devoção, sua invocação he de S. Gervasio e S. Protasio. He muy antiga, e muito antes dos Portugueses virem para India se fez a dita Igreia. El Rey da terra fez huma descortesia a dita Igreia não deixando ir pordiante a obra della; pelloque foy muy atormentado de huma visão, que tinha sempre de noite, e hera que parecia ver duas pessoas na cabeceira de seu leito con duas canas nas mãos que o ameaçavão; pelloque chamou os christãos, e contandolhes a visão soube da invocação da Igreia e logo mandou ir obra pordiante dando em penitencia a dita Igreia hum grande candieiro de cobre que atee oie se guarda na dita Igreia.

Huns ladrões furtarão certos candieiros da Igreia pequenos, e querendose ir, cuidando que fugião os achou o samchristão da Igreia pela menhàa no lugar donde fiserão o furto, dando com as mãos na area, como que estavão nadando na agoa, ou remavão com as mãos alguma embarcação. O que vendo o dito samchristão compadecendose delles, ê || [97r] accodindo outros Christãos os lançarão fora, e os puserão em salvo, peroque não os matassem; os ladrões que erão gentios.

Estando hum dia muitos Christãos ecclesiasticos e seculares na dita Igreia, e ao redor della comendo conforme seu costume o pão bento, que dissemos arriba, começou a chouver, pelloque na metade da festa ficarão todos muy tristes, porque não tinhao donde se agasalhar se viera a chuivà. O qual vendo a molher christaa, a cuias custas se fasia adita

the king of the country came together with many heathens to see the cross and greatly admired it.

The same thing happened when the hermitage of the Holy Cross at Mangate caught fire. While the whole church was on flames, a very big wooden cross remained unharmed in the fire. Many persons come to this church and make various vows to the Virgin for particular favours. And they get them from her.

Against a Christian woman of Mangate they brought a false accusation that she had committed adultery. She was a person of honour and she felt it very badly. She fasted forty days, confessed and received communion; and then she took in her hands a red hot iron in that church and held it for a good length of time in the palms of her hands without being burned, saying that she was innocent of what they had accused her. And when that hot iron was dropped off her hands, they threw some green leaves over it, which were at once destroyed by the heat.[15]

[h] The great Church of Paru[r] is held in great devotion. It is in the name of SS. Gervasis and Protasis. It is very ancient, and it was built much before the Portuguese came to India. The king of the country did an act of discourtesy to the church, not allowing its works to go ahead. Therefore, he was very much tormented by a vision which he had every night: he saw two persons at the head of his bed with canes in the hands threatening him. For that reason he called the Christians. On talking to them about the vision he was informed of the patrons of the church. At once he gave orders to continue the work, and gave also as penance to that church a big lamp of copper, which is kept in the church till today.

Some thieves stole some small lamps of the church. As they were trying to make off, the sacristan of the church came upon them in the morning at the very place they had committed the theft. They were throwing their hands into the air, as though they were swimming in water or rowing a boat with their hands. Seeing this the sacristan had pity on them, but [97r] the other Christians came rushing in and drove them out, just letting them go free without killing them. The thieves were heathens.

One day many Christians, both ecclesiastics and secular, were in and around the said church, eating the blessed bread according to their custom, as we said above. Then it began to rain, and so in the middle of the feast all turned sad, as there was no place for all to take shelter if it were to rain. Seeing this the Christian woman, at whose cost the feast was

---

[15] This incident is narrated in the Jesuit annual letters of 1593 (*Documenta Indica*, XVI, pp. 336-337).

festa, entrou na Igreia, e pondose de giolhos rogou a Nosso Senhor que detinesse a chuiva, e assendeo hum candieiro diante do altar, e não choveo consolando Nosso Senhor a todos aosque se tinhão aiuntados na dita Igreia e cabavão sua festa com muita alegrìa.

[i] A Igreia de Corlengate [Kuravilangad] foy feita antes muito dos Portugueses uirem a India. Sua invocação he de Madre de Deus. Foy fundada por esta causa. Appareçeo a Virgem em sonhos a hum christão mandandolhe que fisesse no dito lugar huma Igreia, e não obedecendo o christão lhe appareçeo por outras duas vezes dandolhe na cabeça com huma cana por estas duas veses e com tudo não fez a Igreia, depois do qual logo outro dia foy hum christão arrebatado do bom espirito, e falando em nome de Nossa Senhora, disse que edificasse no dito lugar huma Igreia. A qual edificarão en nome da Virgem Madre de Deus. O nomem do christão que fez a dita Igreia não he conhecido, porque não onomeando por seu nome o chamão, o christão da Igreia.

Nesta Igreia offerecerão os Christãos, muito dinheiro para o edificio della, o qual sabendo hum reisinho da terra veo de noite para roubar o dito dinheiro, e batendo na porta da igreia, hum sacerdote que dentro della estava, numqua lhe quis abrir, e porfiando elles que arombarian as portas, o dito sacerdote lhes disse que fisessem o que quisessem que elle morreria primeiro nas suas mãos, antes que levassem o dinheiro da dita igreia. E disendo esto lhes deu huns poucos de reales por hum buraco da porta, os quaes elles tomavão; e se forão sem bulir com a Igreia; e logo descendo da Igreia mordeo huma cobra a hum dos soldados do dito rey, que logo morreo e tomando o corpo morto, o levarão na casa dhum seu idolo, e estando o dito rey nella com os mais soldados, e o corpo do defunto, cahio huma trave darriba do templo, e deu na cabeça do dito rey, ao qual postoque não matou, feriou muito mal, pello que arrependião do sacrilegio, numqua mais, nem elle, nem seus herdeiros, ousarão bulir com a dita igreia.

Costume he no Malavar, não se poderem as Igreias nem casas dos Christãos cubrirem de telhas sem licençaa do Rey da terra. Porem os Christãos de Quorlengate não tendo que ver com isto, cubrirão sua Igreia de telhas. Pello que o Rey da terra agastado foy a dita Igreia e quebrou toda a telha della. E logo em chegando o dito Rey a sua casa depois disto feito, logo se tornou doundo, e deitando seu proprio esterco polla boca, morreo em breve miseravelmente. E sua molher, que estava prenha nao podendo parir, ainda depois dos dez meses, lhe abrirão a barriga e lhe

being celebrated, entered the church and falling on her knees prayed Our Lord to delay the rain. She lighted a lamp before the altar, and it did not rain any more. Thus Our Lord consoled everyone assembled in the church, and they made the feast with great joy.

[i] The Church of Corlengate [Kuravilangadu] was built much before the Portuguese reached India. It is in the name of the Mother of God. It was founded for the following reason. The Virgin appeared to a Christian in his sleep and ordered him to build a church at that place. But he did not obey, and she appeared to him twice more, beating him on the head with a cane. Yet he did not build the church. Soon after that one day a Christian was moved by a good spirit, and speaking in the name of Our Lady, he said that a church should be built at the said place. And they built it in the name of the Virgin Mother of God. The name of the Christian who built the church is not known, because he is not called by his name but he is called "the Christian of the Church."

In this church the Christians had collected much money as offerings for its edifice. Having learnt of this a kinglet of the land came by night to steal that money. He knocked at the door of the church. A priest was inside but he did not want to open it. But as they were trying to break open the door, the priest said to them that they might do whatever they wanted, but not before he died by their hands would they get away with the money of that church. Saying this he gave them a few reals through a hole in the door. They took them and went away doing no harm to the church. As they were going down from the church, one of the soldiers of the said king was bitten by a cobra and he died at once. They carried the dead man to the house of an idol. As the king and his soldiers were there with the corpse, a beam fell on the head of the king from the top of the temple. Though it did not kill him, it wounded him very badly. Hence repenting of the sacrilege, never did he dare to meddle with that church again, nor his heirs.

It is the custom in Malavar that the churches or the houses of the Christians cannot be thatched with tiles without the permission of the king of the country. However, the Christians of Quorlengate, not wanting to go along with it any more, thatched their church with tiles. Piqued by this, the king of the country went to the church and broke all its tiles. On reaching home soon after this deed, this king became mad, and discharging the excrement through his mouth he died miserably in a short time. His wife, who was pregnant, did not give birth even after ten months. So they opened her belly and took out the child, but she died. After that for

tirarão a criança, e ella morreo, depois do qual por medo ainda que mais lhes pezou, derão licença para se telhar a dita Igreia.

|| [97v] Hum dia o senhor da terra fechou a dita Igreia não deixando entrar nella peçoa alguma por odio que tinha aos Christãos. Estavão naquella hora dous candieiros grandes accesos con pouco ageite, e dali a quarenta dias abrindo a dita Igreia os acharão da mesma maneira con o mesmo ageite e torcidas que se não tinhão desminuido cousa alguma, o qual vendo o dito senhor, admirado do milagre, deixou de afliguir aos Christãos.

Hum sacerdote schismatico, porque nem obedecia ao prelado, nem quis tomar o chalendario Gregoriano, como tinha tomada toda esta Christiandade, tendo de sua parte quinhentos homens todos rebeldes a Igreia. Este sacerdote foy illuso do demonio do para si que era santo, e emendou, digo desmanchou a resa e as oraçoes da missa, como quis, sendo idiota, e muy soberbo, e andava *com habito de religioso* sem serlo, e ainda se iactava que era Bispo, disendo que hum Simeão, que antigamente se fisera qua Bispo, e depois foy daqui botado, o tocara com certo vestido, com que ficara Bispo, e mais disia que lhe apparecerã Nossa Senhora, que lhe dissera que estivesse nos seus treze. Este sacerdote, como digo, continuava na dita Igreia de Quorlengate, sendo tal, escomungado nominatim. Não podendo resistirlhe os outros Christãos, que todos neste Malavar são governados de senhores gentios, todavia ninguem lhe ouvia a sua missa senão os de sua parcelealidade. Hum dia estando-o hum sacerdote de seminario de Vaypicotta, confundindo con rezões, disse o dito schismatico, que Noss Senhora no partu, não fora virgem porfiando nisto, por mais que com rezões claras, outro sacerdote o confundia. E dalli a pouco pella balasphemia, que disse, lhe deu huma infermidade na lingua; que se lhe meteo para dentro de pouco em poco, e durando isto alguns meses foy perdendo a falla de modo que não se podia perceber o que disia, e morreo com a lingua podre, e com muitos dores, inobediente, e escomungado, e desemparado de todos, porque antes delle morrer, todos, os que erão de sua parcelealidade, se reduzirão por meio dos padres da Companhia.

Hum gentio determinado de roubar o dinheiro da dita Igreia foy tres noites a meia noite, e entrando dentro do muro da Igreia vio muitas matronas, que estavão fasendo oração na dita Igreia, e todas estas tres anoites vendo a dita visão, ficou tam pasmado, pelloque não ousou mais tornar aella, e apregoou isto en muitas partes con muito medo e admiração.

the fear which weighed ever more on them, they gave permission to thatch that church with tiles.

[97v] One day the lord of the land closed the said church and would not allow anyone to enter it out of the hatred he had for the Christians. At that hour two big lamps remained lit in the church but with little oil. Opening that church after forty days they saw the lamps in the same condition, still burning, and the oil had not diminished at all. Seeing this, the said lord marvelled at the miracle and stopped vexing the Christians.

There was a schismatic priest, who neither obeyed the prelate nor wanted to accept the Gregorian calendar, which this whole Christianity had accepted. He had in his party five hundred rebels of the church. He was under the illusion of the devil that he was a saint. And he corrected, I say deformed, the Liturgy of the Hours and the prayers of the Mass as he wanted. Being stupid and very proud he was going about in the habit of a Religious, which he was not. He even used to boast to be a bishop, saying that one Simon, who formerly was a bishop here but was later sacked from here, had donned him with a robe and thus made him bishop. He said also that Our Lady had appeared to him and told him not to yield. This priest stayed on at the church of Quorlengate, though he had been excommunicated by name. The other Christians could not oppose him, because in Malavar they are governed by heathen lords. However, no one went to hear his Mass, except those who were of his clique. One day a priest of the Vaypicotta seminary was confuting him with reasons. The schismatic priest maintained that Our Lady was not a virgin *in partu*[16] and he maintained his position with stubbornness than clear reasons, while the other priest confuted him. Shortly after that, for the blasphemy he had uttered she gave him an infirmity on the tongue, which drew back little by little. In a few months he gradually lost his speech, so that no one could understand what he was saying. He died with a putrid tongue and suffering many pains, disobedient, excommunicated, and forsaken by all. For before his death all those who were of his clique had been brought back by the Fathers of the Society.

Determined to steal the money of that church, a heathen went there at midnight on three nights. But when he got within the walls, he saw many matrons reciting prayers in the church. As he saw this vision on all three nights, he became so amazed that he never again dared to return there. And he has avowed this here and there with great fear and amazement.

---

[16] *In partu*, Latin, meaning while giving birth to Jesus. According to Catholic belief, Mary was a virgin *ante partum, in partu, et post partum*: before, in, and after giving birth to Jesus.

Hum ladrão tomou certa cousa da Igreia, e levando-a andando toda noite atee pola menhã, não pode andar mais, que hum quarto de legoa, e achando o senhor da terra o mandou spetar. Outros muitos castigos de diversas maneiras que seria largo contar, tem dado Deus Nosso Senhor aos que tiverão pouco respeito a dita Igreia.

[j] A Igreia de Molanodurte [Mulanthuruthy] tem a invocação do Apostolo S. Thome. Foy feita depois dos Portugueses virem a India, hauerà [deest numerus] annos. Hum gentio pagava cada anno certo censu para a Igreia darros, e havia ia tempo que não queria pagar. Pello qual accostumando os Christãos nos tre dias de ieium que tem antes da quaresma comerem todos iuntos no pateo da Igreia, por causa do dito gentio não querer pagar, estavão ia para deixar sua solemnidade. Mas o Apostolo S. Thome || [98r] teve cuidado dos seus, porque como o dito gentio confessou, lhe appareceo de noite em visão huma pessoa veneravel, que não o deixava dormir ameaçando-o, pelloque o dito gentio ame-amedrontado confessou seu peccado, e pagou logo a Igreia, e tiverão naquelle anno os Christãos oque bastava para fazer sua solemnidade.

Estando na dita Igreia os carpinteiros trabalhando cahirão sobre elles muitas traves, as quaes virão que huma pessoa, vestida como clerigo, as detinha, como fez de modo que nenhum padeçeo trabalho. Estando os Christãos aiudando a subir huma pedra muy grande arriba para edificar a Igreia, estando ia no alto se virou e cahindo em dereito donde elles estavão, estando elles descuidados, lhes appareeço que os botarão a cada hum por seu cabo, de modo que a pedra não os achou, e cahio em riba dhum banco, que fez em pedacos.

O Regedor de Molanodurte, por mais que os Christãos lhe impidirão, não quiz senão mandar fazer espingardas para seu Rey no alpendre da dita igreia. Depois doqual indo a guerra com seu Rey ficarão todos perdidos, e o dito Regedor com muitas feridas no corpo: e no tempo que se curava dellas, via todas as noites huma visão dhuma pessoa, que o ameaçava com huma cana na cabeceira. E confessando que os ditos malos lhe asocederão por causa de pouca reverencia que tivera a Igreia de S. Thome, fez hum voto a ella dando conta disto aos Christãos, e cesou a inquietação, que tinha.

Hum ferreiro levou da igreia huma rripa, e disendolhe os Christãos que não fizesse aquillo, despreçou os, e foy se. Denoite lhe appareçeo huma pessoa que lhe dava com huma cana, porque tomarà a dita ripa. E com grande medo contou isto aos Christãos e tornou arripa, e fez hum voto a Igreia, e foy livre de inquietação.

A thief took away something of that church. But carrying it and walking all the night till the morning he could not go more than a quarter of a league. And the lord of the land saw him and pierced him with a spit. Many other punishments of various kinds, which God Our Lord gave to those who held little respect to that church, will be too long to narrate.

[j] The Church of Molandurte [Mulanthuruthy] is under the patronage of St Thomas the Apostle. It was built [... blank] years ago, after the Portuguese came to India. A heathen used to pay a rent of rice to the church. However, for some time he refused to pay it. On the Three Day Fast before the Lent, the Christians were accustomed to assemble and take a meal at the churchyard. But as the heathen refused to pay the rent, they were about to give up their festivity. The Apostle St Thomas, however, [98r] had care for his people. As the said heathen confessed, a venerable person appeared to him in a vision at night and threatened him without letting him sleep. Frightened by this, the said heathen admitted his sin and soon paid to the church. And the Christians got what was necessary for them to celebrate the feast that year.

When the carpenters were at work in the church, many beams fell down over them. But they saw a person dressed as a cleric holding up the beams, so that none of them got hurt. Some Christians were once helping to hoist a very big stone for the construction of a church. When it was well at the top they saw it fall in the direction where they were standing. Being unprotected they thought that it would hit them on their head, but the stone fell on a bench and broke it into pieces.

The governor of Molandurte gave orders to construct guns for his king at the portico of that church. But the Christians objected to it. Afterwards going for war with their king, they lost everything, and the governor was left with many wounds on the body. While getting cured of the wounds, he saw every night in a vision a man menacing him with a cane at the bedside. And he admitted that the said evils had befallen him due to the little reverence he had for the church of St Thomas. He made a vow to the church, informing also the Christians about it. Thus ended all his disturbance.

A blacksmith took away a small plank (*ripa*) of the church. When the Christians said that he should not do it, he disregarded them and went away. At night a person appeared to him and beat him with a cane for having taken the plank. And he narrated this to the Christians with great fear, returned the plank and made a vow to the church, and he was freed of the disturbance.

Hum christão disse que elle tomava hum dia huma poucachinha de chumaya, que era da Igreia e a puzera em riba dhuma trave na sua casa. Depois do qual huns meninos piquenos, que tinha, choravão e gritavão denoite, que os queimavão na dita chumaya. O christão vendo isto tornou a chumaya a Igreia, e fez lhe hum voto, e cessou a inquietação dos meninos.

[k] A Igreia de Caramatete [Kadamattathu], hoie ha sesenta annos que se edificou, tem por invocação S. Jorge. Faz muitos milagres, assy com os gentios, como com os Christãos, os quaes todos fazem muitos votos a dita Igreia. Hum dia não estando ainda acabada a dita Igreia se ouvio hum som da campana tres vezes, que ouvirão ainda os gentios, que pouzavão longe. E hum bom velho, que pousava alli perto se alevantou, hera meia noite, e foy a dita Igreia, e vio muitos lumens, e vozes de instromentos musicos muito suaves; e pasmado da vizão, se retirou, e pubricou oque viram.

Furtou hum ladrão da dita Igreia cinco || [98v] cruzesinhas e quatro candieiros. E indo por seu caminho com o furto nas mãos, pareçeolhe que vinha tras delle hum grande tropel de gente, e desviandose do caminho escondeo oque furtara dentro do mato, e depois tornado ao caminho e não vendo ninguem dos que evidava, tornou a buscar o furto, que tinha escondido, e numqua pode acharlo, e dalli a treis dias ficou doundo, e perguntado pollo furto e donde estava, disia que não sabia. E que aquillo que elle furtara, o poõ o comeria, e aelle os peixes. Dalli a duzentos dias revelou Nosso Senhor a hum sacerdote velho, o modo de achar o dito furto, e a pessoa que o avia de em caminhar, que acharia en tal parte, foy o dito sacerdote, e achou tudo, como lhe fora dito, depois o senhor da terra, matou ao dito ladrão, e deitando seu corpo no rio ficou comido de peixes, como elle mesmo dissera.

Matarão os Christãos dalli hum gentio principal, por faser certa iniuria a hum clerigo, depois do qual os soldados do morto queimarao as casas dos Christãos, mas não tocavão na Igreia, e porque estava edificada no senhorio do dito defunto, não podião os clerigos frequentarla; todavia hum delles determinou de ir là a resar, como fez. E encomendouse a Nosso Senhor que o livrasse de os imigos e desse lugar, para se frequentar a Igreia. E foy se. Dalli a pouco de noite estando hum soldado principal do gentio que matarão dormindo, sentio que lhe derão huma grande pancada, com aqual se alevantou, e correndo logo a dita Igreia tremendo, acordou ao samchristão della, e lhe disse que falasse com o clerigo e com

A Christian said that one day he took a little lime (*chumaya*) beloning to the church and placed it over a beam of his house. After that his little children began to cry and shout at night that they were burning in that lime. He returned the lime to the church, gave an offering to the church and the disturbance of his children ended.

[k] The Church of Caramatete [Kadamattathu] was built sixty years ago. Its patron is St George. He performs many miracles for the heathens as well as for the Christians, and they all give many offerings to the church. One day when the church was not yet completed, someone heard the sound of a bell three times, which was heard also by the heathens living at a long distance. And a good old man who was living close by got up at midnight and went to the church and saw many lights and [heard] the sweet sound of musical instruments. Struck with wonder at the vision, he returned home and made public what he saw.

A thief stole from the church five [98v] small crosses and four lamps. As he was going to get away carrying the stolen goods in his hands, it seemed to him that a crowd of people were following him. And so he slipped off the road and hid the stolen goods in a thicket. Returning to the road, he found no one of those he had thought were following him. So he retreated his steps to take back what he had hidden. But he could not find it. After three days he became mad. On being asked about the stolen goods and their whereabouts, he said he did not know, and that he who stole it will eat the dust and him the fishes. Two hundred days later Our Lord revealed to an old priest the way to find out the stolen goods, the person who had them, in which road and spot he would find them. That priest went to search and found everything as he was told. After that the lord of the land executed the said thief and threw his body into the river, and fishes ate it, as he himself had said.

The Christians of the place killed a heathen chief for having done some injury to a cleric. After that the soldiers of the dead man burned the houses of the Christians, but they did not touch the church because it was in the principality of the said dead man. But the clerics could not go to the church. But one of them determined to go there and recite the Office. Before doing so he recommended himself to Our Lord to deliver him from his enemies and to give them a chance to frequent the church. And so it happened shortly. One night, when the principal soldier of the murdered heathen was asleep, he thought they gave him a big push. At this he got up, and running to the church trembling, woke up the sacristan of the church and told him to speak with the cleric and the others that they might come to the church, that he was taking them at his risk

os mais, que viessem a Igreia que elle mesmo os tomava a sua conta e não temessem. Com o qual ficarão frequentando a Igreia, como primeiro.

[l] A Igreia de Coligere [Kõlanchery], averà cincoenta annos, que foy edificada, tem por a invocação de S. Pedro e S. Paulo, tem todos Christãos e gentios muita devação na dita Igreia. Hum homem furtou huma cruz da dita igreia e ficou doudo, de modo que por mais meisinhas que lhe fiserão numqua pode o sarar. E disia elle mesmo que não havia para que falar em meisinhas, pois elle era aquelle que furtarà a cruz da dita Igreia.

[m] A Igreia de Muttão [Muttam] he de Nossa Senhora, quiserão os gentios queimarla, como fiserão a outras casas, e puzerão fogo nadita Igreia, mas não se queimou, dizendo muitas pessoas gentias, que estavão de longe que virão accodir muitos passeros, que com as alas apagarão o fogo. Ha pouco tempo que se edificou.

[n] A *hermida* de S Gervasio e Protasio, que està en Angamale tem a invocação de S. Gervasio e S. Protasio. He muy antiga; hum bramene quis tirarla dalli pello qual para enfadar os Christãos mandava certos polleas (pulayas), que são hum genero de gente do Malavar, que não podem chegar perto com os outros, e tocando-os aelles, he necessario lavaremse. O dito bramene || [99r] por despreço da Igreia mandava trabalhar os ditos polleas pegados com ella, pelloque lhe morrerão todos os herdeiros que tinha, e sua molher ficou steril. E preguntando a causa destes males aos feiticeiros todos lhe disserão que era a ira de Deus sobre elle. Hum todavia lhe disse en particular que a causa era ter feito algum mal a alguma Igreia de Christãos de S. Thome. Do qual o bramene arrependido, porque de noite duas pessoas com canas nas mãos pondose na sua cabeceira não o deixavão dormir, com os quaes sonhos elle afligido contou o negoceo aos Christãos e sua mã intenção, de tirar dalli a igreia e fazendo hum voto a ella ficou livre da dita vexação e sua molher teve logo hum filho.

|| [99v] [o] Da sobredita Ygreia de Molandurte, furtou huma vez hum Christão huma cruzezinha de prata como ninguem o sabia; d'alli a dous meses, dia de paschoa estando todo o povo na Ygreia foi arrebatado do demonio e com os gritos continou a gritar dizendo, Eu sou o que furtei a cruz, esta em tal partes repetindo; isto com muytos gritos, como forão donde dizia, como a acharão. E o dito arrependido do que tinha feito, sarou.

Gav. N. 42

This page is in Bishop Ros' hand ||

and they should not be afraid. With this they began to frequent the church as before.

[l] The Church of Colingere [Kolanchery] was built fifty years ago, and is in the patronage of SS. Peter and Paul. All the Christians and heathens have great devotion to that church. A man stole a cross of the said church. And he became so mad that afterwards the medicines given him could not cure him. He himself said not to speak to him of any medicine, because he was the one who stole the cross of that church.

[m] The Church of Muttâo [Muttam] is of Our Lady. The heathens wanted to set it on fire as they had burned other houses. They set fire to the church, but it was not burned. Many heathens staying at a distance said that they saw many sparrows come and put out the fire flapping their wings. The church had been built a short time ago.

[n] The hermitage of SS. Gervasis and Protasis, which exists at Angamale, is dedicated to SS. Gervasis and Protasis. It is very ancient. A Brahmin wanted to remove it from there, and so in order to molest the Christians he sent some *Polleas* [Pulayas]. These are a kind of people of Malavar, who cannot come close to others, and if touched by them it is necessary to wash oneself. The said Brahmin [99r] had, out of disrespect for the church, sent those *Polleas* to work in discord with the church. Therefore, all his heirs died and his wife remained sterile. On consulting the sorcerers for the cause of these evils they all said it was the anger of God over him. However, one in particular said that the cause was that he had done some evil to a church of the Christians of St Thomas. The Brahmin repented of it; because two persons, with a cane in their hands and standing at his bedside, were not letting him sleep at night. Afflicted by such dreams he told the Christians about the matter and of his evil intention to remove the church from there. Giving an offering to the church, he was freed of the said vexation, and his wife soon had a son.

[o] [99v] [In the hand-writing of Bishop Francis Ros] Once a Christian stole a small cross of silver from the above said church of Molandurte without any one knowing about it. Two months later on the day of Easter, while all the people were in the church, he was hurled down on the ground by the devil and he began to cry out saying, "I am the one who stole the cross, it is in such a place." While he was repeating it and continuing to shout, they went to the place he indicated and found it. And he repented of his deed and was healed.

Gav. n. 42

Appendix V

COMMON DECLARATION OF POPE JOHN PAUL II AND PATRIARCH MAR DINKHA IV (11 NOVEMBER 1994)

We reproduce below the original English text of the common christological declaration between the Catholic Church and the Assyrian Church of the East signed by His Holiness Pope John Paul II and His Holiness Patriarch Mar Dinkha IV on 11 November 1994 (*Acta Apostolicæ Sedis* 87 July (1995) 685-687).

On behalf of their respective Churches the pope and the patriarch declare that, though full communion has not yet been achieved in all necessary respects, as regards the mystery of the Incarnation the same *faith* has been proclaimed by both the Churches all along in the past in spite of misunderstandings caused by differing *theologies*. In other words, in defence of the same christological faith conflicting theologies fought each other on the Catholic and the Nestorian or Assyrian sides. "The Lord's Spirit permits us to understand better today that the divisions brought about in this way were due in large part to *misunderstandings*."

The importance of this common declaration is all too evident. It supplies a bifocal lens to look at historical Nestorianism and Catholic judgements of it without, however, demanding of the past the enlightenment of the present.

DECLARATIO

De mysterio Incarnationis Domini nostri Iesu Christi.

COMMON CHRISTOLOGICAL DECLARATION BETWEEN THE CATHOLIC CHURCH AND THE ASSYRIAN CHURCH OF THE EAST

His Holiness John Paul II, Bishop of Rome and Pope of the Catholic Church, and His Holiness Mar Dinkha IV, Catholicos-Patriarch of the Assyrian Church of the East, give thanks to God who has prompted them to this new brotherly meeting.

Both of them consider this meeting as a basic step on the way towards the full communion to be restored between their Churches. They can indeed, from now on, proclaim together before the world their common faith in the mystery of the Incarnation.

As heirs and guardians of the faith received from the Apostles as formulated by our common Fathers in the Nicene Creed, we confess one Lord Jesus Christ, the only Son of God, begotten of the Father from all eternity who, in the fullness of time, came down from heaven and became man for our salvation. The Word of God, second Person of the Holy Trinity, became incarnate by the power of the Holy Spirit in assuming from the holy Virgin Mary a body animated by a rational soul, with which he was indissolubly united from the moment of his conception.

Therefore our Lord Jesus Christ is true God and true man, perfect in his divinity and perfect in his humanity, consubstantial with the Father and consubstantial with us in all things but sin. His divinity and his humanity are united in one person, without confusion or change, without division or separation. In him has been preserved the difference of the natures of divinity and humanity, with all their properties, faculties and operations. But far from constituting "one and another", the divinity and humanity are united in the person of the same and unique Son of God and Lord Jesus Christ, who is the object of a single adoration.

Christ therefore is not an "ordinary man" whom God adopted in order to reside in him and inspire him, as in the righteous ones and the prophets. But the same God the Word, begotten of his Father before all worlds without beginning according to his divinity, was born of a mother without a father in the last times according to his humanity. The humanity to which the Blessed Virgin Mary gave birth always was that of the Son of God himself. That is the reason why the Assyrian Church of the East is praying the Virgin Mary as "the Mother of Christ our God and Saviour". In the light of this same faith the Catholic tradition addresses the Virgin Mary as "the Mother of God" and also as "the Mother of Christ". We both recognize the legitimacy and rightness of these expressions of the same faith and we both respect the preference of each Church in her liturgical life and piety.

This is the unique faith that we profess in the mystery of Christ. The controversies of the past led to anathemas, bearing on persons and on formulas. The Lord's Spirit permits us to understand better today that the divisions brought about in this way were due in large part to misunderstandings.

Whatever our christological divergences have been, we experience ourselves united today in the confession of the same faith in the Son of God who became man so that we might become children of God by his grace. We wish from now on to witness together to this faith in the One who is the Way, the Truth and the Life, proclaiming it in appropriate ways to our contemporaries, so that the world may believe in the Gospel of salvation.

The mystery of the Incarnation which we profess in common is not an abstract and isolated truth. It refers to the Son of God sent to save us.

The economy of salvation, which has its origin in the mystery of communion of the Holy Trinity — Father, Son and Holy Spirit —, is brought to its fulfilment through the sharing in this communion, by grace, within the one, holy, catholic and apostolic Church, which is the People of God, the Body of Christ and the Temple of the Spirit.

Believers become members of this Body through the sacrament of Baptism, through which, by water and the working of the Holy Spirit, they are born again as new creatures. They are confirmed by the seal of the Holy Spirit who bestows the sacrament of Anointing. Their communion with God and among themselves is brought to full realization by the celebration of the unique offering of Christ in the sacrament of the Eucharist. This communion is restored for the sinful members of the Church when they are reconciled with God and with one another through the sacrament of Forgiveness. The sacrament of Ordination to the ministerial priesthood in the apostolic succession assures the authenticity of the faith, the sacraments and the communion in each local Church.

Living by this faith and these sacraments, it follows as a consequence that the particular Catholic churches and the particular Assyrian churches can recognize each other as sister Churches. To be full and entire, communion presupposes the unanimity concerning the content of the faith, the sacraments and the constitution of the Church. Since this unanimity for which we aim has not yet been attained, we cannot unfortunately celebrate together the Eucharist which is the sign of the ecclesial communion already fully restored.

Nevertheless, the deep spiritual communion in the faith and the mutual trust already existing between our Churches entitle us from now on to consider witnessing together to the Gospel message and co-operating in particular pastoral situations, including especially the areas of catechesis and the formation of future priests.

In thanking God for having made us rediscover what already unites us in the faith and the sacraments, we pledge ourselves to do everything possible to dispel the obstacles of the past which still prevent the attainment of full communion between our Churches, so that we can better respond to the Lord's call for the unity of his own, a unity which has of course to be expressed visibly. To overcome these obstacles, we now establish a Mixed Committee for theological dialogue between the Catholic Church and the Assyrian Church of the East.

Given at Saint Peter's, on 11 November 1994

† K. MAR DINKHA IOANNES PAULUS PP. II

Index

By Sunny Kokkaravalayil, S.J.

Note: Only the more important terms are entered in this index. We use the abbreviation SD for the Synod of Diamper, and TC for Thomaschristians. A number followed by an (n.) signifies that the reference is to a footnote in the page mentioned.

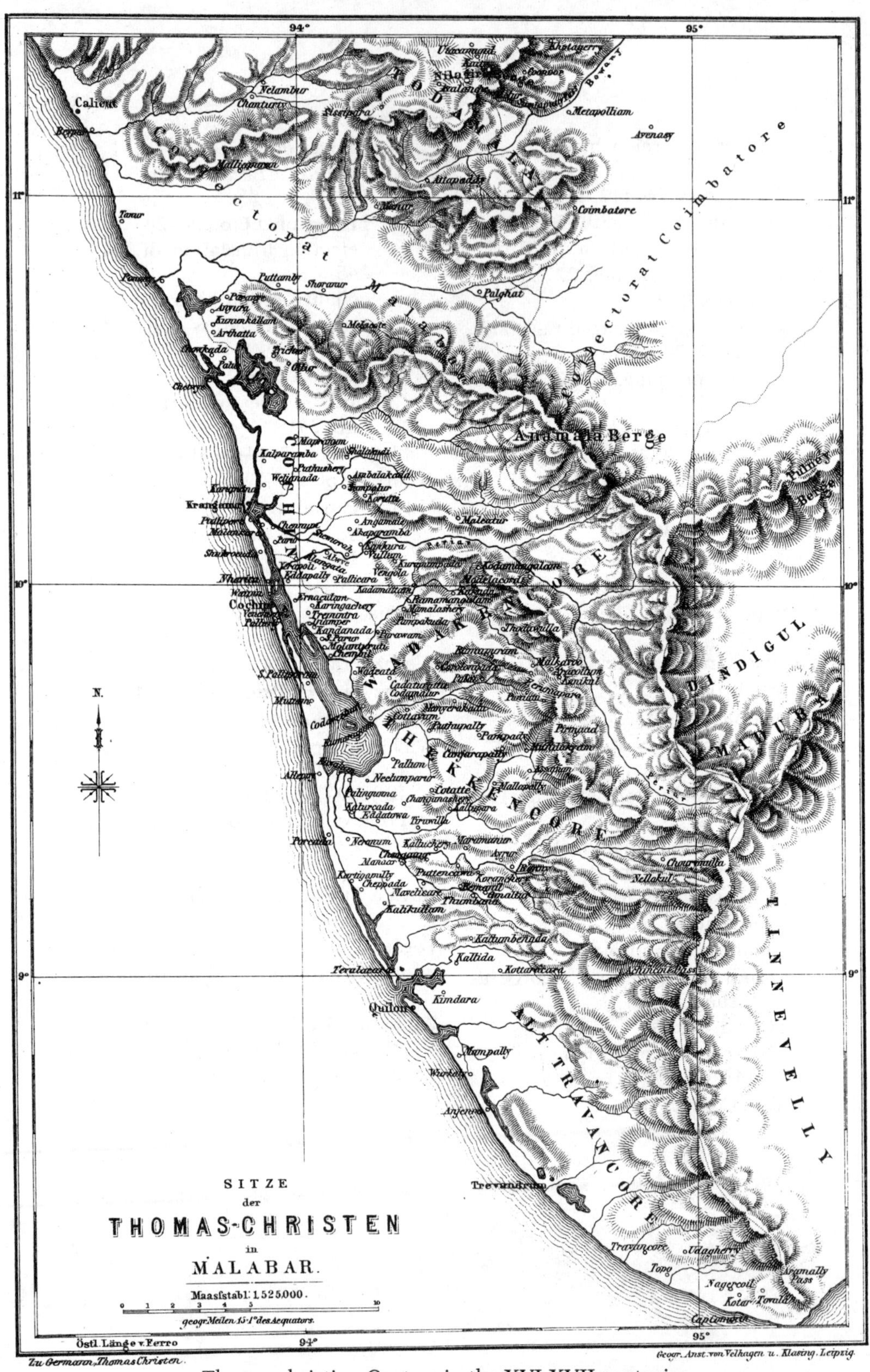

Thomaschristian Centers in the XVI-XVII centuries.
Reproduced from W. Germann, *Die Kirche der Thomaschristen: ein Beitrag zur Geschichte der Orientalischen Kirchen,* Gütersloh 1877.